Fathers Under Fire

Fathers Under Fire

The Revolution in Child Support Enforcement

Irwin Garfinkel, Sara S. McLanahan,
Daniel R. Meyer, and Judith A. Seltzer
Editors

Russell Sage Foundation ♦ New York

The Russell Sage Foundation

Library of Congress Cataloging-in-Publication Data

Fathers under fire : the revolution in child support enforcement /
   Irwin Garfinkel . . . [et al.], editors.
       p.   cm.
   Includes bibliographical references and index.
   ISBN 0-87154-303-6
    1. Child support—Government policy—United States.   2. Absentee
      fathers—United States.   3. Fatherless family—United States.
I. Garfinkel, Irwin.
HV741.F38   1998
306.874'2—dc21

98-23324
CIP

Text design by Suzanne Nichols.

RUSSELL SAGE FOUNDATION
112 East 64th Street, New York, New York 10021
10 9 8 7 6 5 4 3 2 1

This book is dedicated to Ronald B. Mincy

Contents

Contents

Contributors

IRWIN GARFINKEL is M. I. Ginsberg Professor of Continuing Urban Problems in the School of Social Work at Columbia University.

SARA S. MCLANAHAN is professor of sociology and public affairs at Princeton University.

DANIEL R. MEYER is associate professor in the School of Social Work at the University of Wisconsin, Madison, and an affiliate of the Institute for Research on Poverty.

JUDITH A. SELTZER is professor of sociology at the University of California, Los Angeles.

DAVID E. BLOOM is professor of population and health economics at Harvard University's School of Public Health and deputy director of the Harvard Institute for International Development.

ANNE CASE is professor of economics and public affairs at Princeton University.

CECILIA CONRAD is associate professor of economics at Pomona College and senior research associate with the Joint Center for Political Economic Studies in Washington, D.C.

FRED DOOLITTLE is deputy director of research at Manpower Demonstration Research Corporation, New York and San Francisco.

RICHARD B. FREEMAN is Herbert Ascherman Chair in Economics at Harvard University. He is also director of the Labor Studies Program at the National Bureau of Economic Research and executive director of the Program in Discontinuous Economics at the London School of Economics Centre for Economic Performance.

THOMAS L. HANSON is assistant research psychologist in the Department of Psychology, University of California, Riverside.

EARL S. JOHNSON is research associate at Manpower Demonstration Research Corporation, New York and San Francisco.

CYNTHIA MILLER is research associate at Manpower Demonstration Research Corporation.

Contributors

MARTHA MINOW is professor of law at Harvard University.

JESSICA PEARSON is director of the Center for Policy Research in Denver, Colorado.

NANCY THOENNES is associate director of the Center for Policy Research in Denver, Colorado.

JANE WALDFOGEL is assistant professor of social work and public affairs at the Columbia University School of Social Work.

Conference Participants

Elijah Anderson, University of Pennsylvania
Sheila D. Ards, Benedict College
Katharine Bartlett, Duke University
Andrea Beller, University of Illinois
David E. Bloom, Harvard University
Jeanne Brooks-Gunn, Columbia University
Anne Case, Princeton University
David Chambers, University of Michigan
Cecilia Conrad, Pomona College
Fred Doolittle, Manpower Demonstration Research Corporation
Kathryn Edin, University of Pennsylvania
Jeffery Evans, National Institutes of Health
Ron Ferguson, Harvard University
Ed Freeland, Response Analysis
Richard B. Freeman, Harvard University
Frank F. Furstenberg, University of Pennsylvania
Irwin Garfinkel, Columbia University
John Graham, Rutgers University
Maria Hanratty, Council of Economic Advisers
Thomas L. Hanson, University of California, Riverside
Pedro Hernandez, University of Wisconsin, Madison
James Hyman, Fannie Mae Foundation
Mori Insinger, University of Pennsylvania
Aurora Jackson, Columbia University
Earl S. Johnson, Manpower Demonstration Research Corporation
Waldo E. Johnson, Jr., University of Chicago
Lawrence Katz, Harvard University
Alan Krueger, Princeton University
Michael Laracy, Annie E. Casey Foundation
Robert Lerman, Urban Institute
Robert Mare, University of California, Los Angeles
Sara S. McLanahan, Princeton University
Linda Mellgren, U.S. Department of Health and Human Services
Daniel R. Meyer, University of Wisconsin, Madison
Cynthia Miller, Manpower Demonstration Research Corporation
Ronald Mincy, Ford Foundation
Martha Minow, Harvard University
Robert Moffitt, Johns Hopkins University

Conference Participants

Shawn Mooring, Ford Foundation
Donald Oellerich, U.S. Department of Health and Human Services
Elizabeth Peters, Cornell University
Richard Peterson, New York City Criminal Justice Agency
Nancy Reichman, Princeton University
Lauren M. Rich, University of Pennsylvania
John Robertson, Washington University
Philip K. Robins, University of Miami
Judith A. Seltzer, University of California, Los Angeles
Freya Sonenstein, Urban Institute
Elaine Sorenson, Urban Institute
Julien Teitler, Princeton University
Mark D. Turner, Urban Institute
Jane Waldfogel, Columbia University
Maureen Waller, Public Policy Institute of California
Melvin Wilson, University of Virginia

Acknowledgments

Funding for organizing and editing *Fathers Under Fire* was provided by grants from the Russell Sage Foundation, the Ford Foundation, and the Annie E. Casey Foundation. Support also came from grants from the National Institute of Child Health and Human Development (HD-24571 and HD-30913-02), the Office of Population Research at Princeton University, and the Institute for Research on Poverty at the University of Wisconsin. The volume benefitted from the thoughtful criticisms of two anonymous reviewers. Irwin Garfinkel and Sara McLanahan are grateful to the Centre for Analysis of Social Exclusion at the London School of Economics, and Daniel Meyer is grateful to the Social Policy Research Unit at the University of York for providing comfortable and stimulating intellectual homes for them to complete work on revisions to the manuscript. We are especially grateful to Eric Wanner, president of the Russell Sage Foundation, who in 1989 first encouraged Irwin Garfinkel and Sara McLanahan to enrich their research on single mothers and their children by a study of nonresident fathers. We are also grateful to Ronald Mincy, senior program officer in the Human Development and Reproductive Health Program at the Ford Foundation, who has strategically promoted research on nonresident fathers and articulately championed father responsibility and involvement.

IRWIN GARFINKEL
SARA S. MCLANAHAN
DANIEL R. MEYER
JUDITH A. SELTZER

Introduction

Irwin Garfinkel, Sara S. McLanahan,
Daniel R. Meyer, and Judith A. Seltzer

The American family has undergone a dramatic restructuring during the past four decades. At the beginning of the 1950s, a large majority of children in the United States lived with both of their biological parents from the time they were born to the age of maturity. Only one of five children born in the 1950s lived apart from their father before reaching adulthood.[1] Today the picture is dramatically different. Over 50 percent of children will live apart from at least one of their parents, usually the father,[2] before reaching adulthood (Bumpass 1984; Bumpass and Sweet 1989). These changes represent a fundamental shift in the living arrangements of both children and parents.

Although a significant minority of children have lived apart from their fathers throughout American history, what is truly new today is the proportion of *fathers* who are living apart from their children. Up until the twentieth century, mortality rates were high, and many children lost fathers as well as mothers through death. Peter R. Uhlenberg (1980) estimates that about 24 percent of children born in 1900 experienced the death of a parent before reaching age fifteen. While mortality rates have declined steadily throughout the twentieth century, divorce and out-of-wedlock births have increased, and both have skyrocketed since the 1960s, dramatically altering the nature and prevalence of father absence. Today's absent fathers live apart from their children by choice—their own choice, or the mother's, or both. That children in single-mother families have a living father who could contribute to their economic support and upbringing has important implications for these families, for the broader society, and for fathers themselves.

The changes in the causes of father absence are just part of today's markedly different landscape. Significant, too, is the sheer growth in the numbers of children who do not live with their fathers and who never have lived with their fathers. In 1965, when Senator Daniel Patrick Moynihan of New York wrote his famous report *The Negro Family: The Case for National Action*, births outside marriage accounted for 5 percent of all births and for 23 percent of all births to African American women. Today the numbers are 30 percent and 70 percent, respectively.[3] These are sobering statistics.

The greater number of children living apart from their fathers has important consequences for children, parents, and society at large. Half of all children living in mother-only households have incomes below the poverty line, and another quarter have incomes between the poverty threshold and 200 percent of the poverty line (U.S. Bureau of the Census 1996, P60–194). Not surprisingly in view of the high poverty rates of single-mother households, the increase in their numbers led to a dramatic expansion of the welfare system (Garfinkel and McLanahan 1986). The rise in single-parent families also has lasting consequences for the social mobility of the next generation: growing up with a single parent has been found to increase children's risk of dropping out of high school, becoming teen mothers, and finding themselves out of school and out of steady work as young adults (McLanahan and Sandefur 1994).

FATHERS UNDER FIRE

In response to the increase in divorce and nonmarital childbearing, and the resulting impact on public expenditures, poverty, and child welfare, policymakers passed a series of laws aimed at forcing nonresident fathers to provide more economic support for their children. In the mid-1970s, the federal government established the Office of Child Support Enforcement and directed states to do the same. Twice in the 1980s, major federal legislation was passed requiring states to strengthen paternity establishment, to create legislative guidelines for setting child support orders, and to withhold obligations from fathers' wages. This process continued into the 1990s, with child support enforcement being a major component of the new welfare legislation—the Personal Responsibility and Work Opportunity and Reconciliation Act, (PRWORA) of 1996. Coupled with the decline in the value of welfare benefits that occurred over this same period, the child support legislation may be seen as an attempt to privatize the cost of children and to shift some of the burden from the state and from mothers onto the shoulders of fathers.

Nonresident fathers, as a consequence, face a very different, more invasive, world. A man who parents a child outside marriage and denies paternity can be required to take a blood or genetic test. The amount of child support that all fathers must pay is increasingly determined by government regulations. Their obligations are increasingly withheld from their paychecks. Fathers who fail to pay may have their income tax refunds and property seized and their driver's, professional, and trade licenses revoked, and they may no longer receive food stamps. The ultimate sanction for non-payment continues to be jail. It is no exaggeration, therefore, to say that nonresident fathers are now under fire.

Nonresident fathers have become money objects. Fathers who fail to pay child support are labeled "deadbeat dads" without regard to other contributions they may be making to their children. Furthermore, concern about the effects of child support enforcement on the fathers themselves has been minimal. Until recently, researchers have made little attempt to understand fathers in a broader perspective.[4] What are fathers' capabilities and responsibilities? How do they react to stricter enforcement? What are their needs and concerns?

Despite more than twenty years of increasingly strong legislation, child support collections, on average, have not shown much improvement. The lack of attention to the fathers, coupled with the disappointing child support record to date, suggests that it is time to reappraise child support enforcement policy by examining its impact on nonresident fathers.

Three overarching questions must be addressed in this reappraisal. First, are the new child support policies consistent with the capacities and circumstances of nonresident fathers? Second, do child support policies have adverse unintended effects on the fathers? Finally, should policy be reoriented to do more to assist nonresident fathers?

THE QUESTIONS ADDRESSED

What Are the Policies, and Are They Consistent with Fathers' Capabilities?

In order to assess the effects of the new child support system on fathers, we must first understand the different components of the legislation, how they have evolved over time, and the extent to which they are being implemented throughout the country. Although the federal government has been pushing the states to strengthen their child support enforcement systems for more than twenty years, federal authority is relatively weak. When it comes to family matters, federal officials must rely on incentives and moral persuasion to move states in the direction they would have them go. Hence, at any point in time, there is enormous variation across the states with respect to their political will and their capacity (both financial and managerial) to enforce child support obligations. Equally important, although the federal legislation is universal in word, in practice states have a strong incentive to treat different groups of fathers differently. On the one hand, collecting support from low-income fathers is much harder than collecting from middle-income fathers, so the child support agency's performance will look better to the extent that it focuses on middle-income fathers. On the other hand, pursuing the fathers of children on welfare is likely to reduce welfare costs, whereas pursuing middle- and upper-income fathers has no such benefit. Moreover, whereas reducing welfare costs is politically popular, pursuing middle- and upper-income fathers is less acceptable to the electorate. Indeed, fathers with financial resources are well organized and have been waging strong campaigns in state legislatures throughout the country to protect their rights and lower their financial obligations.

Unfortunately, although we know a great deal about single mothers and their children,[5] we know comparatively little about nonresident fathers. And we know even less about nonresident fathers at the bottom of the income distribution. In part, our ignorance is due to the fact that we are dealing with a relatively new phenomenon and we lack good data on these men. Many nonresident fathers are missing from our social surveys, and others do not want to be identified and therefore misreport their status. In part, our ignorance may be due to the fact that we, as a society, care more about the status of children, whom we see as having little control over their lives, than adults, whom we view as, by and large, "getting what they deserve."

The need for a better understanding of nonresident fathers goes beyond intellectual curiosity. The knowledge gaps must be filled if social scientists and policymakers are to understand the effect of twenty years of policy changes, estimate the likely effectiveness of new changes on the horizon, and devise new measures that work. What are the lives of the full spectrum of nonresident fathers like? How much income do they have? With whom do they live? How does their situation compare to that of resident fathers? To that of single mothers and children? How do those fathers who fail to pay child support differ from fathers who pay? What percentage of these men are potentially dangerous or undesirable as fathers? These questions are addressed in part 1 of this volume.

What Are the Likely Repercussions of Stronger Child Support Enforcement?

Since the mid-1970s, opponents of child support enforcement have argued that forcing fathers to pay more child support will only impoverish their new families and that the new laws are simply "robbing Peter to pay Paul." This critique has not been adequately addressed because most research examines the benefits associated with the receipt of increased child support payments but does not look at the costs associated with the payment of child support dollars.[6]

Other critics worry that strong child support enforcement may discourage nonresident fathers from marrying and starting new families and, in particular, from marrying single mothers with children. There is evidence, though still controversial, that marriage has several benefits for men, including decreased mortality, lower alcohol use, and higher earnings (Akerlof 1998; Waite 1995). Certainly, marriage or cohabitation with a single mother increases the standard of living of the mother and child. Indeed, twenty-five years ago, when the growth of single motherhood was first becoming apparent, many people believed that the best solution to the economic problems of these families was remarriage, which, in those days, was quite common (Ross and Sawhill 1975).

Still other critics worry that stronger enforcement will have the unintended effect of reducing fathers' work effort or forcing them into the underground economy. If this happened, everyone would be worse off, including the father's first family, his subsequent or current family, and the government, which would collect less in taxes. Whether this fear is well founded depends in part on whether fathers see child support obligations as a tax that may encourage them to work less or as a reduction in income that may encourage them to work more.

Another concern is that stronger enforcement will increase contact between the parents and possibly exacerbate conflict or violence. The latter would undoubtedly be harmful to children. Fathers who pay child support see their children more often than fathers who do not pay, and one might expect that new fathers who are brought into the system would follow suit. Because greater contact increases the opportunity for conflict, and because these men may have strong feelings about not paying support, the risk of conflict would seem to be high in these families. This problem may be especially acute in low-income families where the mother is receiving welfare and the child support dollars go toward reducing welfare costs rather than to the child. In response to the new welfare legislation, many advocates for women and children have presented numbers suggesting that a large proportion of welfare mothers have been exposed to domestic violence in the past; their data include links between violence and disputes over child support (Allard et al. 1997; Raphael and Tolman 1997). Thus, the answer to this question has important implications not only for child support policy but for welfare policy more generally.

Finally, stronger child support enforcement may have benefits as well as costs. First, strengthening fathers' obligations to their children is likely to also strengthen their rights to be involved with their children. As noted earlier, a father who pays child support is more likely to spend time with his child and to help make decisions about how his child is raised (Seltzer 1991). When parents get along, more contact with the father and greater father involvement is likely to have benefits for the child (Amato and Rezac 1994; Hetherington, Cox, and Cox 1982). Second, stronger child support enforcement may have an important deterrent effect on nonmarital fertility. Once young men realize that fathering a child incurs a financial obligation, lasting for up to eighteen years, they may take more precautions to avoid an unintended pregnancy. We know that the vast majority of nonmarital births are due to unintended pregnancies (Brown and Eisenberg 1995). We also know that women bear most of the responsibility for contraception. Thus, if fathers were to change their behaviors in this regard, the number of unintended pregnancies would probably decline, as would the number of nonmarital births.

The chapters in part II assess the effects of stronger child support enforcement on nonresident fathers' income, employment, marriage, fertility, and relationships with their child's mother.

Should We Be Doing More for Nonresident Fathers?

A final question we address in the book is whether society should be doing more to help nonresident fathers meet their obligations and assert their parental rights. Up until recently, fathers in general have been viewed primarily as breadwinners, and child support policies have incorporated this rather limited view. Nonresident fathers have been treated more or less as objects from which money can be extracted, and little thought has been given to their rights as fathers, or to how we might help them meet their obligations, both financial and otherwise.

Perhaps the most frequently expressed concern of fathers is that they are denied access to their children. When child support enforcement was lax, nonresident fathers had the option of trading child support for access to their child. As enforcement has become more rigorous, nonresident fathers have relatively less bargaining power, and therefore they have been lobbying for government to enforce their visitation rights. In response, several demonstration programs that seek to improve fathers' access to their children have been funded in different parts of the country.

Another concern of fathers and their advocates is that many men are unable to meet their financial obligations and need help in gaining jobs and job skills. Again, the federal government has responded to their concerns by funding demonstrations in several states. The Parents' Fair Share programs provide employment and training services, peer group support, counseling, assistance in establishing paternity and child support orders, and, if necessary, help in arranging mediation between the father and his child's mother. The programs also help fathers obtain temporary reductions in their child support obligations while they are in the program.

To answer the question of whether government should be supporting these kinds of programs, we need to know whether they actually work. If they do not work, supporting them would simply be wasting the taxpayer's money, regardless of their appeal. Answering the question also requires stepping back from the practical problems and reassessing the basic premise underlying the child support policies that have been legislated during the past twenty years. These policies treat all fathers alike in terms of holding them financially responsible for their biological children. No exceptions are made for fathers who are very poor, and no exceptions are made for fathers who are supporting new families. Is this appropriate? Part III addresses these questions of whether we should be doing more to help fathers.

A SPECIAL FOCUS ON LOW-INCOME FATHERS

A theme running throughout the chapters in this volume is an interest in and concern for low-income fathers. Most discussions today assume that nonresident fathers are a homogeneous group, at least in terms of their ability to provide for their children. Hence the term "deadbeat dad" is applied rather indiscriminately to all nonpaying fathers. In truth, the reasons for failing to pay child support may be very different, ranging from the inadequate resources of poor fathers who are doing all they can to the attitudes of very wealthy fathers who are, as the term "deadbeat dad" suggests, shirking their responsibilities.

Whether a father is poor also affects his experiences with the child support system. Although universal in principle, in practice the new child support laws treat fathers from different income strata differently. Whereas middle- and upper-income fathers usually negotiate their child support agreements in private and with the services of a lawyer who represents their interests, poor fathers often find themselves without counsel and confronted by public officials who represent the interests of the state. Poor fathers are treated differently in part because they cannot afford a lawyer. Even more important, however, children of poor fathers are likely to be on welfare, and therefore state officials have a much stronger incentive to collect child support payments as a way of reducing welfare costs. Indeed, middle-class mothers often report that they have a hard time getting state agencies to help them collect unpaid child support since the money goes to the mother rather than to the state.[7]

Finally, we might expect low-income fathers to respond differently to stronger child support enforcement, in part because they are less able to meet their obligations, in part because their contributions are less likely to go directly to their child, and in part because of differences in social norms regarding the obligations of fathers who never were married to their child's mother. Although nonmarital child-bearing occurs among all social classes, low-income fathers are less likely to marry than fathers from other income strata. To make sure that we would have information on poor fathers, we asked each of the authors to look not only at nonresident fathers in general but also at poor nonresident fathers in particular. Thus, each of the analyses in this book contains information that improves our understanding of the conditions and responses of poor nonresident fathers.

A CONFERENCE ON NONRESIDENT FATHERS

To answer the questions we have posed, the editors of this volume, with funding from the Annie E. Casey Foundation, the Ford Foundation, and the Russell Sage Foundation, commissioned a large group of social scientists and a small group of legal scholars to write and discuss a set of papers. The papers were subjected to written criticism by two formal discussants and to open discussion by all participants at a conference held September 14–16, 1995, at Princeton University. (See xi for a list of conference participants, along with their institutional affiliations.) The papers were revised in light of the criticisms and suggestions of the discussants, outside reviewers commissioned by the Russell Sage Foundation, and the editors, and they are presented in final form as chapters 1 through 10 of this book. Two teams of authors were asked to write about the policies and the fathers' capabilities. Their chapters are in part I of this volume. Five were asked to examine the possible side effects of stronger child support enforcement, and their chapters make up part II. Finally, three were asked to address the question "Should we do more?" and their chapters are in part III. Each of the chapters is described in more detail in the preface to each part. In the concluding chapter, we revisit the original questions and make policy recommendations, using evidence from the ten chapters in this volume.

NOTES

1. Our measure of living apart from a father excludes children who lost a father because of death. Information on the exposure to father absence among women born during the 1950s comes from the National Survey of Family Growth (1995) and was provided by Dana Glei at Princeton University.

2. The proportion of children in single-parent families who live with their fathers rather than their mothers is only 15 percent but has been growing (see Garasky and Meyer 1996).

3. However, 25 percent of children born nonmaritally are born to cohabiting parents (Bumpass, Raley, and Sweet 1995), so these children do live with their fathers for at least part of their lives.

4. *Making Fathers Pay* by David Chambers is an early notable exception (1979). For more recent exceptions, see Nichols-Casebolt (1986), Haskins (1988), Braver, Fitzpatrick, and Bay (1991), Lerman and Ooms (1993), Sullivan (1993), Seltzer and Brandreth (1995), Sorensen (1997), and Sorensen and Mincy (1998).

5. See, for example, Garfinkel and McLanahan (1986), Ross and Sawhill (1975), Kamerman and Kahn (1988), Cherlin and Furstenberg (1993), Furstenberg and Harris (1993), and Seltzer (1994).

6. For an exception, see Nichols-Casebolt (1986).

7. Some evidence is provided by court cases. In *Carter v. Morrow*, 526 F. Supp. 1225 (W.D.N.C. 1981), nonwelfare mothers sued the state of North Carolina to get child support services comparable to those being provided to welfare mothers. In *Clay v. Austin*, Civ. No. 85–86 (E.D. Ky. 1986), the state of Kentucky was sued because it would not modify awards for nonwelfare mothers. We also have very recent anecdotal evidence from a number of personal acquaintances in different states that documents the unwillingness of the child support offices in those states to provide services to mothers who are not on welfare. Finally, Current Population Survey (CPS) data indicate a big increase in the proportion of AFDC (Aid to Families with Dependent Children) cases with child support payments over time, but no comparable increase for non-AFDC cases.

REFERENCES

Akerlof, George. 1998. "Men Without Children." *Economic Journal* 108(447): 287–309.

Allard, Mary Ann, Randy Albelda, Mary Ellen Colten, and Carol Cosenza. 1997. *In Harm's Way? Domestic Violence, AFDC Receipt, and Welfare Reform in Massachusetts.* Boston: University of Massachusetts Press.

Amato, P. R., and S. J. Rezac. 1994. "Contact with Nonresident Parents, Interparental Conflict, and Children's Behavior." *Journal of Family Issues* 15(2): 191–207.

Braver, Sanford L., Pamela J. Fitzpatrick, and R. Curtis Bay. 1991. "Noncustodial Parent's Report of Child Support Payments." *Family Relations* 40(2): 180–85.

Brown, Sarah S., and Leon Eisenberg, eds. 1995. *The Best Intentions: Unintended Pregnancy and the Well-being of Children and Families.* Committee on Unintended Pregnancy, Division of Health Promotion and Disease Prevention, Institute of Medicine. Washington: National Academy Press.

Bumpass, Larry L. 1984. "Children and Marital Disruption: A Replication Update." *Demography* 21: 71–82.

Bumpass, Larry L., and James A. Sweet. 1989. "Children's Experience in Single-Parent Families: Implications of Cohabitation and Marital Transitions." *Family Planning Perspectives* 21(6): 256–60.

Bumpass, Larry L., Kelly Raley, and James A. Sweet. 1995. "The Changing Character of Stepfamilies: Implications of Cohabitation and Nonmarital Childbearing." *Demography* 32(3): 425–36.

Chambers, David L. 1979. *Making Fathers Pay: The Enforcement of Child Support.* Chicago: University of Chicago Press.

Cherlin, A. J., and F. F. Furstenberg Jr. 1993. "Current Research and Controversies on Stepfamilies in the United States." Paper presented at the International Meeting, Les Récompositions Familiales Aujourd'hui, Paris (December 2–3).

Furstenberg, Frank F., Jr., and Kathleen Millan Harris. 1993. "When and Why Fathers Matter: Impacts of Father Involvement on the Children of Adolescent Mothers." In *Young Unwed Fathers: Changing Roles and Emerging Policies,* edited by Robert I. Lerman and Theodora J. Ooms. Philadelphia: Temple University Press.

Garasky, Steven, and Daniel R. Meyer. 1996. "Reconsidering the Increase in Father-only Families." *Demography* 33(3): 385–93.

Garfinkel, Irwin, and Sara S. McLanahan. 1986. *Single Mothers and Their Children: A New American Dilemma.* Washington: Urban Institute Press.

Haskins, Ron. 1988. "Child Support: A Father's View." In *Child Support: From Debt Collection to Social Policy,* edited by Alfred J. Kahn and Sheila B. Kamerman. Newbury Park, Calif.: Sage Publications.

Hetherington, Eileen Mavis, Martha Cox, and Roger Cox. 1982. "Effects of Divorce on Parents and Children." In *Nontraditional Families: Parenting and Child Development,* edited by Michael E. Lamb. Hillsdale, N.J.: Erlbaum.

Kamerman, Sheila, and Alfred Kahn, eds. 1988. *Child Support: From Debt Collection to Social Policy.* Newbury Park, Calif.: Sage Publications.

Lerman, Robert I., and Theodora J. Ooms, eds. 1993. *Young Unwed Fathers: Changing Roles and Emerging Policies.* Philadelphia: Temple University Press.

McLanahan, Sara S., and Gary Sandefur. 1994. *Growing up with a Single Parent: What Hurts, What Helps.* Cambridge, Mass.: Harvard University Press.

Moynihan, Daniel Patrick. 1965. *The Negro Family: The Case for National Action.* Washington: U.S. Department of Labor, Office of Planning and Research.

Nichols-Casebolt, Ann. 1986. "The Economic Impact of Child Support Reform on the Poverty Status of Custodial and Noncustodial Families." *Journal of Marriage and the Family* 48 (November): 875–80.

Raphael, Jacqueline, and Richard M. Tolman. 1997. "Trapped by Poverty and Trapped by Abuse: New Evidence Documenting the Relationship Between Domestic Violence and Welfare." Executive summary. Chicago: Taylor Institute.

Ross, Heather L., and Isabel V. Sawhill. 1975. *Time of Transition: The Growth of Families Headed by Women.* Washington: Urban Institute Press.

Seltzer, Judith A. 1991. "Relationships Between Fathers and Children Who Live Apart: The Father's Role After Separation." *Journal of Marriage and the Family* 53(1): 79–101.

———. 1994. "Consequences of Marital Dissolution for Children." *Annual Review of Sociology* 20(20): 235–66.

Seltzer, Judith A., and Yvonne Brandreth. 1995. "What Fathers Say About Involvement with Children After Separation." In *Fatherhood: Contemporary Theory, Research, and Social Policy,* edited by William Marsiglio. Thousand Oaks, Calif.: Sage Publications.

Sorensen, Elaine. 1997. "A National Profile of Nonresident Fathers and Their Ability to Pay Child Support." *Journal of Marriage and the Family* 59 (November): 785–97.

Sorensen, Elaine, and Ronald B. Mincy. 1998. "Deadbeats and Turnips in Child Support Reform." *Journal of Policy Analysis and Management* 17(1): 44–51.

Sullivan, Mercer L. 1993. "Young Fathers and Parenting in Two Inner-City Neighborhoods." In *Young Unwed Fathers: Changing Roles and Emerging Policies,* edited by Robert I. Lerman and Theodora J. Ooms. Philadelphia: Temple University Press.

Uhlenberg, Peter. 1980. "Death and the Family." *Journal of Family History* 5(3): 313–20.

U.S. Bureau of the Census. 1996. *Marital Status and Living Arrangements.* Current Population Reports, series P20–491. Washington: U.S. Government Printing Office, March.

Waite, Linda J. 1995. "Does Marriage Matter?" *Demography* 32(4): 483–507.

Part I

What Are the Policies and
Who Are the Fathers?

The chapters in this part ask whether our current child support policies are consistent with fathers' capabilities and responsibilities. In chapter 1, Irwin Garfinkel, Daniel Meyer, and Sara McLanahan provide a brief history of social policies for nonresident fathers. Prior to the 1940s, the vast majority of single mothers were widows, and thus it made sense that protecting them and their children from poverty and economic insecurity was a public responsibility. After 1960, however, in response to soaring divorce and out-of-wedlock birth rates and rising public expenditures, policy-makers began to reassess their policies and to try to shift more of the costs of supporting single mothers and their children from the state to nonresident fathers. Since the mid-1970s, the federal government has passed a series of laws aimed at increasing the proportion of eligible children with a child support order, increasing and standardizing order levels, and increasing collection rates. The authors describe these legislative changes and examine their possible effects on trends in federal and state child support statistics. They find that the aggregate trends show little improvement during the 1980s, suggesting that the new legislation has been unsuccessful in the short term. However, a more careful look at the trends suggests improvement in both collections and order rates. Paternity establishment rates have risen dramatically, and there is some evidence that particular policies, such as guidelines and income-withholding, are working in some states.

What is worrisome about these statistics is that child support enforcement agencies are targeting low-income fathers to try to offset public expenditures, such as AFDC and other welfare programs, on children with single mothers. Thus, the increase in orders and collections may be occurring among the men at the bottom end of the income distribution who can least afford to meet these obligations. Most of the child support dollars coming into the system as a result of increased enforcement among low-income fathers go toward reducing welfare costs rather than toward increasing the living standards of single mothers and their children.[1] Finally, very little money is being spent on programs to help poor fathers meet their new obligations. The chapter ends with a discussion of two such programs that were implemented in the 1990s: the Parents' Fair Share programs, which were designed to improve fathers' ability to pay support, and the Access Demonstrations, which were designed to increase both low-income and higher-income fathers' access to their children.

Evaluating the effects of child support enforcement on nonresident fathers requires a general understanding of fathers as well as their work and family situations. Unfortunately, although we have a wealth of information about single mothers and their children, we know very little about nonresident fathers. One reason for this oversight is a lack of good data. Many nonresident fathers are not represented in our national surveys. In chapter 2, "A Patchwork Portrait of Nonresident Fathers," Irwin Garfinkel, Sara McLanahan, and Thomas Hanson use data from the 1987 to 1988 National Survey of Families and Households (NSFH) and several other sources to adjust for the underrepresentation of nonresident fathers and to provide a more accurate picture of their resources and constraints. By using adjustment procedures that provide a range of estimates, the authors recognize that reasonable persons may disagree about how fathers who are missing from the survey differ from those who are included and acknowledge paternity.

They find that nonresident fathers have less education and lower wages than fathers who live with their children. They also find that nonresident fathers are less likely to be in good health and more likely to abuse alcohol and drugs than fathers who live with their children.

Not surprisingly, nonresident fathers, on average, have lower incomes than resident fathers. The mean personal income for all nonresident fathers ranges from about $26,900 to $33,400 (in 1995 dollars), compared to $40,700 for resident fathers. These results are similar to those in other studies of nonresident fathers' incomes. To the extent that the estimates are reasonably consistent across data sources and techniques of compensating for nonresident fathers' low rates of participation in surveys, the results provide valuable information for assessing what nonresident fathers are able to contribute in child support.

Consistent with claims that scarce economic resources are partly to blame for the failure of nonresident fathers to pay child support, the authors find that fathers who do not pay child support are even worse off than fathers who pay.

Although nonresident fathers have less income than resident fathers, after taking account of child support payments and the number of people in their home, Garfinkel and his colleagues conclude that nonresident fathers have roughly the same standard of living as resident fathers. Both are substantially better off than resident mothers and their children, more than 70 percent of whom are poor or near-poor.

These authors also examine nonresident fathers' living arrangements. They find that only one-third of these men are supporting new families that include children. The same is true for the subset of fathers who pay no child support. These findings suggest that living with other children may not be a significant cause of nonpayment.

Only a small percentage of nonresident fathers have serious alcohol or drug problems, but these problems appear to be more common among nonresident fathers than among resident fathers. Moreover, the proportion of fathers with problems is even higher among men who do not pay child support. This pattern suggests that tougher child support enforcement may bring more troubled fathers into the system, but that these fathers would still comprise only a small percentage of the whole. Garfinkel, McLanahan, and Hanson, however, are careful to note that because substance abuse is likely to be underreported, the true percentage could easily be much higher.

The chapters on child support policies and practices and the portrait of non-resident fathers set the stage for part II, in which the chapters extrapolate from what is to ask what will be: How does child support enforcement change nonresident fathers' circumstances and behaviors?

NOTE

1. Of the $2.9 billion collected for AFDC families in 1996, $500 million was paid to families as a result of the disregard policy, and the rest went to offset public costs (U.S. Department of Health and Human Services 1997). For several reasons, these figures underestimate the proportion of the child support paid by low-income fathers that goes to their children via the passthrough. First, child support collections for AFDC cases are more likely to come from non-low-income fathers than from low-income fathers. Second, collections from low-income fathers are likely to be lower and therefore more likely to be passed through to the mothers than collections from non-low-income fathers. Finally, some mothers and children of low-income fathers will not be receiving welfare, and any child support collected from these fathers will go directly to the mothers and children.

REFERENCE

U.S. Department of Health and Human Services, Office of Child Support Enforcement. 1997. *Twentieth Annual Report to Congress.* Washington: U.S. Department of Health and Human Services.

Chapter 1

A Brief History of Child Support Policies in the United States

Irwin Garfinkel, Daniel R. Meyer, and Sara S. McLanahan

Throughout the history of the United States, some children have lived apart from their fathers, and government has always assumed at least some responsibility for these children. One mechanism that has protected children from the economic consequences of the loss of a father is the private child support system, which is regulated by state law. Another mechanism is the public assistance system—or welfare system—which provides cash support to poor children who live apart from their fathers and which may pursue private child support on behalf of the child. During the past twenty-five years, the federal government has taken a number of rather dramatic steps to strengthen the private child support system, particularly with respect to the treatment of poor children. At the same time, the value of public assistance for poor children has declined by nearly one-third (U.S. House of Representatives 1996). Together, these changes in social policies have had profound effects on poor mothers and children and on low-income non-resident fathers. In effect, the new legislation has privatized the costs of children and shifted some of the financial burden from mothers to fathers. Although most of these new policies have been aimed at increasing the amount of child support that nonresident fathers owe and the regularity with which they pay, at least some attention has been given to policies and programs that increase fathers' rights and their ability to meet their new obligations. In this chapter, we review the major child support policies affecting nonresident fathers and their children and briefly describe evidence on the effects of these policies. We pay special attention to how child support policies affect low-income fathers, both in terms of the laws themselves and the manner in which the laws are implemented.

THE PRIVATE CHILD SUPPORT SYSTEM

The terms "single parent" and "single mother" are almost synonymous. Yet there was a time in this country when people assumed that fathers, rather than mothers, would bear the primary responsibility for children. Prior to the nineteenth century, in the relatively rare event of divorce or separation, fathers expected to be granted custody of their children.[1] Around the mid-1800s, this expectation began to change, and a "tender years" doctrine, which held that mothers were better caretakers of children than fathers, became increasingly popular. State statutes dealing with custody often contained an explicit preference for the mother. As a result, by the twentieth century the dominant arrangement was one in which children of divorced parents lived with their mothers.

Starting in the 1960s, states began to remove the explicit gender preferences from their custody statutes; since then, joint and shared custody arrangements have gained varying degrees of acceptance. However, the only one of these new arrangements that has become widespread—joint legal custody—has no implications for where the child lives, since it deals only with a father's right to have equal legal status in making decisions about the child. Thus, although the explicit gender preferences have been removed from custody statutes, the vast majority of single-parent households continue to be headed by mothers.[2]

As noted earlier, government has long played a role in regulating the extent to which nonresident parents contribute privately to their children's welfare. Traditionally, child support law has come under family law, a province of state government, and so child support systems have varied dramatically. Courts were the main actors in the system. Although state law established the duty of nonresident parents to support their children, decision-making power and administrative authority were delegated to local courts, and judges had the authority to decide whether a nonresident father would be required to pay child support, and if so, how much. Judges also decided what actions would be taken if the father failed to meet his obligation (Krause 1981). In addition, the courts were responsible for establishing paternity for children born outside marriage, partly because extramarital sexual intercourse was seen as a crime (Melli 1992).

In most parts of the country, the existence and level of a child support order were the outcomes of private negotiations between the father and mother (and their lawyers if they could afford them) and thus varied significantly among similar types of families. The degree of enforcement varied widely, too. In many counties, little was done about fathers who fell behind in their payments. Rather, the burden of collecting overdue support fell to the resident mother, who had little recourse but to pay for a lawyer and take the father to court.[3]

The case-by-case handling of child support orders resulted in a system that worked quite differently for low-income and high-income fathers. Some fathers who could afford a good lawyer were able to avoid a child support order; some who could not afford a lawyer were saddled with a large obligation. Because the system was court-based, a lawyer was needed to make adjustments to the amount of the child support. Thus, poor fathers who could not afford a lawyer often could not get relief from their obligation even if they lost their job. Another compounding factor was that child support orders were often based on an estimate of the minimum cost to raise a child. Because that minimum cost was relatively fixed, the amount of child support required of poor fathers was a much higher percentage of their income than the amount required of middle- and upper-income fathers (Garfinkel 1992; Cancian and Meyer 1996). A final difficulty with the system, from a poor father's point of view, was that the money he paid did not necessarily go to his child. Mothers who received public assistance (see the discussion later in this chapter) were required to report whatever child support they received to the welfare office, which, in turn, typically lowered their AFDC checks dollar for dollar. Thus, the fathers of poor children, who were mostly poor themselves, had very little incentive to pay child support, and many of these men simply disappeared.

In general, the policy toward nonresident fathers was either to punish them if they did not pay or to ignore them; the policy furnished few if any incentives to pay. The federal income tax system, for example, did not allow fathers who paid child support to deduct the payment from their taxable income. In many states, middle- and upper-income fathers had the option of paying family support, a combination of child support and alimony that was deductible to the father. Low-income fathers, however, were rarely able to take advantage of this option, which was disallowed by the Tax Reform Act of 1984.

Just as fathers' financial obligations to their children were treated on a case-by-case basis, visitation agreements and arrangements for nonresident fathers to see their children were also handled case by case. Even if a legal agreement indicated that a father could see his children, the arrangement seldom specified a particular amount or schedule. If a resident mother did not facilitate a father's access to his child, the father generally had no recourse other than to hire a lawyer and take the mother to court. Again, poor fathers were disadvantaged by the system, since they were less likely than a middle-income father to be able to afford a lawyer.

THE *OTHER* CHILD SUPPORT SYSTEM—PUBLIC SUPPORT

Government has always provided economic support for poor children in single-parent families (Garfinkel and McLanahan 1986). From colonial times through the turn of the twentieth century, these types of assistance provided to these families varied: some local communities provided cash and in-kind benefits; in others, mothers and children were put in poorhouses; and in still others, children were sent to orphanages because the poorhouses could not accommodate families (Katz 1986).

In general, there was no special policy for the nonresident fathers of these poor single-parent families. In cases in which a poor nonresident father requested assistance on his own, he was generally treated just like a single man with no children; that is, the community offered only temporary relief—work or transportation out of town.

This policy of ignoring nonresident fathers made sense because few of the poor single-parent families requesting assistance had a living nonresident father whose whereabouts were known. Most of the single mothers were widows; a few were abandoned or never married, and even fewer were legally divorced or separated.

In the families in which there was a nonresident father, or in which there was a father who sometimes lived with the family, policies had the effect of marginalizing the fathers. In the 1800s, poor families requesting assistance were often treated differently depending on whether the father was around. If the father was present, he may have been offered a job; but otherwise, the family was not eligible for assistance. If the father was not around, the mother and children may have been offered cash because the mother would not have been expected to work. Thus fathers who were unable or unwilling to work might have concluded that the only way for their children to receive regular cash assistance was for them to abandon the family. Even in the twentieth century, because cash economic support was generally available only to single-mother families, fathers who lost their jobs were often forced to abandon their family in order for their children to receive help.[4]

In the early part of the twentieth century, the commitment to provide support for children in single-mother families expanded as states began enacting mothers' pension laws. In the 1930s, the federal government assumed greater responsibility for children by creating the Aid to Dependent Children (ADC) program (later to become Aid to Families with Dependent Children, or AFDC), followed by the Survivor's Insurance Program, which provided aid to all insured widowed mothers and their children, irrespective of income. As the AFDC caseload shifted from widows to divorced, separated, and never-married mothers throughout the 1940s, 1950s, and 1960s, state and federal policy-makers became increasingly concerned about nonresident fathers and the fact that they were not supporting their children. The first federal child support legislation was enacted in 1950 and required welfare departments to notify local law enforcement agencies of the existence of a dependent child with a living nonresident father. Further minor legislation was enacted in 1965 and 1967, but little was accomplished (Cassetty 1978).

Indeed, up through most of the 1970s, welfare policies continued to discourage nonresident fathers from seeing their children and from maintaining relationships with the mothers of their children. Under the "man of the house" rule, caseworkers conducted surprise home visits to ensure that a father (or other male) was not living with the family. These visits reinforced a message that nonresident fathers were not to be involved once the state had taken on the support of the family.

EMPIRICAL EVIDENCE ON THE PRIVATE SUPPORT SYSTEM

Prior to the 1970s, we have very little systematic data on how the private child support system was working. In 1979 the Census Bureau added a child support module to its Current Population Survey (CPS), and the evidence from this survey provides a fairly comprehensive picture of the system as of the late 1970s (U.S. Bureau of the Census 1983).[5] According to the data, only 60 percent of mothers with children potentially eligible for child support had a legal arrangement in which the father was obliged to pay support. Divorced fathers were much more likely to owe and pay child support than fathers of children born out of wedlock. While about three-quarters of divorced mothers reported that fathers had a child support obligation (U.S. Bureau of the Census 1983, 1995), only 10 percent of never-married mothers reported that the fathers of their children owed child support.

Of the 60 percent of fathers with child support orders, only about one-half paid the full amount due, one-fourth paid only a portion of what was due, and another fourth paid nothing (U.S. Bureau of the Census 1983). Of the 40 percent of fathers with no formal obligation, estimates indicate that less than 20 percent paid informal support (Seltzer 1995; Teachman 1991).

Well-to-do fathers were much more likely to owe and to pay child support than poor fathers under the old system. Yet poor fathers who did have a legal obligation usually faced a far more onerous child support burden than their wealthier counterparts. On average, order levels of poor fathers represented a higher proportion of their income than order levels of middle- and upper-income fathers (Oellerich, Garfinkel, and Robins 1991).

FEDERAL REFORMS OF THE PRIVATE CHILD SUPPORT SYSTEM

After 1960 rapid social change began to alter fundamentally the nature of father absence and society's willingness to support the children of nonresident fathers. Rates of divorce, separation, and out-of-wedlock births, which had been growing steadily throughout the century, accelerated. The dramatic growth of mother-only families, coupled with the equally dramatic growth in the level of public provision per female-headed family, led to an explosion in public spending. Between 1955 and 1975, public expenditures on the welfare benefits package (AFDC, food stamps, and Medicaid) tripled (Garfinkel and McLanahan 1986).[6] The public and policy-makers objected not only to the cost but to the realization that many fathers were not doing their part to help support their children.

While publicly funded child support had always been associated with people in the lower economic strata, the mounting divorce rates of middle-class women after 1960 brought a new element to the equation: namely, middle-class mothers and women's rights organizations, like the National Organization of Women (NOW). NOW gathered evidence that child support orders and compliance rates were low (Cassetty 1978). In response to both the mounting strain on government resources and the perception that fathers were not paying their fair share, lawmakers at the federal and state levels sought to shift a greater share of the costs of child-rearing from the mothers and the public purse to nonresident fathers.

Despite initial opposition from both ends of the political spectrum, strengthening child support enforcement has become increasingly popular and now enjoys broad bipartisan support. Although critics on the right continue to worry about the invasion of family privacy and to urge policy-makers to focus their attention on welfare recipients only, their support for ideas like family values and personal responsibility predominates over their concerns for privacy. Similarly, although critics on the left continue to worry about the harsh treatment of poor fathers and the potential danger to poor mothers, their concern for women's economic status and for gender equity has led them to support most of the recent reforms. Today some of the most vocal opposition to stronger child support enforcement comes from middle- and upper-income fathers who argue that they are not being treated fairly by the courts, that they lack sufficient access to their children, and/or that their new families are suffering because order levels are set too high. Even so, these fathers are not arguing against child support per se but rather for more access to their children and more equity in the setting of child support obligations. Today there is near-universal agreement among policy-makers that children have a right to financial support from their biological fathers. Thus, the recent debates are generally about how to make child support policies as fair as possible, how to ensure fathers' access to their children, and how to protect the relatively small but significant group of mothers who are potentially at risk of domestic violence.

FEDERAL CHILD SUPPORT LEGISLATION, 1974 TO 1996

The first major federal child support legislation was passed by Congress in 1974—the addition of part D to Title IV of the Social Security Act. This act established the Child Support Enforcement (CSE) (or IV-D) program, created the federal Office of Child Support Enforcement (OCSE), required all states to establish comparable state offices, and authorized federal funding for three-quarters of the states' expenditures on child support enforcement. While the initial concern of the bill's sponsors was to ensure that public child support was not going to families that could be supported by nonresident fathers, they tried to broaden its appeal by also including assistance for middle-class single mothers. This was accomplished through the addition of funding for the child support offices to serve nonwelfare cases, albeit for only one year (as opposed to the permanent funding for welfare cases). Thanks perhaps in part to this particular addition, the 1974 landmark legislation passed narrowly. After a series of one-year extensions, in 1980 federal support was extended permanently to all children eligible for support, irrespective of income or welfare status. Legislation in 1984 required states to provide services on a universal basis.

Major federal laws in the area of child support policy were passed nearly unanimously by both houses of Congress in 1984 (the CSE amendments) and with overwhelming support in 1988 (the Family Support Act [FSA]). Although the provisions affecting income support in the Personal Responsibility and Work Opportunity Reconciliation Act (PRWORA) of 1996 were quite controversial, its child support provisions were not. Rather than discussing the child support provisions of each of these acts separately, we group the legislation by topic. To focus the discussion, we present the changes in three areas: policies that establish the legal obligation of fathers to pay child support, particularly policies to establish paternity; policies that affect the level of the child support orders; and policies aimed at enforcing child support obligations. Finally, we also review policies that provide fathers with services that help them meet their child support obligations and gain access to their children. Child support policy is still a province of state-based family law, and many states have passed significant policy reforms as well during this period; some of the most significant of these policies are also discussed in each policy area.

Policies Affecting Child Support Order Rates

As pointed out previously, in the 1970s most divorced fathers already had a child support order, and therefore no explicit legislation was passed to increase the order rates of these men. Instead, the major federal and state legislation in this area has focused on obtaining child support orders from men who have fathered children outside marriage. For these men, paternity must be formally established before a legally enforceable child support order can be issued. The 1975 landmark child support legislation had required mothers to cooperate with child support enforcement officials to establish paternity and child support orders. As of the late 1970s, however, paternity had been established in less than 20 percent of all eligible cases. At that time, some states had statutes of limitations that resulted in a relatively short time frame after a nonmarital child was born in which paternity could be established. The 1984 legislation changed this situation, requiring that states change their laws so that paternity could be established at any time up until the child's eighteenth birthday. Numerous states also enacted "long arm" statutes in the 1980s that allowed them to initiate paternity actions across state lines. Probably the most important change related to blood tests. In the late 1970s, blood tests were admissible as evidence in paternity cases only if they excluded the father. By the end of the 1980s, however, nearly all states had changed their laws to admit probabilistic evidence of paternity. The 1988 Family Support Act required states to utilize blood and genetic testing in disputed cases. After successful experiments in the states of Washington and Virginia, the Clinton administration began urging states to establish voluntary paternity acknowledgment programs at birth in hospitals. Most recently, the 1996 PRWORA requires states to have available in hospitals and birth record agencies a paternity acknowledgment form, which becomes a legal finding of paternity after sixty days. It also requires states to accept forms signed in other states. Finally, the 1996 legislation requires states to establish paternity in 90 percent of all nonmarital births or to increase the percentage by a defined rate each year until they are at 90 percent.

Insofar as low-income men are much more likely to father children outside marriage, the new paternity policies have disproportionately affected low-income fathers. Moreover, since these men are much more likely than other fathers to have children on welfare, their child support dollars are likely to go toward reducing welfare costs rather than to helping their child. Thus, fathers have little incentive to cooperate with the system. Indeed, as some ethnographic studies suggest, children may actually have less income if paternity is established and their fathers are paying support through the formal system instead of informally.

New efforts to establish paternity create a serious dilemma for these parents. If the father cares for his child and wants to stay in close contact, he runs the risk of being ordered to pay child support and thereby having less income to spend on the child. Similarly, the mother is often forced to choose between protecting the father (and his relationship with the child) and cooperating with the child support agency to maintain her welfare benefit. Of course, this dilemma may become less important under the new welfare regime, which limits welfare receipt to a maximum of five years, and even fewer years in some states. If these time limits are strictly enforced, single mothers will not be able to rely on welfare as a permanent source of support for their children. Once a mother is no longer eligible for welfare, any child support paid by the father will go directly toward the child. It is far too soon to say how these changes in the two systems will affect the relationship between the parents and between fathers and children. But the loss of options for mothers and the increased pressure on nonresident fathers are likely to have profound effects.

Thus far, attempts to increase the proportion of never-married mothers with a child support order have been quite successful. The annual number of paternities established by the federal Office of Child Support Enforcement increased from 111,000 in 1978 to 661,000 in 1996 (U.S. Department of Health and Human Services 1997; U.S. House of Representatives 1996). OCSE also estimates that in 1996 more than 200,000 fathers signed voluntary paternity acknowledgments. The extent to which these voluntary acknowledgments are also counted in the formal establishment numbers is unknown.[7] Being conservative and assuming that all voluntary acknowledgments are counted, the number of paternities formally established, divided by the number of out-of-wedlock births per year, suggests that the paternity establishment ratio has increased from 19 percent in 1979 to 52 percent in 1996. Thus, paternity is now being established in the majority of nonmarital births. Not surprisingly, the proportion of never-married mothers with a child support order has gone from 8 percent in 1979 to 23 percent in 1991 (U.S. Bureau of the Census 1983, 1995). Thus, men who father children out of wedlock are increasingly obligated to pay child support, and this trend is likely to intensify.

Despite the increase in child support orders among poor, never-married mothers, the overall order rate remained rather flat throughout the 1980s. In the early 1990s, the proportion of eligible families with a child support order remained at about 60 percent, which is where it was at the beginning of the 1980s. The explanation for this apparent anomaly is that divorce and separation cases, which generate a high proportion of child support orders, are making up a smaller share of the child support caseload, whereas cases due to out-of-wedlock births, which have a low, albeit growing, proportion of child support orders, are making up a larger share of the caseload. Thus, the overall order rate of 60 percent masks the gains realized in the rate of orders among children born outside marriage. If paternity establishment rates continue to increase at their present rate, we should soon witness a sharp increase in the proportion of nonresident fathers bound by child support orders.

Policies Affecting Order Levels

Because child support orders were generally set on a case-by-case basis in the pre-reform era, similar cases were often treated differently, and poor fathers with legal obligations may have been treated more harshly than their more well-to-do counterparts. The old system was also criticized for producing unacceptably low child support orders and for failing to keep orders on a par with inflation. The 1984

CSE amendments required states to adopt numeric child support guidelines that courts could use to determine child support obligations. The 1988 FSA went further, requiring states to make these guidelines presumptive. Judges who departed from the suggested amount were required to provide written justification.

In every state, the individual, cost-oriented perspective was replaced with an income-sharing perspective, which held that nonresident fathers were to share a particular percentage of their income with their children, with the percentage based on what was typically spent in two-parent families rather than on the minimum cost of a child. Finally, the Family Support Act of 1988 required states to examine all child support orders in welfare cases every three years (starting in 1993) and to update them in accordance with the guidelines. It also required states to review child support orders for non-welfare cases that fell under the jurisdiction of the Office of Child Support Enforcement if either parent requested the review.

The empirical evidence on the effects of the new state guidelines on how much nonresident fathers are ordered to pay is ambiguous. The gross trends in child support orders between 1979 and 1991, as reported by the CPS Child Support Supplements, suggest that in the period from 1978 to 1985, just before most states began establishing guidelines, the real value of child support orders declined by 25 percent (Beller and Graham 1993; Garfinkel 1992; Robins 1992). This precipitous decline coincided with unusually high inflation between 1978 and 1981 and with unusually high unemployment rates between 1981 and 1983 (Hanson et al. 1996). Since the guidelines were implemented (after 1985), order levels have increased somewhat, but it is too soon to tell whether the increase is due to the guidelines themselves or to the fact that men's incomes have been increasing. Whether the new guidelines will increase child support order levels is a question that cannot be answered at this time. The federally mandated policies did not take effect until the mid-1980s, and the data we have from the CPS Child Support Supplement is available only through 1992.

Other research on the potential and actual effects of the guidelines suggests that though the potential effects are large, actual effects have been modest. The amounts of child support orders required by the new state guidelines are substantially higher than those issued under the old system (Oellerich, Garfinkel, and Robins 1991). But in a few states studies of the effects of implementing guidelines have found only modest changes (Thoennes, Tjaden, and Pearson 1991; Meyer et al. 1996).

How are low-income fathers being treated under the new guidelines? In many states, these fathers are required to pay a higher percentage of their income than middle- and upper-income fathers. In a few states, guidelines contain a self-support reserve, which results in smaller orders for low-income nonresident parents. In other states, the orders are either progressive or proportional to fathers' income. However, one national study of guidelines indicates that low-income fathers are more likely to be ordered to pay amounts that exceed those set out in the guidelines (Argys, Peters, and Waldman 1995) than middle- and high-income fathers, a finding that is replicated in a more detailed study of a single state (Meyer, Cancian, and Melli 1997). This happens in part because courts sometimes base child support orders on imputed income rather than actual income, assuming that any father could have earnings equal to full-time work at the minimum wage. If a father cannot attain this level of earnings, his child support order will be a very high percentage of his income. Moreover, many states require a minimum child support order, and in others there is a suggested minimum amount (Meyer, Cancian, and Melli 1997). Fathers with very low incomes will thus have orders that are a very high percentage of their income. In addition to these high orders, fathers of children receiving welfare may be ordered to pay back all of the money the state has paid to their children in Medicaid and welfare benefits. The overall effect of the implementation of the new child support guidelines, as of the early 1990s, appears to be a continuation of regressivity: fathers in the lowest-income group pay a much higher percentage of their income (if they pay at all) than fathers in the highest-income category—28 percent versus 10 percent (Sorensen 1995).[8]

Federal legislation to update child support orders also affects poor nonresident fathers disproportionately. In the old child support system, orders were seldom changed to reflect new circumstances, and thus fathers who lost their job or otherwise experienced an income decline were likely to accumulate large child support debts, or arrearages. On the other hand, those who had income increases also seldom had their orders increased. The 1988 FSA required states, beginning in 1993, to review all child support orders of AFDC cases at least every three years and to offer to review any other cases being handled by the child support state offices (OCSE). Since low-income fathers are much more likely to have a child under the auspices of the OCSE, they are more likely to have their child support orders updated.

The effects of the 1988 legislation on a father may be either positive or negative, depending upon whether his income has increased or decreased. Evidence from Wisconsin indicates that fathers of children on welfare who have child support obligations are more likely to experience income increases than decreases, suggesting that many more fathers will experience increased obligations (Phillips and Garfinkel 1993).[9] Moreover, downward modifications cost the state money, while upward modifications save state dollars. So states have an incentive to apply modifications selectively. Evidence from studies of review and modification procedures in several states indicates that states did not update orders that would have decreased (Caliber Associates 1992; Kost et al. 1996). Finally, the PRWORA of 1996 allows states to determine for themselves whether welfare cases will be reviewed and modified, in effect giving them permission to update only orders when the father's income has increased.

Policies Affecting Whether Fathers Pay Child Support

The way child support is collected is also changing dramatically. After the landmark 1974 legislation, the first significant step toward tighter enforcement was passage of the 1984 CSE amendments, which required states to withhold child support obligations from the wages and other income of nonresident parents who were more than one month delinquent in their child support payments. The 1988 legislation went a step further, requiring automatic withholding of child support obligations from the outset for all IV-D cases as of 1990 and for all child support cases as of 1994. Many states, however, failed to implement withholding for non-IV-D cases because they neither had nor wanted to develop the bureaucratic capacity to administer universal withholding of payments. The 1996 PRWORA requires all states to develop the bureaucratic capacity to monitor all child support payments and to administer universal withholding.

The withholding of child support from the wages of nonresident parents will be effective only to the extent that the child support system can keep track of employment changes. Recently, some states have attempted to improve their ability to track employment changes by requiring employers to report their recent hires. The PRWORA goes further, establishing a national directory of new hires and requiring each state to maintain a directory of child support orders; these directories will be matched to facilitate the collection of orders.

Congress has also enacted legislation to improve the collection of child support in interstate cases. The PRWORA goes the furthest; it requires each state to enact the Uniform Interstate Family Support Act, ensuring that states have comparable collection policies. States must also provide information on motor vehicle registrations and law enforcement records to other states and to the federal government so that nonresident parents who move across state lines can be found.

The penalties for not paying support have also been increased. Legislation in 1981 allowed the interception of income tax refunds when a nonresident parent was behind in child support payments. The 1984 CSE required states to have procedures for imposing liens against property of nonresident parents who were delinquent. A new round of penalties was instituted by PRWORA, which requires states to have in place procedures for revoking driver's licenses and professional licenses of delinquent obligors.

Federal legislation has severely restricted the ability of nonresident fathers who are behind in their payments to have their obligations altered. Since 1975 federal law has required that child support obligations remain in place even if the nonresident father declares bankruptcy. More serious for poor nonresident fathers, since the late 1980s the ability of courts to decrease the amount of child support arrearages, even in response to a decreased ability to pay, has been significantly curtailed. A final dramatic policy change came with the PRWORA: states for the first time are allowed to deny food stamps to nonresident parents who are behind in their child support payments. While previous policies have sought to force nonresident parents to pay their support obligations, the new law is the first effort to withhold benefits from poor nonresident parents as a means of penalizing nonpayment.

In sum, public enforcement of the private child support obligations of nonresident fathers has undergone substantial tightening in the last twenty years. Most of the reforms have been aimed at forcing fathers to pay more child support, with each round of legislation giving the state new methods of enforcing existing child support orders and new punishments for those not paying. Avoiding those orders is more difficult already, and it will become increasingly so in the future.

Evaluating the effects of the legislation on the degree to which fathers are meeting their obligations is difficult because, as with order rates and guidelines, the strongest legislation has been implemented too recently. By the early 1990s, the average percentage of orders paid had increased only slightly—from 65 percent in 1978 to 68 percent in 1991 (U.S. Bureau of the Census 1995). But more than likely, collection rates today are already higher than they were in 1991, and the stringent new legislation makes it likely that they will continue to climb. Of the policies discussed in this chapter, only immediate withholding has been evaluated by research based on differences across states and before/after comparisons within states. This research indicates that immediate withholding of child support obligations increases collection rates by between 5 and 30 percent (Garfinkel and Klawitter 1990; Garfinkel and Robins 1994).

Policies to Assist Nonresident Fathers

Like the traditional system, most recent child support reforms have focused nearly exclusively on increasing child support payments rather than on offering incentives to pay or on helping fathers increase their earnings capacity. For example, the earned income tax credit, which provides a refundable tax credit to working low-income parents and was dramatically expanded in the 1980s and 1990s, is not available to nonresident parents even if they are paying substantial amounts of child support.[10] Similarly, a nonresident father cannot claim his children as dependents on his income tax return, no matter how much child support he pays, unless the resident mother has waived the right to the exemption.

However, in 1984 as a first step toward incentives for low-income fathers, a disincentive to pay was recognized and lessened. Individuals receiving AFDC have long been required to sign over any child support collected on their behalf to the state; these collections were then used to offset AFDC expenditures, and children on AFDC did not receive any benefit from child support paid by their nonresident father. To counteract this disincentive, the legislation stipulated that the first fifty dollars of child support paid each month was to go to the family, with the remainder directed to the state to offset AFDC costs. There is some ethnographic evidence that the fifty-dollar incentive was not enough to encourage payment through the formal system (see, for example, Edin 1995). The 1996 PRWORA reversed direction and gave states the flexibility to determine whether they wanted to continue the fifty-dollars-per-month incentive, eliminate it, or increase it. As of this writing, most states have chosen to either continue or eliminate the set-aside. In contrast, Wisconsin is experimenting with allowing recipients to keep the entire amount of child support collected.

The only federal policy aimed at actually helping low-income nonresident fathers pay child support has been funding for a group of state demonstrations established by the 1988 Family Support Act. The Parents' Fair Share demonstrations provide work and training opportunities to unemployed and poor nonresident fathers, and they hold child support obligations in abeyance while fathers participate in the program. They also provide services to help men become better fathers.

As support enforcement has been strengthened, fathers' bargaining position in gaining access to their children has been weakened. A critical feature of enforcement policy has been a firm separation between the financial side of child support arrangements and the amount of visitation; that is, meeting their child support obligations did not guarantee nonresident parents the right to visit their children, and failure to pay did not give resident parents the right to refuse visits. Moreover, a breakdown in visitation provided no excuse for nonpayment. Fathers' groups have complained bitterly about the one-sidedness of child support enforcement policy in that a nonresident parent's failure to pay brings him serious consequences, whereas a resident mother's failure to provide access to the children carries no formal consequences. The increase in joint legal custody may be viewed as one response to these complaints. The federal government responded by including in the 1988 FSA funding for several state demonstrations that were aimed at helping fathers gain access to their children, and funds were made available to all states in the 1996 legislation.

The Access Projects, together with the Parents' Fair Share demonstrations, are notable departures from previous policy. During the first few years of the federal CSE amendments, federal and state officials prided themselves on their pure law enforcement approach to child support. Now some offices are being asked to provide social services as well. The demonstrations are also notable in that the child support office's "clients" in the past have always been seen as the resident parent and children; Parents' Fair Share and the Access Projects ask child support workers to provide services to nonresident parents as well. These are marked changes in policy direction.

For many fathers, these new policy efforts are not enough. To them, policy still seems focused on forcing them to pay what they sometimes view as unreasonable amounts and imposing increasingly severe penalties if they do not comply. The steps toward dealing with access issues and providing limited training seem tiny in comparison; in terms of governmental expenditures, they are indeed tiny.

Still others view current child support policies as too lenient. They point out that in many states judges have great discretion in setting the amount of child support orders, and that most often judges deviate from the guidelines only to lower the order (CSR, Inc. 1996). Moreover, nonresident parents can still manage to avoid their financial responsibilities (by working for cash, voluntarily taking lower-paid jobs, and so forth).

The resolution of these debates, and thus the future of policy toward nonresident fathers, is unclear. Representatives of federal agencies are now systematically reviewing various policies to determine their effect on fathers; a variety of new initiatives may result from these reviews. With what criteria should new initiatives affecting nonresident fathers be judged? While equity concerns are one input into policy formation, another input could be information on how current policies are working. This review and the other chapters in this volume provide valuable new information on nonresident fathers and how current policy affects them. As is always true of social science research, the chapters are best at describing how the child support system of the recent past has affected fathers, mothers, and children. They are less definitive in recommending policies, assessing long-term effects of child support reforms, or predicting how the most recent changes (or changes still to be considered) will affect fathers, mothers, and children. Nonetheless, they represent what is currently known about a critical topic affecting millions of children, nonresident parents, resident parents, and taxpayers, and we hope they affect future policies for nonresident fathers.

The authors thank Paula Roberts and Linda Mellgren for discussion of these issues and comments on an earlier version. Any errors that remain are the responsibility of the authors alone.

NOTES

1. Reviews of the history of child custody determinations include Buehler and Gerard (1995), Emery, Hetherington, and Dilalla (1984), Furstenberg (1988), Kelly (1994), Mason (1994), and Pearson, Munson, and Thoennes (1982).

2. Although Garasky and Meyer (1996) find a large increase in the proportion of single-parent families headed by fathers, Hernandez and Garfinkel (1998) find no trend in custody at divorce toward fathers. There are several possible explanations for these findings. Perhaps the increase in father-only families is due to a decrease in remarriage among fathers who gain custody; perhaps it is due to children moving from living with their mother to living with their father as they age; or perhaps it is due to fathers who share custody reporting children as living with them (see also Cancian and Meyer 1998).

3. In a few states, like Wisconsin and Michigan, child support payments were made to the courts, but even in these states the courts usually only monitored payments and did not take action to enforce compliance with an existing order unless specifically requested to do so by the resident parent (Cassetty 1978; Chambers 1979).

4. While the direction of the incentive is clear (Aid to Dependent Children created an incentive for families to break up), the magnitude is not. A body of empirical research has examined the relationship between the level of welfare benefits and both the divorce rate and the rate of nonmarital births. While more recent studies have found larger and more consistent effects, the effects are still small (Moffitt 1998).

5. Though the CPS data are based on mothers, the discussion in the text is framed in terms of the effects on fathers. Because some mothers may have children by more than one nonresident father, and some nonresident fathers may have children by more than one mother, the number of resident mothers will not exactly match the number of nonresident fathers. However, the numbers should be close enough to be a reasonableapproximation.

6. Only a small part of the increase was due to an increase in the real value of cash AFDC benefits. Most of the increase was due to the addition of new in-kind benefits (food stamps and Medicaid) and to the increase in the proportion of single mothers who received welfare benefits.

7. About one-third of nonmarital births are to cohabiting couples (Bumpass and Raley 1995). Fathers in these couples may be particularly likely to acknowledge paternity voluntarily.

8. Because research indicates that upper-income fathers pay a greater proportion of what they owe, the data in the text underestimate the extent to which orders are regressive.

9. There are two reasons for this. First, fathers of children on welfare tend to be young, and so their incomes increase as they grow older. Second, some fathers of children on welfare are temporarily unemployed. Reemployment leads to an increase in income (see Phillips and Garfinkel 1993).

10. Prior to 1990, the parent providing more than half of a child's support could claim the credit, but in 1990 the eligibility requirements changed, limiting the eligibility of nonresident parents. In 1993 a very small credit for those not living with children (childless individuals as well as nonresident parents) was instituted.

REFERENCES

Argys, Laura M., H. Elizabeth Peters, and Donald M. Waldman. 1995. "Can the Family Support Act Put Some Life Back into Deadbeat Dads: An Analysis of Child Support Guidelines, Award Rates, and Levels." Paper presented at the American Economic Association meetings, Washington (January).

Beller, Andrea H., and John W. Graham. 1993. *Small Change: The Economics of Child Support.* New Haven, Conn.: Yale University Press.

Buehler, Cheryl, and Jean M. Gerard. 1995. "Divorce Law in the United States: A Focus on Child Custody." *Family Relations* 44(4): 439–58.

Bumpass, Larry L., and R. Kelly Raley. 1995. "Redefining Single-Parent Families: Cohabitation and Changing Family Reality." *Demography* 32(1): 97–109.

Caliber Associates. 1992. "Evaluation of Child Support Review and Modification Demonstration Projects in Four States." Cross-site final report. Fairfax, Va.: Caliber Associates.

Cancian, Maria, and Daniel R. Meyer. 1996. "Changing Policy, Changing Practice: Mothers' Incomes and Child Support Orders." *Journal of Marriage and the Family* 58(3): 618–27.

———. 1998. "Who Gets Custody?" *Demography* 35(2):147–57.

Cassetty, Judith. 1978. *Child Support and Public Policy: Securing Support from Absent Fathers.* Lexington, Mass.: Lexington Books.

Chambers, David L. 1979. *Making Fathers Pay: The Enforcement of Child Support.* Chicago: University of Chicago Press.

CSR, Inc. 1996. *Evaluation of Child Support Guidelines.* Report to the U.S. Office of Child Support Enforcement. Washington: CSR, Inc.

Edin, Kathryn. 1995. "Single Mothers and Child Support: The Possibilities and Limits of Child Support Policy." *Children and Youth Services Review* 17(1–2): 203–30.

Emery, Robert E., E. Mavis Hetherington, and Lisabeth F. Dilalla. 1984. "Divorce, Children, and Social Policy." In *Child Development Research and Social Policy,* vol. 1, edited by Harold W. Stevenson and Alberta E. Siegel. Chicago: University of Chicago Press.

Furstenberg, Frank F., Jr. 1988. "Good Dads—Bad Dads: Two Faces of Fatherhood." In *The Changing American Family and Public Policy,* edited by Andrew Cherlin. Washington: Urban Institute Press.

Garasky, Steven, and Daniel R. Meyer. 1996. "Reconsidering the Increase in Father-Only Families." *Demography* 33(3): 385–93.

Garfinkel, Irwin. 1992. *Assuring Child Support: An Extension of Social Security.* New York: Russell Sage Foundation.

Garfinkel, Irwin, and Marieka M. Klawitter. 1990. "The Effect of Routine Income Withholding of Child Support Collections." *Journal of Policy Analysis and Management* 9(2): 155–77.

Garfinkel, Irwin, and Sara S. McLanahan. 1986. *Single Mothers and Their Children.* Washington: Urban Institute Press.

Garfinkel, Irwin, and Philip K. Robins. 1994. "The Relationship Between Child Support Enforcement Tools and Child Support Outcomes." In *Child Support and Child Well-being,* edited by Irwin Garfinkel, Sara S. McLanahan, and Philip K. Robins. Washington: Urban Institute Press.

Hanson, Thomas L., Irwin Garfinkel, Sara S. McLanahan, and Cynthia K. Miller. 1996. "Trends in Child Support Outcomes." *Demography* 33(4): 483–96.

Hernandez, Pedro, and Irwin Garfinkel. 1998. "Gender Differences in Child Custody and Child Support Orders." Unpublished paper.

Katz, Michael B. 1986. *In the Shadow of the Poorhouse.* New York: Basic Books.

Kelly, Joan B. 1994. "The Determination of Child Custody." *Future of Children* 4 (Spring): 121–42.

Kost, Kate, Tom Corbett, Dan Meyer, and Pat Brown. 1996. "Revising Child Support Orders: The Wisconsin Experience." *Family Relations* 45(1): 19–26.

Krause, Harry D. 1981. *Child Support in America: The Legal Perspective.* Charlottesville, Va.: Michie.

Mason, Mary Ann. 1994. *From Father's Property to Children's Rights: The History of Child Custody in the United States.* New York: Columbia University Press.

Melli, Marygold S. 1992. "A Brief History of the Legal Structure for Paternity Establishment in the United States." In *Institute for Research on Poverty: Special Report 56A: Paternity Establishment: A Public Policy Conference.* Madison, Wisc.: Institute for Research on Poverty.

Meyer, Daniel R., Judi Bartfeld, Irwin Garfinkel, and Patricia Brown. 1996. "Child Support Reform: Lessons from Wisconsin." *Family Relations* 45(1): 11–18.

Meyer, Daniel R., Maria Cancian, and Marygold S. Melli. 1997. "Low-Income Fathers and Child Support Orders." Final Report to the Wisconsin Department of Workforce Development. Madison, Wisc.: Institute for Research on Poverty (June).

Moffitt, Robert. 1998. "The Effect of Welfare on Marriage and Fertility." In *Welfare, the Family, and Reproductive Behavior,* edited by Robert Moffitt. Washington, D.C.: National Academy Press.

Oellerich, Donald, Irwin Garfinkel, and Philip Robins. 1991. "Private Child Support: Current and Potential Impacts." *Journal of Sociology and Social Welfare* 18(1): 3–24.

Pearson, Jessica, Paul Munson, and Nancy Thoennes. 1982. "Legal Change and Child Custody Awards." *Journal of Family Issues* 3(1): 5–24.

Phillips, Elizabeth, and Irwin Garfinkel. 1993. "Income Growth Among Nonresident Fathers: Evidence from Wisconsin." *Demography* 30(2): 227–41.

Robins, Philip K. 1992. "Why Did Child Support Award Levels Decline from 1978 to 1985?" *Journal of Human Resources* 27(2): 362–79.

Seltzer, Judith A. 1995. "Demographic Change, Children's Families, and Child Support Policy in the United States." In *Families, Human Resources, and Social Development,* edited by Hsiao-hung, Nancy Chen, Yia-ling Liu, and Mei-o Hsueh. Taipei, Taiwan: National Chengchi University.

Sorensen, Elaine. 1995. "A National Profile of Noncustodial Fathers and Their Ability to Pay Child Support." Urban Institute, Washington. Unpublished paper.

Teachman, Jay D. 1991. "Contributions to Children by Divorced Fathers." *Social Problems* 38(3): 358–71.

Thoennes, Nancy, Patricia Tjaden, and Jessica Pearson. 1991. "The Impact of Child Support Guidelines on Award Adequacy, Award Variability, and Case Processing Efficiency." *Family Law Quarterly* 25(3): 325–45.

U.S. Bureau of the Census. 1983. *Child Support and Alimony: 1978.* Current Population Reports, series P23–112. Washington: U.S. Government Printing Office.

————. 1995. *Child Support for Custodial Mothers and Fathers: 1991.* Current Population Reports, series P60–187. Washington: U.S. Government Printing Office.

U.S. Department of Health and Human Services, Office of Child Support Enforcement. 1997. *Twentieth Annual Report to Congress.* Washington: U.S. Department of Health and Human Services.

U.S. House of Representatives, Committee on Ways and Means. 1996. *Overview of Entitlement Programs: 1996 Green Book.* Washington: U.S. Government Printing Office.

Chapter 2

A Patchwork Portrait of Nonresident Fathers

Irwin Garfinkel, Sara S. McLanahan, and Thomas L. Hanson

Nonresident fathers who fail to pay child support are often depicted in the media either as wealthy scoundrels who go to great lengths to escape their parental responsibility or as penniless victims who are willing but unable to support their children. Still others describe these fathers as men with serious drug and alcohol problems who are potentially dangerous to mothers and children. While cases such as these can be found in every community, most nonpaying fathers probably do not fit any of these stereotypes. More likely, their incomes fall somewhere in between extreme poverty and wealth and their personality flaws are not serious enough to disqualify them from the parental role.

Unfortunately, the data needed to determine how many fathers fit the stereotypes and how many fall somewhere in between are not readily available. Although several national surveys have attempted to identify nonresident fathers, the evidence suggests that a substantial proportion of these men are either underrepresented in the surveys or do not admit to being fathers. Thus, men who acknowledge their parental status are a somewhat select group of fathers who probably do not represent the average nonresident father. Andrew Cherlin, Jeanne Griffith, and James McCarthy (1983) were the first researchers to draw attention to the problem of "missing fathers" in survey data. Using the June 1980 Current Population Survey (CPS), which collected fertility histories from men as well as women, they found that the proportion of divorced and separated men who acknowledged being fathers was about half as large as the proportion of divorced and separated women who acknowledged being mothers. More recently, researchers have shown that the problem exists in other data sets as well, including surveys designed explicitly to study family relationships and interhousehold exchanges (Sorensen 1995; Robertson 1995; Seltzer and Brandreth 1994; Rendall et al. 1997).[1]

In sharp contrast to the data on nonresident fathers, our national surveys contain very good information on resident mothers and children.[2] Soon after the landmark 1974 child support legislation was signed into law, the U.S. Census Bureau added a child support supplement to the April 1979 Current Population Survey (CPS-CSS). The CPS-CSS has been repeated every other year since 1982. Combined with information from the March CPS, these data provide a very good picture of the economic and social circumstances of resident mothers and their children. In addition, the National Survey of Families and Households (NSFH) and the Survey of Income and Program Participation (SIPP) contain excellent samples of child support–eligible households.

The absence of a nationally representative sample of nonresident fathers does not mean that we are completely ignorant about these men. Since women tend to mate with men like themselves—what demographers call assortative mating—we can infer some things about the fathers by looking at the characteristics of the mothers (Sweet and Bumpass 1987; Miller, Garfinkel, and McLanahan 1997). Assuming assortative mating, the NSFH data on mothers indicate that nonresident fathers come from all walks of life, from the highest to the lowest echelons. At the same time, when we compare resident fathers with what we assume nonresident fathers are like (based on the characteristics of resident mothers), we find that nonresident fathers are disproportionately black (31 percent), more likely to be high school dropouts (31 percent), and less likely to have been married to their child's mother when their child was born (53 percent).[3] Statistics such as these are useful in giving us a general picture of nonresident fathers. They also tell us something about which fathers are missing from our nationally representative surveys. For example, if 80 percent of the nonresident fathers in a particular sample are white, we know that the sample underrepresents disadvantaged fathers.

Although using mothers' characteristics as a proxy for fathers' characteristics is useful for some purposes (for example, to estimate education, race, and even earnings capacity), this approach is not very useful for obtaining information on characteristics and behaviors that change over time (such as labor-force behavior, health status, and living arrangements). To get information on the latter, we need data taken directly from the fathers themselves.

In this chapter, we present information on several different characteristics of nonresident fathers. We use the National Survey of Families and Households, and we adjust these data to take account of fathers who are underrepresented in the survey and fathers who are in the survey but have misreported their parental status. We focus on three sets of questions:

1. How much income do nonresident fathers have? In other words, can they afford to pay more child support?

2. What are their current living arrangements? Have they formed new families? Are they supporting new children?

3. What are their personal characteristics? Do they have serious alcohol or drug problems? Are they likely to be good parents to their children?

In the next section, we review previous research that touches on these questions. In following sections, we discuss our data and the methods we use to adjust the NSFH data to take account of missing fathers, and we report the results. Unlike the clean, crisp picture of resident mothers that emerges from the CPS-CSS and other surveys, the picture of nonresident fathers must be patched together from various data sources. Nonetheless, we believe that trying to adjust for the missing fathers is useful insofar as it gets us closer to the truth about some of the characteristics we are most concerned about.

PREVIOUS RESEARCH

Nonresident Fathers' Income

How much child support nonresident fathers can afford to pay is probably the single most important question concerning policy-makers. Not surprisingly, most of the research on nonresident fathers tries to address this question. Table 2.1 (prepared by Dan Meyer) presents a summary of the findings of several major studies that have attempted to estimate the incomes of nonresident fathers. All results are reported in 1995 dollars.

The studies are grouped according to whether they focus on (1) divorced and separated fathers, (2) young and unwed fathers, (3) fathers of children on welfare or fathers of children receiving child support enforcement services, or (4) all fathers. Notice the wide range of incomes across the different subgroups. Most studies show that divorced and separated fathers have average incomes in the $30,000 to $40,000 range; two studies show incomes in the mid to high forties. In contrast, young, unwed fathers have incomes in the high teens—about half that of the average divorced or separated father. Fathers of children on welfare have the lowest incomes, ranging from $10,000 to $15,000. Obviously, one cannot generalize from any one of these groups to nonresident fathers as a whole.

Even within these subgroups, generalization is problematic. The studies of fathers of children on welfare, for example, are based on men who are identified as fathers in official child support enforcement records. Less than half of the nonresident fathers in this subgroup are identified (McDonald, Moran, and Garfinkel 1990). Studies of young, unwed fathers fail to identify about 20 percent of the fathers, and the problem is even more acute among minority fathers. Longitudinal studies of divorced and separated fathers are probably the most complete, but even these suffer from non-inclusion and nonresponse biases.[4]

The last section of table 2.1 reports the results from three studies that estimate the incomes of all nonresident fathers. All three of these studies attempt to deal with the problem of missing fathers. Irwin Garfinkel and Donald Oellerich (1989) and Cynthia Miller, Irwin Garfinkel, and Sara McLanahan (1997) use information on resident mothers in the CPS to predict the personal incomes of nonresident fathers. Elaine Sorensen (1995) uses information on men's fertility in the SIPP to identify nonresident fathers and to measure their income directly.[5] Although these studies use different approaches, they reach very similar conclusions.[6] Garfinkel and Ollerich (1989) estimate that the average income of nonresident fathers is about $30,000, whereas Miller and her colleagues (1997) conclude that it is about $28,000. According to both studies, white fathers have about twice as much income as nonwhite

TABLE 2.1 / Estimates of the Income of Nonresident Fathers

Study	Data Set	Sample	Mean Annual Income (in 1995 Dollars)	Type of Income
Divorced or Separated Nonresident Fathers				
1. Oellerich (1984)	SIE 1976	Divorced and separated fathers	34,369 D 25,749 S	—
2. O'Neill (1985)	CPS 1980	Fathers reporting a child from a disrupted marriage living elsewhere	39,803	Family income
3. Nichols-Casebolt (1986)	PSID 1980	Nonresident fathers who were married by 1968 but experienced divorce by 1980	37,911 D 41,887 D-W 22,766 D-NW	Family income the year after divorce
4. Cassety (1978)	PSID 1975	Nonresident fathers who were married by 1968 but experienced divorce by 1974	31,924 D	Personal income
5. Hill (1988)	PSID 1982	Nonresident fathers who were married by 1968 but experienced divorce by 1981	45,107 D	Average family income in the years between the divorce and 1981
6. Teachman and Polanko (1989)	NLS-HSC72 1986	Fathers who, by 1986, had divorced a woman who had graduated from high school in 1972	29,728 D	Personal earnings the year of divorce

Study	Data source	Sample	Value	Income measure
7. Maccoby and Mnookin (1992)	Surveys of Californians with children, filing for divorce in 1984 to 1985	Fathers who filed for divorce in 1984 to 1985	48,667 D	Median personal income fifteen months after filing for divorce
Young Nonresident Fathers				
8. Lerman (1990)	NLSY 1987	Unmarried fathers in 1984 age twenty-three to thirty in 1987	16,228 18,620 W 17,325 H 14,679 B	Personal earnings in 1987
9. Mincy and Sorensen (1998)	SIPP 1990	Nonresident fathers age eighteen and thirty-four (using two different weighing schemes)	17,257–21,338	Personal earnings in 1987
Nonresident Fathers of Children on AFDC (or with Active Case at the CSE)				
10. Oellerich (1984)	SIE 1976	All nonresident fathers on AFDC in Wisconsin	14,695	Personal income
11. Haskins, Schwartz, and Akin (1985)	Survey of nonresident fathers with active cases at North Carolina's Child Support Enforcement Agency	AFDC recipients AFDC recipients	10,341–13,952 12,472–14,807	Mean personal income
12. Sonenstein and Calhoun (1988)	SOAP	Nonresident fathers with active cases at the Child Support Enforcement Agency in Florida	14,164	Median personal income

(Table continues on p. 36.)

TABLE 2.1 / Continued

Study	Data Set	Sample	Mean Annual Income (in 1995 Dollars)	Type of Income
All Nonresident Fathers				
13. Garfinkel and Oellerich (1989)	CPS-CSS 1979	Mothers with children potentially eligible for child support	29,602 34,378 W 17,267 NW	Estimated personal income based on characteristics of mothers
14. Sorensen (1995)	SIPP	Nonresident fathers	26,507–27,722	Personal income
15. Miller, Garfinkel, and McLanahan (1997)	CPS-CSS 1990	Mothers with children potentially eligible for child support	28,193 21,427 B 30,697 NB 32,912 RM 32,186 D 26,911 S 20,143 NM	Estimated personal income based on characteristics of mothers

Data set abbreviations: AFDC: Aid to Families with Dependent Children; CPS: Current Population Survey; CPS-CSS: Current Population Survey—Child Support Supplement; ESC: Employment Securities Commission (of North Carolina); NLS-HSC72: National Longitudinal Survey—; NLS-YW: National Longitudinal Survey—Young Women; NLSY: National Longitudinal Survey—Youth Cohort; PSID: Panel Study of Income Dynamics; SOAP: Survey of Absent Parents; SIE: Survey of Income and Education; SIPP: Survey of Income and Program Participation.

Other codes: B = Black; D = Divorced; H = Hispanic; M = Married; NB = Non-Black; NM = Never Married; NW = Non-White; RM = Remarried; S = Separated; W = White.

fathers, and divorced fathers have about twice as much income as never-married fathers. Sorensen reports that the average personal income of nonresident fathers is about $27,000, with nonpayers having about $8,000 to $10,000 less income than payers. She also finds that between 8 and 14 percent of all nonresident fathers are poor, and that between 14 and 40 percent of all black nonresident fathers are poor.

These three studies also applied child support guidelines to the estimated incomes of nonresident fathers to develop estimates of how much child support nonresident fathers should be paying. The estimates indicate that according to these guidelines the nonresident fathers should have paid more than three times the amount they did pay. In 1990 fathers should have paid between $45 billion and $50 billion, but they actually paid only about $14 billion (Sorensen 1995; Miller, Garfinkel, and McLanahan 1997). Some policy-makers have misinterpreted these results to suggest that the potential savings in welfare from strict enforcement of child support are huge. In fact, this research documents that the bulk of the payment gap is attributable not to the very poor nonresident fathers whose children are on welfare but rather to the more well-to-do fathers, whose children are rarely on welfare. Only 13 percent of the payment gap is due to the fathers of children on welfare (Oellerich, Garfinkel, and Robins 1991).

Nonresident Fathers' New Families

Also important to policy-makers are the living arrangements of nonresident fathers. What proportion of these men are supporting new families, particularly families with children? What is the economic status of their "second" families? If the proportion is high and the economic status is precarious, stricter child support enforcement could lead to a substantial reshuffling of poverty—from first to second families—rather than a reduction of poverty. Even if we believe that the needs of the first family should take precedence over the needs of the second, we still would want to know how many children from second families are likely to be affected.

Unfortunately, there is very little information about the living arrangements of nonresident fathers or the proportion that are remarried and raising children. Research based on young adults in the National Longitudinal Survey of Youth (NLSY) indicates that at least 25 percent of nonresident fathers are living with their own parents (Robertson 1995). These data, however, overrepresent young men and poor families, and therefore the results cannot be generalized to the whole population. Sorensen (1995) finds that nearly half of the nonresident fathers identified in the SIPP are currently married and more than one-third are living with new children. Finally, Judith Seltzer and Yvonne Brandreth (1994) report that about 46 percent of nonresident fathers in the NSFH are remarried and about 24 percent have new children. While the latter two studies are based on nationally representative data sets, Seltzer and Brandreth do not take account of missing nonresident fathers; moreover, as described later in this chapter, the Sorensen study includes some fathers whose children are over eighteen.

Nonresident Fathers' Personal Characteristics

A final question facing policy-makers is whether nonresident fathers are potentially dangerous to resident mothers and children. Clearly, most mothers and children in first families are likely to benefit from the greater economic security that comes with regular child support payments. Yet many people fear that forcing reluctant fathers to pay may have negative consequences as well. Much of their concern is based on the belief that many nonresident fathers are "unsavory characters" who have serious mental health problems, problems with drugs and alcohol abuse, or problems with physical abuse and violence. According to this scenario, the current system is preferable to a new system because it allows the mothers to avoid all contact with these fathers and allows the men to virtually disappear.

Previous research tells us very little about the potential for violence among nonresident fathers. Several recent studies have reported high rates of domestic violence among mothers on welfare, with current prevalence rates ranging from 15 to 32 percent and lifetime prevalence ranging from 34 to 65 percent (Raphael and Tolman 1997). But these studies are limited to mothers on welfare and do not distinguish between nonresident fathers and other partners. Several other studies have looked at parental conflict before and after divorce. Hanson and his colleagues find that about 25 percent of couples engage in high conflict after separation, and another 22 percent report moderate conflict (Hanson, McLanahan, and Thomson 1996).[7] These percentages may understate the potential problem, however, since the most conflict-prone couples are likely to avoid all contact with each other after a divorce, thereby minimizing the chance of conflict. If child support enforcement were increased, these parents would have more reason and opportunity to communicate with one another, and the child would probably be exposed to more high conflict.

Evidence from Qualitative Studies

In addition to the quantitative studies, there is an emerging set of qualitative studies that look at nonresident fathers. These studies provide rich detail about the economic and social circumstances of nonresident fathers, about their relationships with their children, and about their views of fatherhood and paternal responsibility. Nearly all of this research focuses on young, black, inner-city fathers, and the portraits that emerge are of men who are weakly attached to the labor force and who lack the resources to make regular child support payments.

The findings are mixed with respect to whether these young fathers *want* to support their children. Elijah Anderson's (1993) study of "sexual games" describes a situation in which young men take advantage of young women to fulfill their own sexual needs. These young fathers appear to have little concern for their children's well-being. In contrast, other researchers report that fathers do care about their children and that many are making irregular (informal) contributions, including buying diapers and baby-sitting for the mother (Furstenberg, Sherwood, and Sullivan

1992; Edin 1995; Edin and Lein 1997). Maureen Waller (1995) argues that poor mothers and fathers have defined the role of fatherhood to emphasize emotional support and guidance over economic responsibility. Her research indicates that poor, unwed fathers place considerable value on the importance of biological parenthood.

With respect to the mental health and problem behavior of nonresident fathers, the ethnographies suggest that while many young fathers have trouble holding a job and may even spend time in jail, most have something to offer their children. The overwhelming impression of these young men conveyed by the literature is one of immaturity and irresponsibility rather than pathology or dangerousness. Indeed, many of the fathers who are not paying child support are maintaining contact with their children and are still involved with the mothers, although often intermittently. Similarly, most mothers indicate that they would like the fathers to be more involved with their children, although they recognize that they cannot depend on them for financial support (Furstenberg, Sherwood, and Sullivan 1992; Waller 1995; Edin 1995).

DATA AND METHODS

To create a portrait of nonresident fathers, we use the National Survey of Families and Households, a nationally representative sample of approximately thirteen thousand adult men and women interviewed in 1987. The NSFH has several advantages over the SIPP and other data that have been used to examine nonresident fathers' characteristics (see chapter 2). First, like the SIPP, the NSFH is representative of all noninstitutionalized, adult men who are permanent residents of households in the United States.[8] Second, the NSFH data contain complete fertility histories for all male and female respondents. Finally, the NSFH contains a screener that asks respondents whether they have a minor child living outside the household, and if so, where the child lives. The screener can be used to identify and exclude nonresident fathers whose child is living with someone other than the mother. No other survey asks these questions.[9] In the NSFH, 522 men over the age of twenty-one report living apart from a biological child who resides with his or her mother.[10]

Although the NSFH does a better job of identifying nonresident fathers than other surveys, these data still miss a substantial number of fathers. According to table 2.2, 9.4 million women report having a child eligible for support, whereas only 5.8 million men report being nonresident fathers. Assuming that the number of nonresident fathers should match the number of resident mothers, the discrepancy suggests that as many as 3.6 million fathers are missing from the NSFH sample. Furthermore, assuming assortative mating, the numbers in table 2.2 suggest that the missing fathers are disproportionately nonwhite, poorly educated, and unmarried at the child's birth. They also are less likely to pay child support than the fathers who are represented in the survey. Whereas only 41 percent of the mothers report receiving child support (mean of $3,259), 70 percent of nonresident fathers report paying support (mean of $3,735). Although previous research (Schaeffer,

TABLE 2.2 / Differences in Mothers' and Fathers' Reports About Nonresident Fathers

	Mothers' Reports	Fathers' Reports	Ratio Father/Mother
All fathers (weighted)	9,399,535[a]	5,838,366	62%
White[b]	6,555,928	4,621,667	70
Black	2,843,626	1,216,669	43
Education			
< high school	2,199,126	1,062,797	48
= high school	4,253,039	2,292,254	54
> high school degree	2,947,370	2,483,315	84
Age			
<28	1,614,999	806,059	50
28–38	3,942,393	2,550,958	65
38+	3,842,143	2,481,349	65
One or more nonmarital births	4,974,575	2,404,132	48
Number of marital births	4,424,978	3,434,204	78
Father's income	—	$33,479	
Father pays some support	41%	70.2%	
Mean payment[c]	$3,259	$3,735	
Sample size	1,565	522	

Source: National Survey of Families and Households (1987).

Notes:

[a] Number of nonresident fathers according to mothers' reports, assuming all children in household have same father.

[b] Includes Asians and Hispanics.

[c] Among those who paid any child support.

Seltzer, and Klawitter 1991) indicates that nonresident fathers tend to overstate their child support contributions, the magnitude of these differences suggests that the missing fathers in the NSFH are principally nonpayers.[11] Indeed, if one assumes that all of the missing fathers are nonpayers, this brings the proportion of paying fathers down to 43.5 percent, or only two and a half percentage points higher than the percentage reported by the mothers. For this reason, our method of correcting the data for missing fathers imposes the assumption that all of the missing fathers are nonpayers.

If men are more likely to have children with different partners than women, the difference between the number of nonresident fathers and the number of resident mothers in table 2.2 may overstate the number of missing fathers. We found, however, that our results were the same regardless of whether we matched on the number of mothers and fathers or on the number of children reported by men and women. For ease of exposition, we describe our methodology and present our results using a strategy that equalizes the number of fathers and mothers.

The nonresident fathers who are missing from the NSFH survey can be divided into two groups: men who are missing because they are underrepresented in the sample, and men who are missing because they misreport their parental status. The latter group is sampled by the NSFH, but these men are misclassified, either because they do not know they are fathers or because they do not want to disclose this information. Our strategy for correcting for both underrepresentation and misreporting is to identify subgroups of nonresident fathers in the NSFH who resemble the missing fathers in terms of age, race, and income and to reweight these subgroups so that the sample is more representative of all nonresident fathers.

Adjusting for Underrepresentation

We adjust our sample for three groups of men who are underrepresented in the NSFH: men in the military, men undercounted in the U.S. census, and men in jail or prison. We do not adjust for men in mental hospitals or college dormitories, since men and women are very nearly equally represented in these two institutions. We begin by identifying the number of men in each of these groups who are not represented in the NSFH. Next, we use data from other sources to estimate the proportion of men in these groups who are nonresident fathers. And finally, we reweight the men in the NSFH sample to take account of underrepresented fathers.

Household surveys typically undercount men who are only loosely attached to particular households. In extreme cases, these men are homeless. It is well known that the census undercounts these individuals. Since the NSFH is weighted to the CPS, which in turn is weighted to the census, it follows that the NSFH undersamples these men as well. Although the proportion of white men who are undercounted in the census is much smaller than the proportion of black men who are missed, the absolute number of whites is larger than the absolute number of blacks. We estimate that about 900,000 black men and 1,227,000 white men between the ages of twenty-two and sixty are missing from the NSFH because of the failure to adjust for the census undercount.[12] (Although women are also undercounted in the census, very few resident mothers are missed, and therefore we do not adjust our sample to take account of women in the undercount.) In addition to the men who are underrepresented because of the undercount, in 1987 there were about 700,000 men in jail or prison, all of whom were missing from the NSFH survey. Finally, we estimate that the NSFH misses about one million men who were in the military at the time of the survey.[13]

The next step in our procedure was to determine how many of the missing men were nonresident fathers. We assume that the percentage of missing military men who are nonresident fathers is the same as the percentage of sample men who are nonresident fathers—approximately 10 percent. Based on this assumption, we estimate that about 100,000 of the 3.6 million missing nonresident fathers were in the military.

Based on data from Richard Freeman and Jane Waldfogel (see chapter 4), we estimate that 44.8 percent of the men in jail are fathers,[14] and we assume the same proportion for the men in the census undercount. Evidence for the plausibility of this assumption comes from survey data on homeless men that indicate that nearly one-half of these men report they are fathers (Rossi 1989). Based on these assumptions, we estimate that close to 1.2 million of the 3.6 million nonresident fathers who are missing from the NSFH survey were either in jail or not counted by the census.

The last step in our procedure was to identify subgroups of nonresident fathers in the NSFH similar to the men in the military, in jail, or in the undercount and to reweight the former to take account of the latter. For those in the military, we assume that the missing men are similar to the average man in the NSFH (between eighteen and fifty-five), and we reweight the latter to take account of the former.[15] The overwhelming majority of men in jail earn little to nothing. Although we are less certain about men in the undercount, we also assume that most of these men are also extremely impoverished. Thus, to adjust for the fathers who are in jail or in the undercount, we reweight the NSFH nonresident, nonpaying fathers who are in the bottom decile of the income distribution for their age and race category.

Adjusting for Misreporting

Correcting for the underrepresentation of men in the NSFH accounts for about 36 percent of the nonresident fathers who are missing in the NSFH. Thus, we conclude that another 64 percent of these men are likely to be in the NSFH but are not classified as fathers. To adjust the NSFH sample for misreporting by nonresident fathers, we begin by assuming assortative mating. Then we classify both resident mothers and nonresident fathers into twelve broad race, age, and education categories. By subtracting the number of nonresident fathers (reweighted to take account of men in jail and in the undercount) from the number of resident mothers in each cell, we can estimate how many nonresident fathers in each cell are likely to be misreporting their status. Next, we reweight the nonresident fathers in each cell so that the total number of nonresident fathers matches the total number of resident mothers.

At this stage, we make two alternative, but equally plausible, assumptions about the characteristics of the missing fathers:

1. We assume that fathers who misreport their status have the same characteristics *as the average nonresident father in their age, education, and race group.*[16]

2. We assume that fathers who misreport their status have the same characteristics *as the average nonpaying nonresident father in their age, education, and race group.*

These two assumptions lead to very different estimates of the income of the missing fathers. As shown in the next section, nonresident fathers who do not pay child support have less income than fathers who pay. Note that although both assumptions are reasonable, they do not provide upper and lower bounds around the possibilities. We might have assumed that the average father who misreports his status is even more advantaged than the average nonresident father. There are at least two reasons for expecting fathers who deny their parenthood to have higher-than-average incomes. First, the more income a man has the more he has to lose by admitting paternity and making himself liable for support. Second, men who have remarried and started new families are more likely to have a stake in denying paternity from a previous relationship. They also have higher-than-average incomes.

There are also reasons for believing that the men who misreport their status have lower incomes than the average nonpayer. Fathers who are ignorant of their paternity status are likely to have below-average incomes. If their prospects were better, the mothers would have kept them better informed. Moreover, while fathers with above-average income have more to lose absolutely, because child support obligations are regressive, poorer fathers have more to lose proportionately. Although our two assumptions do not bound the possibilities, as we shall see later, they produce quite different estimates of the incomes of nonresident fathers who pay no child support.

RESULTS

To provide a context in which to interpret the data on nonresident fathers, tables 2.3 through 2.8 include data on resident fathers in addition to data on nonresident fathers. By resident father we mean a father who lives with at least one biological child and has no minor children living in another household. In addition, many of the tables break down both nonresident and resident fathers into those who have had at least one child outside marriage and those who have never had a child outside marriage. Nearly all of the resident fathers are married, but a small minority are unmarried and cohabiting with their partner and child.

The distinction between births in marriage and births outside marriage is important for a number of reasons. First, as the tables indicate, the characteristics of these two groups of fathers differ. Second, fathers are likely to be less committed to a child born outside marriage. Finally, in order to enforce child support for a child born outside marriage, paternity must first be established.

For nonresident fathers, we present three estimates: an unadjusted estimate, which is derived only from nonresident fathers who acknowledge their status in the NSFH; and two adjusted estimates, which are based on different assumptions about whether the fathers who misreport are like the average nonpayer or like the average nonresident father in their race-age-education group. The unadjusted estimates are obviously inaccurate, but they are presented for information purposes and are used for tests of statistical significance. Differences between resident and nonresident fathers (unadjusted) that are statistically significant at the 10 percent and 5 percent levels, respectively, are noted in the unadjusted column. Because the unadjusted estimates for nonresident fathers understate the differences between resident and nonresident fathers, and because the sample sizes are often small, the tests of statistical significance are very conservative. Despite this, we find a large number of statistically significant differences. Finally, because of missing data on particular variables, sample sizes differ for each variable analyzed.[17] The range of unweighted sample sizes across all variables is presented in each table for the resident fathers and nonresident fathers as a whole and for the breakdowns by birth status of the child.

Fathers' Age, Education, and Health

Many people claim that nonresident fathers cannot afford to pay more child support than they are currently paying and that stricter child support enforcement is unrealistic and perhaps unjust. We begin our analysis by examining three aspects of fathers' human capital: their age, education, and health.

Table 2.3 indicates that nonresident fathers are younger, less educated, and less healthy than resident fathers. (Compare columns 3 and 4 with column 1.) Although the difference in the mean age of the two groups is only one year, the proportion of nonresident fathers who are under age twenty-five is higher than the proportion for resident fathers—9 to 10 percent versus 4 percent. Differences in education are even more striking. The mean difference in years of schooling is a full year; nonresident fathers drop out of high school at much higher rates (21 to 22 percent versus 13 percent) and have much lower rates of college graduation (11 to 12 percent versus 29 percent).

Health differences between the two groups of fathers are also notable. Only 80 percent of nonresident fathers report good health, as compared to 86 percent of resident fathers. And a much higher percentage of the nonresident fathers are disabled or depressed than resident fathers. Finally, drug and alcohol abuse are much more common among nonresident fathers than resident fathers, 7 to 8 percent versus 3 percent.

Insofar as drug and alcohol abuse are the only measures we have for assessing whether nonresident fathers are potentially dangerous to mothers and children, it is worth examining these numbers in more detail. Note that we do not assume that all fathers who abuse alcohol or drugs are violent, or that all fathers who are violent also abuse alcohol and drugs. However, since these two behaviors are correlated (Leonard and Blane 1992; Kantor and Straus 1989; Kantor and Blane 1987), we believe the information on alcohol and drugs may be useful in providing evidence of the potential risk of violence. According to table 2.3, the proportion of nonresident fathers who report alcohol or drug problems is about twice as high as the number of resident fathers who report such problems. Even so, the number is still under 10 percent, suggesting that only a small minority of nonresident fathers pose a serious threat to their families.

Yet, for two reasons, the numbers reported in table 2.3 almost certainly underestimate the proportion of fathers, especially nonresident fathers, who have problems with drugs or alcohol. First, people are likely to underreport their own problems with drugs and alcohol (Lemmens, Tan, and Knibbe 1990). Second, our assumption that nonresident fathers who are in jail or loosely attached to a household (in the census undercount) are just like other fathers in the bottom 10 percent of the income

TABLE 2.3 / Fathers' Age, Education, and Health

	Resident Fathers	Nonresident Fathers		
		Unadjusted	Adjusted Low	Adjusted High
All fathers[a]				
Mean age	37	36[b]	36	36
Under twenty-five (percentage)	4	6[b]	10	9
Mean education (years)	13	12[b]	12	12
Education < high school (percentage)	13	17[b]	22	21
College graduate	29	16[b]	12	11
Good health	86	79[b]	80	80
Disabled	6	9	14	12
Depressed	7	11[b]	12	12
Substance abuse	3	7[b]	8	7
Fathers with no nonmarital births[a]				
Mean age	37	38	38	38
Under twenty-five (percentage)	3	1[b]	1	1
Mean education (years)	13	13	13	13
Education < high school (percentage)	11	9	10	12
College graduate	31	22[b]	19	17
Good health	88	85	85	85
Disabled	6	5	8	8
Depressed	7	10[b]	10	10
Substance abuse	3	6[b]	6	6
Fathers with one or more nonmarital births[a]				
Mean age	37	34[b]	33	33
Under twenty-five (percentage)	9	13	19	19
Mean education (years)	12	12	11	12
Education < high school (percentage)	26	28	34	33
College graduate	12	6[c]	3	4
Good health	81	71[c]	73	72
Disabled	11	14	20	18

(Table continues on p. 46.)

TABLE 2.3 / *Continued*

	Resident Fathers	Nonresident Fathers		
		Unadjusted	Adjusted Low	Adjusted High
Depressed	11	12	15	15
Substance abuse	7	9	9	9

Source: NSFH (1987).

[a] Due to missing data, sample sizes differ for each variable. Ranges for all the variables are as follows: sample sizes for all fathers are 1,170 to 1,344 (resident fathers) and 438 to 522 (nonresident fathers). Sample sizes for fathers with no nonmarital births are 1,028 to 1,181 (resident fathers) and 260 to 292 (nonresident fathers). Sample sizes for fathers with one or more nonmarital birth are 142 to 152 (resident fathers) and 178 to 211 (nonresident fathers).

[b] Difference between resident fathers and nonresident fathers is statistically significant at the .05 level (two-tailed test).

[c] Difference between resident fathers and nonresident fathers is statistically significant at the .10 level (two-tailed test).

distribution of their race-age-education cell could severely underestimate the prevalence of addiction problems in these groups. If all the nonresident fathers in jail or loosely attached to households had drug or alcohol problems, the total proportion of nonresident fathers with this problem would increase by about twelve percentage points, to between 19 and 20 percent.[18]

If we compare the difference between the numbers in the bottom two sections of table 2.3 with the differences between columns 1 and 2 through 4, we see that the differences associated with nonresident fathers' marital status are even larger than the differences between resident and nonresident fathers. Only 1 percent of nonresident fathers who were married when their child was born are under the age of twenty-five, whereas nearly 20 percent of fathers who had a child outside marriage are under age twenty-five. Similarly, whereas 10 to 12 percent of divorced and separated fathers have less than a high school education, 33 to 34 percent of unwed fathers fall into this category. And while 85 percent of divorced and separated fathers report good health, only 72 to 73 percent of unmarried fathers do so. Finally, the prevalence of depression and drug and alcohol abuse are about 50 percent higher among fathers whose children were born outside marriage.

It is worth noting that most of the differences between these two groups of fathers are due to the fact that race and marital status at birth are highly correlated. White fathers are more likely to marry and then divorce or separate, whereas black fathers are more likely to father a child outside marriage. Indeed, in results not shown here, we divided nonresident fathers into whites and blacks, and the differences were very similar to those reported in table 2.3.

Fathers' Wage Rates and Employment

Table 2.4 presents data on fathers' wage rates, a good measure of earnings capacity, and fathers' weeks and hours worked, good measures of the utilization of earnings capacity. The age, education, and health differences reported in table 2.3 should be manifested in differences in wage rates and hours worked. For the most part, they are. While resident fathers earn twenty dollars per hour on average, nonresident fathers earn between fourteen and fifteen dollars per hour. (The numbers reported in table 2.4 are based on fathers who reported working during the past year.)

The difference between resident and nonresident fathers with marital births (twenty-one dollars per hour versus seventeen dollars) is quite substantial and larger than the difference between resident and nonresident fathers with non-

TABLE 2.4 / Fathers' Wage Rates, Hours Worked, and Weeks Worked

		Nonresident Fathers		
	Resident Fathers[c]	Unadjusted	Adjusted Low	Adjusted High
All fathers[a]				
Wage rate	$20	$15[b]	$14	$15
Hours worked	43	41[b]	36	37
Weeks worked	49	49	48	48
Fathers with no nonmarital births[a]				
Wage rate	$21	$17[b]	$17	$17
Hours worked	43	42	39	40
Weeks worked	50	50	48	48
Fathers with one or more nonmarital births[a]				
Wage rate	$14	$13	$12	$13
Hours worked	40	38	32	33
Weeks worked	47	48	47	48

Source: NSFH (1987).

[a] Due to missing data, sample sizes differ for each variable. Ranges for all the variables are as follows: samples sizes for all fathers are 977 to 1,331 (resident fathers) and 328 to 517 (nonresident fathers). Samples sizes for fathers with no nonmarital births are 869 to 1,130 (resident fathers) and 189 to 291 (nonresident fathers). Sample sizes for fathers with one or more nonmarital birth are 108 to 150 (resident fathers) and 139 to 208 (nonresident fathers).

[b] Difference between resident fathers and nonresident fathers is statistically significant at the .05 level (two-tailed test).

[c] Difference between resident fathers and nonresident fathers is statistically significant at the .10 level (two-tailed test)

marital births. Notice that the variation within the two groups of nonresident fathers (those with marital births and those with nonmarital births) is much greater than the variation between resident and nonresident fathers, underscoring the fact that not all nonresident fathers are the same. Finally, while differences in weeks worked are small to nonexistent, there are significant differences between resident and nonresident fathers in hours worked per week—forty-three versus thirty-six to thirty-seven. Again, the differences among nonresident fathers are larger than the difference between nonresident and resident fathers.

Fathers' Income and Assets

Table 2.5 compares the income and assets of fathers. It also compares fathers' incomes at each decile of their respective income distributions. Our measure of income includes personal earnings, pensions, transfers, and all other sources of personal income. Because earnings are the predominant source of income, however, we expect the differences in income to be similar to the differences in wage rates and hours worked in table 2.4. Not surprisingly, nonresident fathers have considerably less income than resident fathers. Their mean income is between $26,864 and $28,823, which is 29 to 34 percent less than the mean income of resident fathers, $40,694.

These estimates of the mean income of nonresident fathers are in the same range as the estimates presented in the bottom section of table 2.1. They are somewhat lower than the Garfinkel and Oellerich (1989) estimate; they bracket the estimate of Miller and her colleagues (1997); and they are somewhat higher than the Sorensen (1995) estimates.

Nonresident fathers also have fewer assets than do resident fathers. They are less likely to own a car (77 to 80 percent versus 97 percent), and they are only about half as likely to own their own home (38 to 39 percent versus 77 percent).

Finally, the data on the income distributions of nonresident fathers show substantial variation in fathers' economic status. A large minority of fathers have quite high incomes. Over 20 percent have annual incomes over $40,000. At the opposite end of the distribution, however, a large minority of nonresident fathers have very low incomes. More than 40 percent of these men have incomes less than $20,000. More than 20 percent have incomes below $6,000!

To put these numbers in perspective, consider that as of the mid-1990s roughly 40 percent of female-headed families with children received welfare benefits. Assuming that the fathers of these children are drawn from the bottom of the income distribution, which is a pretty reasonable assumption, our numbers imply that virtually all of the fathers of children on welfare have incomes below $20,000, and one-half of those fathers have incomes below $6,000. Even the most efficient child support enforcement system imaginable will not be able to get much money from these fathers. Some of these fathers are quite young, and their incomes will grow as they get older (Phillips and Garfinkel 1993; Brien and Willis 1997). Still, our findings reinforce previous research that indicates that although nonresident fathers as a whole can pay substantially more child support than they are cur-

TABLE 2.5 / Fathers' Income and Home and Car Ownership

	Resident Fathers[c]	Nonresident Fathers		
		Unadjusted	Adjusted Low	Adjusted High
All fathers[a]				
Mean income	$40,694	$33,415[b]	$26,864	$28,823
First decile	8,203	5,512	0	546
Second decile	16,405	13,124	2,734	5,605
Third decile	21,874	16,405	12,304	13,671
Fourth decile	27,342	22,538	16,405	17,773
Fifth decile	32,811	26,932	20,507	23,241
Sixth decile	38,279	31,444	25,975	27,342
Seventh decile	43,748	38,279	31,444	34,178
Eighth decile	51,267	46,482	41,014	42,380
Ninth decile	65,622	60,974	54,685	57,419
Own home (percentage)	77	43[b]	38	39
Own car	97	85[b]	77	80
Fathers with no nonmarital births[a]				
Mean income	$42,306	$36,460[b]	$31,016	$32,317
Own home (percentage)	80	50[b]	46	47
Own car	97	89[b]	84	87
Fathers with one or more nonmarital births[a]				
Mean income	$25,603	$29,140	$22,135	$24,699
Own home (percentage)	54	32[b]	30	28
Own car	94	79[b]	69	71

Source: NSFH (1987).

[a] Due to missing data, sample sizes differ for each variable. Ranges for all the variables are as follows: sample sizes for all fathers are 1,220 to 1,325 (resident fathers) and 455 to 501 (nonresident fathers). Sample sizes for fathers with no nonmarital births are 1,081 to 1,175 (resident fathers) and 259 to 292 (nonresident fathers). Sample sizes for fathers with one or more nonmarital birth are 140 to 150 (resident fathers) and 196 to 209 (nonresident fathers).

[b] Difference between resident fathers and nonresident fathers is statistically significant at the .05 level (two-tailed test).

[c] Difference between resident fathers and nonresident fathers is statistically significant at the .10 level (two-tailed test).

rently paying, only a small portion of this gap is attributable to fathers of children on welfare.

Up to this point, our entire discussion has focused on the adjusted estimates of nonresident fathers' characteristics and attributes because we believe that the adjusted estimates are more accurate. It is worth comparing the unadjusted estimates to the adjusted estimates, however, to gain some insight into how important the adjustments are. The mean unadjusted income estimate of $33,415 is $4,600 to $6,600—or 16 to 24 percent—higher than the adjusted estimates. These differences are not trivial, but neither are they huge. By way of contrast, the differences at the bottom of the income distribution are huge. The unadjusted estimates suggest that less than 10 percent of nonresident fathers have incomes under $5,600. The adjusted estimates suggest that at least 20 percent have such low incomes. Failing to take account of missing fathers underestimates the proportion of extremely poor fathers by at least 100 percent.

Fathers' and Mothers' Standard of Living

The income comparisons between resident and nonresident fathers understate the relative well-being of nonresident fathers because fewer of these men are support- ing children. For similar reasons, a comparison of the personal incomes of non- resident fathers and resident mothers would be misleading. Thus, in table 2.6, we compare the ratio of household income to family needs, as determined by the poverty level for a specified family size. An income-to-need ratio of 1.00 is equiva- lent to what a family needs to live above the poverty line. A ratio of less than 1.00 means that the family's standard of living is below the poverty line.

TABLE 2.6 / Fathers' and Mothers' Standard of Living

		Nonresident Fathers			
All Fathers[a]	Resident Fathers	Unadjusted	Adjusted Low	Adjusted High	Resident Mothers and Children
Mean income/ needs ratio (percentage)	3.9[a]	4.8	4.2	4.3	2.2[b]
First decile	0.9	1.2	0.5	0.8	0.3
Second decile	1.5	1.7	1.5	1.6	0.5
Third decile	2.0	2.2	1.9	2.1	0.7
Fourth decile	2.5	3.0	2.4	2.5	1.0
Fifth decile	3.0	3.6	3.1	3.4	1.3
Sixth decile	3.5	4.5	3.9	4.1	1.8
Seventh decile	4.2	5.3	4.9	5.0	2.4
Eighth decile	5.0	6.5	6.1	6.2	3.1
Ninth decile	6.5	8.5	8.3	8.3	4.1

Source: NSFH (1987).

[a] Due to missing data , sample sizes differ for each variable. Ranges for all the variables are as fol- lows: sample sizes for all fathers are 1,173 (resident fathers) and 393 (nonresident fathers).

[b] Mean is statistically different from unadjusted nonresident mean at the .05 level.

According to table 2.6, the standard of living enjoyed by nonresident fathers is actually somewhat higher than the standard of living enjoyed by resident fathers, between 4.2 and 4.3 versus 3.9. But if we subtract the child support paid by approximately 43 percent of these fathers (not shown in the table), the average standard of living of all nonresident fathers is nearly the same as the standard of living of resident fathers.

A substantial minority of nonresident fathers are poor or near-poor. Near-poor is defined as having an income-to-need ratio of between 1 and 2. Over 10 percent of nonresident fathers are poor, and another 20 percent are near-poor. Not surprisingly, given the similarity in means, these figures are virtually identical to those for resident fathers.

In contrast, the living standard of mothers and children who are eligible for child support is *much* lower than the standard of living of nonresident fathers. The average income-to-needs ratio among mothers and children is 2.2, which is about half that of nonresident fathers. Over 60 percent of the mothers and children are poor or near-poor. And 40 percent live below the poverty line!

In sum, nonresident fathers are younger, less educated, and in poorer health than resident fathers. In addition, their hourly wage rates are lower, and they work fewer hours per week. As a consequence, they earn only about two-thirds as much income as resident fathers, and they have fewer assets. Yet, because they live with fewer dependents and therefore share their income with fewer dependents, nonresident fathers' standard of living is equal to that of resident fathers. And although a large minority of these men are poor or near-poor, the proportion of resident fathers who are poor or near-poor is just as large. Moreover, nonresident fathers enjoy a *much* higher standard of living than their children and their children's mothers.

Fathers' Living Arrangements

Many people argue that forcing nonresident fathers to pay child support makes one set of children better off and another set worse off. This argument presupposes that most nonresident fathers are living with children. Table 2.7 suggests otherwise. Less than one-third of nonresident fathers are living with a new partner and children. About one-third of these children are stepchildren. (These data are not shown in the table.)

The living arrangements of the other two-thirds of nonresident fathers are also of interest. Almost one-quarter of nonresident fathers live with a partner of the opposite sex (without children); 15 percent live alone, 19 percent live with their parents, 8 percent share a residence with another adult (not a partner), and 4 percent are in jail, homeless, or loosely attached to any household. The living arrangements of the last three groups, which together constitute about one-third of all nonresident fathers, are likely to be attributable to low income. Thus, it is worth looking at the proportion of fathers who have either started new families or are so poor that they neither start new families nor contribute much to the support of their existing families.

TABLE 2.7 / Living Arrangements of Nonresident Fathers (Percentage)

	Unadjusted	Adjusted Low	Adjusted High
All fathers[a]			
Partner and children	36	31	31
Partner/no children	25	23	21
Parents	12	19	23
Others	9	8	8
Alone	18	15	13
Jail/homeless or loosely attached	0	4	4
Fathers with no nonmarital births[a]			
Partner and children	37	33	35
Partner/no children	30	32	31
Parents	6	9	8
Others	7	5	5
Alone	20	19	19
Jail/homeless or loosely attached	0	2	2
Fathers with one or more nonmarital births[a]			
Partner and children	35	27	29
Partner/no children	17	14	13
Parents	20	30	29
Others	13	11	11
Alone	15	11	11
Jail/homeless or loosely attached	0	6	6

Source: NSFH (1987).

[a] Due to missing data, sample sizes differ for each variable. Ranges for all variables are as follows: sample size is 396 for all fathers, 231 for fathers with no nonmarital births, and 165 for fathers with a nonmarital birth.

Payers Versus Nonpayers

For a number of reasons, it is useful to distinguish among nonresident fathers who do and do not pay child support. First, it is useful to know whether payers and nonpayers are different in terms of their earnings capacity, their living arrangements, and their personal problems. If these differences are large, they might help explain why these fathers do not pay. Second, child support enforcement reforms have been directed primarily at fathers who are not paying support. Most of these fathers—about two-thirds—are not required to pay support because they do not have a court order. The bulk of these fathers have not had paternity established or have abandoned their wives without securing a divorce. Thus, examining the benefits and costs of strengthening enforcement requires an examination of the characteristics of nonpayers.

The first six rows of table 2.8 present data on the incomes, living standards, living arrangements, and alcohol and drug problems of nonresident fathers who do and do not pay child support. As described earlier, we assume that all fathers who pay child support acknowledge their status as nonresident fathers and that all of the fathers who misreport their status do not pay child support. Thus, the low and high bounds apply only to the nonpayers.

The difference in personal income between nonresident fathers who do and do not pay child support is striking. Nonpayers have only about half the income of payers, between $16,782 and $21,700 versus $37,993. In results not shown in the table, we found that between 30 and 40 percent of nonpayers had annual incomes below $6,500! Obviously, unless their incomes can be increased, these fathers can not pay much child support.

Nonresident fathers who pay child support not only have much higher income than nonresident fathers who pay no support, but their income is nearly as high as

TABLE 2.8 / Differences Between Payers and Nonpayers and Unduplicated Count of Proportions of Fathers Who Might Be Excused from Paying Support

			Nonresident Fathers		
				Nonpayers	
	Resident Fathers	Payers	Unadjusted	Adjusted Low	Adjusted High
Income	$40,694	$37,993	$22,210[a]	$16,782	$21,700
Living standards	3.9[a]	5.3	3.3[a]	2.8	3.1
Home ownership (percentage)	77[a]	42	42	34	38
New children	100[a]	37	36	28	33
Jail or homeless	0	0	0	7	7
Alcohol or drug abuse	3[b]	5	13[a]	12	9
Poor	9	7	12[b]	27	19
Poor or substance abuser	13	12	20[b]	40	31
Poor, substance abuser, or living with new children	100[a]	42	53[a]	61	58

Source: NSFH (1987).

Notes: Due to missing data, sample sizes differ for each variable. Ranges for all variables are as follows: sample size is 1,170 to 1,344 for resident fathers.

[a] Difference between nonresident payers and nonresident nonpayers is statistically significant at the .05 level.

[b] Difference between nonresident payers and nonresident nonpayers is statistically significant at the .10 level.

the average income of resident fathers. Moreover, the standard of living of payers is substantially higher than the standard of living of resident fathers. Yet, nonresident fathers who pay child support are still much less likely to own their own home. At least part of this difference is probably attributable to the fact that, for most couples, the family home is the major financial asset. Thus, when a divorce occurs, the home is usually sold in order to divide the assets. In some divorce settlements, the mother may be given the home.

Fathers who pay child support are more likely to be living with children than nonpayers, 37 percent versus 28 to 33 percent. In view of the lower incomes of nonpayers, this difference is not surprising. The data do suggest, however, that having new children does not prevent a substantial proportion of nonresident fathers from supporting children from a former union.

Note that we estimate that 7 percent of the nonpayers are in jail, homeless, or so loosely attached to any household that they are not counted in the census. This figure climbs to 19 percent, or nearly one of five of the fathers with children born outside marriage! (This figure is not presented in the table.) These men have been overlooked in previous research on fathers precisely because of their living conditions.

Finally, nonpayers are more likely than payers to report problems with alcohol and drugs, between 9 and 12 percent versus 5 percent. While this percentage is still rather low, note that the unadjusted figure for nonpayers is larger than both adjusted estimates. This is the only instance where the adjusted estimates give a more favorable portrait of nonresident fathers than the unadjusted estimates. Furthermore, among the nonpayers with nonmarital births, the unadjusted figure is 20 percent. This anomaly, along with the high figure for nonpayers with children born outside marriage, reinforces our earlier argument that these results should be interpreted with great caution.

Fathers' Cumulative Problems

Up to this point, we have examined various characteristics of nonresident fathers one at a time. But critics of strengthening child support enforcement have argued that most fathers who fail to pay child support are either poor, supporting other children, or not good candidates for fatherhood. Rows 7 through 9 of table 2.8 address this issue by indicating what proportion of fathers have at least one of these constraints and therefore might be exempted from paying child support. For this exercise, the presence of a drug abuse or alcohol problem is taken as an indicator of poor prospects for fatherhood.

The last two columns of the table indicate that about 60 percent of nonpayers fall into at least one of the categories. While these data provide some support for the critics of stronger enforcement, we are skeptical for two reasons. First, a large proportion of nonpayers, nearly half, would not be exempt on the grounds of poverty, other commitments, or personal problems. Second, among fathers who pay child support, 42 percent would be exempt on these grounds.

SUMMARY AND CONCLUSION

Getting a clear picture of nonresident fathers is difficult because a large group of them are not included in household surveys and an even larger group is included but do not acknowledge their paternity. In the NSFH, which is the best national survey for identifying nonresident fathers, we estimate that nearly 40 percent are missing, one-third of whom are in jail or so loosely attached to a household that they are not interviewed. To develop estimates of the characteristics of the missing fathers, we rely heavily on other data and a number of reasonable assumptions, which are nevertheless quite strong. Most important, we assume that, owing to assortative mating, the missing fathers are like the mothers of their children in terms of race, education, and age. In addition, we assume that the fathers in jail or loosely attached to a household have the same characteristics as the poorest 10 percent of nonresident fathers who do not pay child support in their race-education-age group. Finally, we assume that the nonresident fathers who misreport their status have the same characteristics as either the average nonresident father or the average nonpaying nonresident father in their age-education-race group. Taking account of and correcting for missing fathers makes a big difference to our image of nonresident fathers because the missing fathers are so disproportionately disadvantaged. For example, we estimate that correcting for missing fathers at least doubles the number of nonresident fathers with incomes below $5,600. While these corrections are necessary, they are subject to error. That is why we entitled this chapter "A Patchwork Portrait."

As compared to fathers who live with all their biological children, nonresident fathers are more likely to be very young, high school dropouts, and unhealthy. They have lower hourly wages and work fewer hours per week. As a consequence, the average income of nonresident fathers is only about two-thirds that of resident fathers, and they are much less likely to own their own homes. Yet, because they have fewer dependents to support, the living standards of nonresident fathers are virtually identical to the living standards of resident fathers. Furthermore, the living standards of nonresident fathers are substantially higher than the living standards of their children and the mothers of their children.

Equally important, there is a wide distribution in the circumstances of nonresident fathers. Their incomes and living standards range from very high to very low. Ten percent of these fathers have incomes above $55,000, and 20 percent have incomes below $6,000. The differences in income between fathers who have parented children within and outside wedlock are striking. The average income of the latter is only about three-quarters of the average income of the former. The income differences between nonresident fathers who do and do not pay child support are even greater. Nonpayers earn only about half as much as payers. Even so, there is also a wide distribution of circumstances within each group of fathers. Extreme poverty and affluence is present in each group—although in vastly different proportions.

The notion that most nonresident fathers have started new families is not supported by the data. Only one-third of nonresident fathers live with children.

Although we find no evidence in the data that a large proportion of nonresident fathers are potentially dangerous to their children, the data are very weak in this area.

In short, what emerges from our analysis is not a single portrait of nonresident fathers but a set of different portraits. As a whole, the portraits do not suggest that stronger enforcement of child support should be abandoned. But this investigation's discovery of a large minority of very poor fathers suggests that the most important political motive for reform—substantially reducing public expenditures—is not likely to be realized.

Future research on nonresident fathers should address the issue of dangerousness, use more recent data, and focus on unwed fathers. As we have noted repeatedly, the NSFH provides insufficient data to assess the extent to which nonresident fathers are a potential threat to the mothers of their children. Both the population of nonresident fathers and their economic and social circumstances have undoubtedly changed since 1987. The number of men in jail in 1997, for example, is nearly twice what it was in 1987. Finally, future research should focus on unwed fathers because that is the group we know the least about, and it is also the most rapidly growing group.

We are grateful to the conference participants for their helpful comments, to Joshua Goldstein and Elaine Sorensen for catching errors in earlier drafts, to Barbara Vaughan for programming assistance and for help with the weighting procedures, to Melanie Adams and Amy Worlton for technical assistance and table production, to David Harding for tables and tests of significance, and to Jennifer Manfredonia for proofreading and bibliographic assistance.

NOTES

1. In the mid-1980s, the federal Office of Child Support Enforcement attempted to address the problem by commissioning the Survey of Absent Parents (SOAP), a trial survey of absent parents. Plans to conduct a full-scale survey were abandoned, however, because of the high costs of locating nonresident fathers (Sonenstein and Calhoun 1988).

2. The quality of the data for resident mothers who receive AFDC is less clear. See Meyer (1995).

3. These proportions are lower in the latest CPS-CSS (1992)—27 percent, 23 percent, and 33 percent. Some of the differences may reflect the fact that the CPS numbers are from a recent time period and draw on a somewhat different sample. Note, however, that there are also inconsistencies between the CPS-CSS and the SIPP (U.S. Bureau of the Census 1995, appendix A).

4. Studies based on longitudinal data like the PSID (Panel Study of Income Dynamics) and NLS (National Longitudinal Survey) suffer from attrition bias but can adjust for this bias by using pre-split data. Studies based on cross-sectional data like the CPS and SIE (Survey of Income and Education) are more likely to suffer from fathers who fail to acknowledge their status and to some degree from fathers not being represented in the sample because they are homeless, loosely attached to a household, or in jail. This latter

problem of underrepresentation is less serious for divorced and separated fathers than for unwed fathers.

5. Similarly, Mincy and Sorensen (1998) have a more recent published version of the 1995 paper reported in table 2.1. Unfortunately, the more recent version reports only income figures net of child support payments and is therefore not comparable to the other income estimates reported in the table.

6. Garfinkel and Oellerich (1989) and, more recently, Miller, Garfinkel, and McLanahan (1997) rely on the assumption of assortative mating. They begin with a representative sample of residential mothers (from the CPS-CSS) and then impute the income of all the missing nonresident fathers. Divorced and separated fathers are assumed to earn as much as the average divorced or separated father of the same race, age, years of schooling, and location. Unwed fathers are assumed to earn as much as the average never-married man of similar race, age, years of schooling, and location. The fathers are assumed to be of the same race, have equivalent schooling, be located in the same place, and be 2.7 years older than the mothers. The imputation methods in the two papers differ. For more detail, see Miller, Garfinkel, and McLanahan (1997).

Sorensen uses the Survey of Income and Program Participation (SIPP), which asks men if they pay child support. The SIPP also asks men how many children they have fathered, and Sorensen uses this information to identify men who report having more children than they are currently living with. Based on a comparison of the numbers of children reported by nonresident fathers and resident mothers, Sorensen estimates that approximately 30 percent of black nonresident fathers are missing from the SIPP and develops upper and lower bound estimates of their incomes. She finds no missing white fathers.

7. Fathers were classified as high on conflict if the mother reported that the couple disagrees "several times a week" or more about any of the items asked about, or if they argue heatedly "very often" or "always," or if they ever engage in violence.

8. In this dimension the NSFH is superior to the NLSY, which contains complete fertility histories of all men and women but is limited to individuals born between 1956 and 1964. As of 1993, male respondents are still too young (less than thirty-seven years old) to constitute a representative sample of nonresident fathers. As table 2.2 indicates, 40 percent of nonresident fathers are over age thirty-eight. Brien and Willis (1997) utilize the NLSY to estimate the earnings of partners of young mothers who are receiving welfare.

9. The SIPP asks men whether they pay child support, and it asks how many children a man has fathered. The child support question, however, misses fathers who do not pay support, and the fertility question does not ask children's ages, making it difficult to determine whether a nonresident child is under nineteen and eligible for support. Nor is there any follow-up question in the SIPP, once a nonresident child has been identified, as to where the child lives; it is thus impossible to ascertain whether the child is living with the mother. As a consequence, fathers with children over age eighteen, children who live with someone other than the mother, or children who have died are inappropriately included. For an excellent discussion of the problem and an inventive, detailed way of dealing with it, see Sorensen (1997).

10. The age cutoff is necessary because in the NSFH resident mothers can be identified only if they are eighteen or older. In general, fathers are older than mothers. We assumed that the difference was on average three years, hence the restriction to age twenty-one. Without a restriction, we would be comparing different groups of mothers and fathers and would underestimate how many missing fathers there are.

11. To the extent that fathers count expenses during a visit as "child support," or to the extent that fathers report informal support but mothers do not, the percentage of fathers who report paying child support would be higher than the percentage of mothers who report receiving support.

12. To determine the size of the undercount in 1987, we multiply the estimates of the percentage undercount in 1980 by the projected population estimates for 1987. See U.S. Bureau of the Census (1988), tables A-1 and A-2.

13. An attempt was made by the NSFH staff to include in the sample young adults who were in the military. Persons "currently away in the Armed Forces" were included as members of households and were thus eligible to be selected as respondents. Of course, the respondent for the screening questions would have had to acknowledge that these persons were at least loosely attached to the household for them to be included on the roster. Persons in the military were also part of the sampling frame if they were permanent residents of households. Unfortunately, the procedures used to identify military personnel were not very successful, and the numbers of military personnel reported in the NSFH is much smaller than what we would expect based on population estimates.

14. We obtained this estimate by applying Freeman and Waldfogel's report of the proportion of inmates with children under age eighteen—56 percent—by the proportion of inmates who are not married—80 percent (U.S. Bureau of the Census, 1995).

15. Because men in the military are younger than all men ages eighteen to fifty-five, this adjustment overestimates the earnings of the missing fathers in the military. Because only 100,000 of 3.6 million missing fathers are deemed to be in the military, however, the overall overestimate will be quite small.

16. The exception is that we assume that none of the misreporting fathers pay child support. We are fairly confident that fathers who pay are unlikely to deny paternity.

17. The results presented in tables 2.3 through 2.8 omit observations with missing values. To see how sensitive the results were to missing values, we utilized the 471 nonresident father observations with reported income values to obtain predictions for the 51 nonresident father observations with missing income values. The predictions were based on a regression with age, education, race or ethnicity, and child support payment status as the independent variables. (In some cases, some independent variables also had to be coded missing.) The difference in the mean income between the sample of 471 cases with reported values and the sample of 522 with reported plus imputed values was only 1.5 percent ($33,414 versus $32,915) and not statistically significant. The difference in the distributions of income was equally small.

18. The fathers in jail and loosely attached to households account for 1.1 million of the total population of 9.4 million nonresident fathers, or about 12 percent of the total.

REFERENCES

Anderson, Elijah. 1993. "Sex Codes and Family Life Among Poor Inner-City Youths." In *The Ghetto Underclass*, edited by William Julius Wilson. Newbury Park, Calif.: Sage Publications.

Brien, Michael J., and Robert J. Willis. 1997. "The Partners of Welfare Mothers: Potential Earnings and Child Support Enforcement." *Future of Children* 7(1): 65–73.

Cassety, Judith. 1978. *Child Support and Public Policy*. Lexington, Mass.: Lexington Books.

Cherlin, Andrew, Jeanne Griffith, and James McCarthy. 1983. "A Note on Maritally-Disrupted Men's Reports of Child Support in the June 1980 Current Population Survey." *Demography* 20(3): 385–89.

Edin, Kathryn. 1995. "Single Mothers and Child Support: The Possibilities and Limits of Child Support Policy." *Children and Youth Services Review* 17(1–2): 203–30.

Edin, Kathryn, and Laura Lein. 1997. "Work, Welfare, and Single Mothers' Economic Survival Strategies." *American Sociological Review* 62(2): 253–66.

Furstenberg, Frank F., Kay Sherwood, and Mercer Sullivan. 1992. *Caring and Paying: What Fathers and Mothers Say About Child Support.* New York: Manpower Demonstration Research Corporation.

Garfinkel, Irwin, and Donald T. Oellerich. 1989. "Noncustodial Fathers' Ability to Pay Child Support." *Demography* (May).

———. 1992. "Noncustodial Fathers' Ability to Pay Child Support." In *Child Support Assurance,* edited by Irwin Garfinkel, Sara S. McLanahan, and Philip K. Robins. Washington: Urban Institute Press.

Hanson, Thomas L., Sara S. McLanahan, and Elizabeth Thomson. 1996. "Double Jeopardy: Parental Conflict and Stepfamily Outcomes for Children." *Journal of Marriage and the Family* 58(1): 141–54.

Haskins, Ronald, J. Schwartz, and John S. Akin. 1985. "How Much Child Support Can Absent Fathers Pay?" *Policy Studies Journal* 14: 201–22.

Hill, Martha S. 1988. "The Role of Economic Resources and Dual Family Status in Child Support Payments." Revised paper originally presented at the Population Association meeting (April 1988).

Kantor, Glenda-Kaufman, and Howard T. Blane. 1987. "The 'Drunken Bum' Theory of Wife Beating." *Social Problems* 34(3): 213–30.

Kantor, Glenda-Kaufman, and Murray A. Straus. 1989. "Substance Abuse as a Precipitant of Wife Abuse Vicitimizations." *American Journal of Drug and Alcohol Abuse* 15(2): 173–89.

Lemmens, Paul, E. S. Tan, and R. A. Knibbe. 1990. "Measuring Quantity and Frequency of Drinking in a General Population Survey: A Comparison of Five Indices." *Journal of Studies on Alcohol* 53(5): 476–86.

Leonard, Kenneth E., and Howard T. Blane. 1992. "Alcohol and Marital Aggression in a National Sample of Young Men." *Journal of Interpersonal Violence* 7(1): 19–30.

Lerman, Robert I. 1990. "Fatherhood, Child Support, and Earnings: A Report on the Links Between Family Responsibilities and Job Market Outcomes." Draft report for the U.S. Department of Health and Human Services, Office of the Assistant Secretary for Policy Evaluation (June 27, 1990).

Maccoby, Eleanor E., and Robert H. Mnookin. 1992. *Dividing the Child: Social and Legal Dilemmas of Custody.* Cambridge: Harvard University Press.

McDonald, Thomas P., James R. Moran, and Irwin Garfinkel. 1990. "Absent Fathers' Ability to Pay More Child Support." *Journal of Social Service Research* 13(4):.

Meyer, Daniel R. 1993. "Child Support and Welfare Dynamics: Evidence from Wisconsin." *Demography* 30(1): 45–62.

———. 1995. "Supporting Children Born Outside of Marriage: Do Child Support Awards Keep Pace with Changes in Fathers' Incomes?" *Social Science Quarterly* 76(3): 577–93.

Miller, Cynthia, Irwin Garfinkel, and Sara McLanahan. 1997. "Child Support in the U.S.: Can Fathers Afford to Pay More?" *Review of Income and Wealth* 43(3): 261–81.

Mincy, Ronald B., and Elaine J. Sorensen. 1998. "Deadbeats and Turnips in Child Support Reform." *Journal of Policy Analysis and Management* 17(1): 44–51.

Nichols-Casebolt, Ann. 1986. "The Economic Impact of Child Support Reform on the Poverty Status of Custodial and Noncustodial Families." *Journal of Marriage and Family.* 48(4): 875–80.

Oellerich, Donald T. 1984. "The Effects of Potential Child Support Transfers on Wisconsin AFDC Costs, Caseloads, and Recipient Well-Being." Institute for Research on Poverty Special Report 35. Madison, Wisc.: Institute for Research on Poverty, University of Wisconsin-Madison.

Oellerich, Donald T., Irwin Garfinkel, and Philip K. Robins. 1991. "Private Child Support: Current and Potential Impacts." *Journal of Sociology and Social Welfare* 18(1): 3–23.

O'Neill, June. 1985. "Determinants of Child Support." 1-R01-HD16840-01. Washington, D.C.: The Urban Institute under contract for the National Institutes of Health.

Phillips, Elizabeth, and Irwin Garfinkel. 1993. "Income Growth Among Nonresident Fathers: Evidence from Wisconsin." *Demography* 30(2): 227–41.

Raphael, J., and R. M. Tolman. 1997. *Trapped by Poverty and Trapped by Abuse: New Evidence Documenting the Relationships Between Domestic Violence and Welfare: Executive Summary.* Chicago: Taylor Institute.

Rendall, Michael S., Lynda Clarke, Elizabeth H. Peters, Nalini Ranjit, and Georgia Verropoulou. 1997. "Incomplete Reporting of Male Fertility in the United States and Britain." Population and Development Program Working Paper #97.03. Ithaca, N.Y.: Population and Development Program, Cornell University.

Robertson, John. 1995. "Are Young Noncustodial Fathers Left Behind in the Labor Market?" Ph.D. diss., Columbia University.

Rossi, Peter H. 1989. *Down and Out in America: The Origins of Homelessness.* Chicago: University of Chicago Press.

Schaeffer, Nora Cate, Judith A. Seltzer, and Marieka Klawitter. 1991. "Estimating Nonresponse and Response Bias: Resident and Nonresident Parents' Reports About Child Support." *Sociological Methods and Research* 20(1): 30–59.

Seltzer, Judith A., and Yvonne Brandreth. 1994. "What Fathers Say About Involvement with Children After Separation." *Journal of Family Issues* 15(1): 49–77.

Sonenstein, Freya L., and Charles Calhoun. 1988. *The Survey of Absent Parents: Pilot Results.* Washington: U.S. Department of Health and Human Services.

Sorensen, Elaine. 1995. "A National Profile of Nonresident Fathers and Their Ability to Pay Child Support." Urban Institute, Washington. Unpublished paper.

———. 1997. "A National Profile of Nonresident Fathers and Their Ability to Pay Child Support." *Journal of Marriage and the Family* 59 (November): 785–97.

Sweet, James, and Larry Bumpass. 1987. *American Families and Households.* New York: Russell Sage Foundation.

Teachman, Jay D., and Karen Polanko. 1989. "Providing for the Children: Socioeconomic Resources of Parents and Child Support in the United States." Paper presented at the Institute foe Research on Poverty, Small Grants Conference (May 1989).

U.S. Bureau of the Census. 1988. "United States Population Estimates by Age, Sex, and Race, 1980–1987." *Current Population Reports,* series P-25, no. 1022 (March). Washington: U.S. Government Printing Office.

———. 1995. "Child Support for Custodial Mothers and Fathers." *Current Population Reports.* Series P-60, no. 187. Washington: U.S. Government Printing Office.

Waller, Maureen. 1995. "Claiming Fatherhood: Paternity, Culture, and Public Policy." Department of Sociology Working Paper No. 4-95. Princeton, N.J.: Princeton University.

Part II

How Does Child Support Enforcement Affect Fathers?

The five chapters in this part investigate some potential side effects of rigorous child support enforcement. The authors pay particular attention to whether heightened enforcement produces a different reaction among low-income fathers, whose financial circumstances limit their ability to pay child support, than among higher-income fathers.

Chapter 3 examines whether stronger enforcement is likely to reduce the standard of living and increase poverty rates in fathers' new families. Chapters 4 through 7 investigate possible behavioral responses of nonresident fathers, including whether stronger child support enforcement is likely to reduce fathers' labor-force participation and the number of hours they work (chapter 4), whether it would reduce marriage and remarriage (chapter 5), whether it would increase fathers' involvement with their children and parental conflict (chapter 6), and whether it would reduce the rate of nonmarital childbearing (chapter 7). To assess the effects of stronger enforcement on fathers' behavior, the last four chapters use research designs that take advantage of variations across states and time periods in the adoption and implementation of child support enforcement policies.

In chapter 3, Daniel Meyer uses data from the National Survey of Families and Households (NSFH) to describe the effect of child support enforcement on nonresident fathers' economic circumstances. He simulates the effects of various child support guidelines and enforcement regimes on fathers' income and ability to help provide for their children. He estimates the number of fathers who would fall into poverty as a result of paying child support and how many more fathers would be poor if all fathers paid their child support orders in full.

Meyer's analysis uses data from a snapshot of fathers' income and family responsibilities and asks what would happen if fathers did not change their behavior in response to stricter child support enforcement (that is, fathers did not increase their employment hours, avoid remarriage, and so on). Like Garfinkel and his colleagues (see chapter 2), Meyer takes account of the underrepresentation of nonresident fathers in his data by assuming that fathers who are not interviewed pay no child support. As a result, Meyer presents a range of estimates of the effects of child support enforcement on fathers' economic welfare.

He shows that the amount of child support that nonresident fathers currently pay has little effect on the distribution of their incomes at the lower end of the personal income distribution. Child support payments do lower the median and the seventy-fifth percentile of the distribution of fathers' incomes by about $2,500 (1995 dollars) each. If all of current child support orders were paid in full, the personal incomes of fathers at the lower end of the income distribution would decrease further, but there would be little effect on the upper end, because more of those fathers already report paying all of the child support due. Nonresident fathers with high incomes owe and pay more child support than fathers at the lower end of the scale. However, fathers with low incomes, as noted in chapter 1, have orders that are higher relative to their incomes.

Ignoring income spent on child support, between 14 and 24 percent of nonresident fathers have household incomes below the poverty level. Meyer's estimates (based on NSFH data) are quite similar to those that Elaine Sorensen (1997) reports using SIPP data. Poverty rates of fathers whose children were born outside of marriage are higher than those of divorced fathers. Once current child support payments are taken into account, an additional 1 percent of nonresident fathers fall into poverty. If all nonresident fathers paid the support due according to their orders, up to 0.4 percent more would fall into poverty. Meyer shows that a proportional standard for child support orders would reduce economic hardship among poor fathers compared to orders established under the system current at the time of the NSFH survey. A proportional system would also reduce the economic advantage that fathers with high or moderate incomes experience compared to fathers with low incomes. Although his data cannot assess the effect of child support on the magnitude of the trade-off between creating poverty among nonresident fathers' new families and alleviating poverty in resident mothers' families, Meyer concludes that a guideline that ignores self-support and the economic claims of new families would not result in a massive reshuffling of poverty among children, even if enforcement of child support orders were perfect. His findings about the varying effects of adjustments for self-support, household income, and second families inform a normative assessment of the competing interests of nonresident fathers, children from first and subsequent relationships, and resident mothers, issues we address in the third part of this volume.

In chapter 4, Richard Freeman and Jane Waldfogel ask how more rigorous child support enforcement would alter nonresident fathers' labor-force participation and employment patterns. Anticipating the effects of child support enforcement on fathers' labor activity is crucial for understanding the effects of child support policies on nonresident fathers' economic welfare and on the welfare of their children. The authors contrast two scenarios. Under the first, more common scenario, child support payments are a fixed amount that the nonresident father owes for an extended period of time. Enforcement reduces the father's income but has no effect on the marginal value of an additional hour of work. To make up for the loss in income, the father is expected to increase the amount of paid work. Under the second scenario, child support obligations are adjusted in response to changes in the father's income. Enforcement operates like an income tax, both reducing the father's income and the value or price of working more. Under either scenario, nonresident fathers may also respond to child support enforcement by trying to evade the government and taking jobs in the informal economy, by working off the books, or by becoming self-employed.[1]

Freeman and Waldfogel use data from the 1986 and 1991 Surveys of Income and Program Participation (SIPP). Even though the SIPP is a large national sample similar to the NSFH, the SIPP data include small numbers of nonresident fathers, particularly small numbers of low-income fathers and never-married fathers. The data do not identify the important subset of men who had a child outside of marriage but subsequently married. Despite the disadvantages of small sample sizes and some ambiguity in the identification of nonresident fathers, the combination of SIPP data and information from the Office of Child Support Enforcement about child support policies and practices provide a valuable opportunity to examine the effects of child support on nonresident fathers' labor supply responses.

Freeman and Waldfogel's main finding is that policies about child support payments do not reduce nonresident fathers' labor-force participation. There is some chance that the policies increase labor supply, particularly for never-married fathers, although these results vary across samples and so are much less reliable than the main finding of no labor supply effect. Self-employment or work on casual jobs does not respond to more rigorous child support policies. The authors interpret their findings as evidence that child support obligations do not have an adverse effect on labor supply for low-income fathers; instead, they argue, low wage rates are a source of low child support transfers.

Critics of strict child support enforcement claim that heavy financial obligations to children from a previous relationship limit nonresident fathers' ability to remarry and father additional children. Because nonresident fathers who remarry often share their incomes with stepchildren, strict child support enforcement may transfer money out of stepfamily households, thereby helping some children at the expense of others. In chapter 5, David Bloom, Cecilia Conrad, and Cynthia Miller investigate the effects of child support enforcement on the remarriage rates of nonresident fathers and on the likelihood that they will have children in new marriages. Using data from the SIPP and the National Longitudinal Survey of Youth (NLSY), they show that effective child support enforcement reduces the likelihood of remarriage for low-income men. As evidence that these findings are not the result of state differences that account for both child support policies and remarriage rates, the authors show there is no effect of child support enforcement on remarriage rates for men who did not have children when they divorced.

Bloom and his colleagues also find that child support enforcement is unlikely to prevent nonresident fathers from having children in subsequent marriages, given that they remarry. Enforcement, however, may reduce the chance that a nonresident father who has already had one child outside of marriage will have another child out of wedlock. This finding applies to all nonresident fathers but appears to be somewhat stronger for low-income nonresident fathers.

As in the other large surveys used to study nonresident fathers, the NLSY and SIPP data used in the remarriage analysis have small numbers of nonresident fathers, especially in important subgroups, such as those with low incomes or those who have had a child out of wedlock. By conducting parallel analyses with data from two sources, Bloom and his colleagues provide a range of estimates of the likely effects of rigorous child support enforcement on nonresident fathers' remarriage. Although they find reasonably consistent effects of child support enforcement variables, such as collection rates, on remarriage for low-income fathers, they also find that whether fathers will actually pay support has no effect on remarriage. The authors attribute the difference between the findings for individual fathers' behavior and the findings for the effects of aggregate-level enforcement variables to the weak statistical instruments they use.

Bloom and his colleagues emphasize their finding that a 10 percent increase in the child support collection rate will decrease the annual rate of remarriage by 3 to 9 percent among low-income fathers. Building on this estimate, the authors simulate the effect of a 10 percent increase in child support collections on the financial gain to all children, including those who live with remarried mothers. They interpret their results as showing that the increase in child support payments is largely offset by the reduction in remarriage, by which nonresident fathers share income with their stepchildren. The authors conclude that the economic benefits of child support enforcement for children are overstated because they do not take account of the negative effects of more rigorous enforcement on children in stepfamilies.

In chapter 6, Judith Seltzer, Sara McLanahan, and Thomas Hanson also ask how child support enforcement affects nonresident fathers' relationships with their children. They use data from the NSFH to examine the effects of child support enforcement on the amount of time nonresident fathers spend with children, on fathers' influence in child-rearing decisions after separation, and on the amount of conflict between parents. By increasing nonresident fathers' financial investments in their children, stricter child support enforcement may increase fathers' incentive to spend time with their children and to participate in decisions about their children's lives. Also, a father paying support is likely to want to ensure that the mother spends the support money on the children. However, stricter enforcement measures—particularly the automatic withholding of child support—takes from fathers the ability to trade child support to the mother for visits with their children. As a result of this change in the bargaining playing field, stricter enforcement may have the effect of reducing the amount of time the father spends with the children; the mother can count on child support being collected through withholding whether she facilitates visits or not. Finally, by bringing more fathers into the system, including those who have dropped out to avoid conflict with their children's mother, more rigorous child support enforcement may increase children's exposure to high levels of conflict between their parents.

Seltzer and her colleagues use two strategies to assess the effects of stricter enforcement on nonresident fathers' relationships with children. Like several of the other authors in this part of the book, they take advantage of state and temporal variation in child support policies to estimate the effects of child support payments on visiting, taking account of unmeasured characteristics that may explain both child support payments and frequency of visits. They also use data from a longitudinal sample of families observed both before and after a separation to control statistically for the fathers' income and the quality of the parents' relationship and the father-child relationship before divorce. By taking account of economic resources and the quality of family relationships, their longitudinal analysis explicitly controls for many of the characteristics that might explain both child support and other aspects of fathers' involvement with children after separation. Both analyses rely almost exclusively on information provided by resident mothers about nonresident fathers' behavior, because of the underrepresentation of non-resident fathers in the NSFH data.

The authors find that fathers who pay support have more influence in child-rearing decisions and may see their children more frequently than fathers who do not pay support. Their findings also suggest that stricter enforcement of child support obligations is likely to increase children's exposure to the type of serious disagreement between their parents that is generally considered to be harmful to children. For fathers as a whole, paying some support seems to have no effect on conflict, but when payments increase beyond $2,000 a year (in 1993 dollars), the incidence of more serious conflict rises.

A common finding in chapters 4 through 6 is that more rigorous enforcement may have a greater effect on the behavior of low-income fathers than on that of fathers with more economic resources. This pattern is consistent with the more difficult experiences that low-income fathers have in the child support system and the higher percentage of these fathers who have children out of wedlock and are therefore subject to increased efforts to establish legal paternity, compared to higher-income fathers. An alternative explanation is that the indicators of child support enforcement used in the statistical analyses are measured more appropriately for low- than higher-income fathers. All three of these chapters rely heavily on data about enforcement from the Office of Child Support Enforcement and other statistics from IV-D offices. Because these state and federal agencies have generally focused their efforts on nonresident fathers whose children are supported by public welfare programs, the statistics they use to evaluate their effectiveness are likely to be better measures of performance among low-income fathers than among all nonresident fathers, even though many child support reforms have universalistic goals. Conclusions about the relative impact of child support enforcement on low- and high-income fathers would be strengthened by improved measures of enforcement for fathers at all income levels.

In the last chapter of this part of the book, Anne Case steps back from the question of how child support enforcement affects nonresident fathers to ask whether enforcement affects the nonresident status of fathers in the first place. Case examines the effects of child support enforcement on the rate of nonmarital childbearing. She argues that states with low rates of nonmarital births may have certain characteristics that also lead to strict child support enforcement policies, that is, a conservative electorate.[2] Also, states with rapidly rising nonmarital birth rates may adopt stricter child support enforcement policies as a reaction to these demographic trends. In either instance, a study exploring the effects of child support enforcement on nonmarital childbearing must take account of these alternative explanations. Case does this by showing that state child support policies are a function of changes in states' economic and demographic conditions and the political forces at work in the state, including the proportion of women in state legislatures. She then demonstrates that even after taking account of the factors that predict state policies, nonmarital childbearing rates are curbed by tougher enforcement policies. Case's aggregate-level finding that enforcement may reduce childbearing outside of marriage is consistent with the individual-level results reported by Bloom and his colleagues on the likely reduction in nonmarital childbearing among fathers who already have one out-of-wedlock child. Thus, at least some aspects of child support enforcement are likely to alter men's fertility, reducing the chance of their becoming nonresident fathers.

These chapters on the effects of stronger child support enforcement set the stage for the chapters in part III, in which the authors explore whether we should be doing more to help nonresident fathers.

NOTES

1. To try to disentangle the effect of child support enforcement on labor supply from the effects of labor-force participation on the ability to pay child support, Freeman and Waldfogel examine the effect on labor supply of child support policies across states and over time. By comparing the effects of policies on the labor supply of nonresident fathers to that for resident fathers in the same states, Freeman and Waldfogel test the validity of their conclusions. This strategy addresses the problem that state policies and labor supply may be determined by the same factors.

2. This concern is similar to that addressed in other chapters by using men without children or resident fathers as a control group to test whether the effects of child support enforcement affect only nonresident fathers. To the extent that the enforcement variables affect men not subject to these rules, other state differences than child support policies account for the association between child support enforcement and nonresident fathers' behavior.

REFERENCE

Sorenson, Elaine. 1997. "A National Profile of Nonresident Fathers and Their Ability to Pay Child Support." *Journal of Marriage and the Family* 59(4): 785–97.

Chapter 3

The Effect of Child Support on the Economic Status of Nonresident Fathers

Daniel R. Meyer

Children in mother-only families are in severe economic straits, with poverty rates near 50 percent (Baugher and Lamison-White 1996). This fact, along with a growing public dissatisfaction with welfare expenditures on mother-only families, has spurred scrutiny of the child support system to determine whether nonresident parents (mostly fathers) are providing appropriate amounts of financial support to their children. One of the results of this scrutiny has been the introduction of significant reforms in the child support system. Some of the changes are aimed at increasing the amount of child support that is owed. Each state has now developed a numerical formula, or guideline, that is used to determine the amount owed in new child support orders unless it is found that the guideline would be inappropriate in a particular case. These guidelines have been quite controversial in many states. Two controversial questions have been: (1) Should child support orders be set at a lower level for low-income nonresident parents? and (2) Should child support orders be decreased for nonresident parents with new family responsibilities?

Of course, even if the guidelines increase the amount owed, it may not be paid, particularly if the nonresident father has a very low income. While some research has estimated that a great deal more child support could be collected (see, for example, Garfinkel and Oellerich 1989; Miller, Garfinkel, and McLanahan 1997; Sorensen 1997), little of this research has looked explicitly at potential orders and payments among low-income nonresident fathers or at potential orders and payments among fathers with new families. If a large proportion of fathers have low incomes themselves, then extracting more child support from them may cause more poverty among them in an effort to alleviate poverty among mothers and children. Moreover, if a large proportion of low- or moderate-income fathers have remarried and have new dependents, then increasing the amount of child support paid may merely reshuffle poverty among children, decreasing poverty among children in resident-mother families but increasing it among children in nonresident-father families.

This chapter focuses on the effect of different child support scenarios on the economic well-being of nonresident fathers and their families. Specifically, it addresses three sets of questions:

1. What is the current economic status of nonresident fathers before they pay child support? What is their economic status after they pay support? How many fathers fall into poverty as a result of paying child support?

2. What would the economic status of nonresident fathers be if they paid everything they currently are ordered to pay? Would this cause additional fathers to fall into poverty?

3. If all child support orders were set according to a particular guideline, and new orders were fully paid, what effect would this have on nonresident fathers' economic well-being?

I present results from straightforward simulations that assume that fathers did not (or would not) change their labor supply patterns, their living arrangements, or their fertility as a result of child support policy. Thus, the estimates presented here can be viewed as short-term effects rather than necessarily long-term equilibrium effects. Other chapters in this volume address potential behavioral effects of child support. For the third question, dealing with the effects of potential guidelines, I test six different guidelines, including the Wisconsin percentage-of-income guideline and several variations that make special adjustments for low-income nonresident parents or for new families of nonresident parents.[1] This chapter begins with brief reviews of the policy context and of the prior research on the economic status of nonresident fathers. Data and methods, results, and conclusions are presented in the final three sections.

POLICY CONTEXT

Historically, child support orders were based on the amount needed to meet the child's needs and were set on a case-by-case basis. This policy regime resulted in a large percentage of resident mothers without orders, or with relatively low orders, and in inconsistent orders among similar cases (Garfinkel 1992). The Child Support Enforcement amendments of 1984 required each state to develop a numeric formula (guideline) that could be used to calculate child support orders. The Family Support Act of 1988 went further, requiring that the guideline be used unless it was explicitly determined that it would be inappropriate in a given case.

The guidelines that the states have instituted fall into three categories: percentage-of-income, income-shares, and Melson. In percentage-of-income guidelines, order amounts are calculated by multiplying the income of the nonresident parent by a percentage specific to the number of children being supported. Income-shares guidelines incorporate the income of both the resident and nonresident parents, as well as the number of children. The Melson guidelines are the most complicated, allowing each parent to set aside a portion of their income for their own needs before child support is assessed. The issues involved in selecting a guideline type have been discussed elsewhere (see, for example, Garfinkel and Melli 1990; Haynes 1994; chapter 10 of this volume; and Williams 1987). While the calculations based on these three guidelines differ, they can result in similar order levels (Lewin/ICF 1990).

Some states have made special provisions for low-income nonresident parents. The Melson guidelines do this automatically, but special adjustments to the other guidelines are also in place in some locations. These typically set no order or only a token order if the nonresident parent's income is below a certain level, called a "self-support reserve."

Some states have also made special provisions for nonresident parents who remarry or who have new children. Marianne Takas (1994) has recently discussed two potential types of adjustments: one of these follows the self-support reserve concept but sets aside a family reserve, so that the needs of the nonresident parent's new family are considered. She prefers this type and suggests that the family reserve be set at the poverty line for the appropriate family size, divided by the number of potential earners in the new family. This reflects the idea that the nonresident parent and his or her spouse are jointly responsible for the needs of any new children. A second type of adjustment is to set aside an amount for new children based on what the child support order for them would be if the nonresident parent left the new family. The amount of the original child support order is then set based on any remaining income.[2]

While some empirical research has examined the effect of different guidelines on the incomes of resident mothers (see Garfinkel, Oellerich, and Robins 1991), little has been done to examine the effect of different guidelines on the economic status of nonresident fathers.

PRIOR RESEARCH ON THE ECONOMIC STATUS OF NONRESIDENT FATHERS

Estimates of the economic status of nonresident fathers have been completed by several researchers (for further discussion, see chapter 2). One set of recent estimates has been completed by Elaine Sorensen (1997). She combines two data sets, the Survey of Income and Program Participation (SIPP) and the National Survey of Families and Households (NSFH). Estimates from SIPP are more recent, but the NSFH is better at identifying nonresident fathers. Both data sets are limited in that the number of nonresident fathers identified is substantially lower than the number of resident mothers; Sorensen reweights the data to account for the missing nonresident fathers.[3] She estimates mean annual personal income as about $23,000 (1996 dollars). The two data sources provide rather different estimates of poverty, from 15 percent in the SIPP to 25 percent in the NSFH.

Generalizations about nonresident fathers' incomes from the prior research are difficult because of data problems. Nonetheless, estimates of income for divorced or separated fathers are much higher than for never-married fathers; young nonresident fathers generally have lower incomes than older nonresident fathers; and the incomes of fathers of children receiving welfare are particularly low (see chapter 2).

Some research has examined whether paying child support increases the poverty of fathers. Ann Nichols-Casebolt (1986) found that full collection of a percentage-of-income standard among white divorced fathers would increase their poverty level from 4.8 percent to 6.3 percent, and among nonwhite fathers from 26.1 percent to 35 percent. Even then, however, these fathers would be economically better off than the mothers and children, whose poverty rates would decrease from 28.7 percent to 21.8 percent among whites, and from 44.3 percent to 36.1 percent among nonwhites.

This research extends the previous literature in several ways. It presents new information on the effects of different child support scenarios on the economic status of nonresident fathers and on the effects of different scenarios on different groups of fathers. It also provides information on the extent to which child support reform increases poverty among children because children currently living with nonresident fathers become impoverished.

DATA AND METHODS

Data

The ideal data set would enable the researcher to identify nonresident fathers and would include information on their income, family status, child support payments, and child support orders. If the researcher wanted to test the effects of a guideline that includes the income of both parents, then information about the income of the resident-parent family would also be needed. I believe the first wave of the National Survey of Families and Households, conducted in 1987 and 1988, is the best data set for this research because it provides a straightforward method of identifying nonresident fathers, contains a nationally representative sample of the non-institutionalized population, and includes information on the economic status, living arrangements, and child support situations of nonresident fathers.[4] NSFH has three main limitations: (1) its data are from 1986 and thus do not reflect the effects of recent child support reforms; (2) it contains a fairly small sample (425) of nonresident fathers with full information, making estimates for some subgroups imprecise; and (3) no income information is available on the resident mothers who were partnered with the nonresident fathers in the data set, so guidelines that require information on the income of both parents cannot be tested.[5]

Methods

IDENTIFYING NONRESIDENT FATHERS The NSFH asks respondents: "Do you have any biological or adopted children age eighteen or younger who do not live in this household at least half the time?" Affirmative responses were given by 634 men. Each child was listed, and a "focal child" was selected from the list. The current living arrangements of the focal child were then asked. When the focal child was living with the other parent, the entire sequence of child support questions was asked. Respondents whose child was not living with the other parent were not asked information about potential child support orders. For this research, I have selected any father whose focal child lives with the mother, a total sample of 532 fathers.[6] (Also meeting these selection criteria would be 92 nonresident mothers, but they are not the focus of this chapter.) I have further limited the sample by requiring that the information on child support payments and orders and personal income of the nonresident father be known. This leaves a final sample of 425 fathers. In the full sample of nonresident fathers, 71 percent are black, 20 percent are under age thirty, and 38 percent had a nonmarital birth (unweighted). The final sample is quite similar, with 71 percent black, 22 percent under age thirty, and 35 percent with a nonmarital birth.

UNDERCOUNT OF NONRESIDENT FATHERS   The NSFH has substantially fewer nonresident (noncustodial) fathers than resident (custodial) mothers (Seltzer and Brandreth 1995; chapter 2 of this volume). Because of this discrepancy, in this chapter I present two sets of results. I report results using the NSFH weights, which correct for the oversampling of certain groups in the design of the survey and make basic descriptive statistics from the NSFH match those of the U.S. Census Bureau's Current Population Survey (CPS). These weights essentially assume that the nonresident fathers who are not in the data are similar to those who are. But they make no adjustments for nonresident fathers who are not in the sampling frame (men in prison, for example) or for the Census Bureau's known limitation of undercounting men who are loosely attached to a household, nor is there an adjustment for fathers who are in the sampling frame but deny that they have nonresident children. Because many of the missing fathers are likely to have low incomes, the NSFH weights overestimate fathers' economic status. Thus, for the main results, I use weights developed by Garfinkel and his colleagues (see chapter 2). The first step in the construction of these weights is an adjustment for the fathers not in the sample (primarily men in prison, in the military, or loosely attached to a household). This is done by increasing the weights of NSFH-identified nonresident fathers who are likely to be similar to these missing fathers. (Men in prison or loosely attached to a household are assumed to have very low incomes, and men in the military are assumed to have average incomes, with child support orders and payments consistent with these income groups.) The second step is to adjust for fathers in the sampling frame who do not admit fatherhood. This step involves increasing the weights of some of the identified nonresident fathers so that the number of nonresident fathers and resident mothers is equal within race-age-education groups. Garfinkel and his colleagues consider two methods of selecting the fathers to increase; the alternative I choose is their "conservative" method, which assumes that the fathers have the same characteristics as nonpaying, nonresident fathers within each group. In my view, this estimate is closer to the truth than the estimates using NSFH weights. The adjusted weights may, however, underestimate fathers' economic status, so the true results may be in between the upper and lower bounds presented here.

CHILD SUPPORT ORDERS AND PAYMENTS   The amount of the current child support order was asked specifically, and thus its calculation is generally straightforward.[7] Those with current orders are asked how much is paid. Even fathers who do not have a current order are asked whether they paid anything toward the child's support, so informal payments are captured. Because I want to examine fathers' incomes in a scenario in which they pay their entire obligation and do not want to underestimate the burden this would cause, I assume fathers who are paying more than they currently owe have an "informal" order for the amount they are paying.[8] Note that there are some differences in timing: income information is from the calendar year 1986, child support orders are from the date of the interview, and child support payments are calculated over the twelve months prior to the interview.[9]

When the calculations are completed, between 48 percent (adjusted weights) and 63 percent (unadjusted weights) of the fathers have a formal child support order. The percentage with orders can be compared to mothers' reports using a national survey of resident mothers, the Current Population Survey. In the CPS of 1987, about 60 percent of resident mothers reported having a child support order (Lester 1991). Similarly, in my data 53 to 74 percent of fathers report paying child support. In the CPS, about 40 percent of resident mothers report receiving some child support (Lester 1991). The differential reporting of whether child support is being paid or received is consistent with the findings of previous analyses that fathers report paying more child support than mothers report receiving, and that fathers report paying more than shown in an administrative record of payments (Braver, Fitzpatrick, and Bay 1991; Schaeffer, Seltzer, and Klawitter 1991).[10]

INCOME AND POVERTY STATUS   I use several measures of income, all of which include an annual time period, and thus my number of low-income fathers is higher than the number of those who are persistently poor over several years, and lower than the number who experience a short spell of low income. I examine both the father's personal income (the basis for child support calculations in every state) and his "family" income, calculated as a combination of the personal incomes of the father, his spouse or partner if he has one, and the children living with him or them. This definition of family income is thought to be a better reflection of economic status than income measures that ignore cohabitors (for example, Citro and Michael 1995). I compare family income to the poverty line because this provides a measure of economic well-being that is widely recognized and used. I also calculate the poverty "gap," the total amount of money needed to bring all poor families up to the poverty line. If the father was neither the householder nor the spouse of the householder, he was asked about only his own income, and the householder was asked to provide for the income of all related individuals in the household. This kind of father presents a difficulty in calculating poverty status: if he is pooling income with others in the household, the incomes of everyone in the household and the entire number of people in the household should be used to calculate poverty; if he is not, his poverty status should be based only on his own income and family size. In the base results presented here, I calculate poverty status based only on the income of the nonresident father; later in the chapter I provide selected results that show the effect of this decision. All income figures in the results have been adjusted to 1995 dollars using the consumer price index (CPI-U).[11]

SCENARIOS OF CHILD SUPPORT REGIMES   In the first scenario, I examine the economic status of nonresident fathers if they paid no child support. This straightforward calculation uses the typical definition of income and does not consider the possibility that a father might work less if he were not paying child support. The second scenario examines the economic status of fathers *after* they pay child support, simply subtracting the child support paid to get "disposable income." In the third scenario, I assume that current child support orders are fully paid. (In this scenario and the scenarios that follow, I ignore the possibility that fathers living with a new spouse and her children may have higher family incomes because their spouse could be receiving increased child support.) I then test six scenarios with potential guidelines, summarized in table 3.1. In each scenario, I assume that orders are set based on a specific guideline and are fully paid. All guidelines tested are variants of the Wisconsin percentage-of-income guideline because income information on the resident parent is required by other guidelines and is not available.

Guideline 1 is the Wisconsin percentage-of-income guideline, in which orders are based only on the number of children and the nonresident father's personal gross cash income, as follows: 17 percent of income for those with one nonresident child; 25 percent for two children; 29 percent for three children; 31 percent for four children; and 34 percent for five or more.[12] Guideline 2 attempts to capture the way the child support system works in some locations (Johnson and Doolittle 1996): if a father's income is less than the earnings that would be received by a full-time minimum-wage earner, the child support order is based on "imputed income" (full-time work at the minimum wage). The Wisconsin percentages are applied either to actual income or to this imputed income, whichever is greater. Guideline 3 makes an explicit adjustment for the nonresident father's needs. It is identical to guideline 1 except that no child support is due until the father's income is higher than the poverty line for a family of one ($5,702 in 1986); the Wisconsin percentages apply to all income above this amount.

Guidelines 4 through 6 all make an adjustment for the father's new family. Both 4 and 5 allow for a family reserve. Guideline 4 is that suggested by Takas (1994): there is a self-support reserve equal to the family poverty line divided by the number of potential earners. I calculate the reserve assuming all adults in the home are potential earners, and I apply the Wisconsin percentages to the nonresident father's personal income if it is above the self-support reserve. Guideline 5 also uses a family support reserve equal to the family poverty line. The income of others in the family (primarily the new spouse) counts toward the reserve but, once the reserve amount is reached, does not affect orders. This is different from most current guidelines, which assume that child support can be assessed only on the nonresident father's personal income (Gold-Bikin and Hammond 1994). Guideline 6 takes a different approach, which could be called "second children first." If the father has new children, an amount is set aside for them based on the Wisconsin percentages and his gross income. The amount of the child support order is then based on the Wisconsin percentages times the remaining income.

Table 3.1 also provides the order amounts that would result from these guidelines for six potential nonresident fathers (A throughF), all of whom have one non-resident child. I vary the fathers by income status (three have very low incomes,

TABLE 3.1 / Yearly Child Support Order Amounts for Six Potential Guidelines

Potential Order Guideline	Income Base	Self-Support Reserve	Order Amount One Nonresident Child					
			A	B	C	D	E	F
			Father's Income $6,000; Lives Alone	Father's Income $6,000; New Spouse's Income $0; One New Child	Father's Income $6,000; New Spouse's Income $6,000; One New Child	Father's Income $60,000; Lives Alone	Father's Income $60,000; New Spouse's Income $0; One New Child	Father's Income $60,000; New Spouse's Income $60,000; One New Child
1. Basic Guideline	Personal income	None	$1,020	$1,020	$1,020	$10,200	$10,200	$10,200
2. Imputed income	Personal income or full-time minimum-wage earnings, whichever is more	None	$1,185	$1,185	$1,185	$10,200	$10,200	$10,200
3. Personal reserve	Personal income over self-support reserve	Poverty line for family of one	$51	$51	$51	$9,231	$9,231	$9,231
4. Adjusted family reserve 1	Personal income over self-support reserve	Poverty line, based on actual family size divided by number of	$51	$277	$277	$9,231	$9,457	$9,457

			$51	$0	$555	$9,231	$8,715	$10,200
5. Adjusted family reserve 2	Personal income over self-support reserve	Poverty line, based on actual family size; spouse income goes toward self-support reserve (adults)						
6. Second children first	Personal income after subtracting amount set aside for new children (Wisconsin percentages times personal income)	None	$1,020	$847	$847	$10,200	$8,466	$8,466

$6,000, and three have ten times that much, $60,000), family status, and the income status of the new spouse. In guideline 1, family status and spousal income do not matter and order amounts are proportional to income. Guideline 2 increases the order amount of poor fathers because it assumes that any father could be making minimum wage ($3.35 per hour in 1986) and working full-time; it calculates the order based on this "imputed income." This guideline results in the highest orders for low-income fathers. Compared with the first guideline, guideline 3 reduces the order of poor fathers (A through C) to a token amount and also reduces the orders of upper-income fathers by a similar dollar amount. Guideline 4 adjusts for new families and is based on personal income. For fathers B and C, orders are slightly higher than for father A because even though the needs of the new family are greater, the new spouse is expected to contribute something. Guideline 5 adjusts for new families in a different way, allowing for a larger self-support reserve but counting the spouse's income toward the self-support reserve. Thus, orders are lower when there is a new spouse who is not working (compare B to A, and E to D), but higher when the new spouse is working (compare C to A, and F to D). Finally, guideline 6 results in higher orders than guidelines 3 through 5 in the low-income case but not necessarily in the upper-income case. It is the only guideline tested that varies based on whether the father has children but is not affected by the presence of a new wife.

RESULTS

Current and Potential Effects of Child Support on Fathers' Incomes

Figure 3.1 displays fathers' pre–child support incomes and allows a comparison of the effects on the income estimates of using the adjusted weights based on Garfinkel and his colleagues (see chapter 2) versus the unadjusted (NSFH) weights. As expected, there are more low-income fathers when using the adjusted incomes: twice as many fathers have incomes below $5,000 when the adjusted weights are used, and the number of fathers with incomes below $10,000 rises from 17 percent to 28 percent. In both cases, there are a substantial number of fathers with moderate incomes: about 50 to 65 percent have incomes over $20,000, and about 22 to 30 percent have incomes over $40,000.

Figure 3.2 provides information on the distribution of fathers' personal incomes under several child support scenarios using the adjusted weights; figure 3.3 shows identical information using unadjusted weights. The first set of bars on the left reflects the first scenario—income before child support is paid. The median income, shown in the middle bar of the set, is $22,200 (adjusted) or $27,800 (unadjusted). The mean income (not shown) is $27,000 to $33,500, with the adjusted estimate somewhat higher than Sorensen's estimate of $23,000. There is significant variation in incomes: one-quarter of the fathers have incomes above $37,500 (adjusted) or $41,700 (unadjusted), and one-quarter have incomes below $6,700 (adjusted) or $13,900 (unadjusted).

FIGURE 3.1 / Personal Income of Nonresident Fathers (in 1995 Dollars)
(Adjusted and Unadjusted Weights)

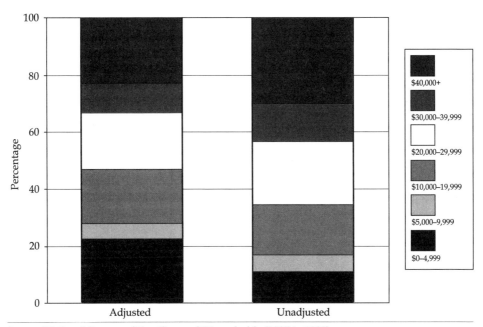

Source: National Survey of Families and Households (1997 to 1998).

The second set of bars shows income after current child support has been subtracted. Because low-income fathers do not pay much child support, paying current child support has little effect on income at the twenty-fifth percentile. However, fathers at the top of the income distribution report paying substantial amounts (between $3,000 and $4,000 at the seventy-fifth percentile). The third set of bars shows what the distribution of incomes would be if current child support orders were fully paid. Incomes decrease further, but not by a large amount because many fathers report that they are already paying the full amount due.

The effects of the six potential guidelines are shown as the last sets of bars. Guideline 1 (and indeed, all guidelines) requires substantially more of fathers in the middle- and upper-income ranges than current orders require; this can be seen by the sharp drop between the "paying amount due" and "basic guideline" (1) scenarios. In contrast, lower-income fathers would not be required to pay a great deal more. The next set of bars shows the effect of the "imputed income" guideline (2): in figure 3.2, income at the twenty-fifth percentile falls because child support orders are increased among poor fathers. The next set of bars shows the effects of a guideline with a "personal reserve" (3). Compared to guideline 1, the personal reserve guideline sets orders among the lowest-income fathers at zero;

FIGURE 3.2 / Personal Income of Nonresident Fathers (Adjusted Weights)

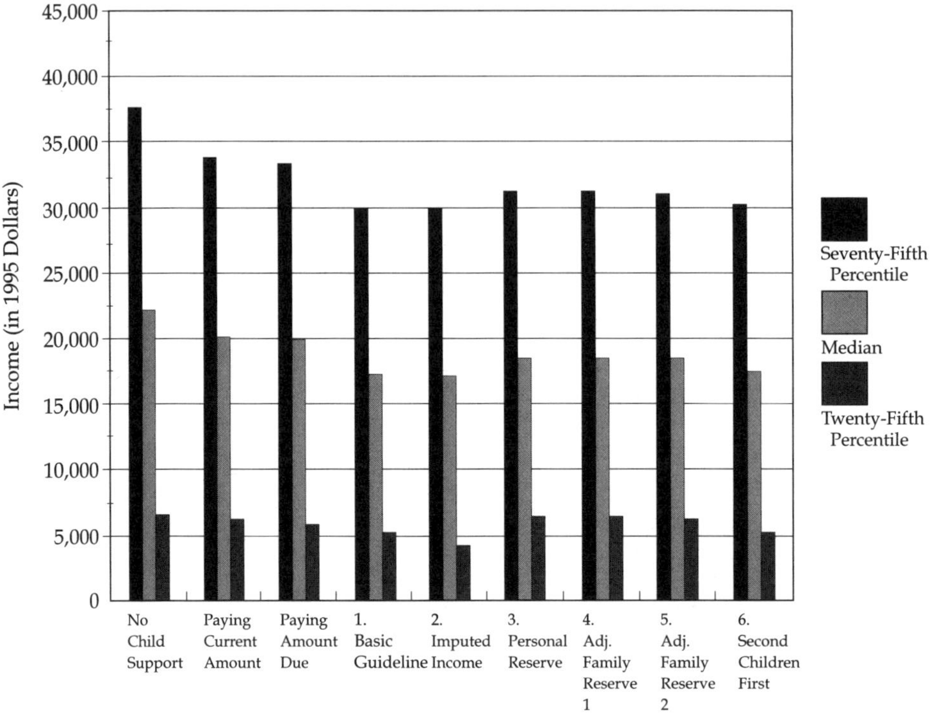

Source: National Survey of Families and Households (1987 to 1988).

thus, incomes of the lowest-income fathers in figure 3.2 are unchanged from the "no child support" scenario. Because the guideline treats all fathers with the same number of nonresident children as having the same needs, the incomes of all fathers increase (not just those of the low-income fathers) compared to guideline 1. Guidelines 4 and 5 have similar effects, in both cases increasing incomes over guideline 1. Guideline 6 is similar to guideline 1 in that it does not incorporate a reserve for the father's own needs; it does, however, lower orders among fathers living with children. The aggregate effects are quite similar to those of guideline 1.

Current and Potential Effects of Child Support on Fathers' Poverty Status

Table 3.2 shows the poverty status of the fathers' families under several child support regimes, using the federal government's official poverty line. (The table shows zero-order relationships; no multivariate analyses are presented.) The first column

FIGURE 3.3 / Personal Income of Nonresident Fathers (Unadjusted Weights)

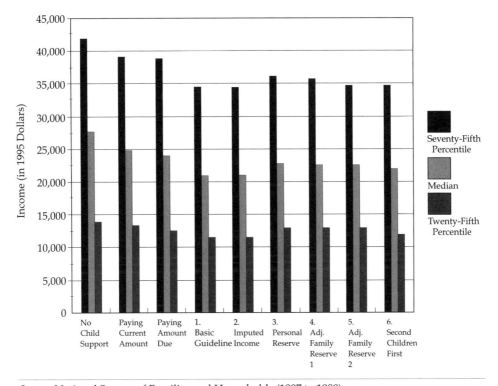

Source: National Survey of Families and Households (1987 to 1988).

shows the scenario in which no child support is paid: 14.4 to 23.6 percent of fathers have household incomes below the poverty level, with the higher percentage based on the adjusted weights. The percentages are generally consistent with Sorensen's estimate of 15 to 25 percent.

The next two sections present poverty rates among different types of family units. Nonresident fathers who are currently living with their own children have poverty rates of 11 to 16 percent. Poverty rates are a little higher among fathers who live with stepchildren or other children not their own (14 to 19 percent), and still higher among fathers who live in households without children (16 to 28 percent). Poverty rates among fathers with a wife or partner and no children are substantially lower than those of all nonresident fathers, while even among fathers with a wife or partner *and* children, rates are somewhat lower than among all fathers, about 11 percent.[13]

The fourth section shows that fathers of marital children are much better off than fathers of nonmarital children, with poverty rates of 8 to 16 percent, compared to 25 to 36 percent.[14] But even though many fathers of nonmarital children have low

TABLE 3.2 / Child Support and the Poverty Rate of Nonresident Fathers

	Percentage Poor[a]									
	Before Child Support Is Paid	After Current Child Support Is Paid	If Current Order Is Fully Paid	If Potential Order 1 Is Paid	If Potential Order 2 Is Paid	If Potential Order 3 Is Paid	If Potential Order 4 Is Paid	If Potential Order 5 Is Paid	If Potential Order 6 Is Paid	Unweighted N
All Fathers	23.6 *14.4*	24.6 *15.7*	24.8 *16.1*	25.6 *16.7*	25.6 *16.7*	24.2 *14.9*	24.4 *15.1*	23.6 *14.4*	25.6 *16.7*	425
Children in current household										
Any own children	16.3 *10.6*	17.3 *11.8*	17.3 *11.8*	18.2 *11.6*	18.2 *11.6*	18.2 *11.6*	18.2 *11.6*	16.3 *10.6*	18.2 *11.6*	100
Other children	19.0 *13.7*	20.8 *16.4*	20.8 *16.4*	22.4 *18.6*	22.4 *18.6*	20.1 *15.4*	20.1 *15.4*	19.0 *13.7*	22.4 *18.6*	79
No children	28.0 *16.3*	28.7 *17.3*	29.1 *17.9*	29.6 *18.5*	29.6 *18.5*	28.0 *16.3*	28.3 *16.7*	28.0 *16.3*	29.6 *18.5*	246
Living situation										
Wife/partner and children	11.5 *10.9*	12.6 *12.2*	12.6 *12.2*	13.9 *12.8*	13.9 *12.8*	13.3 *12.3*	13.3 *12.3*	11.5 *10.9*	13.9 *12.8*	149
Wife/partner and no children	10.4 *3.6*	11.4 *4.9*	12.1 *5.8*	11.4 *4.9*	11.4 *4.9*	10.4 *3.6*	11.4 *4.9*	10.4 *3.6*	11.4 *4.9*	80
Living alone	26.4 *10.8*	27.7 *12.7*	28.4 *13.6*	28.2 *12.9*	28.2 *12.9*	26.4 *10.8*	26.4 *10.8*	26.4 *10.8*	28.2 *12.9*	114
Marital birth										
Yes	15.5 *8.4*	16.6 *9.9*	17.0 *10.4*	17.7 *11.2*	17.7 *11.2*	15.9 *8.9*	16.2 *9.3*	15.5 *8.4*	17.7 *11.2*	270
No	35.5 *25.0*	36.2 *26.1*	36.2 *26.1*	37.3 *26.7*	37.3 *26.7*	36.5 *25.6*	36.5 *25.6*	35.5 *25.0*	37.3 *26.7*	149

									N
Race									
Black	40.1	40.6	42.1	42.1	41.6	41.6	40.1	42.1	122
	27.3	*28.3*	*29.4*	*29.4*	*28.5*	*28.5*	*27.3*	*29.4*	
Nonblack	17.4	18.8	19.4	19.4	17.9	17.7	17.4	19.4	303
	10.9	*12.8*	*13.4*	*13.4*	*11.6*	*11.3*	*10.9*	*13.4*	
Current marital status									
Married	7.5	7.9	9.4	9.4	8.9	8.9	7.5	9.4	169
	6.7	*7.1*	*8.1*	*8.1*	*7.7*	*7.7*	*6.7*	*8.1*	
Formerly married	34.0	35.5	36.6	36.6	34.6	34.2	34.0	36.6	196
	16.1	*18.3*	*19.8*	*19.8*	*16.9*	*16.4*	*16.1*	*19.8*	
Never married	34.8	36.5	35.6	35.6	34.8	34.8	34.8	35.6	60
	33.1	*36.0*	*34.5*	*34.5*	*33.1*	*33.1*	*33.1*	*34.5*	
Age									
Under thirty	24.1	27.6	29.8	29.8	27.4	26.6	24.1	29.8	93
	25.6	*30.7*	*32.0*	*32.0*	*28.6*	*27.3*	*25.6*	*32.0*	
Thirty to thirty-nine	24.1	25.1	24.8	24.8	24.4	24.4	24.1	24.8	199
	11.6	*13.4*	*12.5*	*12.5*	*12.1*	*12.1*	*11.6*	*12.5*	
Over forty	22.6	22.6	24.4	24.4	22.6	22.6	22.6	24.4	133
	11.6	*11.6*	*13.8*	*13.8*	*11.6*	*11.6*	*11.6*	*13.8*	
Number of nonresident children									
One	20.5	21.8	21.9	21.9	21.1	20.9	20.5	21.9	250
	15.1	*17.0*	*16.8*	*16.8*	*16.0*	*15.6*	*15.1*	*16.8*	
Two	24.6	26.1	29.1	29.1	26.2	26.2	24.6	29.1	119
	8.7	*10.8*	*13.6*	*13.6*	*9.6*	*9.6*	*8.7*	*13.6*	
Three or more	37.5	37.5	37.5	37.5	37.5	37.5	37.5	37.5	56
	23.7	*23.7*	*23.7*	*23.7*	*23.7*	*23.7*	*23.7*	*23.7*	

Source: National Survey of Families and Households (1987 to 1988).

[a] Percentages using adjusted weights are shown first, followed by percentages using unadjusted weights in italics.

incomes, poor fathers and nonmarital fathers are not identical groups. For example, of the fathers with incomes under $10,000, about half had nonmarital births and half had marital births. Alternatively, of fathers with nonmarital births, about two-thirds have income above $10,000.

The remaining sections show poverty rates for fathers with different characteristics. African American fathers have poverty rates more than twice as high as those of other fathers. Table 3.2 also shows particularly high poverty rates for fathers who are not married and fathers with three or more nonresident children.

The remaining columns show poverty rates after deducting the amount of child support that is paid (column 2), the amount that should be paid under current orders (column 3), and the amount that would be required to be paid under different guidelines (columns 4 through 9). By comparing the poverty rates in column 1 with those in other columns, we can see the percentage who fall into poverty because of child support.

Current child support increases the poverty rate of nonresident fathers by 1 to 1.3 percentage points. Three groups have more than a two-percentage-point increase in poverty rates as a result of current child support: men living with stepchildren or other children (unadjusted weights only), never-married men (unadjusted weights only), and young men (both adjusted and unadjusted weights). While the level of poverty is substantially higher using the adjusted weights, the percentage-point differences due to current child support are generally higher using the unadjusted rates.

If fathers paid everything they report they owe, poverty rates would increase over the rates that reflect current payments by an additional 0.2 to 0.4 percentage points (seen by comparing columns 2 and 3). No group shows an increase in poverty rates of more than two percentage points. The general lack of change between columns 2 and 3 reflects fathers reporting that they pay almost all of what is due.

Poverty rates after potential child support is paid are shown in the final columns. If orders set according to guideline 1 were fully paid, poverty rates among nonresident fathers would increase by 2 to 2.3 percentage points (compare columns 1 and 4). Because this guideline makes no special allowances for low-income fathers, groups with a higher proportion of fathers with incomes close to the poverty line show larger increases in poverty. Guideline 2 differs from the first only in its effect on poor fathers, so the actual poverty rates are identical.

Guideline 3 is intended to decrease the burden on low-income fathers, and a comparison of columns 1, 4, and 6 reveals that the self-support reserve guideline generates less than one-third the increase in poverty rates that is created by guideline 1. Guidelines 4 and 5 adjust for new families and do so in a way that is also beneficial to low-income fathers. In fact, guideline 5 results in the largest self-support reserve, and this guideline would not increase poverty at all compared to the pre–child support rate because most poor fathers would not be asked to pay child support. Guideline 6 makes an adjustment for new children but not for a new spouse or partner, nor does its adjustment result in an advantage to low-income men who have not fathered new children. Thus, overall poverty rates are identical to the rates based on guideline 1.

The data in table 3.2 merely show whether fathers fall below the poverty line; the table does not address whether child support is deepening poverty among fathers already poor. Table 3.3 shows the poverty gap under various scenarios. The adjustments for undercounting and misreporting make a large difference to the poverty gap, as the unadjusted gap before the payment of child support is $4 billion and the adjusted gap is $10 billion. Current child support increases the total gap by between $1.2 billion and $1.3 billion, an average of $700 to $1,600 for every father who was poor prior to paying child support. If all current orders were fully paid, the aggregate gap would increase another $400 million to $700 million, with the average gap increasing another $400 to $500. The poverty gap under guideline 1, a proportional guideline, is actually smaller than under current child support (column 2) or current orders (column 3), showing that the current system asks more of poor fathers than a proposed proportional system would. The effects of counting imputed income can be seen by comparing potential orders 1 and 2; the poverty gap increases by $900 million to $2.6 billion, from an average of between $6,100 and $6,700 per poor father to between $7,300 and $8,200. The remaining potential orders would all have lower poverty gaps than the proportional order (guideline 1) because they require less of lower-income fathers.

As discussed earlier, these results are based on the assumption that the appropriate family income for fathers who live in someone else's household is only his own income. I conduct two sensitivity tests to check the robustness of the results under this assumption. First, I compare the poverty rates calculated under this assumption to poverty rates among the subsample of fathers for whom family income is not subject to this assumption (fathers who are the head of the household or whose partner or spouse is the head). The poverty rates for the subsample are substantially lower (for adjusted weights, 14.9 percent instead of 23.6 percent, and for unadjusted weights, 8.6 percent instead of 14.4 percent). However, while some of this difference is due to my assumption, a large part is probably attributable to the fact that fathers who are the head of the household or living with a spouse or partner who is the head have higher incomes than fathers who are neither. But even in the smaller sample, the effect of child support regimes on poverty rates are quite similar: for example, paying child support increases poverty rates among those with known incomes by 0.9 to 1.2 percentage points, compared to 1 to 1.3 percentage points for all cases.

The second test differs from the basic calculations in that I assume household income is an appropriate approximation for family income in twenty-two cases in which the father is not the householder but the householder provided an estimate of household income. Pre–child support poverty rates are lower (19.6 percent adjusted, instead of 23.6 percent; 11.2 percent unadjusted, instead of 14.4 percent). The effects of child support on poverty are generally similar: increasing the poverty rate by 0.8 to 1.2 percentage points, compared to the base effect of 1 to 1.3 percentage points.

In summary, the poverty rates among nonresident fathers of 14.4 to 23.6 percent are either somewhat or substantially above the rates of the population as a whole—13.6 percent among all persons in 1986 (Baugher and Lamison-White 1996). Poverty

TABLE 3.3 / Child Support and the Poverty Gap for Nonresident Fathers

	Poverty Gap (Billions of 1995 Dollars)[a]									
	Before Child Support Is Paid	After Current Child Support Is Paid	If Current Order Is Fully Paid	If Potential Order 1 Is Paid	If Potential Order 2 Is Paid	If Potential Order 3 Is Paid	If Potential Order 4 Is Paid	If Potential Order 5 Is Paid	If Potential Order 6 Is Paid	Unweighted N
All fathers	10.4	11.7	12.4	11.5	14.1	10.5	10.5	10.4	11.4	425
	4.2	*5.4*	*5.8*	*4.9*	*5.8*	*4.3*	*4.3*	*4.2*	*4.8*	
Children in current household										
Any own children	2.4	2.5	2.6	2.7	3.0	2.5	2.5	2.4	2.6	100
	1.1	*1.3*	*1.3*	*1.3*	*1.4*	*1.2*	*1.2*	*1.1*	*1.2*	
Other children	2.0	2.2	2.3	2.2	2.8	2.0	2.0	2.0	2.2	79
	0.9	*1.1*	*1.2*	*1.1*	*1.3*	*0.9*	*0.9*	*0.9*	*1.1*	
No children	6.1	6.9	7.5	6.6	8.3	6.1	6.1	6.1	6.6	246
	2.2	*3.1*	*3.2*	*2.5*	*3.1*	*2.2*	*2.2*	*2.2*	*2.5*	
Living situation										
Wife/partner and children	2.6	3.0	3.1	3.1	3.3	2.7	2.7	2.6	3.0	149
	1.6	*2.0*	*2.1*	*2.0*	*2.1*	*1.7*	*1.7*	*1.6*	*1.9*	
Wife/partner and no children	1.1	1.2	1.2	1.1	1.4	1.1	1.1	1.1	1.1	80
	0.2	*0.3*	*0.3*	*0.3*	*0.3*	*0.3*	*0.3*	*0.3*	*0.3*	
Living alone	1.3	1.4	1.5	1.5	1.9	1.3	1.3	1.3	1.5	114
	0.3	*0.5*	*0.5*	*0.4*	*0.5*	*0.3*	*0.3*	*0.3*	*0.4*	
Marital birth										
Yes	4.1	4.9	5.0	4.6	5.6	4.2	4.2	4.2	4.6	270
	1.7	*2.4*	*2.5*	*2.0*	*2.3*	*1.7*	*1.7*	*1.7*	*1.9*	
No	5.8	6.3	7.0	6.4	8.0	5.9	5.9	5.8	6.4	149
	2.3	*2.8*	*3.0*	*2.7*	*3.2*	*2.4*	*2.4*	*2.3*	*2.6*	

										N
Race										
Black	4.5	4.8	5.4	4.9	6.3	4.6	4.6	4.5	4.9	122
(unadjusted)	*1.6*	*1.9*	*2.0*	*1.9*	*2.3*	*1.7*	*1.7*	*1.6*	*1.8*	
Nonblack	5.9	6.9	7.0	6.5	7.7	5.9	5.9	5.9	6.5	303
	2.6	*3.5*	*3.7*	*3.0*	*3.5*	*2.6*	*2.6*	*2.6*	*2.9*	
Current marital status										
Married	2.0	2.2	2.3	2.4	2.6	2.1	2.1	2.0	2.3	169
	1.1	*1.3*	*1.4*	*1.4*	*1.5*	*1.2*	*1.2*	*1.1*	*1.3*	
Formerly married	6.6	7.3	7.4	7.1	8.9	6.6	6.6	6.6	7.1	196
	1.9	*2.6*	*2.7*	*2.2*	*2.7*	*2.0*	*2.0*	*1.9*	*2.2*	
Never married	1.8	2.2	2.8	2.0	2.5	1.8	1.8	1.8	2.0	60
	1.1	*1.5*	*1.6*	*1.3*	*1.5*	*1.1*	*1.1*	*1.1*	*1.3*	
Age										
Under thirty	1.6	1.9	2.1	2.0	2.4	1.7	1.7	1.6	2.0	93
	1.3	*1.6*	*1.8*	*1.6*	*1.9*	*1.3*	*1.3*	*1.3*	*1.6*	
Thirty to thirty-nine	5.7	6.3	6.8	6.1	7.7	5.8	5.8	5.7	6.0	199
	1.8	*2.3*	*2.5*	*2.0*	*2.4*	*1.9*	*1.8*	*1.8*	*2.0*	
Over forty	3.1	3.5	3.6	3.3	4.0	3.1	3.1	3.1	3.3	133
	1.1	*1.5*	*1.6*	*1.3*	*1.5*	*1.1*	*1.1*	*1.1*	*1.2*	
Number of nonresident children										
One	5.2	6.1	6.8	5.7	6.7	5.3	5.3	5.2	5.7	250
	2.7	*3.6*	*3.8*	*3.0*	*3.5*	*2.7*	*2.7*	*2.7*	*3.0*	
Two	3.0	3.1	3.1	3.3	4.2	3.1	3.0	3.0	3.3	119
	0.6	*0.7*	*0.7*	*0.8*	*1.0*	*0.6*	*0.6*	*0.6*	*0.7*	
Three or more	2.2	2.5	2.5	2.4	3.1	2.2	2.2	2.2	2.4	56
	0.9	*1.2*	*1.3*	*1.1*	*1.3*	*0.9*	*1.0*	*0.9*	*1.0*	

Source: National Survey of Families and Households (1987 to 1988).

[a] Poverty gaps using adjusted weights are shown first, followed by poverty gaps using unadjusted weights in italics.

rates among some groups of fathers are quite high: fathers of nonmarital children, formerly married fathers, never-married fathers, and fathers of three or more nonresident children all have poverty rates around 35 percent (adjusted weights), and African American nonresident fathers have a rate of 40 percent (adjusted weight). On the other hand, poverty rates among resident mothers were *even higher* in 1986 than the rates for fathers: 46 percent for all female-headed households with children under eighteen, and 58 percent for African American female-headed households with children (Baugher and Lamison-White 1996).

Child support is not currently throwing many fathers below the poverty line, nor would it even if selected potential guidelines were fully paid. On the other hand, the poverty gap is fairly large and increases under almost all these potential guidelines—substantially so in the scenario in which imputed income is used to calculate orders.

Differential Effects of Current and Potential Child Support

Table 3.4 examines median child support orders and payments for fathers in different parts of the income distribution and fathers with different levels of responsibility for new families. The top row shows median child support payments and orders among all fathers. Median current payments vary from $584 (adjusted) to $2,136 (unadjusted), with median current orders being $1,668 to $2,503. Potential guidelines vary from requiring $2,671 to $4,172 (adjusted) or $3,736 to $5,437 (unadjusted); the lowest amounts are associated with the guidelines that incorporate self-support or family support reserves.

Current payments and current orders generally rise as income rises, as can be seen in the first two columns of the first section. But increases in current payments and orders are not proportional to the income of fathers: fathers with lower incomes are paying (and are asked to pay) a higher percentage of their income. By comparing columns 1 and 3, we see that the lowest-income fathers are currently paying almost as much as they would be asked to pay under a proportional guideline (1), while all other groups of fathers are paying quite a bit less than they would be required to pay under this basic guideline. Upper-income fathers in particular would be required to pay substantially more than their current payments. By comparing columns 2 and 3, we can see that higher-income fathers are not currently ordered to pay proportional amounts, since their orders would increase the most under the basic guideline. In fact, the orders of upper-income fathers would increase dramatically under this first guideline, from $3,337 to over $11,000.

The orders based on imputed income (potential order 2) increase orders among the poorest men, requiring an average of $1,647 instead of the order of $189 to $567 that would be asked under a basic guideline. Compared to the basic guideline (potential order 1), the guideline with a self-support reserve (3) decreases orders across all income ranges, eliminating orders for the average father with an income under $10,000. It also lowers orders for fathers in all family situations. The adjustment for new families under guideline 4 results in median orders quite similar to

TABLE 3.4 / Median Annual Child Support Paid and Due (in 1995 Dollars)

	Current Child Support Paid[a]	Current Child Support Due	Potential Order 1	Potential Order 2	Potential Order 3	Potential Order 4	Potential Order 5	Potential Order 6	Unweighted N
All fathers	584	1,668	4,172	4,172	2,671	2,709	3,168	3,728	425
	2,136	*2,503*	*5,437*	*5,437*	*3,736*	*3,860*	*4,508*	*4,728*	
Father's income									
Under $10,000	0	0	189	1,647	0	0	0	142	70
	417	*1,418*	*567*	*1,647*	*0*	*0*	*0*	*567*	
$10,000 to $19,999	0	0	2,837	2,837	1,489	1,489	2,364	2,718	83
	626	*1,435*	*2,837*	*2,837*	*1,489*	*1,489*	*1,794*	*2,600*	
$20,000 to $29,999	1,460	1,669	4,728	4,728	3,380	3,388	3,737	4,693	87
	1,669	*2,153*	*4,728*	*4,728*	*3,380*	*3,447*	*4,019*	*4,491*	
$30,000 to $39,999	2,336	2,503	6,619	6,619	5,271	5,279	5,717	6,619	64
	2,503	*2,920*	*6,619*	*6,619*	*5,271*	*5,596*	*5,910*	*6,524*	
More than $40,000	3,337	3,337	11,157	11,157	9,490	9,526	9,999	10,429	121
	3,337	*3,337*	*11,472*	*11,472*	*9,526*	*9,763*	*10,085*	*10,429*	
Children in home									
Any own children	1,334	1,669	4,964	4,964	3,380	3,414	4,019	4,042	100
	1,669	*2,002*	*5,910*	*5,910*	*4,275*	*4,326*	*4,728*	*4,693*	
Other children	0	0	3,357	3,357	2,009	2,198	1,905	2,786	79
	1,752	*2,503*	*3,357*	*3,357*	*2,671*	*2,705*	*3,199*	*3,545*	
No children	667	1,669	4,172	4,172	2,671	2,671	3,233	4,172	246
	2,503	*2,870*	*5,673*	*5,673*	*4,089*	*4,127*	*4,728*	*5,562*	
Living situation									
Wife/partner and children	834	1,435	4,651	4,651	3,021	3,346	3,886	3,546	149
	1,679	*2,153*	*5,437*	*5,437*	*3,616*	*3,661*	*4,346*	*4,078*	

(Table continues on p. 88.)

TABLE 3.4 / *Continued*

	Current Child Support Paid[a]	Current Child Support Due	Potential Order 1	Potential Order 2	Potential Order 3	Potential Order 4	Potential Order 5	Potential Order 6	Unweighted N
Wife/partner and no	1,669	2,336	6,572	6,572	4,562	5,271	4,884	6,572	80
children	*2,503*	*2,503*	*6,953*	*6,953*	*4,970*	*5,677*	*6,255*	*6,953*	
Living alone	1,112	1,785	4,255	4,255	2,647	2,647	2,647	4,255	114
	2,837	*3,337*	*6,987*	*6,987*	*5,177*	*5,177*	*5,177*	*6,987*	

Source: National Survey of Families and Households (1987 to 1988).

[a] Child support amounts using adjusted weights are shown first, followed by amounts using unadjusted weights in italics.

those resulting from the guideline with the self-support reserve. Guideline 5 contains a different type of adjustment that generally increases orders over those under guideline 4 except among families with stepchildren (adjusted weights only) and fathers who live with a wife or partner but no children (adjusted weights only). The final potential guideline (6) adjusts for new children but not a new partner. Among cases with new children, the median order declines by $900 to $1,200 (compare potential order 1 to potential order 6).

CONCLUSIONS

While my ability to draw firm conclusions is limited because the range of estimates of economic status is fairly wide, I do find that, whereas some nonresident fathers have very low incomes, others have at least moderate incomes, and more than one-third have incomes over $30,000. While a fairly high percentage of fathers are poor using one set of weights, very few fathers fell into poverty because of the amount of child support they paid in 1986, and very few would have fallen into poverty even if they had paid everything they owed. On the other hand, current child support does increase the poverty gap by $1.2 billion to $1.3 billion, worsening the poverty of those already poor.

The focus of this chapter has been whether nonresident fathers appear to be able to afford to pay child support under alternative guidelines. But determining whether guidelines should incorporate a self-support reserve and whether they should incorporate an adjustment for new families are normative issues whose answers should be based on standards of equity, not just pragmatic concerns. A discussion of this issue is beyond the scope of this chapter (for a review of this and related issues, see chapter 10). Nonetheless, these results suggest that an unadjusted basic guideline would not throw many nonresident fathers and children into poverty. In fact, an unadjusted basic guideline would ask poor fathers to pay *less* than they are currently asked to pay, so the poverty gap would actually be *smaller* under the unadjusted proportional guideline than under the current support system. On the other hand, a child support system in which orders are based on "potential" or "imputed" income results in a large increase in the poverty gap, substantially increasing the depth of poverty among fathers who are already poor.

With these data, I cannot answer the question of whether increasing the amount of child support would create poverty in fathers' new families to the extent that it would alleviate poverty in mothers' families, because I do not have information on the mother's income for each father in the sample. Still, I find that few of the nonresident fathers who live with children (either their own children or the children of others) become poor when they pay child support or would become poor even if they paid child support set according to several potential guidelines. This suggests that a reshuffling of poverty among children is not a major concern.

The finding that few fathers fall into poverty is somewhat misleading because it examines only the question of whether fathers' incomes cross an arbitrary line. A closer examination shows that the current child support system asks a substantially higher percentage of income from lower-income fathers than from higher-income fathers. Fathers with moderate or high incomes are treated much more generously by the current child support system than if they were required to pay proportional amounts, or, indeed, the amounts required by any of the potential guidelines tested here. For example, the average father with an annual income of more than $40,000 reported paying $3,300 in current child support; under one potential guideline, he should be paying more than $11,000.

As noted, the conclusions are limited by the number of missing nonresident fathers. An important complement to this research would be administrative data, which would enable the researcher to identify divorced nonresident fathers without having to rely on self-reports. For example, recent research using Wisconsin data on the incomes of nonresident fathers (Phillips and Garfinkel 1993; Meyer 1995) and on the relationship between fathers' incomes and child support payments (Bartfeld and Meyer 1994; Meyer and Bartfeld 1996) provide complements to this national study. To date, no study that I am aware of has used an approach comparable to that conducted in this chapter and included a look at administrative data to examine the effect of child support on the economic status of nonresident fathers. Another useful extension of this work would be to examine panel data (either from administrative sources or from surveys). This would enable researchers to explore whether child support has different effects among those whose low-income status is temporary and those who have longer-term difficulties with income.

Finally, the conclusions are limited by the time period studied, which preceded several child support reforms. Perhaps a more recent analysis would show that more child support is being ordered and paid and that some of the regressivity of child support has been lessened.

An earlier version of this chapter was presented at the Population Association of America annual conference, April 1995. I thank Stuart Kipnis and Mary Eamon for excellent research assistance, Elizabeth Evanson for editing assistance, and Judi Bartfeld and the participants at a session of the Population Association of America conference for comments. The Institute for Research on Poverty provided partial funding for this research. Opinions expressed are those of the author and not necessarily those of the sponsoring institution.

NOTES

1. Income shares and Melson guidelines require that the income of both the resident parent and the nonresident parent be known. Thus, simulating the effects of these alternate guidelines cannot be completed with the main data used in this chapter.

2. Takas (1994) describes this as the current Wisconsin treatment of second families. This was not the intent of the Wisconsin guidelines, but they were somewhat ambiguous, causing some to interpret them in this way. The Wisconsin guidelines have recently been changed to clarify that this treatment applies not to the general case of second families but only when there is more than one support order required of the same person.

3. Underreporting of fatherhood among nonresident fathers has been found in other surveys as well (Cherlin, Griffith, and McCarthy 1983; O'Neill 1985).

4. The undercount of nonresident fathers in the NSFH appears at first glance to be larger than the SIPP, the main alternative dataset that could be used. But because the identification of nonresident fathers in the SIPP is imprecise, researchers using SIPP may incorrectly count some as nonresident fathers who are not, and thus the undercount in the SIPP may be as great or greater than that in NSFH.

5. A final limitation is that the determination of the amount of child support paid is somewhat imprecise for those with formal child support orders: after the order amount has been ascertained, respondents are asked how many payments have been missed (none, less than one-quarter, about one-quarter, one-half, three-quarters, or all), and how much they usually pay when they do pay. I use the responses to calculate an approximate amount of child support paid: for example, if the order is $400/month ($4,800/year), usual amounts paid are $200, and half the payments are missed, I assume that a total of $1,200 was paid. For a discussion of the accuracy of self-reported child support amounts and related issues, see Schaeffer (1994) and Schaeffer, Seltzer, and Klawitter (1991). Another way in which the information on child support is limited is that fathers who have both child support and alimony orders are asked about order amounts separately, but the amount-paid question refers to both. I therefore cannot distinguish between child support and alimony payments and thus count it all as child support. This affects twenty-five cases, but in most of these the amount of alimony ordered is fairly low.

6. Although fathers whose children are living with grandparents, other relatives, or foster parents could be asked to pay child support, this is not a frequent occurrence, and these cases are not included in the information that follows. Of the 102 fathers whose children were not living with their mother, the largest four categories were: living with grandparents ($n = 28$), living with other relatives ($n = 13$), living at college ($n = 13$), and living with his or her spouse ($n = 9$). If the focal child was living at college or living with a spouse, interviewers were instructed to select another focal child if one was available.

7. One limitation is that fathers with more than one child were asked the amount of child support they were "supposed to pay to [the child's mother]." If a man had children with two different partners, he was not asked to include any information on orders and payments to the family of the nonfocal child. In these cases, I may underestimate the amount of child support a man pays or should pay. I also underestimate the amount he would be required to pay under different guidelines.

8. Men paying more than their formal order could be paying arrearages; to the extent that this is the cause of the "overpayment," I overstate orders but not payments.

9. In addition to the obvious problem of matching child support payments and income, an additional problem may occur among those who became separated from their child within the twelve months preceding the interview. For example, a father who separated from his family six months prior to the interview and paid $200 in child support in each month since the separation may have responded to the child support questions in two different ways. He may have annualized his report, stating that he would have paid $2,400 over the past year. Or he may have reported that he made payments in six of the past twelve months averaging $200 each. In the second scenario, I would calculate total annual child support paid to be $200 times six, or $1,200 annually, or the equivalent of $100/month, not the $200 actually paid. This decision makes very little difference to the conclusions described here; moreover, a simple regression of the amount paid showed

that there is no significant difference in this calculation of child support paid between those who last lived with their child in 1987 to 1988, in 1986, or prior to 1986.

10. If fathers overestimate payments, this would bias my findings about the number of fathers thrown into poverty by paying child support. But because I find only a few fathers whose current child support payments cause them to fall into poverty, any *overestimate* of payments does not change this conclusion.

11. Note that this may overstate fathers' incomes in that the incomes of those working in low-wage jobs have not generally kept up with the inflation rate.

12. The number of children under age nineteen who live elsewhere is used, even though not all these children may be living with their mother or the same mother. Note also that while Wisconsin uses different guidelines when one or more child lives with each parent (split custody), when the child or children live with both parents at least 30 percent of the time (shared custody), and when the obligor is subject to a previous child support order; my simulations use the basic guideline only.

13. Two groups of fathers are not included in this breakdown because there are few unweighted cases: fathers living with children but without a spouse or partner ($N = 30$), and fathers living with children and without a spouse or partner but with other adults ($N = 52$).

14. Determining whether the focal child's parents were married or not married is straightforward if the father was never married (the child is nonmarital) or if the father has a nonresident child living with its mother and the father has been married only once and is currently married (the child is nonmarital). In all other situations, the approximate birth date was compared to the range of months in which the father was married, after making allowances for uncertainties over the exact month of birth for children conceived prior to a divorce but born after a divorce (called "marital") and for children born within three months prior to the marriage date (also called "marital").

REFERENCES

Bartfeld, Judi, and Daniel R. Meyer. 1994. "Are There Really Dead-Beat Dads? The Relationship Between Enforcement, Ability to Pay, and Compliance in Nonmarital Child Support Cases." *Social Service Review* 68(2): 219–35.

Baugher, Eleanor, and Leatha Lamison-White. 1996. "Poverty in the United States: 1995." *Current Population Reports*, series P-60, no. 194. Washington: U.S. Government Printing Office for the U.S. Bureau of the Census.

Braver, Sanford L., Pamela J. Fitzpatrick, and R. Curtis Bay. 1991. "Noncustodial Parents' Report of Child Support Payments." *Family Relations* 40(2): 180–85.

Cherlin, Andrew, Jeanne Griffith, and James McCarthy. 1983. "A Note on Maritally-Disrupted Men's Reports of Child Support in the June 1980 Current Population Survey." *Demography* 20(3): 385–89.

Citro, Constance F., and Robert T. Michael, eds. 1995. *Measuring Poverty: A New Approach.* Washington: National Academy Press.

Garfinkel, Irwin. 1992. *Assuring Child Support: An Extension of Social Security.* New York: Russell Sage Foundation.

Garfinkel, Irwin, and Marygold S. Melli. 1990. "The Use of Normative Standards in Family Law Decisions: Developing Mathematical Standards for Child Support." *Family Law Quarterly* 24(2): 157–78.

Garfinkel, Irwin, and Donald T. Oellerich. 1989. "Noncustodial Fathers' Ability to Pay Child Support." *Demography* 26(2): 219–33.

Garfinkel, Irwin, Donald Oellerich, and Philip K. Robins. 1991. "Child Support Guidelines: Will They Make a Difference?" *Journal of Family Issues* 12(4): 404–29.

Gold-Bikin, Lynne, and Linda Ann Hammond. 1994. "Determination of Income Under Guidelines." In *Child Support Guidelines: The Next Generation*, edited by Margaret Campbell Haynes. Washington: U.S. Department of Health and Human Services.

Haynes, Margaret Campbell, ed. 1994. *Child Support Guidelines: The Next Generation*. Washington: U.S. Department of Health and Human Services.

Johnson, Earl, and Fred Doolittle. 1996. "Low-Income Parents and the Parents' Fair Share Demonstration: An Early Qualitative Look at Low-Income Parents (NCPs) and How Policy Initiatives Have Attempted to Improve Their Ability to Pay Child Support." New York: Manpower Demonstration Research Corporation.

Lester, Gordon. 1991. "Child Support and Alimony: 1989." *Current Population Reports*, series P-60, no. 173. Washington: U.S. Government Printing Office for the U.S. Bureau of the Census.

Lewin/ICF. 1990. "Estimates of Expenditures on Children and Child Support Guidelines." Report to U.S. Department of Health and Human Services. Washington: Lewin/ICF.

Meyer, Daniel R. 1995. "Supporting Children Born Outside of Marriage: Do Child Support Awards Keep Pace with Changes in Fathers' Incomes?" *Social Science Quarterly* 76(5): 577–93.

Meyer, Daniel R., and Judi Bartfeld. 1996. "Compliance with Child Support Orders in Divorce Cases." *Journal of Marriage and the Family* 58(1): 201–12.

Miller, Cynthia, Irwin Garfinkel, and Sara McLanahan. 1997. "Child Support in the U.S.: Can Fathers Afford to Pay More?" *Review of Income and Wealth* 43(3): 261–81.

Nichols-Casebolt, Ann. 1986. "The Economic Impact of Child Support Reform on the Poverty Status of Custodial and Noncustodial Families." *Journal of Marriage and the Family* 48(4): 875–80.

O'Neill, June. 1985. "Determinants of Child Support." Report for the National Institute of Health. Washington: Urban Institute.

Phillips, Elizabeth, and Irwin Garfinkel. 1993. "Income Growth Among Nonresident Fathers: Evidence from Wisconsin." *Demography* 30(2): 227–41.

Schaeffer, Nora Cate. 1994. "Errors of Experience: Response Errors in Reports About Child Support and Their Implications for Questionnaire Design." In *Autobiographical Memory and the Validity of Retrospective Reports*, edited by Norbert Schwarz and Seymour Sudman. New York: Springer-Verlag.

Schaeffer, Nora Cate, Judith A. Seltzer, and Marieka Klawitter. 1991. "Estimating Nonresponse and Response Bias: Resident and Nonresident Parents' Reports About Child Support." *Sociological Methods and Research* 20(1): 30–59.

Seltzer, Judith A., and Yvonne Brandreth. 1995. "What Fathers Say About Involvement with Children After Separation." In *Fatherhood: Contemporary Theory, Research, and Social Policy*, edited by William Marsiglio. Thousand Oaks, Calif.: Sage Publications.

Sorensen, Elaine. 1997. "A National Profile of Nonresident Fathers and Their Ability to Pay Child Support." *Journal of Marriage and the Family* 59(4): 785–97.

Takas, Marianne. 1994. "Addressing Subsequent Families in Child Support Guidelines." In *Child Support Guidelines: The Next Generation*, edited by Margaret Campbell Haynes. Washington: U.S. Department of Health and Human Services.

Williams, Robert G. 1987. "Guidelines for Setting Levels of Child Support Orders." *Family Law Quarterly* 21(3): 281–324.

Chapter 4

Does Child Support Enforcement Policy Affect Male Labor Supply?

Richard B. Freeman and Jane Waldfogel

S ince the mid-1970s, the U.S. government has tried to increase child support payments from noncustodial parents. Originally, the federal effort concentrated on the fathers of children receiving cash assistance (known in this period as Aid to Families with Dependent Children [AFDC], after 1996 as Temporary Assistance to Needy Families [TANF]). The goal was to save on the welfare budget and to make these men responsible for the children they had fathered. In 1984 federal legislation required states to provide child support enforcement services for non-AFDC families as well. In 1988 the federal government required states to make a greater effort to establish paternity for the children of unwed mothers and pressed states to use wage-withholding as a mode of ensuring payment of child support orders.

Government-induced child support payments transfer money from noncustodial fathers to the family or to the state. Child support moneys collected by child support enforcement (CSE) agencies for non-AFDC families go to the custodial parent. Child support moneys collected for AFDC families go largely to the state, to cover the costs of AFDC checks. In the former case, custodial parents have an incentive to help the government collect moneys. In the latter case, they may have the opposite incentive. This will be the case if the noncustodial parent is providing funds that are not reported to the state and that parent would no longer make such payments if dunned by a CSE agency (Edin 1995). In both cases, the payments reduce the take-home pay of noncustodial fathers. What effect is this reduction likely to have on noncustodial fathers' labor supply—that is, whether they work and the number of hours they work per week?

To the extent that child support payments are effectively a fixed levy on a noncustodial father—with the amount paid maintained for an extended period—the government-enforced payments will reduce the noncustodial father's income but not the marginal value of an extra hour of his work. In this model, child support enforcement should increase the labor supply of the noncustodial father. But if the father can avoid this levy by engaging in self-employment, casual work, or off-the-books work, or by "disappearing" to some other locale, there may be a huge substitution effect in work activity, from wage and salary employment to less readily observable activities.[1]

To the extent that child support payments operate like an income tax, rising with wages or hours worked because the amount a man owes is altered quickly as his economic circumstances change, child support enforcement will have both income and substitution effects. This could induce either more or less work on existing jobs, as well as induce a shift toward informal activities that would make collection difficult.

In short, the labor supply responses of noncustodial fathers to government enforcement of child support are a potentially important determinant of the success of the government's efforts to transfer money to custodial parents or the state. Government child support policies could increase noncustodial male labor supply or reduce it, or they could lead noncustodial fathers to do different types of work.

What effects do government-induced collection efforts have on the labor supply of noncustodial fathers? Does the effect of child support policies differ between low-income noncustodial fathers and other noncustodial fathers?

In this chapter, we examine these questions using data on fathers from the 1986 and 1991 Surveys of Income and Program Participation (SIPP), together with data on state expenditures and policies from the annual reports of the Office of Child Support Enforcement at the U.S. Department of Health and Human Services. Our empirical strategy is to estimate the effects of state expenditures and policies on noncustodial fathers' labor supply, using custodial fathers and nonfathers as control groups. We use control groups to make sure that our state expenditure and enforcement variables are truly picking up the effects of child support enforcement, which should affect the labor supply of noncustodial fathers only and not some other state conditions that affect the labor supply of all men.

Our major finding is that child support payment policies have no discernible adverse effect on male labor supply; if anything, these policies are associated with increases in labor supply. The problem in getting low-income noncustodial fathers to contribute substantially to the upkeep of their children is not adverse labor supply responses to child support enforcement but rather these men's low earnings and commensurately low support payments.[2]

DATA AND METHODOLOGY

We use data on fathers from the Survey of Income and Program Participation, a large and nationally representative data set that is very well suited to our analysis.[3] The SIPP follows panels over a period of thirty-two months, with interviews every four months. We use data from two points in time: 1986, the earliest year that the SIPP collected fertility data on men; and 1991, a more recent year. Using these two points in time is useful because new policies were introduced over the time period, and thus we are able to estimate the effects of various child support enforcement measures.

Our 1986 sample uses data on child support from the May 1986 interviews of two different panels: the 1984 panel (interview wave 8) and the 1985 panel (interview wave 4). By combining these two panels, both of whom responded to the same basic child support and support-for-household-members module administered in May

1986, we are able to create a larger sample of fathers with data on child support payments than if we used just one panel for that year. Our 1991 sample uses data on child support from the September 1991 interview of the 1991 panel (interview wave 3). The 1991 child support and support-for-household-members module is an expanded version of the basic module and includes more detailed questions about the use of state CSE agencies and methods of payment of child support. For this reason, and because the data capture a more recent time period, we make more use of the 1991 data in our analysis.

In addition to gathering data about child support payments, the SIPP includes a fertility module that asks men how many children they have fathered. The SIPP also asks men about the number of children living with them (we refer to these as custodial children), but unfortunately the SIPP does not ask about the ages and whereabouts of all the children the man has fathered. Thus, we have to estimate the number of noncustodial children that a man has by subtracting the number of custodial children from the total number ever fathered. For men with any noncustodial children, we then estimate the probability that those children are old enough to no longer depend on their parents; the inverse of this is the probability that a man is a noncustodial father of dependent children.[4]

The annual reports of the Office of Child Support Enforcement provide data on the number of collections and paternity establishments made by the states, two important indicators of state CSE activity. In addition, we make use of differences in state laws regarding wage-withholding and enforcement on non-AFDC cases as two other indicators of state CSE activity.[5]

We begin our analysis by contrasting the labor supply of men in the SIPP by their status as fathers—whether they are custodial, noncustodial, or not fathers at all, and, if noncustodial, whether they pay child support. These comparisons show that noncustodial fathers who pay child support work a lot, nearly as much as custodial fathers and more than the noncustodial fathers who don't pay child support, presumably in part because those who work more are more likely to make payments.[6]

This reverse causality suggests that it will be difficult to isolate the effects of child support payments on labor supply in these data: the predominant causal link is likely to run from labor supply to payments rather than in the other direction. Because of this problem, we do not attempt to identify the effects of child support policy on labor supply behavior by relating individual labor supply to individual child support payments. Instead, we examine the relation between child support *policies* across states and work by noncustodial fathers.

Since a sine qua non for child support policies to have an effect on labor supply is that they affect payments (and since prior research has found that not all policies do affect payments), we first identify policy variables that raise the rate of child support payments. Then we examine the effect of these policies on the work activity of noncustodial fathers, both directly and indirectly as "instruments" for child support payments.

To avoid confounding the effects of the policies with other unobserved variables that may be correlated with those policies, we use custodial fathers and non-fathers in the same states as controls for the noncustodial fathers. A control group is essential because what we interpret as the effects of government child support enforcement efforts may instead be the effect of other state conditions that are correlated with child support enforcement efforts. If our state policy variables are truly picking up the effects of child support enforcement and not some other state conditions, then these variables should have an effect on the labor supply of noncustodial fathers who have child support obligations but not on custodial fathers and nonfathers, who have no obligation to pay government-enforced child support.

FATHER STATUS, CHILD SUPPORT PAYMENTS, AND LABOR SUPPLY

We use the 1986 and 1991 SIPP data to examine the labor supply of men age eighteen to fifty-five by father status and child support payment status. We distinguish between four types of men: custodial fathers; noncustodial fathers who pay child support; noncustodial fathers who do not pay child support; and men who are not fathers.[7] Because noncustodial fathers might respond to child support enforcement by changing their type of work activity as well as by changing their amount of work activity, we measure labor supply activity by the type of employment—whether it is standard employment with an employer (and thus presumably discoverable and possibly liable to wage-withholding) or self-employment or casual employment[8]— as well as by whether a man works and his hours worked.

Tables 4.1 and 4.2 show the relationship between fatherhood, child support payments, and labor supply for all men in our sample, for men with a high school education or less, and for men who have never been married. These latter two groups are of interest because they are most likely to be low-income; the never-married are of particular interest because they have the lowest child support payment rate and because they should be most affected by child support enforcement policies such as paternity establishment.

The basic story for all men is clear: custodial fathers and noncustodial fathers who pay child support work the most. Men who are not fathers work the least, while those who are noncustodial fathers and who do not pay child support have work behavior between the high-work custodial fathers and child support–paying noncustodial fathers, on the one hand, and the low-work nonfathers, on the other. Among noncustodial fathers, those who are working but not paying child support are more likely to be self-employed or casual workers than those who are paying child support; this suggests that men who wish to avoid child support payments may be substituting informal work activities. Still, the nonpaying, noncustodial fathers are no more likely to be self-employed or casual workers than are custodial fathers. The pattern among men with a high school education or less is similar to the pattern for men overall. The pattern among never-married men is dominated by men who are not fathers; there are too few men in most other categories to merit much attention.

Could the pattern of results in tables 4.1 and 4.2 be due to differences in observable personal characteristics of the men in the four categories? Noncustodial fathers

TABLE 4.1 / Labor Supply of Men Age Eighteen to Fifty-Five in 1991, by Father Status

	Custodial Father	Noncustodial Father	Noncustodial Father Paying Child Support	Noncustodial Father Not Paying Child Support	Not a Father
All men					
Total working (percentage)	93.59	90.20	95.62	88.15	82.65
Working for an employer	81.32	82.32	84.44	81.46	86.75
Self-employed	17.14	16.11	13.27	17.28	10.32
Casual	1.54	1.56	2.29	1.26	2.93
Mean hours/week	42.39	42.05	42.55	41.85	39.74
N	3,157	1,668	457	1,211	2,979
Men with high school education or less					
Total working (percentage)	90.93	87.06	93.94	84.84	77.48
Working for an employer	83.14	84.65	86.64	83.79	88.62
Self-employed	15.02	13.53	10.60	14.58	7.82
Casual	1.86	1.92	2.76	1.63	3.56
Mean hours/week	41.81	41.08	40.62	41.24	38.97
N	1,503	948	231	717	1,270
Never-married men					
Total working (percentage)	71.84	81.69	95.65	78.48	77.82
Working for an employer	86.28	88.32	77.27	91.41	88.18
Self-employed	1.60	4.71	4.55	4.77	7.98
Casual	12.12	6.97	18.18	3.82	3.94
Mean hours/week	42.30	36.33	33.74	37.08	38.20
N	23	123	23	100	1,966

Source: Survey of Income and Program Participation (1991).

Notes: Data in columns 1 through 4 are weighted by the probability that a man is either a noncustodial father or custodial father (see the appendix for details). Working for an employer, self-employed, and casual are percentages of total working.

TABLE 4.2 / Labor Supply of Men Age Eighteen to Fifty-Five in 1986, by Father Status

	Custodial Father	Noncustodial Father	Noncustodial Father Paying Child Support	Noncustodial Father Not Paying Child Support	Not a Father
All men					
Total working (percentage)	94.17	91.04	95.39	88.81	82.55
Working for an employer	81.16	82.49	85.41	80.90	90.09
Self-employed	18.57	17.22	14.27	18.84	9.35
Casual	0.27	0.29	0.32	0.26	0.56
Mean hours/week	41.12	40.18	40.61	39.94	35.98
N	5,577	2,822	955	1,867	5,806
Men with high school education or less					
Total working (percentage)	91.20	88.38	94.69	85.38	78.27
Working for an employer	84.31	84.99	88.78	82.98	92.63
Self-employed	15.39	14.73	11.03	16.69	6.81
Casual	0.30	0.28	0.19	0.33	0.56
Mean hours/week	39.80	38.97	39.69	38.57	35.41
N	2,866	1,694	546	1,148	2,665
Never-married men					
Total working (percentage)	60.06	80.16	92.98	73.37	76.97
Working for an employer	95.78	91.74	94.34	89.98	92.56
Self-employed	4.21	8.26	5.66	10.02	6.63
Casual	0.00	0.00	0.00	0.00	0.81
Mean hours/week	35.81	36.33	36.91	35.90	33.52
N	43	165	57	108	3,939

Source: SIPP (1986).

Notes: Data in columns 1 through 4 are weighted by the probability that a man is either a noncustodial father or custodial father (see the appendix for details). Working for an employer, self-employed, and casual are percentages of total working.

who pay child support tend to be more educated and older than those who do not pay child support,[9] so it is plausible that at least some of the differences between these two groups could be attributed to differences in measurable characteristics.

To see whether this is the case, we examine in table 4.3 the relationship between father status and labor supply conditional on a host of personal characteristics. We estimate probit equations for working, as well as for working for an employer, as opposed to being self-employed or casually employed, among those who are working. We condition on age, education, ethnicity, marital status, year, and one indicator of labor market conditions, the state unemployment rate. We use ordinary least squares (OLS) regression for our analysis of hours worked, controlling for the same set of variables. In columns 1 and 2, we report the marginal effects of the father-status dummy variables from the employment and type of employment probits, along with the standard error of the estimated effects. Coefficients from the OLS models of hours worked, and the standard errors of these estimates, are shown in column 3. The estimated coefficients on the father-status dummy variables in these three models show that the relations in tables 4.1 and 4.2 are not the result of differences in observable characteristics between men in the various sets. Controlling for those characteristics, custodial fathers and noncustodial fathers who pay child support are more likely to be working (in model 1) and to work more hours per week (in model 3) than the reference group (nonfathers), while noncustodial fathers who are not paying child support work less than the other two groups of fathers and, in some models, less than the men who are not fathers. To the extent that the "raw" linkage between child support payments and work is positive because it is easier to collect support from fathers who work more (or because there is some unobserved characteristic that is correlated both with working and with paying child support), these results suggest that we cannot simply estimate the effect of child support payments on labor supply and assume that this represents the true effect that enforcing child support orders would have on the labor supply of noncustodial fathers not currently making such payments. Rather, we use the strategy of relating the labor supply of noncustodial fathers to variation in state child support enforcement policies, not to their individual support payments.

GOVERNMENT POLICIES TO INCREASE CHILD SUPPORT PAYMENTS

Government efforts to increase child support payments take four forms (see table 4.4):

1. *Establishing paternity:* In 1992 paternity was established for only about one-third of the nearly 1.2 million births to unmarried women, and some 3.1 million children in total had no legal father (U.S. Department of Health and Human Services, 1994, p. 11). The percentage of children born out of wedlock for whom paternity has been established varies greatly among states. From 1989 to 1992, it ranged from 3 percent in the District of Columbia to 87 percent in West Virginia. The 1988 Family Support Act requires states to increase the proportion of children born out

TABLE 4.3 / The Relationship Between Father Status, Child Support, and Men's Labor Supply, 1986 and 1991

	Working Model	Working-for-Employer Model	Hours-Worked-per-Week Model
All men			
Custodial fathers	.0222[a]	−.0207[a]	.3922
	(.0071)	(.0083)	(.2985)
Noncustodial fathers paying child support	.0640[a]	.0036	1.6229[a]
	(.0077)	(.0127)	(.4528)
Noncustodial fathers not paying child support	−.0115	−.0030	−.1858
	(.0081)	(.0117)	(.4140)
Observations	20,523	18,227	16,032
Men with high school education or less			
Custodial fathers	−.0289[a]	−.0299[a]	.4508
	(.0118)	(.0120)	(.4365)
Noncustodial fathers paying child support	.0880[a]	−.0138	1.3764[a]
	(.0125)	(.0176)	(.6112)
Noncustodial fathers not paying child support	−.0076	−.0233	−.2693
	(.0125)	(.0149)	(.5447)
Observations	10,126	8,675	7,748
Never-married men			
Noncustodial fathers paying child support	.1921[a]	−.0613	1.1014
	(.0391)	(.0380)	(1.5944)
Noncustodial fathers not paying child support	.0502	−.0166	1.0273
	(.0311)	(.0235)	(1.2002)
Observations	5,893	4,561	4,259

Source: SIPP (1986, 1991).

Notes: In the first model, the dependent variable is a dummy variable for working at all versus not working. In the second model, the dependent variable is a dummy variable for working for an employer versus working self-employed or casually, among those working at all. Both models are estimated using probit, and the marginal effects (and standard errors in parentheses) are shown. In the third model, the dependent variable is hours worked, among those working at all and reporting positive hours. All three models also include controls for age, education, black, Hispanic, marital status, year, and state unemployment rate. The omitted father status category is "not a father." Coefficients for never-married custodial fathers are not shown because of that group's small sample size.

[a] Statistically significant ($p < .01$).

TABLE 4.4 / Child Support Agency Activities to Dun Absent Fathers

	All Families (in Thousands)	AFDC Families	Non-AFDC Families
Total number of cases			
All IV-D program cases	17,110	7,472	7,491
Paternities			
Needing establishment	3,471	2,303	1,169
Established	554	396	159
Percentage established	16	17	14
Support orders			
Needing establishment	2,962	1,740	1,222
Established	1,045	604	440
Requiring obligation to be enforced or modified	3,392	1,739	1,653
Absent parents			
Needing to be located	4,802	2,893	2,332
Located	4,484	2,571	1,912
Cases with orders			
Established	9,484	4,937	4,547
Collected	3,120	1,164	1,956

Sources: U.S. Department of Health and Human Services (1995), tables 2, 3, 35, 36, 37, 38, 40, 45, and 47.

of wedlock for whom paternity has been established. Table 4.4 shows that by 1993 state governments on average were establishing paternity in 16 percent of the cases that needed paternity established. The number of paternities established by CSE offices increased from 307,135 in 1988 to 554,205 in 1993.

2. *Obtaining a support order:* Some single-parent families make arrangements for informal child support, but about two-thirds of those who obtain support do so through formal court or CSE agency arrangements. The federal government requires states to establish child support guidelines and to use them in setting child support orders. The agencies established more than one million orders in 1993 and enforced or modified more than five million orders.

3. *Locating the absent father:* Locating the absent father is important in obtaining a support order and in enforcing one. In 1993 states allocated 15 percent of their budgets to finding absent parents and determining their income or assets (U.S. Department of Health and Human Services 1994). As of 1993, CSE agencies had located nearly 4.5 million absent parents. Many absent fathers are not, however,

in the workforce. Roughly 840,000 absent fathers are incarcerated.[10] This is roughly 10 percent of all absent fathers!

4. *Collecting money:* In 1993 the Child Support Enforcement program collected $8.9 billion, of which nearly three-quarters was from non-AFDC families. Figure 4.1 shows that collections, expenditures, and cases increased more rapidly among non-AFDC families than among AFDC families, particularly following the 1984 Child Support Enforcement amendments, which mandated that state CSE agencies provide collection services for non-AFDC families. In figure 4.1, the higher level of the ratio of non-AFDC to AFDC collections than of cases or expenditures shows that, per case or per dollar spent, CSE agencies collect more money for non-AFDC activity than for activities for AFDC families.

Withholding, largely of wages, has become a major tool for collecting child support moneys. Initially, withholding was limited to delinquent fathers (delinquent withholding), but the Family Support Act of 1988 requires immediate withholding on all new and modified child support orders in AFDC cases, with the requirement phased in for non-AFDC cases. In 1993, over half of the money collected by CSE agencies took the form of wage-withholding; another 16 percent consisted of withholding of taxes, unemployment insurance, and so on. Only 38 percent of payments were "routine payments" from the absent father to the family or CSE agency. By contrast, in 1985 routine payments constituted nearly all of the total. Over that

FIGURE 4.1 / Ratio of Non-AFDC to AFDC Child Support Cases, Expenditure, and Collections

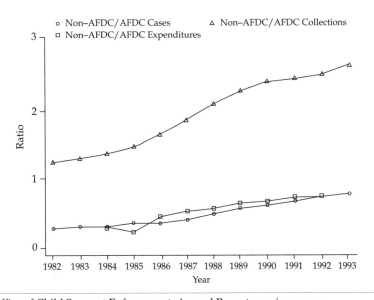

Sources: Office of Child Support Enforcement, Annual Reports, various years.

period, wage-withholding increased from $300 million to $4.7 billion (U.S. Department of Health and Human Services 1994).

From the variation in CSE policies across states in 1991, we have chosen three policy measures: the collection rate in a state, defined as the number of CSE cases for which any child support was collected, divided by the number of mother-only families in the state;[11] expenditures on paternity establishment per case (as reported by the states to OCSE); and a dummy variable for whether a state had a policy of immediate withholding on all new cases by 1991.[12]

We treat these policy measures as *indicators* of state efforts to obtain child support from noncustodial fathers rather than as well-determined individual policies. None of these measures is ideal. The most comprehensive measure that we use is the collection rate, which we view as an indicator of the policy-induced change in the probability that a noncustodial father will pay support. The collection rate is likely to depend on the states' efforts to increase child support payments, but we recognize that it will also depend in part on the behavior of potentially delinquent fathers. If these fathers can avoid the states' CSE policy by altering their type of employment, collections will be lower than they otherwise would be.[13] In addition, the number of mother-only families (the denominator for our collection rate variable) is obtained by interpolation and extrapolation of census data and is only a rough measure of the potential number of cases with delinquent fathers. Paternity establishment expenditures per case is an indicator of the state effort to find and enforce child support payment from the group most likely to not be paying child support voluntarily. It is independent of fathers' labor supply behavior but includes only one aspect of state activity. Immediate wage-withholding reflects the state effort to take the decision on payments out of the hands of the father; it shows how much the child support system in fact administratively resembles the income tax system. The variable is a 0/1 dummy reflecting the existence or nonexistence of the policy and is presumably exogenous to the labor supply behavior of fathers.

To see whether these policies had any discernible effect on child support payments as reported in the 1991 SIPP data, we added measures of the relevant policy by state to the 1991 SIPP. We then estimated probit equations for noncustodial fathers linking their payment of *any* child support and of *formal* child support, defined as payments made via wage-withholding, a court, or a state CSE office, to the policy measures (along with various demographic characteristics). Our distinction between any child support and formal support is important because child support policies can have different effects on these two measures. Successful child support policies could raise the probability of formal payments but have *no* effect on the probability of any child support being paid in the first place. This would occur if the policies largely affect the form by which payments are made, encouraging payment through legal mechanisms as opposed to informal payments—for instance, Mr. Jones pays his support through withholding instead of with a personal check to his ex-wife or ex-girlfriend.

The results of this analysis are given in table 4.5, where we report the estimated marginal effect of the relevant policy and the standard error of the estimated effect. All three policies have positive effects on the probability that a father pays *formal*

TABLE 4.5 / Marginal Effects of Child Support Enforcement Policies on Child Support Payments by Noncustodial Fathers in 1991

	Paid Formal Child Support	Paid Any Child Support
All noncustodial fathers		
Immediate wage-withholding	.0335[a]	.0033
on all new cases by 1991	(.0142)	(.0266)
Paternity establishment expenditures	.0117	.0068
per case	(.0066)	(.0120)
Collection rate[b]	.1097[a]	.0778
	(.0265)	(.0512)
Observations	1,359	1,359
Men with high school education or less		
Immediate wage-withholding	.0055	−.0083
on all new cases by 1991	(.0230)	(.0355)
Paternity establishment expenditures	.0061	.0028
per case	(.0101)	(.0158)
Collection rate[b]	.0810[a]	.0718
	(.0416)	(.0675)
Observations	1,146	1,146
Never-married men		
Immediate wage-withholding	.2252[a]	.2239[a]
on all new cases by 1991	(.1014)	(.1081)
Paternity establishment expenditures	.0321	.0517
per case	(.0444)	(.0535)
Collection rate[b]	−.0691	−.0704
	(.1713)	(.2121)
Observations	108	108

Source: SIPP (1991).

Notes: The dependent variable for Paid CS is a dummy variable for paying any child support at all. The dependent variable for Paid Formal CS (for 1991 only) is a dummy variable for paying child support via withholding, a court, or an OCSE versus not paying CS at all. Models are estimated using probit, and the marginal effects and standard errors are shown. Models also include controls for age, education, black, Hispanic, marital status, year, state unemployment rate, and log of state median income.

[a] Statistically significant ($p < .01$).

[b] Number of CSE cases with collections divided by the number of single-mother families in the state.

child support. For the total sample, the effects are reasonably well determined, but for men with less than a high school education and for nonmarried men, they show greater variability. By contrast, the effects of the policies on the probability that a father pays *any* child support are smaller and less well determined, probably because, to some extent, government child support policies change the mechanisms by which payments are made from informal payments to more formal, government-sponsored or -monitored payments.[14] The fall in the marginal effect of immediate wage-withholding in the first row of the table presumably reflects this. Since never-married men are the least likely to make voluntary arrangements for child support, the large effect of immediate withholding on the probability that they will make payments, relative to the effect for the total group, also seems plausible: for the group that does less, there is less space for substitution of formal for other payments. The greater effect of paternity establishment expenditures for the never-married men also makes sense, since they are the ones who are least likely to have paternity established in the first place.

The results in table 4.5 show sufficient linkage between the measures of child support policy and the probability of child support payments to suggest that child support policy might affect the net take-home pay of noncustodial fathers and thus their labor supply. Accordingly, we next estimate the relationship between the policy measures and the work activity of noncustodial fathers, where work activity is measured by employment; whether the type of employment is working for an employer, self-employment, or casual work; and hours worked. Since our policy measures vary across states, there is a danger that they might be correlated with some other state-specific factors that influence labor supply decisions. One way to deal with this problem, which we do not follow here, is to add measures of many other state characteristics to the model. As discussed earlier, the way we deal with this problem is to compare the noncustodial fathers within a state to custodial fathers (or, in some instances, nonfathers) in the same state. Since child support policies should influence the behavior of noncustodial fathers only, the effects of child support policy on labor supply should show up in differences between the labor supply behavior of noncustodial fathers and custodial fathers (or nonfathers) within states. In essence, we use custodial fathers (or, in the case of never-married men, nonfathers) as within-state "brothers" for the noncustodial fathers to control for unmeasured state factors that might be related to men's labor supply independent of state child support policies.

Table 4.6 presents the results of these estimations for all men, for those with a high school education or less, and for the never-married. We use probit models to estimate which men work and, for those working, whether they work for an employer or not; we use OLS to estimate hours for men who work and report positive hours. In each of these models, we link the outcome variable to the relevant set of policy variables and to the policy variables interacted with the probability that a man is a noncustodial father, controlling for a set of demographic variables and a few measures of the state's economy. The table reports the coefficients on the policy variables interacted with noncustodial father status and thus shows the differential effect of a policy on noncustodial fathers compared to its effect on custodial fathers, or, in the case of the never-married men, on the noncustodial fathers versus nonfathers. These coefficients are most readily interpreted as "differences in differences": they tell us the effect of a policy on the labor supply of noncustodial fathers, whose behavior is presumably influenced by the CSE policy, after controlling for the effect of that same policy across both noncustodial and custodial fathers (or nonfathers) whose behavior is presumably not influenced by the policy.[15]

TABLE 4.6 / Effects of State Child Support Enforcement Policies on the Labor Supply of Noncustodial Fathers in 1991

	Working Model	Working-for-Employer Model	Hours-Worked-per-Week Model
All men			
Immediate wage-withholding	.0159	.0438	0.4616
	(.0262)	(.0459)	(1.3773)
Paternity establishment expenditures per case	.0082	.0247	0.6842
	(.0124)	(.0212)	(0.6595)
Collection rate	.0369	-.0108	-2.4581
	(.0544)	(.0904)	(2.7071)
Observations	4,061	3,741	3,208
Men with high school education or less			
Immediate wage-withholding	.0844	.0293	0.5729
	(.0454)	(.0642)	(1.9740)
Paternity establishment expenditures per case	.0271	.0400	1.2751
	(.0218)	(.0302)	(0.9504)
Collection rate	.0051	.0595	-2.8212
	(.0951)	(.1259)	(3.9476)
Observations	2,020	1,794	1,563
Never-married men			
Immediate wage-withholding	.2250	.0424	-6.0342
	(.1370)	(.1053)	(4.1949)
Paternity establishment expenditures per case	.1195	-.0763	0.0843
	(.0628)	(.0795)	(2.3796)

(Table continues on p. 108.)

TABLE 4.6 / Continued

	Working Model	Working-for-Employer Model	Hours-Worked per-Week Model
Collection rate	.7262	-.0040	-5.2409
	(.3804)	(.2207)	(8.7026)
Observations	1,821	1,418	1,281s

Source: SIPP (1991).

Notes: In the first model, the dependent variable is working versus not working. In the second model, the dependent variable is working for an employer versus working self-employed or casually, among those working at all. Both models are estimated using probit, and the marginal effects and standard errors are shown. In the third model, the dependent variable is hours worked, among those working at all and reporting hours in the SIPP. Coefficients shown are for the policy variables interacted with the probability that a man is a noncustodial father. All models also include the policy variables, controls for age, education, black, Hispanic, marital status, year, state unemployment rate, and the log of state median income, and these controls interacted with the probability that a man is a noncustodial father. For all men and men with low education, the reference group is custodial fathers; for never-married men, the reference group is nonfathers.

The results in table 4.6 for the effect of policies on the probability of working at all, shown in column 1, provide no evidence of adverse labor supply effects. They provide some weak support for positive supply effects, in the form of the modestly positive but not significant coefficients on the policy variables for all men and for men with a high school education or less, and more substantially positive coefficients on the policies for the never-married group. In column 2, there are no statistically discernible effects of the various policies on the probability that a noncustodial father works for an employer rather than being self-employed or working casually, but most of these effects tend to be positive. Thus, we find no support for the conjecture that men who are faced with CSE policies try to avoid the obligation by pursuing self-employment or casual work. Column 3 shows the hours results, which are mixed: the coefficients on withholding and paternity establishment tend to be positive, while the coefficients on the collection rate are negative, but none are statistically significant.

The strongest evidence for an effect of CSE policies on noncustodial fathers' labor supply is in the employment results for the never-married men. Here, the coefficients on the collection rate and on withholding are positive and reasonably large; if this effect were duplicated with the 1986 SIPP, we would view it as fairly clear evidence that for the group most likely to avoid child support payments, CSE policies have a positive labor supply effect, but as we shall see, the 1986 results are quite different.

THE 1986 SIPP ANALYSIS

We take advantage of the availability of child support policy data and SIPP data on noncustodial fathers for 1986 to perform a similar analysis for that year. Because the SIPP module on support for non-household members contained less information in 1986 than it did in 1991, our analysis of the effects of CSE policies on child support payment is limited to their effects on *any* child support, which, as we saw, were modest in 1991. In addition, our measures of policy variables for 1986 differ from our 1991 measures, because the policy environment was different that year. Immediate withholding was not federally required in 1986, and there was no federal pressure on states to devote resources to paternity establishment, so these measures are not relevant in 1986. Our policy measures for 1986 are: the collection rate (defined as it was in 1991); whether the state had mandatory withholding of wages on *delinquent* cases prior to 1986 (forty states had such a policy, ten did not); and whether the state offered enforcement to non-AFDC women prior to 1985 (twenty-two states had such a policy, and twenty-eight did not).

Table 4.7 summarizes the results of our analysis of the effects of these three CSE policies on child support payments and on labor supply in the 1986 SIPP. As before, the analysis takes the form of a probit equation linking the outcome measures to the state policies, conditional on demographic characteristics (with the exception of the hours-worked model, which is run using OLS). We report the estimated marginal effects of the policy variables and their standard errors. Column 1

TABLE 4.7 / Marginal Effects of Differences in State Child Support Enforcement Policies on Noncustodial Fathers' Child Support Payments and Labor Supply in 1986

	Paid Any Child Support	Working Model	Working-for-Employer Model	Hours-Worked-per-Week Model
All men				
Mandatory wage-withholding on delinquent cases pre-1986	-.0010	-.0096	.0111	1.0191
	(.0221)	(.0175)	(.0338)	(0.9756)
State enforcement on non-AFDC cases pre-1985	.0195	.0329[a]	-.0121	0.8892
	(.0156)	(.0126)	(.0241)	(0.7057)
Collection rate[b]	.0092	.0568	.0159	-0.8829
	(.0586)	(.0447)	(.0847)	(2.5017)
Observations	4,024	7,848	7,315	6,289
Men with high school education or less				
Mandatory wage-withholding on delinquent cases pre-1986	.0028	-.0025	-.0291	-0.2091
	(.0260)	(.0293)	(.0411)	(1.2628)
State enforcement on non-AFDC cases pre-1985	-.0022	.0387	.0168	0.2988
	(.0195)	(.0218)	(.0307)	(0.9671)
Collection rate[b]	-.0095	.0493	.0110	-2.2045
	(.0721)	(.0770)	(.1061)	(3.3665)
Observations	2,428	4,251	3,838	3,357
Never-married men				
Mandatory wage-withholding on delinquent cases pre-1986	.0852	-.1145	.2660[a]	4.8853
	(.1254)	(.1058)	(.1170)	(3.8232)

State enforcement on non-AFDC cases pre-1985	.0599 (.0902)	.0339 (.0865)	-.0347 (.0491)	-3.8069 (2.8301)
Collection rate[b]	.0158 (.3639)	-.4110 (.3106)	-.2980 (.1668)	0.2747 (11.0066)
Observations	161	3,877	2,972	2,838

Source: SIPP (1986).

Notes: The first model is estimated for noncustodial fathers only, using probit; marginal effects and their standard errors are shown in column 1. This model for the payment of any child support also includes controls for age, education, black, Hispanic, marital status, state unemployment rate, and log of state median income. In the second model, the dependent variable is working versus not working. In the third model, the dependent variable is working for an employer versus working self-employed or casually, among those working at all. Both models 2 and 3 are estimated using probit, and the marginal effects and standard errors are shown. In the fourth model, the dependent variable is hours worked, among those working at all and reporting hours in the SIPP. Coefficients shown in columns 2 through 4 are for the policy variables interacted with the probability that a man is a noncustodial father. Models 2 through 4 also include the policy variables, controls for age, education, black, Hispanic, marital status, year, state unemployment rate, and the log of state median income, and these controls interacted with the probability that a man is a noncustodial father. For all men and men with low education, the reference group in models 2 through 4 is custodial fathers; for never-married men, the reference group is nonfathers.

[a] Statistically significant (*p* < .01).

[b] Number of CSE cases with collections divided by the number of single-mother families in the state.

shows that the policy variables are barely connected to the probability that a non-custodial father makes a child support payment. While this does not rule out any labor supply effects—perhaps the policies do not affect child support because they induce negative labor supply effects—it makes it unlikely that we will find any negative labor supply effects in these data.

The estimates in column 2 show a positive relation between the collection rate and state enforcement of non-AFDC cases and the probability of working for all men and for men with high school or less education. In contrast to the modest positive effects of policy variables on the labor supply of never-married fathers in 1991, relative to their comparison group, never-married men with no children, the coefficients on wage-withholding and the collection rate in column 2 are negative. The estimates in column 3, for the probability of working self-employed or casual, are mixed, as they were in 1991: the only statistically significant effect suggests that wage-withholding raises the likelihood that a never-married noncustodial father works for an employer rather than as a self-employed or casual worker, but there is also a negative effect of the collection rate on never-married noncustodial fathers' regular employment that is nearly significant. The results from the OLS hours-worked models (shown in column 4) are similarly inconclusive; again, there are hints of both negative and positive effects for never-married men.

In sum, the "reduced form" estimates of the link between child support policies and labor supply for 1986 support the findings for 1991 that for all noncustodial fathers, more aggressive state child support policies may be associated with modestly greater probabilities of working. These estimates give different results, however, for noncustodial fathers who have never been married than do the 1991 calculations. Because the sample size of men who report that they are noncustodial fathers and have never been married is small, we read these combined results as additional evidence for the conclusion that child support policies have little discernible effect on labor supply behavior.

SUPPLY ESTIMATES WITH POLICY VARIABLES AS INSTRUMENTS

As a final exercise in assessing the labor supply effects of child support policies, we next undertake an instrumental variable analysis, using our policy measures as instruments for actual payment of child support. Using the 1991 SIPP, we instrument *any* child support payments and *formal* child support payments on the three state policy variables used in table 4.5 and enter the "predicted probability of making support payments" attributable to state policies into the relevant labor supply equation. Using the 1986 SIPP, we perform a similar analysis for any child support. The results of these estimations, given in table 4.8, confirm the generally weak relation between policy-induced child support and the labor supply of noncustodial fathers. Columns 1, 2, and 3 record the coefficients on the predicted probability that a man would pay any child support or formal support from the 1991 SIPP. The coefficients on any child support in the working model (column 1) are weakly positive, with notably larger effects for the never-married men, while those in the

TABLE 4.8 / Marginal Effects of Predicted Child Support Payment on the Labor Supply of Noncustodial Fathers in 1991 and 1986

	1991—Working Model	1991—Working-for-Employer Model	1991—Hours-Worked-per-Week Model	1986—Working Model	1986—Working-for-Employer Model	1986—Hours-Worked-per-Week Model
All men						
Predicted paid any child support	.3721	.2261	−7.8905	.2280	.0039	13.1282
	(.2938)	(.5487)	(16.2463)	(.1406)	(.3023)	(9.2006)
Predicted paid formal child support	.1004	.4323	−11.0593			
	(.1750)	(.3065)	(8.8062)			
Observations	4,061	3,741	3,208	7,848	7,315	6,289
Men with high school education or less						
Predicted paid any child support	.9722	.8357	−25.3408	.4142	.0652	21.5478
	(.5191)	(.7584)	(22.9659)	(.2295)	(.3454)	(11.5308)
Predicted paid formal child support	.4738	.5903	−12.4934			
	(.3028)	(.4169)	(12.4913)			
Observations	2,020	1,794	1,563	4,251	3,838	3,357
Never-married men						
Predicted paid any child support	4.9985[a]	0.6264	−56.0964	3.2955	1.8258	113.6453
	(2.1811)	(1.5028)	(59.7933)	(1.7935)	(1.1788)	(63.8232)

(Table continues on p. 114.)

TABLE 4.8 / Continued

	1991—Working Model	1991—Working-for-Employer Model	1991—Hours-Worked-per-Week Model	1986—Working Model	1986—Working-for-Employer Model	1986—Hours-Worked-per-Week Model
Predicted paid formal child support	4.5917[a] (1.6475)	0.5636 (0.7301)	−29.2248 (26.8177)			
Observations	1,813	1,418	1,281	3,877	2,972	2,838

Source: SIPP (1986, 1991).

Notes: Any child support payment in 1991 and 1986, and formal child support payment in 1991, are predicted from the models shown in tables 4.5 and 4.7. The dependent variable in the first model is a dummy variable for working at all versus not working. In the second model, the dependent variable is a dummy variable for working for an employer versus working self-employed or casually, among those working at all. Both models are estimated using probit, and the marginal effects and standard errors are shown. In the third model, the dependent variable is hours worked, among those working at all and reporting hours in the SIPP. All three models also include controls for age, education, black, Hispanic, marital status, year, state unemployment rate, and the log of state median income.

[a] Statistically significant (*p* < .01).

working-for-an-employer model (column 2) are negligible for all men and modestly positive for the two subgroups. The coefficients on formal child support are similar: weakly positive for working, and negligible for working for an employer for all men, but modestly positive for the subgroups. In this case, our analysis of hours worked per week (see column 3) yielded negative coefficients, which were substantial but with correspondingly large standard errors for the never-married. Columns 4, 5, and 6 give the analogous results for the 1986 SIPP. Given the weak link between the policy variables and individual child support payments in that year, it is not surprising that these calculations show little effect on any of the three labor supply outcomes of the predicted probability of making child support payments driven by policy. Nevertheless, the signs all point to an absence of adverse effects, since the predicted child support payment variable is associated with a higher probability of working, a higher probability of working for an employer rather than being a self-employed or casual worker, and higher hours.

CONCLUSION

Our analysis of child support enforcement policies, child support payments, and the labor supply of fathers suggests that child support enforcement policies have a relatively modest effect on both child support payments and labor supply. We attribute the modest estimated effect of policies on payments in part to the fact that CSE policies produce a substitution of formal for informal modes of payment. Perhaps our most interesting result, and one that deserves further attention, is the implication in table 4.5 that CSE policies largely alter the form by which child support is paid rather than increasing the total amount paid.

The negligible estimated effect of state CSE policies on labor supply is consistent with the general finding in male labor supply studies that male labor supply is relatively unresponsive to variations in wages due, say, to taxes.[16] Since the huge literature on male labor participation and hours has found little if any supply responsiveness, it would have been remarkable indeed if our study had found such. As best we can tell, noncustodial fathers in states with more extensive or stronger CSE policies are, if anything, slightly more likely to be working relative to custodial fathers and slightly less likely to be working "off the books" in casual work or self-employment. Although we did find some evidence that men facing tougher child support enforcement may work fewer hours, we also found some evidence of the opposite effect, and neither effect was very precisely estimated.

It is possible that the low-income noncustodial fathers missing from the SIPP survey, and those who were in the survey but denied ever having children, might be more likely to respond to CSE policies by reducing their labor supply than the men whom we were able to identify in the SIPP. However, we do not believe that the inclusion of the missing men would greatly affect our prime conclusion that the labor supply responses of absent fathers are not a serious bound on child support enforcement collections. The problem in getting absent fathers to contribute to their children appears to be not so much one of adverse labor supply responses to child support enforcement but rather one of noncustodial fathers' low pay and employment. Men who are noncustodial fathers have, on average, poorer employment and earnings prospects than other men, as we saw earlier (see also chapter 9 in this volume). It is these poor labor market prospects, rather than adverse labor supply responses, that are likely to be responsible for the limited success of child support enforcement in getting these fathers to contribute enough to move their children out of poverty and off of welfare.

APPENDIX: IDENTIFYING NONCUSTODIAL FATHERS IN THE SIPP

The SIPP is one of very few nationally representative data sets that asks men about their fertility history. Unfortunately, the SIPP asks only about the number of children ever born; it does not ask about the children's ages, current whereabouts, and so on. By comparing the number of children ever born with the number of children currently in a man's family, we can identify men who have fathered more children than are currently living with them, but we cannot tell from the data in the SIPP whether these missing children are over the age of eighteen or whether they are minors living with a custodial mother. For this reason, we use a two-step process to determine the likelihood that a man is a noncustodial father. First, we identify potential noncustodial fathers, that is, men who have fathered more children than are currently living with them. Second, for these potential noncustodial fathers, we assign a probability that they are really noncustodial, that is, that the missing children are minors not living in their homes as opposed to children over the age of eighteen.

First, we use the fertility history question to determine how many children a man has ever had. This step is fairly straightforward except that some men (14.7 percent in 1986 and 8.9 percent in 1991) are missing data for this question. (We experimented with imputing values for these men but in the end decided to leave them out of the analysis.) For each man who answered the fertility question and reported having had children, we compare the number fathered with the number of children currently living in the family. Men who do not have all their children living with them are identified as potentially noncustodial. Men who do have all their children living with them are identified as definitely custodial (with probability equal to one).

Second, we use fertility data, also from the SIPP, by age and race and ethnicity group to estimate the probability that a potential noncustodial father is a true noncustodial father of minor children as opposed to a father with children over eighteen. We do this by first estimating the probability that he has at least one child over eighteen. This is simply the probability that he began having children at his current age minus eighteen. For example, the probability that a forty-five-year-old white (or black or Hispanic) man who does not have all his children living with him is a parent of children over the age of eighteen (as opposed to a noncustodial parent of minor children) is simply the probability that a twenty-seven-year-old white (or black or Hispanic) man has at least one child. The probability that he is a noncustodial father of minor children is then simply the inverse.

This method assigns to each man who has fathered children a probability of non-custodial fatherhood (which means having at least one minor child not living at home) and a probability of custodial fatherhood (which means having all his minor children living at home although he might also have grown children not living at home). We use these probabilities to generate the percentages of types of fathers in our samples. We also use them in interaction with the policy variables, so that the weight an observation is given in estimating the effect of a policy variable for non-custodial fathers depends on the probability that each man is a true noncustodial father.

TABLE 4A.1 / Summary Statistics for Men Age Eighteen to Fifty-Five in 1991, by Father Status

	Custodial Father	Noncustodial Father	Noncustodial Father Paying Child Support	Noncustodial Father Not Paying Child Support	Not a Father
All men					
Total working (percentage)	93.59	90.20	95.62	88.15	82.65
Working for an employer	81.32	82.32	84.44	81.46	86.75
Self-employed	17.14	16.11	13.27	17.28	10.32
Casual	1.54	1.56	2.29	1.26	2.93
Mean hours/week	42.39	42.05	42.55	41.85	39.74
Age	38.61	40.62	38.12	41.56	29.10
College or higher (percentage)	30.68	21.30	20.57	21.58	28.80
Some college only	21.72	21.88	28.88	19.24	28.57
High school only	35.30	39.57	38.94	39.81	32.70
Less than high school	12.29	17.25	11.60	19.38	9.94
African American	7.25	11.81	10.28	12.39	9.20
Hispanic	8.98	8.95	7.44	9.52	8.09
Married, first marriage	79.28	40.68	8.53	52.80	23.26
Remarried	14.36	26.10	41.79	20.19	3.56
Previously married	5.63	25.84	44.64	18.76	7.18
Never married	0.73	7.37	5.03	8.25	66.00
State unemployment rate	2.75	2.75	2.75	2.75	2.74
State log median income ($)	9.84	9.83	9.82	9.83	9.85
Paid child support (percentage)	NA	27.38	100.00	0.00	NA
Paid formal child support	NA	13.06	47.70	0.00	NA

State immediate withholding?	60.58	59.83	60.28	59.66	58.04
State log paternity expenditures per case ($)	4.61	4.60	4.62	4.59	4.69
State collection rate (percentage)	35.00	35.14	35.89	34.86	34.72
Predicted paid child support	14.74	27.18	42.68	21.40	24.74
Predicted paid formal child support	5.62	12.93	21.43	9.77	11.07
N	3,157	1,668	457	1,212	2,979
Men with high school education or less					
Total working (percentage)	90.93	87.06	93.94	84.84	77.48
Working for an employer	83.14	84.65	86.64	83.79	88.62
Self-employed	15.02	13.53	10.60	14.58	7.82
Casual	1.86	1.92	2.76	1.63	3.56
Mean hours/week	41.81	41.08	40.62	41.24	38.97
Age	38.06	39.61	36.72	40.54	28.15
High school only (percentage)	74.17	69.65	77.06	67.26	76.69
Less than high school	25.83	30.35	22.94	32.74	23.31
African American	9.20	12.83	10.39	13.62	11.65
Hispanic	13.79	12.21	10.39	12.80	12.60
Married, first marriage	76.38	38.84	9.96	48.14	20.55
Remarried	15.38	25.82	41.99	20.62	3.15
Previously married	7.04	25.23	41.99	19.83	7.87
Never married	1.21	10.11	6.06	11.42	68.43
State unemployment rate	2.76	2.76	2.75	2.76	2.74
State log median income ($)	9.82	9.82	9.81	9.83	9.85
Paid child support (percentage)	NA	24.36	100.00	0.00	NA
Paid formal child support	NA	13.60	55.84	0.00	NA
State immediate withholding?	63.31	59.51	59.09	59.65	62.21

(*Table continues on p. 120.*)

TABLE 4A.1 / Continued

	Custodial Father	Noncustodial Father	Noncustodial Father Paying Child Support	Noncustodial Father Not Paying Child Support	Not a Father
State log paternity expenditures per case ($)	4.54	4.57	4.58	4.56	4.60
State collection rate (percentage)	34.59	35.64	36.72	35.29	35.15
Predicted paid child support	15.01	24.65	37.84	20.34	19.62
Predicted paid formal child support	6.87	14.18	23.45	11.16	12.63
N	1,503	948	231	717	1,270
Never-married men					
Total working (percentage)	71.84	81.69	95.65	78.48	77.82
Working for an employer	86.28	88.32	77.27	91.41	88.18
Self-employed	1.60	4.71	4.55	4.77	7.98
Casual	12.12	6.97	18.18	3.82	3.94
Mean hours/week	42.30	36.33	33.74	37.08	38.20
Age	32.18	27.94	28.35	27.85	26.47
College or more (percentage)	2.36	8.52	8.70	8.48	24.36
Some college	18.96	13.53	30.43	9.64	31.43
High school only	33.29	49.06	43.48	50.34	32.91
Less than high school	45.52	28.89	17.39	31.53	11.29
African American	31.93	31.43	39.13	29.66	10.38
Hispanic	23.63	21.60	13.04	23.57	9.10
State unemployment rate	2.76	2.75	2.56	2.79	2.74
State log median income ($)	9.84	9.85	9.82	9.86	9.85

Paid child support (percentage)	NA	18.70	100.00	0.00	NA
Paid formal child support	NA	10.57	56.52	0.00	NA
State immediate withholding?	47.61	50.02	69.57	45.34	57.75
State log paternity expenditures per case ($)	4.83	4.79	4.89	4.77	4.70
State collection rate (percentage)	35.38	37.50	39.15	37.12	34.85
Predicted paid child support	21.63	20.93	36.43	16.81	32.47
Predicted paid formal child support	13.81	15.83	27.04	12.43	28.24
N	23	123	23	100	1,966

Source: SIPP (1991).

TABLE 4A.2 / Summary Statistics for Men Age Eighteen to Fifty-Five in 1986, by Father Status

	Custodial Father	Noncustodial Father	Noncustodial Father Paying Child Support	Noncustodial Father Not Paying Child Support	Not a Father
All men, 1986					
Total working (percentage)	94.17	91.04	95.39	88.81	82.55
Working for an employer	81.16	82.50	85.40	80.90	90.09
Self-employed	18.58	17.22	14.27	18.84	9.35
Casual	0.26	0.28	0.33	0.26	0.56
Mean hours/week	41.12	40.18	40.61	39.94	35.98
Age	38.18	39.94	36.49	41.70	27.35
College or higher (percentage)	27.08	18.27	18.53	18.14	25.56
Some college only	21.54	21.68	24.29	20.35	28.54
High school only	35.78	40.53	42.51	39.51	33.55
Less than high school	15.60	19.52	14.66	22.00	12.35
African American	6.83	11.69	12.36	11.35	8.87
Hispanic	7.00	6.18	5.34	6.61	5.18
Married, first marriage	82.72	41.30	4.50	60.12	23.18
Remarried	12.01	27.32	44.29	18.64	3.22
Previously married	4.49	25.55	45.24	15.47	5.75
Never married	0.78	5.83	5.97	5.76	67.84
State unemployment rate	3.49	3.50	3.50	3.51	3.46
State log median income ($)	9.54	9.53	9.53	9.53	9.55
Paid child support (percentage)	NA	33.85	100.00	0.00	NA
New withholding state?	16.87	16.10	15.80	16.26	16.66

New non-AFDC state?	44.96	46.30	44.19	45.21
State collection rate	20.78	20.02	19.44	21.59
Predicted paid child support	14.12	33.82	56.88	37.93
N	5,577	2,822	955	5,806
Men with high school education or less, 1986				
Total working (percentage)	91.20	88.38	94.69	78.27
Working for an employer	84.31	84.98	88.78	92.62
Self-employed	15.40	14.73	11.03	6.81
Casual	0.30	0.28	0.19	0.58
Mean hours/week	39.80	38.97	39.69	35.41
Age	38.01	39.23	35.25	26.75
High school only (percentage)	69.63	67.50	74.36	73.10
Less than high school	30.37	32.50	25.64	26.90
African-American	8.62	13.16	12.82	12.38
Hispanic	10.29	8.09	6.96	7.05
Married, first marriage	79.81	40.72	4.58	20.41
Remarried	13.11	25.86	41.58	3.04
Previously married	5.65	26.16	46.70	5.40
Never married	1.43	7.26	7.14	71.14
State unemployment rate	3.53	3.52	3.52	3.49
State log median income ($)	9.52	9.52	9.51	9.53
Paid child support (percentage)	NA	32.27	100.00	0.00
New withholding state?	19.16	18.84	19.31	19.53
New non-AFDC state?	44.55	47.36	49.08	46.43
State collection rate	21.07	20.31	19.66	21.78
Predicted paid child support	13.88	32.64	55.31	35.72
N	2,866	1,694	546	2,665

(Table continues on p. 124.)

TABLE 4A.2 / Continued

	Custodial Father	Noncustodial Father	Noncustodial Father Paying Child Support	Noncustodial Father Not Paying Child Support	Not a Father
Never-married men					
Total working (percentage)	60.06	80.16	92.98	73.37	76.97
Working for an employer	95.78	91.74	74.34	89.99	92.55
Self-employed	4.22	8.26	5.66	10.01	6.63
Casual	0.00	0.00	0.00	0.00	0.83
Mean hours/week	35.81	36.33	36.91	35.90	33.52
Age	27.33	27.46	27.74	27.32	25.10
College or more (percentage)	0.45	8.39	10.53	7.26	21.55
Some college	5.18	16.86	21.05	14.64	30.31
High school only	58.37	52.65	49.12	54.52	34.27
Less than high school	36.00	22.10	19.30	23.58	13.86
African American	39.93	44.76	61.40	35.94	10.89
Hispanic	17.81	11.71	8.77	13.26	5.69
State unemployment rate	3.64	3.51	3.40	3.58	3.47
State log median income ($)	9.54	9.53	9.50	9.54	9.56
Paid child support (percentage)	NA	34.64	100.00	0.00	NA
New withholding state?	23.02	13.59	17.54	11.28	16.23
New non-AFDC state?	53.62	42.97	43.86	42.50	44.63
State collection rate	21.51	19.01	16.79	20.32	22.01
Predicted paid child support	35.70	37.30	38.52	36.58	43.39
N	43	165	57	108	1,966

Source: SIPP (1986).

NOTES

1. We do not examine the "disappearance" effect in this chapter, but we note that a large share of absent fathers reside in different states from their ex-partners and children and that enforcement is much more difficult in those cases.

2. Several researchers have found that noncustodial fathers have lower employment and earnings than other men. See, for example, Ferguson (1990); Lerman (1992); Bartfeld and Meyer (1994); Pirog-Good and Good (1994); Robertson (1997); and Sorensen (1993). Sorensen and Wheaton (1994) estimate that even if all custodial mothers had child support awards and received full child support, poverty among mother-only families would fall by just three percentage points, and the state would save 20 percent of AFDC spending (table 2). The modest reduction in poverty is due to the fact that the average award was about $3,000 in 1989 and most additional child support goes to the non-poor.

3. The data are not perfect, however. Identification of absent fathers in the SIPP is subject to error, and some respondents may give inaccurate information on children or child support (Sorensen and Weant 1994), as in other data sets (Cherlin, Griffith, and McCarthy 1983; Seltzer and Brandreth 1994). As with other national surveys, the SIPP has some problems in surveying low-income men, some of whom are likely to be fathers who do not contribute to their children's upbringing. According to Garfinkel, McLanahan, and Hanson (chapter 2 in this volume), approximately 6 percent of noncustodial fathers are missing from the SIPP, and this group includes many (such as the incarcerated and the homeless) who are likely to be low-income.

4. See the appendix for more detail on the SIPP samples and the procedures we use to identify potential noncustodial fathers and to estimate the probability that a man is a noncustodial father of dependent children.

5. The administrative data are incomplete and in some places inconsistent (see U.S. Department of Health and Human Services 1994, appendix C; Guyer, Miller, and Garfinkel 1996).

6. Indeed, Sorensen and Turner (1997) found that noncustodial fathers' labor supply (the number of weeks worked) was the strongest predictor of whether they paid child support.

7. To check the accuracy of noncustodial fathers' reports about child support payments, we compared the proportion of noncustodial fathers who reported that they paid formal support with the proportion of custodial mothers who reported receiving formal support in the 1991 SIPP. The father and mother reports on child support were basically consistent. For instance, in analyses not shown here, we find that 39 percent of previously married women report receiving formal support, while 40 percent of previously married men report paying it, and so on.

8. Casual employment in the SIPP is defined as any work in the preceding four months that is not described as regular work for an employer or self-employment but that is mentioned by the respondent as resulting in earnings, even if the work was for only a few hours.

9. See summary statistics in table 4A.1.

10. The 1991 Survey of State Prison Inmates found that male inmates had more than 770,000 children under the age of eighteen. Fifty-six percent of prison inmates had children (U.S.

Department of Justice 1991). Assuming that men in jail have a similar rate of parentage, we estimate that approximately 840,000 absent fathers are incarcerated.

11. This variable is simply the multiplicand of Garfinkel et al.'s (forthcoming) case collection rate (number of collections per OCSE case) and case enforcement rate (number of OCSE cases per mother-only family in the state). Note that the number of CSE cases is not the same as the number of absent-father families. A child can have more than one case if more than one man has been named as the potential father, and different children in the same family can have different cases if they have different fathers. In 1991 this variable ranged from 13 percent in Texas to 86 percent in Wisconsin, with a mean of 37 percent.

12. In response to the 1988 Family Support Act, thirty-five states had authorized immediate wage-withholding by 1991, while fifteen had not yet done so.

13. And if by altering their type of employment some fathers are able to reduce the impact of the collection rate on their own payments, then the collection rate might not have a negative effect on their hours worked. Thus, across all noncustodial fathers, the estimate of the effect of the collection rate on men's hours worked, which might be negative for those men who did not change their type of employment, would be biased upwards.

14. Substitution of formal child support for informal support helps explain why, despite the national effort to increase child support payments, there is no clear trend in the proportion of absent-father families obtaining support.

15. Because our model includes both the policy variables and the policy variables interacted with being a noncustodial father, we can interpret the coefficient on the policy–noncustodial father interaction variable as being the additive effect of the policy for noncustodial fathers, above and beyond its effect for all fathers whether custodial or noncustodial (or, in the case of never-married men, for all noncustodial fathers and non-fathers). The other variables in the model (age, education, black, Hispanic, marital status, year, state unemployment rate, and the log of state median income) are also entered both directly and interacted with the probability that a man is a noncustodial father.

16. See, for example, Pencavel (1986).

REFERENCES

Bartfeld, Judi, and Daniel Meyer. 1994. "Are There Really Deadbeat Dads? The Relationship Between Ability to Pay, Enforcement, and Compliance in Nonmarital Child Support Cases." *Social Service Review* (June): 219–35.

Cherlin, Andrew, Jeanne Griffith, and James McCarthy. 1983. "A Note on Maritally-Disrupted Men's Reports of Child Support in the June 1980 Current Population Survey." *Demography* 20(3): 385–89.

Edin, Kathryn. 1995. "Single Mothers and Child Support: The Possibilities and Limits of Child Support Policy." *Children and Youth Services Review* 17(1/2): 203–30.

Ferguson, Ron. 1990. "Noncustodial Fathers: Factors That Influence Payment of Child Support." In *Background Materials for the Parents' Fair Share Meeting, November 8, 1990*. New York: Manpower Demonstration Research Corporation.

Garfinkel, Irwin, Cynthia Miller, Sara McLanahan, and Thomas Hanson. Forthcoming. "Deadbeat Dads or Inept States? A Comparison of Child Support Enforcement Systems." *Evaluation Review*.

Guyer, Jocelyn, Cynthia Miller, and Irwin Garfinkel. 1996. "Ranking States Using Child Support Data: A Cautionary Note." *Social Service Review* (December): 635–52.

Lerman, Robert. 1992. "Do the Earnings Deficiencies of Unwed Fathers Account for Their Low Child Support Payments?" In *Paternity Establishment: A Public Policy Conference.* Vol. 2, *Studies of the Circumstances of Mothers and Fathers.* Madison: University of Wisconsin, Institute for Research on Poverty.

Office of Child Support Enforcement. Various years. *Annual Reports.* Washington: U.S. Government Printing Office.

Pencavel, John. 1986. "Labor Supply of Men: A Review." In *The Handbook of Labor Economics,* edited by Orley Ashenfelter and Richard Layard. Amsterdam: North Holland.

Pirog-Good, Maureen, and David Good. 1994. "Child Support Enforcement for Teenage Fathers: Problems and Prospects." *Journal of Policy Analysis and Management* 14(1): 25–42.

Robertson, John. 1997. "Young Nonresidential Fathers Have Lower Earnings: Implications for Child Support Enforcement." *Social Work Research* 21(4): 211–23.

Seltzer, Judith, and Yvonne Brandreth. 1994. "What Fathers Say About Involvement with Children After Separation." *Journal of Family Issues* 15(1): 49–77.

Sorensen, Elaine. 1993. "Noncustodial Fathers: Can They Afford to Pay More Child Support?" Urban Institute, Washington. Unpublished paper (September).

Sorensen, Elaine, and Mark Turner. 1997. "Factors Influencing Nonresident Fathers' Child Support Payments." Urban Institute, Washington. Unpublished paper.

Sorensen, Elaine, and Margaret Weant. 1994. "Estimates of Young Noncustodial Fatherhood: Preliminary Evidence from Two National Surveys." Urban Institute, Washington. Unpublished paper (October).

Sorensen, Elaine, and Laura Wheaton. 1994. "Potential Effects of Child Support Enforcement on Poverty, Welfare Costs, and Welfare Dependency: Preliminary Evidence from Trim2." Urban Institute, Washington. Unpublished paper (October).

U.S. Department of Health and Human Services, Office of Child Support Enforcement. 1994. *Seventeenth Annual Report to Congress.* Washington: U.S. Government Printing Office. 1995.

———. *Eighteenth Annual Report to Congress.* Washington: U.S. Government Printing Office (see also earlier reports).

U.S. Department of Justice, Bureau of Justice Statistics. 1991. *Survey of State Prison Inmates.* Washington: U.S. Government Printing Office.

Chapter 5

Child Support and Fathers' Remarriage and Fertility

David E. Bloom, Cecilia Conrad, and Cynthia Miller

In 1995 one in four children in the United States lived in poverty. The child poverty rate increased steadily during the 1980s, and this increase can be attributed in large part to a rise in the number of children living in female-headed families (Bane and Ellwood 1989; Lerman 1996). More than 50 percent of all children in female-headed families live in poverty. Children in these families must rely on the income of only one parent, and the income of the mother is typically lower than that of the absent father.

This relationship between trends in family structure and child poverty derives from the fact that most absent parents do not continue to share their incomes with their children after divorce. In other words, most fathers do not pay child support. Currently, only half of all nonresident fathers have a legal obligation to pay child support, and only about 38 percent of all fathers make any payments to their nonresident children (U.S. Bureau of the Census 1996).

Statistics on child poverty and child support are often mentioned together to illustrate the potential benefits of a more strictly enforced child support system. In fact, child support has become an enormously popular policy in the effort to improve the economic status of children. An array of increasingly stringent laws has been passed at both the state and federal levels, with the hope of more strictly enforcing payments and improving the lives of children.

What is often neglected in discussions of child support enforcement and child well-being, however, is that a significant fraction of all children eligible to receive child support, although not necessarily receiving support from their biological fathers, are being supported by two parents, a biological mother and a stepfather. In this way, as was illustrated in another context by Greg Duncan and Saul Hoffman (1985), the current status of the child support system understates the well-being of children of divorce by not considering the possibility of remarriage among families headed by custodial mothers.

Another factor that has been ignored in this debate, and one on which we focus in this chapter, is the possibility of an interaction between stricter enforcement and remarriage. In particular, given the increased emphasis on child support as a means to transfer resources to children, we examine whether the effort to enforce these payments more strictly might also reduce resources for some children by altering fathers' remarriage behavior. In this case, a move toward stricter child support enforcement is not unambiguously good for children.

To illustrate, consider the population of children eligible to receive child support. At present, one-half of these children receive no support through child support or through their custodial parents' remarriage. One-quarter of all eligible children receive support through child support but not through remarriage, while the remaining one-quarter receive support through remarriage and may or may not also receive child support payments. One potential trade-off of more strictly enforcing child support can be stated as follows. Will an increase in child support enforcement, in an effort to help the group of children not receiving any support, diminish the number of children who are supported through remarriage?

In this chapter, we examine the association between child support and fathers' new family formation, including (re)marriage and fertility subsequent to remarriage.[1] The pool of men eligible to marry women who head families consists in part of unmarried fathers, many of whom have a legal obligation to pay (and some of whom actually do pay) child support. These child support obligations may diminish a man's willingness or ability to undertake the financial obligations associated with marriage. Such obligations may also diminish a man's desirability as a marriage partner to a prospective spouse seeking a companion who can offer financial support and security. In fact, empirical evidence on the factors that influence remarriage rates suggests that child support payments may significantly reduce a man's probability of remarriage. Two independent samples were used to estimate the effect of a man's income on his yearly hazard (probability) of remarriage. Using these estimates, figure 5.1 reports how a typical child support payment might reduce this probability. In this case, a typical payment is defined as an average of what fathers currently pay. The estimates indicate that child support payments may reduce a man's yearly probability of remarriage by more than 15 percent.

That child support constrains fathers' behavior might also be inferred from recent reports in the popular press. The press commonly reports accounts of fathers' complaints that child support obligations leave them unable to start or support new families.[2] Similar reports are also made by individuals involved in developing child support policy (Williams 1994). Moreover, noncustodial fathers have formed fathers' rights groups to protect their interests in the child custody and child support system.[3] Thus, by studying the impact of child support on fathers' behavior, we hope to assess fathers' claims that these payments represent a significant burden.

Finally, the enforcement of child support payments might also affect fathers' fertility, which we interpret broadly to include both marriage to a woman with children and fertility within a new marriage. Stronger child support enforcement may not only affect fathers' remarriage rates but may also affect their willingness to marry women with children. Such a finding would suggest that stricter enforcement might reduce the flow of resources to children through its effect on this aspect of fathers' behavior.

FIGURE 5.1 / The Expected Change in the Yearly Hazard of Remarriage for Typical Child Support Payments

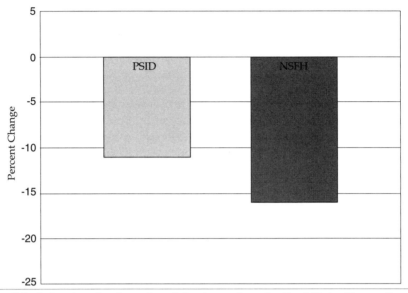

Sources: Calculations based on hazard model estimates from the *Panel Study of Income Dynamics* (PSID 1989) and the *National Survey of Families and Households* (NSFH 1992).

We also examine the effects of child support enforcement on fathers' fertility within new marriages. While the nature of these effects is less relevant to the well-being of children in single-mother families, examining this relationship will provide another clue as to whether child support represents a constraint for fathers. The effect of child support on fertility in new marriages is also interesting in its own right, given that births following remarriage represent an increasing proportion of total births (Wineberg 1990).

To examine the association between child support and new family formation, we use cross-state variation in the level of child support enforcement to identify the effects of the child support system on fathers' remarriage and fertility. When possible, we also examine the association between actual child support payments and these behaviors. In this analysis, we attempt to account for the possibility that the effect of payments on family formation is not causal, but rather that both behaviors are influenced by common factors.

We find that, although stricter enforcement does not appear to affect fathers' fertility, it does reduce remarriage rates among lower-income fathers. In addition, since nonresident fathers are in the pool of men who may potentially marry single mothers and help to provide support for their children, this result suggests that enforcement may not be unambiguously good for children because it may reduce the number of children supported through remarriage. Simple calculations suggest that, at a minimum, the monetary benefits for children of increased enforcement are overstated.

CHILD SUPPORT AND REMARRIAGE

Previous research on the determinants of remarriage has applied labor market search theory to the marriage market (Beller and Graham 1985; Chiswick and Lehrer 1990; Folk, Graham, and Beller 1992; Hutchens 1979). Within this framework, the payment of child support affects the probability of remarriage through its effect on income. As we note later, however, the theory implies that income has an ambiguous effect on the time to remarriage.

In a scenario analogous to wage offers in the labor market, a single individual searching in the marriage market faces a variety of marriage opportunities or offers, the distribution of which depends on how his characteristics are valued by potential spouses. The distribution of offers is likely to depend on his observable characteristics, such as age, education, and income, and on his unobservable characteristics, such as responsibility or character. The existence of children from a previous relationship, for example, may reduce the average marital offer, because it represents a specific investment that is not transferable to a new relationship and may, in the eyes of the potential partner, decrease the quality of the new relationship.

Assuming that marriage offers arrive randomly from this distribution and that search is costly, search theory implies that the individual develops an optimal stopping rule: he will stop searching and accept a marriage offer when the value of this offer is at least as great as some minimum acceptable offer. The marital offer can be viewed as an expected stream of real income or commodities, which includes affection, children, efficiencies from the division of labor, and the realization of scale economies in household production.

Thus, the probability of remarriage within a given period depends on the probability of receiving an acceptable offer within that period. Within this framework, an increase in income, if it is valued positively by potential spouses, alters a man's distribution of marital offers in a way that may decrease his time to remarriage; for a given minimum acceptable offer, he is more likely to accept the next offer received. However, an increase in income may also alter the man's behavior, in that he raises his minimum acceptable offer. A man who alters his minimum acceptable offer, for example, might become more or less likely to marry a woman with children from a previous relationship. An increase in his minimum acceptable offer may result in an increased time to remarriage. Thus, the net effect of a change in income on the time to marriage is ambiguous.

The effect of child support on remarriage is analogous to that of income. As a kind of lump-sum tax, it lowers the father's income, reducing his attractiveness to potential spouses and increasing his time to remarriage. However, this reduction in income may also cause the man to alter his expectations in the marriage market. If, for example, he lowers his minimum acceptable offer, this should reduce his time to remarriage. Thus, a child support award that is strictly enforced has an ambiguous effect on the probability of remarriage within a given period for the noncustodial parent. An additional implication of the theory is that the nature of the matches among men who remarry may be different for men who pay child support and men who do not.

While we treat a child support payment as a tax in this example, it is also likely that the father derives utility, or happiness, from making payments for the support of his children. Thus, the payment of child support is to some extent volitional and to some extent the result of state enforcement.[4] We account for this factor in the empirical analyses.

Although a substantial body of literature exists on the determinants of remarriage (Chiswick and Lehrer 1990; Hutchens 1979; Koo and Suchindran 1980; Spanier and Glick 1980), surprisingly little of this research examines remarriage among men.[5] Among women, however, this research has several major findings: black and Hispanic women remarry more slowly than white women, time to remarriage increases with age at divorce, children lower the probability of remarriage among younger women, and women with higher incomes remarry less rapidly.

The few studies that examine remarriage among men suggest several differences between men and women. Paul Glick (1980) finds that age at divorce and the presence of children at divorce have no effect on men's time to remarriage. Gary Becker, Elisabeth Landes, and Robert Michael (1977) also find that the existence of children from a previous marriage has no effect on a man's likelihood of remarriage. Both studies find that while a woman's income is inversely related to her likelihood of remarriage, a man's income is significantly and positively related to his likelihood of remarriage. Each of these relationships can be easily explained within the search framework described earlier.

Although we are not aware of any studies of the effects of child support on men's remarriage, three recent studies examine the effects of child support receipts on women's remarriage (Beller and Graham 1985; Folk, Graham, and Beller 1992; Yun 1992). The evidence suggests that the receipt of child support tends to reduce a woman's probability of remarriage, but that this effect is small. In theory, the effect of child support receipts on a woman's likelihood of remarriage is ambiguous. Child support receipts may increase her well-being while single and reduce her incentive to search, but they may also make her more attractive as a marriage partner than a woman with children who does not receive such payments.[6] Kwi-Ryung Yun (1992) also finds that, controlling for a range of individual characteristics and the previous husband's income, women who receive higher amounts of child support, as compared with women who receive less or no child support, tend to remarry higher-income men. This effect is interpreted as one in which child support income allows a woman to spend more time searching for a "higher-quality" mate.

In our empirical analyses, we first adopt a reduced-form strategy and model remarriage as a function of the level of state child support enforcement and several individual-level factors that have been found to affect remarriage. Examining the direct effect of enforcement on remarriage allows us to use data that contain no information on actual child support payments. In this model, we expect stricter policies to affect remarriage behavior by increasing the likelihood and amount of child support payments. As mentioned earlier, however, the net effect of stricter enforcement is theoretically indeterminate.

We also examine, when possible, the effects on fathers' remarriage of actual payments. Along with the decisions regarding marital search, the nonresident father will also decide whether to pay child support. As mentioned earlier, whether he makes such payments depends both on his own calculation of the costs and benefits of paying support and on the strictness of state child support enforcement. Thus, if child support payments and the probability of remarriage are both affected by unobservable characteristics of the father (for example, his sense of decency and responsibility), then our estimate of the effect of payments on remarriage will be biased(toward being positive, in this example). We attempt to correct for this possible source of bias in the empirical analysis by using the method of instrumental variables.

DATA AND ANALYSIS

We use individual-level data from two surveys that contain marital and fertility histories. The first data set we use is the Survey of Income and Program Participation (SIPP). The SIPP consists of a series of twenty-eight- to thirty-two-month panels, the first of which was initiated in 1984; for the duration of each panel, interviews are given every four months to a nationally representative sample of households. The survey obtains detailed information about monthly income, program participation, and household composition. Using the marital history, fertility history, and detailed household relationship topical modules from the 1990 SIPP, we construct a cross-sectional sample of nonresident fathers. We follow Elaine Sorensen's (1997) methodology to obtain this sample. Roughly, we identify nonresident fathers by including (1) men who reported making child support payments to nonresident children and (2) men who were divorced, separated, or remarried and reported having fathered more children than were currently living in their household. Additional restrictions on the age of the father and the length of the current marriage are imposed on the latter group to omit those men who are incorrectly included because they had adult children who had left the household. We also restrict the sample to divorces that occurred between 1981 and 1989, given that the child support enforcement variables cover this time period.

We also use data from the 1979 to 1992 National Longitudinal Survey of Youth (NLSY). In 1979 the NLSY interviewed a sample of approximately thirteen thousand women and men age fourteen to twenty-one. Respondents have been reinterviewed in each year thereafter and asked about such topics as labor-force participation, school status, income, marital status, and fertility. We use information from the 1990 and 1991 marital and fertility history questions to construct a sample of men who divorced between 1981 and 1989 and had children at divorce. To examine the effects on remarriage of actual child support payments, we use the subset of these divorces that occurred from 1982 to 1987, given that the NLSY interviewed fathers about payments only during these years.

We also assess the effects of child support enforcement on the marriage behavior of men who had fathered children nonmaritally. To do this, we use a sample of men from the NLSY who reported that they fathered a child at least one year prior to their first marriage or fathered a child during the 1980s but had not yet married as of the 1990 and 1991 surveys.

To measure the level of state child support enforcement, we use information from the annual reports to Congress of the Office of Child Support Enforcement. These reports contain information about caseload size and collections for all cases within the OCSE system.[7] The four variables we use to measure the level of child support enforcement are collections per case (standardized by state per capita income), the percentage of cases in which a collection is made, collections divided by expenditures, and total expenditures divided by the number of female-headed families in the state. These variables are available for every year since 1980. We measure state enforcement for a given father by the level of these variables in the year in which he divorced or separated, or in the case of nonmarital births, the year in which he became a father.[8]

Table 5A.1 presents means for the samples of nonresident fathers from the SIPP and the NLSY. As expected, the SIPP fathers are several years older at divorce and have higher incomes than the NLSY fathers. The NLSY nonmarital fathers are also generally younger and less educated and have lower incomes than the ever-married NLSY fathers. Among the ever-married fathers, over 40 percent were observed to remarry within the survey period, and they remarried, on average, two and a half years after divorce. Fewer of the nonmarital fathers married during the panel, and those who did marry took four and a half years to do so.[9]

Table 5A.1 also indicates that 64 percent of the NLSY fathers report making child support payments to their children sometime during the two years following divorce. This percentage is higher than that found using the Current Population Survey-Child Support Supplement (CPS-CSS) data, the data most commonly used to calculate child support statistics. Judith Seltzer and Yvonne Brandreth (1995) also find that fathers report paying more than mothers report receiving, and Nora Schaeffer, Judith Seltzer, and Marieka Klawitter (1991), using data from mothers' and fathers' reports and court data, find that fathers overreport the payment of child support. Note also that a substantial fraction of fathers' pretax incomes is devoted to the payment of child support, 15 percent of pretax income for the SIPP fathers and 9 percent for the NLSY fathers.

Child Support Enforcement and Remarriage

Table 5.1 examines the effects of child support enforcement on the hazard of remarriage by estimating a proportional hazards model for each of the ever-married samples. In each of the models, we control for several individual characteristics that may affect the hazard of remarriage. For the NLSY sample all of the individual characteristics are measured at the time of divorce, and for the SIPP sample each of the variables, except the father's age, is measured as of the 1990 survey. We also control for an array of state-specific factors that may influence both the level of child support enforcement and men's remarriage. The state variables, measured in the

TABLE 5.1 / The Effect of Child Support Enforcement on the Hazard of Remarriage

Enforcement Measure	SIPP	NLSY
Collections per case	−.058	−.078
	(.048)	(.079)
Collection rate	−.021	−.018
	(.011)	(.019)
Collections/expenditures	−.044	−.007
	(.044)	(.062)
Expenditures per female-headed family	−.001	.002
	(.002)	(.004)
Sample size	563	267

Sources: Survey of Income and Program Participation 1990 and National Longitudinal Survey of Youth 1979 to 1992.

Notes: The data are unweighted. Each coefficient represents a separate regression. Also included are individual and state characteristics and time dummies for year of divorce. See table 5A.2 for full model results. Standard errors are in parentheses.

year of separation or divorce, are the unemployment rate, real per capita income, and the marriage rate in 1980. We also include the real AFDC maximum benefit,[10] given that AFDC generosity may be correlated with child support policy but may also affect men's remarriage through its effect on women's desire to marry. Finally, all models include a series of dummy variables for year of divorce and region (full model results are reported in table 5A.2).

We examine the effects of each enforcement variable separately, given that they are fairly highly correlated with one another. Each of the enforcement variables has a negative coefficient, with the exception of total expenditures per case for the NLSY sample, suggesting that stricter enforcement reduces the probability of remarriage. In addition, the magnitudes of the coefficients are somewhat similar across the samples. However, only one of the coefficients, that for the collection rate for the SIPP sample, is statistically significant.

Thus, the results suggest that stricter enforcement of child support does not have significant effects on fathers' time to remarriage. However, one could imagine that a child support obligation represents a relatively greater burden for lower-income men, in which case we would not observe effects of enforcement for the sample of all fathers, but only for lower-income fathers. We test this hypothesis by interacting each enforcement variable with a dummy variable indicating whether the respondent has income below the sample average. We also examine whether the effects of enforcement differ by education level by interacting each of the variables with a dummy variable indicating whether the father had a high school education or less. The first section of table 5.2 presents the results for the income interactions. In general, the coefficients indicate that enforcement reduces the hazard of remarriage among lower-income fathers and has little effect on higher-income fathers. Collections per case have a significantly negative effect on the remarriage of low-income men, and this effect is consistent across the samples. The coefficient on the

TABLE 5.2 / The Effect of Child Support Enforcement on the Hazard of Remarriage: Interactions with Income and Education Level

Enforcement Measure	SIPP		NLSY	
	(1)	(2)	(1)	(2)
Interactions with low income				
Collections per case	.043	−.197	.092	−.293
	(.063)	(.083)	(.101)	(.128)
Collection rate	.002	−.048	.007	−.042
	(.012)	(.016)	(.025)	(.028)
Collections/expenditures	.006	−.105	.067	−.163
	(.055)	(.074)	(.074)	(.099)
Expenditures per female-	.001	−.003	.003	−.002
headed family	(.003)	(.002)	(.004)	(.004)
Interactions with low education				
Collections per case	−.033	−.051	−.242	.204
	(.060)	(.078)	(.211)	(.229)
Collection rate	−.007	−.026	−.0002	−.024
	(.013)	(.016)	(.032)	(.037)
Collections/expenditures	−.039	−.010	−.306	.302
	(.059)	(.074)	(.306)	(.303)
Expenditures per female-	−.001	−.001	.015	−.014
headed family	(.002)	(.002)	(.006)	(.006)
Sample size	563		267	

Source: SIPP 1990 and NLSY 1979 to 1992.

Notes: The data are unweighted. Columns 1 show the effects of enforcement for fathers with above-average income in the first section and higher education in the second section, and columns 2 show the coefficients on the interactions of each enforcement variable with low-income status and low-education status, respectively. Low income is defined as having income below the sample average ($24,000 for the SIPP and $11,000 for the NLSY). Low education is defined as having completed high school or less. Also included are individual and state characteristics and time dummies for year of divorce. Standard errors are in parentheses.

collection rate is significantly negative only for the SIPP sample, while the coefficient on collections divided by expenditures is significant at the 10 percent level only for the NLSY sample. Finally, although the coefficients on the interaction terms for total expenditures per female-headed family are both negative, they are not significant for either sample. On the whole, however, the pattern of coefficients suggests that stricter child support enforcement reduces remarriage probabilities among lower-income men.

The second section of table 5.2 presents results from the models that include interactions of the enforcement variables with the education level of the father. The results indicate that the effects of enforcement do not vary by education level. The only coefficient that is marginally significant is that for the interaction of the collection rate with low education for the SIPP sample.

The estimates indicate that stricter child support enforcement reduces the hazard of remarriage among lower-income noncustodial fathers. However, the enforcement variables could also be capturing the effect on remarriage of other policies that are common among states that enforce child support. To test whether the enforcement variables are measuring child support enforcement per se, we estimated the models in table 5.1 for samples of men who were not noncustodial fathers. Table 5.3 presents the results. The models are estimated for low-income men without children at divorce and for our samples of low-income, noncustodial fathers. The coefficients indicate that, while collections per case and the collection rate negatively affect remarriage for men with children, they have no such effects for men without children. The coefficients for men without children, in addition to being statistically insignificant, are all very close to zero. These results suggest that the effects of enforcement we observe are related to the child support system and not to other unobservable state characteristics that may be associated with stricter enforcement.[11]

The fact that these coefficients are estimated from a hazard model, coupled with the fact that each of the enforcement variables is measured in different units, makes it difficult to interpret the reported coefficients. Table 5.4 provides the percentage reduction in the yearly hazard of remarriage given a 10 percent increase in two enforcement variables from their sample averages. To calculate these effects, we use the coefficients reported in table 5.3 for the samples of low-income fathers. The results indicate that a 10 percent increase in the level of enforcement reduces yearly remarriage probabilities for low-income fathers between 3.3 and 9.4 percent.

TABLE 5.3 / The Effect of Child Support Enforcement on the Hazard of Remarriage: Men With and Without Children at Divorce

	SIPP		NLSY	
Enforcement Measure	With Children	Without Children	With Children	Without Children
Collections per case	−.142	.006	−.211	−.039
	(.083)	(.083)	(.121)	(.116)
Collection rate	−.062	.008	−.055	−.001
	(.021)	(.019)	(.027)	(.027)
Collections/expenditures	−.089	−.004	−.044	.006
	(.069)	(.078)	(.102)	(.087)
Expenditures per female-	−.005	.003	.003	.007
headed family	(.004)	(.005)	(.005)	(.005)
Sample size	304	180	139	179

Source: SIPP 1990 and NLSY 1979 to 1992.

Notes: The data are unweighted. Each coefficient represents a separate regression. Samples are restricted to men with below-average income ($24,000 for the SIPP and $11,000 for the NLSY). Also included are individual and state characteristics and time dummies for year of divorce. Standard errors are in parentheses.

TABLE 5.4 / The Percentage Reduction in the Yearly Hazard of Remarriage for Low-Income Fathers When Child Support Enforcement Is Increased

Enforcement Change	SIPP	NLSY
10 percent increase in collections per case	3.3	4.8
10 percent increase in collection rate	9.4	8.3
Increase in the collection rate from the thirtieth-ranked state to the tenth-ranked	31.2	27.8

Source: SIPP 1990 and NLSY 1979 to 1992.

Note: Estimates are derived from coefficients reported in table 5.3.

Given the substantial dispersion that exists across states in the level of enforcement, however, we can also examine the percentage reduction in the yearly hazard of remarriage associated with moving from the thirtieth to the tenth most effective state. Using the collection rate, for example, this increase in enforcement implies a change in the collection rate of 5.2 points, which substantially reduces the yearly hazard of remarriage, by about 30 percent.

Child Support Payments and Remarriage

We next examine data on actual payments made by fathers, in an effort to quantify the effects of child support per se on the hazard of remarriage. This analysis is performed using the NLSY sample, given that the SIPP survey contains no information on payments made immediately following divorce. In addition, we must restrict the analysis to fathers who divorced between 1982 and 1987, since questions about child support payments were asked only in the 1982 to 1988 surveys.

Table 5.5 presents the results for the estimated effects of child support payments on the hazard of remarriage. All of the individual and state-level variables included in previous models are included here. The child support variable is coded as 1 if the father paid child support at some point during the two years following divorce,

TABLE 5.5 / The Effect of Child Support Payments on the Hazard of Remarriage

Coefficient on whether paid child support	.159	.624	3.25	1.61
	(.309)	(1.87)	(2.06)	(1.59)
Instruments used	None	1, 2	2, 3	1, 4
First-stage F-statistic for instruments	NA	2.06	1.60	3.99
[p value]		[.36]	[.45]	[.14]

Source: NLSY 1979 to 1992.

Notes: The date are unweighted. The models are estimated using a subsample of NLSY fathers who divorced between 1982 and 1987 (the sample size is 150). Each column represents a separate regression. For row 2, the enforcement variables are coded as follows: 1 = collections per case, 2 = collection rate, 3 = collections/expenditures, and 4 = expenditures per female-headed family. Also included are individual and state characteristics and time dummies for year of divorce. Standard errors are in parentheses.

and 0 otherwise. The results in column 1 indicate that paying child support has no significant effect on time to remarriage. However, this estimate of the effect of child support is likely to be biased, given the existence of unobservable factors that influence both payments and remarriage behavior. To account for this, we employ a two-stage approach and predict child support payments in the first stage using the state enforcement variables as instruments. The second stage examines the effect of predicted payments on the hazard of remarriage.

Columns 2 through 4 of table 5.5 present estimates of the effect of child support payments on remarriage using different pairs of the enforcement variables as instruments. In theory, the coefficient for instrumented, or predicted, payments should suffer from less bias than that for actual payments, since the former variable has been purged of its correlation with unobservable factors that also affect remarriage. As the F-statistics in row 3 indicate, however, the state enforcement variables used in the reduced-form analysis are relatively poor instruments, in that they have very little power to predict payments in this sample. Moreover, the coefficient on predicted payments is not consistent across the columns. The results (not reported) were also statistically insignificant for the sample of low-income fathers and the sample of less-educated fathers.

Thus, although we find that child support enforcement policies affect remarriage probabilities among low-income fathers, these same policies do not seem to affect the likelihood of payment immediately after divorce. We should note that in the SIPP sample the enforcement variables measured in 1990 significantly predict the probability and level of payments among SIPP fathers in 1990. One possible explanation for the results for the NLSY sample is that the enforcement variables may not affect payments immediately following divorce but over a longer horizon. It may also be the case that some lower-income fathers do not make payments but nonetheless build up considerable arrearages that may affect marriage behavior. A state's child support enforcement effort provides information on both the probability that a child support obligation exists and the probability that the father will have to meet this obligation, now or in the future. Earl Johnson and Fred Doolittle (see chapter 9 in this volume) report that fathers in the Parents' Fair Share program who have little or no income to pay child support are often acutely aware of the sometimes large amounts of child support they owe.

The Nature of Matches

We next examine the effects of child support enforcement on another aspect of marriage behavior, the nature of marital matches. As mentioned earlier, one implication of the search model is that a man who faces an altered distribution of marital offers may change his minimum acceptable offer. An analogous situation for women arises, it is argued, when the receipt of child support income allows them to search longer for a more "attractive" mate. This argument is tested by Yun (1992), who examines the impact of child support receipts on the characteristics of a woman's new husband. We examine this issue for fathers by estimating, among fathers who remarry, the effect of child support enforcement on the characteristics of the new spouse. In particular, we consider the new spouse's age, education, and income.

We assume that assortative mating is optimal in the marriage market and use the absolute age difference between the spouses as the dependent variable in the analysis. If child support enforcement affects the nature of marital sorting through its effect on the man's minimum acceptable offer, we would expect it to affect the age difference, as he accepts a less than optimal match. We also use the level of the new wife's education and income as indicators of the quality of the marital offer. The results from these models are presented in table 5.6 (full model results are presented in table 5A.3). The results indicate that child support enforcement

TABLE 5.6 / The Effect of Child Support Enforcement on the Nature of Marital Matches

Enforcement Measure	SIPP	NLSY
Spouses' age difference (absolute value)		
Collections per case	.011	−.016
	(.184)	(.292)
Collection rate	−.014	.007
	(.019)	(.072)
Collections/expenditures	.245	.094
	(.193)	(.014)
Expenditures per female-headed family	−.004	−.001
	(.010)	(.014)
New wife's income		
Collections per case	−84.1	257.4
	(656.4)	(674.1)
Collection rate	−16.3	−22.1
	(175.2)	(135.4)
Collections/expenditures	−50.1	−20.6
	(690.0)	(519.6)
Expenditures per female-headed family	−68.6	23.3
	(36.6)	(27.1)
New wife's education		
Collections per case	−.004	NA
	(.081)	
Collection rate	−.0003	NA
	(.021)	
Collections/expenditures	.082	NA
	(.085)	
Expenditures per female-headed family	−.001	NA
	(.004)	

Source: SIPP 1990 and NLSY 1979 to 1992.

Notes: The data are unweighted. Models are estimated using samples of nonresident fathers who remarried (246 for the SIPP and 124 for the NLSY). Also included are those individual and state variables included in previous models. See table 5A.3 for full model results.

has no effect on the nature of matches. For the age difference, for example, the coefficients are not statistically significant, nor are they consistently signed across enforcement variables or samples. Coefficients from similar models run for the low-income and low-education samples were generally not statistically significant. The exception to these results is that three of the four enforcement variables had significant (at 10 percent) and positive effects on the couple's age difference for the low-income NLSY sample. In general, however, while we find that child support enforcement alters the time to remarriage among some nonresident fathers, it appears to exert no significant effects on this aspect of marriage behavior.

Nonmarital Fertility and First Marriage

As a final look at the effects of child support enforcement on fathers' marriage behavior, we examine the time to first marriage for men who father children nonmaritally. For these men, the obligation to pay child support begins with the birth of the first child. To examine this issue, we use a sample of men from the NLSY who fathered a child prior to their first marriage. Child support enforcement variables are measured as of the year of the child's birth.

The results are presented in table 5.7. The first column of the table presents estimates for the full sample, and the second column presents estimates for a sample of low-income fathers. The results indicate that child support enforcement has no impact on the time to first marriage for nonmarital fathers. None of the coefficients is significantly negative, and one coefficient, that for the collection rate, is positive

TABLE 5.7 / The Effect of Child Support Enforcement on the Hazard of First Marriage Among Men Who Fathered a Child Nonmaritally

Enforcement Measure	All Men	Low-Income Men
Collections per case	−.005	.090
	(.109)	(.079)
Collection rate	.066	.101
	(.043)	(.055)
Collections/expenditures	−.043	.033
	(.105)	(.119)
Expenditures per female-headed family	−.003	−.003
	(.008)	(.010)
Sample size	156	110

Source: NLSY 1979 to 1992.

Notes: The data are unweighted. The sample consists of men who fathered children prior to a first marriage. The low-income sample consists of fathers with incomes of less than $6,000 (the sample average is $4,700). Each coefficient represents a separate regression. Also included are individual and state characteristics and time dummies for year of divorce. Standard errors are in parentheses.

for the low-income sample. When the model was estimated for the sample of low-education fathers, the enforcement variables were also insignificant.[12]

We also examined the effects of payments on time to first marriage, by instrumenting reported payments with the enforcement variables. Although not reported, the first-stage enforcement variables did not significantly predict whether payments were made in the two years following the birth of the child, and the resulting estimates for the effects of payments on time to marriage were insignificant. Thus, there appear to be no discernible effects of child support enforcement on the marriage of men who become liable to pay support through the birth of a non-marital child. This finding is consistent with the fact that child support receipt rates for never-married women are substantially lower than for ever-married women (U.S. Bureau of the Census 1996).

CHILD SUPPORT AND FERTILITY

Another important aspect of new family formation is fertility. We measure fertility in two ways: remarriage to a woman with children and fertility within a new marriage. Of special interest is the effect of child support on the probability of remarriage to a woman with children. As mentioned earlier, remarriage is a common route out of poverty for many poor single-mother families; a father who marries a woman with children typically assumes some of the financial responsibility for those children. Stricter child support enforcement could have unintended consequences if it reduces the likelihood of marriage for women with children.

In theory, child support enforcement has an ambiguous effect on a man's propensity to marry a woman with children. First, children from a previous union represent an investment in marriage-specific capital, which may reduce a woman's attractiveness in the remarriage market. If women with children from a prior marriage are at a disadvantage in the marriage market, we might expect to see them ultimately matched with men who are at a similar disadvantage, that is, those with child support obligations. This factor should increase the likelihood that men who pay child support marry women with children. However, a man with a child support obligation may be less willing or able to assume financial responsibility for the children of a new spouse. Furthermore, strict state enforcement of child support payments may make remarriage less attractive for women with children, as they are more likely to receive regular child support payments.

Table 5.8 presents estimates of the effects of child support enforcement on the probability, among men who remarry, of marrying a woman with children (see table 5A.4 for full model results).[13] The top section of the table presents estimates for the full sample, and the bottom section presents estimates for the low-income subsample. Although all but one of the coefficients are negative, none is statistically significant. The coefficient on expenditures per female-headed family comes the closest to significance, with a *t* value of 1.7 for the NLSY sample.

TABLE 5.8 / The Effect of Child Support Enforcement on the Likelihood of Remarriage to a Woman with Children

Enforcement Measure	SIPP	NLSY
All fathers		
Collections per case	−.068	−.001
	(.063)	(.033)
Collection rate	−.003	−.010
	(.015)	(.008)
Collections/expenditures	−.080	−.033
	(.062)	(.026)
Expenditures per female-headed family	.004	−.0024
	(.005)	(.0015)
Low-income subsample		
Collections per case	−.085	−.030
	(.092)	(.054)
Collection rate	−.016	−.015
	(.023)	(.012)
Collections/expenditures	−.003	−.073
	(.089)	(.048)
Expenditures per female-headed family	−.005	−.001
	(.004)	(.003)

Source: SIPP 1990 and NLSY 1979 to 1992.

Notes: The data are unweighted. The models are estimated using samples of nonresident fathers who remarried (246 for the SIPP and 124 for the NLSY). Probit models are estimated for the SIPP samples, and OLS models are estimated for the NLSY samples. (Attaining convergence for the probit model proved difficult with the small NLSY sample.) Also included are individual and state characteristics. See table 5A.4 for full model results.

Among the low-income samples, the coefficients are generally more negative (bottom section), a pattern that is consistent with the results for time to remarriage. However, they are all statistically insignificant. The coefficients estimated for the samples of low-education fathers (not reported) were very similar, in both sign and significance, to those reported for the full sample.

We also examine, using the NLSY subsample, the effects of actual payments on the probability of remarriage to a woman with children. These estimates are reported in table 5.9. Column 1 presents the results from a model in which the payment of child support is coded as a dummy variable set to 1 if the father paid support in the two years following divorce, and 0 otherwise. The coefficient on payment suggests that, conditional on remarriage, the payment of child support has a negative effect on the probability of marriage to a woman with children. As noted earlier, the coefficient on actual payments is likely to be biased, given the existence of unobservables that affect both the payment of support and remarriage behavior. We also present in columns 2 through 4 the effects of instrumented payments on the proba-

TABLE 5.9 / The Effect of Child Support Payments on the Likelihood of Remarriage to a Woman with Children

Coefficient on whether paid child support	−1.33	−4.38	2.33	−3.38
	(.654)	(3.12)	(4.26)	(3.37)
Instruments used	None	1, 2	2, 3	1, 4
First-stage *F*-statistic for instruments	NA	3.06	.66	1.39
[*p* value]		[.22]	[.72]	[.49]

Source: NLSY 1979 to 1992.

Notes: The data are unweighted. The models are estimated using a subsample of NLSY fathers who divorced between 1982 and 1987. (The sample size is 150.) Each column represents a separate regression. For row 2, the enforcement variables are coded as follows: 1 = collections per case, 2 = collection rate, 3 = collections/expenditures, and 4 = expenditures per female-headed family. Also included are individual and state characteristics and time dummies for year of divorce. Standard errors are in parentheses.

bility of remarriage to a woman with children. Again, however, the results indicate that the enforcement variables are weak instruments, and none of the coefficients for instrumented child support payments is significant.

In sum, we find no strong evidence that among nonresident fathers who remarry, those living in high-enforcement states are less likely to marry a woman with children from a previous relationship. These results suggest that there will be no negative effects of stricter enforcement through this aspect of fathers' behavior for poor single mothers, many of whom leave poverty through remarriage.

We next examine the effects of enforcement on fertility within a new marriage. Fertility after remarriage is yet another aspect of new family formation, and according to recent estimates, an increasingly important one. Howard Wineberg (1990) finds that, among women who have been married twice, 35 percent of total births to these women occurred after remarriage. Examining the effects of child support enforcement on new fertility will help to complete our analysis of how the child support system affects fathers' behavior.

The economic model of fertility assumes that the demand for children, as for any other normal commodity, depends upon income and prices. While the price of children is often measured by the price of the mother's time (Becker 1960; Willis 1973), child support affects the demand for children through its effect on family income, given that the birth of a new child does not typically alter the original child support order.[14] A child support obligation then, as a reduction in income, is expected to reduce the demand for new children.[15]

Table 5.10 presents estimates for the effects of child support enforcement on the likelihood, among fathers who remarried, that they would have fathered one or more children by the time of the survey (full model results are presented in table 5A.5). Each of the models controls for individual and state characteristics and the number of years the couple has been married. In addition, we include the wife's rather than the husband's age and education as covariates to capture the price of children for the mother. The estimates indicate that, among fathers who remarry,

TABLE 5.10   /   The Effect of Child Support Enforcement on the Likelihood of Fertility Within a New Marriage

Enforcement Measure	SIPP	NLSY
Collections per case	−.084	.421
	(.080)	(.217)
Collection rate	−.023	.094
	(.018)	(.036)
Collections/expenditures	.047	.056
	(.066)	(.110)
Expenditures per female-headed family	−.003	.021
	(.003)	(.008)

Source: SIPP 1990 and NLSY 1979 to 1992.

Notes: The data are unweighted. Probit models estimated using samples of nonresident fathers who remarried (246 for the SIPP and 100 for the NLSY). Also included are individual and state variables. See table 5A.5 for full model results.

stricter child support enforcement has no significant negative effects on the likelihood that they will father new children.[16] Although the enforcement variables are measured in the year the father divorced, we also estimated models in which they were recoded to the year of remarriage. The results were similar to those reported here. We also tested whether the effects of enforcement differ by income and education level and found no significant differences.

Child Support Enforcement and Nonmarital Fertility

We next look at the effects of child support on nonmarital fertility. Anne Case (see chapter 7 in this volume) finds that child support enforcement reduces out-of-wedlock birth rates. In this chapter, however, we estimate the likelihood of subsequent fertility after the birth of a first nonresident child, that is, after the existence of a child support obligation. To do this, we use the sample of nonmarital fathers from the NLSY to estimate a hazard model for the time to a second nonmarital birth.

Table 5.11 presents the results for the full sample and the low-income sample. While the coefficients are generally negative, suggesting that stricter enforcement reduces subsequent nonmarital births, most are not statistically significant. The exception to this pattern is for the collection rate, which has a significantly negative effect on fertility for the full sample and a somewhat more negative effect for the low-income sample.

The results in this section suggest that child support enforcement has more substantial effects on remarriage behavior than on fertility behavior. We examined the likelihood of becoming a stepfather among men who remarry. While the results indicate that there may be some negative effects of child support enforcement on this likelihood, the coefficients were generally not statistically significant. With

TABLE 5.11 / The Effect of Child Support Payments on the Hazard of a Second
Nonmarital Birth

Enforcement Measure	All Men	Low-Income Men
Collections per case	−.214	−.234
	(.154)	(.220)
Collection rate	−.074	−.105
	(.037)	(.049)
Collections/expenditures	.081	.058
	(.106)	(.126)
Expenditures per female-headed family	−.003	−.008
	(.006)	(.008)
Sample size	156	110

Source: NLSY 1979 to 1992.

Notes: The data are unweighted. The sample consists of men who fathered children prior to a
first marriage. The low-income sample consists of fathers with incomes of less than $6,000 (the
sample average is $4,700). Each coefficient represents a separate regression. Also included are
individual and state characteristics and time dummies for year of divorce. Standard errors are
in parentheses.

respect to new fertility, both within and outside of marriage, child support enforcement appears to exert no significant influence on this behavior. Only one enforcement variable reduced the likelihood of fathering new children nonmaritally, and
none affected fertility within remarriage. One possible explanation for these findings is that, while stricter enforcement may lower the father's income, it may also
reduce the cost of children for the new wife, given that she is more assured that she
would receive child support upon divorce.

DISCUSSION

This chapter assesses some potential trade-offs of a more strictly enforced child
support system. The principal trade-off we examine, and one that has been hitherto
ignored in the effort to enforce child support, relates to the linkage between child
support and fathers' new family formation. Both child support and remarriage are
important avenues through which children are supported. Stricter child support
enforcement, while attempting to provide more resources for children, may also
have negative effects on children's economic well-being if it discourages or hinders
remarriage behavior among mothers or fathers.

We find that child support enforcement reduces remarriage probabilities
among low-income fathers. A 10 percent increase in enforcement, for example, can
be expected to reduce the yearly probability of remarriage for low-income fathers
by up to 10 percent. This result has two implications for child support reform.
First, assuming that marriage is assortative on income, those female-headed fam-

ilies whose remarriage probabilities may be most affected by child support enforcement are the lower-income families, those who may stand to benefit most from remarriage. Second, given that higher-income fathers have more ability to pay child support yet do not appear to be burdened by these payments, a majority of the resource transfer from fathers to children can occur with little effect on remarriage probabilities.

One somewhat puzzling result is that the child support enforcement policies that were observed to affect remarriage probabilities among low-income fathers did not seem to affect the likelihood that they made payments immediately after divorce. This finding is not inconsistent with the remarriage findings if the enforcement variables affect payments not immediately following divorce but over a longer horizon, or if stricter enforcement is associated with fathers building up considerable arrearages. This is an area for future research.

We also explored the extent to which child support enforcement affects the nature of marital matches, using information on the age, education, and income of the new spouse. Marital search theory suggests that a child support obligation may cause a man to alter his expectations in the marriage market. Our results suggest either that enforcement has no effect on this aspect of remarriage behavior or that it affects the father's acceptable offer and distribution of potential offers in ways that are offsetting.

Finally, we examined the effect of child support enforcement on fertility, including the likelihood of becoming a stepfather and fathering new children. We find little evidence that enforcement has significant effects on the likelihood of marriage to a woman with children or on the likelihood of new fertility subsequent to remarriage. Thus, although stricter child support enforcement may engender costs in terms of fathers' remarriage rates, there appear to be no effects on other aspects of remarriage behavior.[17]

The foregoing analyses highlight two key effects of increases in the enforcement of child support awards. The first effect represents the direct positive effect of increased enforcement on child support received. The second effect is an indirect negative effect that operates by reducing remarriage rates of nonresident fathers, some fraction of whom would presumably have remarried custodial mothers and provided support for their children. Whether the economic well-being of children living with lone custodial mothers is, on average, improved or diminished by increased enforcement of child support depends on the relative magnitudes of these two effects.

In an effort to assess the net gain or loss to children of increased enforcement, we consider a 10 percent increase in enforcement for low-income fathers. To determine the increase in child support payments that would result from increased enforcement, we use two independent samples to regress the dollar value of child support receipts on state child support collection rates. Using the March/April 1990 CPS-CSS, a 10 percent increase in the collection rate increases receipts per household by $87.50 per year. Using the 1990 SIPP sample of nonresident fathers, a 10 percent increase in the collection rate increases payments by $33.

We construct an estimate of financial support forgone as a result of increased enforcement as the product of several variables. First, we use our estimates of the effect of enforcement on yearly remarriage rates (see table 5.4)—a 4 percent reduction using collections per case, and a 9 percent reduction using the collection rate. Second, we calculate the share of nonresident fathers in the pool of marriageable men. Census estimates indicate that nonresident fathers represent 15 percent of all eighteen- to fifty-five-year-old men not currently married.[18] Third, we estimate the income gain for a child from her mother's remarriage. Average income for low-income fathers in the SIPP sample is $13,000. We assume that stepfathers devote one-fourth of their resources to supporting their stepchildren.[19] Under these assumptions, we can calculate the income loss from increased enforcement using the effects of the collection rate: the reduction in the yearly hazard of remarriage (.09) multiplied by the share of fathers in the pool of eligible men (.15), multiplied by the income gain from the mother's remarriage ($3,250). This calculation yields an income loss of $44 from a 10 percent increase in enforcement.

Table 5.12 compares these estimated income losses with the gains from enforcement, for the net income effect. If we assume that marriage is assortative on income, the calculations make it clear that the financial gain to low-income children of increased enforcement may be substantially overstated by looking only at the effect of increased enforcement on child support receipts. Indeed, using the low estimate of the effect of enforcement on receipts—$33—allows the negative remarriage effect to offset the positive payment effect completely. Thus, increased child support enforcement may be far less beneficial to the economic well-being of children than it would otherwise appear. And in some cases, as the calculations illustrate, the benefits may be close to zero.

These simulation results are not intended to provide estimates of the dollar benefits of increased enforcement but rather are meant to be suggestive and to highlight the importance of considering the effects of enforcement on behaviors other than payments. As with any simulations, they are sensitive to the assumptions on which they are based. For example, although nonresident fathers make up 15 percent of all unmarried men, a reduction in the remarriage rate for these fathers, or

TABLE 5.12 / Estimates of the Net Effect of Increased Child Support Enforcement on Financial Support for Low-Income Children

	Scenario 1	Scenario 2
Increase in income from child support payments	$87.50	$33.00
Decrease in income from reduced remarriage probability	−44.00	−44.00
Net effect	43.50	−11.00

Notes: Calculations are based on the estimated effect of enforcement on the hazard of remarriage for low-income fathers from the SIPP sample, presented in table 5.3. The calculations in Scenario 1 assume that a 10 percent increase in enforcement increases receipts by $87.50, while those in Scenario 2 assume that it increases receipts by $33. These estimates were obtained from the 1990 Current Population Survey-Child Support Supplement and the 1990 SIPP sample of nonresident fathers, respectively. See the text for full details.

removing these men from the eligible pool, may have a limited impact on custodial mothers' remarriage rates if other types of men are drawn into the pool or if mothers couple with men who are not noncustodial fathers. This is one example in which the complexities of the marriage market are not captured by a simple simulation.

The movement to strengthen the child support system has gained considerable momentum in recent years, but these findings suggest that there may be more flash than substance to the claim that increased child support enforcement increases the economic well-being of children. While increased enforcement appears to channel more resources from nonresident fathers to their biological children, it may diminish the resources those fathers would devote to stepchildren they would otherwise have had.

We thank Philip Robins, Robert Mare, Irwin Garfinkel, Sherry Glied, participants at the conference "The Effects of Child Support Enforcement on Nonresident Fathers," Princeton University, September 1995, and participants at the Columbia University Labor Economics Seminar for helpful comments.

APPENDIX

TABLE 5A.1 / Characteristics of Nonresident Father Samples

	SIPP	NLSY	NLSY Nonmarital
Father's age at divorce (percent)	32.7	26.4	23.2
Education	12.9	11.7	11.4
Number of children at divorce	1.8	1.4	—
Income at divorce	$26,455	$13,421	$5,573
Black (percent)	.14	.10	.58
Remarried by survey (percent)	.41	.46	.23
Years to remarriage	2.5	2.7	4.5
Paid child support (percent)	.55	.64	.27
Amount paid among payers	$4,021	$1,126	$572
Payments as percent of income	.15	.09	.22
Sample size	563	267	156

Source: SIPP 1990 and NLSY 1979 to 1992.

Notes: Sample weights used. Income, education, and child support payments for the SIPP sample are measured as of the 1990 survey. Information about child support payments for the NLSY samples is calculated using subsamples of fathers who divorced or fathered a nonmarital child between 1982 and 1987 and refers to payments during the two years following divorce. For the SIPP sample, payment data refer to the year prior to the survey.

TABLE 5A.2 / Estimates for the Effects of Child Support Enforcement on the Hazard of Remarriage

	SIPP	NLSY
Father's age at divorce	−.006	−.036
	(.012)	(.052)
Education	.044	.113
	(.027)	(.057)
Number of children at divorce	.006	−.258
	(.072)	(.181)
Income at divorce/1000	.019	.013
	(.009)	(.013)
Black	−.731	−.301
	(.233)	(.271)
State per capita income/100	.013	.008
	(.006)	(.010)
State unemployment rate	.067	.158
	(.038)	(.069)
State AFDC maximum benefit/10	−.008	−.011
	(.009)	(.012)
State marriage rate—1980	−.062	.099
	(.051)	(.074)
Log-likelihood	−1,406.0	−571.2
Sample size	563	267

Source: SIPP 1990 and NLSY 1979 to 1992.

Notes: The data are unweighted. Also included are variables for region, year of divorce, and income squared for the SIPP. Income and education for the SIPP sample are measured as of the 1990 survey. Standard errors are in parentheses.

TABLE 5A.3 / Estimates for the Effects of Child Support Enforcement on the Nature of Matches

	Age Difference		Wife's Income (in Thousands of Dollars)	
	SIPP	NLSY	SIPP	NLSY
Constant	6.3	2.8	−25.6	10.0
	(5.4)	(8.5)	(19.2)	(1.81)
Father's age at divorce	.20	.27	.38	.29
	(.05)	(.15)	(.17)	(.31)
Father's education	.17	−.63	−.37	−.51
	(.12)	(.27)	(.42)	(.55)
Number of children at divorce	.52	−.85	−1.26	.59
	(.32)	(.69)	(1.15)	(1.45)
Income at divorce/1,000	.04	−.02	.25	.09
	(.17)	(.04)	(.05)	(.08)
Black	−.84	−.12	6.07	1.48
	(1.0)	(1.0)	(3.67)	(2.19)
State per capita income/100	−.05	−.05	.002	.001
	(.03)	(.04)	(.001)	(.001)
State unemployment rate	−.19	.69	.18	.42
	(.16)	(.26)	(.56)	(.57)
State AFDC maximum benefit/10	−.05	.08	−.007	−.011
	(.04)	(.04)	(.013)	(.010)
State marriage rate—1980	−.32	.04	.19	−.68
	(.22)	(.23)	(.77)	(.48)
Sample size	246	124		

Sources: SIPP 1990 and NLSY 1979 to 1992.

Notes: The data are unweighted. Also included are dummy variables for region and year of divorce. Standard errors are in parentheses. Income and education for the SIPP sample are measured as of the 1990 survey.

TABLE 5A.4 / Estimates for the Effects of Child Support Enforcement on the
Likelihood of Remarriage to a Woman with Children

	SIPP	NLSY
Constant	.041	−3.19
	(1.67)	(3.44)
Father's age at divorce	−.001	.096
	(.014)	(.061)
Education	−.006	.049
	(.037)	(.091)
Number of children at divorce	.109	.336
	(.101)	(.267)
Income at divorce/1,000	−.011	−.017
	(.005)	(.014)
Black	−.267	.516
	(.314)	(.378)
State per capita income/100	.007	.022
	(.009)	(.021)
State unemployment rate	.051	−.148
	(.049)	(.101)
State AFDC maximum benefit/10	−.024	−.038
	(.011)	(.019)
State marriage rate—1980	−.069	−.091
	(.067)	(.092)
Sample size	246	124

Sources: SIPP 1990 and NLSY 1979 to 1992.

Notes: The data are unweighted. Also included are dummy variables for region and year of divorce. Standard errors are in parentheses. Income and education for the SIPP sample are measured as of the 1990 survey.

TABLE 5A.5 / Probit Model Estimates for the Effects of Child Support Enforcement on the Likelihood of Fertility Within Remarriage

	SIPP	NLSY
New wife's age at remarriage	−.067	−.085
	(.015)	(.037)
New wife's education	−.062	−.199
	(.052)	(.130)
Number of father's children at divorce	−.161	−.009
	(.113)	(.377)
Number of mother's children at remarriage	−.185	.652
	(.117)	(.223)
Father's income at remarriage/1,000	.041	−.004
	(.062)	(.020)
Black	.794	.646
	(.355)	(.526)
State per capita income/100	.019	.003
	(.010)	(.022)
State unemployment rate	.053	.154
	(.049)	(.131)
State AFDC maximum benefit/10	−.031	.003
	(.112)	(.003)
State marriage rate—1980	.089	−.037
	(.074)	(.088)
Sample size	250	100

Sources: SIPP 1990 and NLSY 1979 to 1992.

Notes: The data are unweighted. Also included are dummy variables for region and year of remarriage. Income and education for the SIPP sample are measured as of the 1990 survey. For the NLSY sample, education is the father's education, and age and income are measured as of the year of remarriage. Standard errors are in parentheses.

NOTES

1. Child support may also affect the remarriage behavior of custodial mothers, as discussed later in this chapter.

2. See, for example, Stevenson (1994) and National Public Radio (1996).

3. An example of such a group is the Children's Rights Council.

4. It is interesting to note, in this context, that on average fathers who have child support obligations pay about 60 percent of what they owe, and virtually none pay more than the amount owed.

5. One exception is Glick (1980). Becker, Landes, and Michael (1977) also estimate the determinants of remarriage among men as part of a larger study on marriage behavior.

6. While in practice the mother's remarriage has been found to have a negative impact on child support receipts (Hill 1992), child support award levels are typically not formally changed when the mother remarries.

7. The OCSE caseload includes all women receiving AFDC and any non-AFDC-eligible women who request assistance.

8. The behavioral response of fathers to state enforcement will be lessened to the extent that some fathers do not live in the state in which their noncustodial children reside.

9. Although some of the fathers may enter into cohabitational unions rather than formal marriages, we cannot observe cohabitation in these data. Thus, we focus our analyses on entry into formal marriage.

10. These data were provided by Robert Moffitt.

11. The results in table 5.3 also suggest that the negative effect of stricter enforcement on fathers' remarriage is not caused by the fact that enforcement may reduce custodial mothers' desire to marry. If remarriage behavior on the other side of the market were driving our results, we would expect stricter enforcement to have negative effects on the remarriage of men without children. We assume here that men with and without children at divorce are equally likely to marry single mothers.

12. Given that we define our sample based on self-reported nonmarital fertility, this sample may be a somewhat select group of nonmarital fathers.

13. The models of fertility subsequent to marriage were not estimated for the nonmarital fathers, given that so few of them were observed to marry during the panel.

14. Only a handful of state child support guidelines allow an adjustment to the child support award following the birth of a new child to the nonresident parent (Williams 1994).

15. When the traditional fertility model is expanded to include both the quantity and quality of children, an increase in nonwage income may have no effect on the number of children demanded. Here we do not distinguish between quality and quantity and assume that the wealth elasticity for a first child within the new marriage is positive.

16. We also estimated a model in which the dependent variable was the number of new children. The results were similar to those reported in table 5.10.

17. The fertility models we estimate are conditional upon remarriage and do not account for the possibility that the fathers who remarry are a select group. The estimates may provide little information, therefore, on the effects of enforcement on the fertility behavior of those men who are not observed to remarry.

18. Census data indicate that in 1990 the number of unmarried men age eighteen to fifty-five was approximately thirty-one million (U.S. Bureau of the Census 1996). Census data also indicate that approximately four and a half million of the women eligible to receive child support were divorced or separated. We assume that the marital status of the nonresident father is the same as that of the custodial mother, suggesting that previously married nonresident fathers make up 15 percent of the pool of unmarried men (or four and a half million divided by thirty-one million).

19. As no data are available on the share of income devoted to stepchildren, we base this assumption on Lazear and Michael (1988) and Gronau (1991), who report that parents devote 25 to 38 percent of family expenditures to the children with whom they reside.

REFERENCES

Bane, Mary Jo, and David Ellwood. 1989. "One-Fifth of the Nation's Children: Why Are They Poor?" *Science* 245(September): 1047–53.

Becker, Gary. 1960. "An Economic Analysis of Fertility." In *Demographic and Economic Change in Developing Countries*. Universities–National Bureau of Economic Research conference series 11. Princeton, N.J.: Princeton University Press.

Becker, Gary, Elisabeth Landes, and Robert Michael. 1977. "An Economic Analysis of Marital Instability." *Journal of Political Economy* 85(6): 1141–87.

Beller, Andrea, and John Graham. 1985. "Variations in the Economic Well-being of Women and Their Children: The Role of Child Support Income." In *Horizontal Equity, Uncertainty, and Economic Well-being*, edited by Martin David and Timothy Smeeding. Chicago: University of Chicago Press.

Chiswick, Carmel, and Evelyn Lehrer. 1990. "On Marriage-Specific Human Capital: Its Role as a Determinant of Remarriage." *Journal of Population Economics* 3(3): 193–213.

Duncan, Greg, and Saul Hoffman. 1985. "A Reconsideration of the Economic Consequences of Marital Dissolution." *Demography* 22(4): 485–98.

Folk, Karen, John Graham, and Andrea Beller. 1992. "Child Support and Remarriage: Implications for the Economic Well-being of Children." *Journal of Family Issues* 13(2): 142–57.

Glick, Paul. 1980. "Remarriage: Some Recent Changes and Variations." *Journal of Family Issues* 1(4): 455–78.

Gronau, Reuben. 1991. "The Intrafamily Allocation of Goods—How to Separate the Adult from the Child." *Journal of Labor Economics* 9(3): 207–35.

Hill, Martha. 1992. "The Role of Economic Resources and Remarriage in Financial Assistance for Children of Divorce." *Journal of Family Issues* 13(2): 158–78.

Hutchens, Robert. 1979. "Welfare, Remarriage, and Marital Search." *American Economic Review* 69(3): 369–79.

Koo, Helen, and C. M. Suchindran. 1980. "Effects of Children on Women's Remarriage Prospects." *Journal of Family Issues* 1(4): 497–515.

Lazear, Edward, and Robert Michael. 1988. *Allocation of Income Within the Household*. Chicago: University of Chicago Press.

Lerman, Robert. 1996. "The Impact of the Changing U.S. Family Structure on Child Poverty and Income Inequality." *Economica* 63(250): S119–39.

National Public Radio. 1996. "Morning Edition" (April 22).

Schaeffer, Nora C., Judith Seltzer, and Marieka Klawitter. 1991. "Estimating Nonresponse and Response Bias: Resident and Nonresident Parents' Reports About Child Support." *Sociological Methods and Research* 20(1): 30–59.

Seltzer, Judith, and Yvonne Brandreth. 1995. "What Fathers Say About Involvement with Children After Separation." In *Fatherhood*, edited by William Marsiglio. Thousand Oaks, Calif.: Sage Publications.

Sorensen, Elaine. 1997. "A National Profile of Nonresident Fathers and Their Ability to Pay Child Support." *Journal of Marriage and the Family* 59 (November): 785–97.

Spanier, Graham, and Paul Glick. 1980. "Paths to Remarriage." *Journal of Divorce* 3(3): 283–98.

Stevenson, Richard W. 1994. "In Tough Mood, Britain Pursues Absent Parents." *New York Times*, February 7, p. A1.

U.S. Bureau of the Census. 1996. *Statistical Abstract of the United States: 1996*. Washington: U.S. Government Printing Office.

Williams, Robert. 1994. "An Overview of Child Support Guidelines in the United States." In *Child Support Guidelines: The Next Generation*. Washington: U.S. Department of Health and Human Services, Office of Child Support Enforcement.

Willis, Robert. 1973. "A New Approach to the Economic Theory of Fertility Behavior." *Journal of Political Economy* 81(2): S14–64.

Wineberg, Howard. 1990. "Childbearing after Remarriage." *Journal of Marriage and the Family* 52(February): 31–38.

Yun, Kwi-Ryung. 1992. "Effects of Child Support on Remarriage of Single Mothers." In *Child Support Assurance: Design Issues, Expected Impacts, and Political Barriers as Seen from Wisconsin*, edited by Irwin Garfinkel, Sara McLanahan, and Philip Robins. Washington: Urban Institute Press.

Chapter 6

Will Child Support Enforcement Increase Father-Child Contact and Parental Conflict After Separation?

Judith A. Seltzer, Sara S. McLanahan, and Thomas L. Hanson

Parents who live with their children contribute to their offsprings' welfare by spending time with them and spending money on them. When parents live together, they must balance competing demands and limited resources to decide what mix of time and money to devote to their children. When they live in separate households, they must also balance competing demands, but agreements about these matters are more costly to reach and more difficult to sustain.

Recent changes in the child support system have altered the context in which parents who live apart make decisions about allocating time and money to their children. By making it more difficult for nonresident parents to avoid paying child support, by increasing the amount of child support paid, and by strengthening paternity establishment for children born outside of marriage, the new system creates incentives for nonresident parents, usually fathers (Scoon-Rogers and Lester 1995), to spend more time with their children. Stronger child support enforcement may also increase parental conflict, either by increasing contact between parents who would otherwise avoid one another, by encouraging resident mothers to be more assertive in obtaining child support, or by increasing nonresident fathers' dissatisfaction with the system.

In this chapter, we examine the effects of child support enforcement on fathers' involvement with children and on parental conflict. We recognize that physical custody is part of contact. But because sole-father custody and joint physical custody are still relatively rare, we restrict our sample to families in which the children live most of the year with their mothers. We give special attention to low-income families and families in which the parents were never married to each other. While, in principle, the new child support legislation applies to all eligible children, most states have been targeting their efforts on low-income families, in which children are least likely to have child support orders and most likely to receive public assistance.[1] States are also required to increase rates of paternity establishment for children born outside of marriage to increase child support collections for this population. Because child support dollars have been used to offset welfare expenditures, states have a strong incentive to concentrate their efforts on these populations.

Our research is motivated by concern for children's welfare. Implicit in recent child support legislation is the assumption that children benefit directly from the income from child support transfers. Children may also benefit from spending more time with nonresident parents, although the evidence for this is mixed. Some studies based on small, clinical samples show that time with nonresident fathers improves children's adjustment (Hess and Camara 1979; Lund 1987; Wallerstein and Kelly 1980). Other studies based on national surveys find no relationship between father-child contact and children's well-being (King 1994; Furstenberg, Morgan, and Allison 1987; McLanahan et al. 1994).

Compared to increased contact, the potential side effects of parental conflict are more likely to be negative. When parents cannot cooperate on child-rearing issues, increased visitation may be harmful to children because it exposes them to more parental conflict. Numerous studies show that parental conflict reduces children's well-being (Emery 1982; Camara and Resnick 1988; Buchanan, Maccoby, and Dornbusch 1991; Cummings and Cummings 1988). Thus, if stricter child support enforcement leads to more parental conflict, especially high conflict, children may be worse off. Indeed, the inconsistent findings regarding the relationship between parental contact and child well-being may result from a failure to consider the quality of parents' relationships with each other (Amato and Rezac 1994; Hetherington, Cox, and Cox 1982).

The first section of this chapter discusses the different rationales for why child support payments should increase fathers' involvement with their children and why it might increase parental conflict. The second section describes the methods of analysis, data, and variables used. The third section presents results based on two samples, one cross-sectional and the other longitudinal. In the final section, we discuss the implications of our findings for child support policy.

THEORY AND PREVIOUS RESEARCH

Child Support and Father Involvement

Whether stricter child support enforcement will increase or decrease a nonresident father's involvement with his children cannot be predicted from theory. On the one hand, theory suggests that paying support increases visitation because fathers will want to monitor how the mother uses the child support dollars (Weiss and Willis 1985). According to this argument, fathers who live apart from their children are uncertain about how much of their child support payment is spent on the children versus how much is spent on the mother herself (Sherwood 1992; Arendell 1992). Even if the money is spent on the children, the father may not trust the mother to purchase the things he believes are good for the child. Divorced fathers who feel that they cannot control how their children are raised are less likely to pay support (Braver et al. 1993). Thus, fathers who pay child support will see their children more often to reduce uncertainty and to increase their control over how child support money is spent.

Child support enforcement may also increase contact between nonresident fathers and their children by altering fathers' views about themselves and their place in their children's lives. Fathers who pay support may come to see themselves as "good" fathers and may change other aspects of their behavior to conform with their new image of themselves. This may include pushing for more time with their children and for more decision-making authority. Similarly, mothers who receive child support on a regular basis may come to see the nonresident father in a more positive light and to view his claims to access and influence as more legitimate (Sen 1990).

On the other hand, if fathers trade off investments of time and money, stricter child support enforcement may reduce contact between nonresident fathers and children. Just as resident parents sometimes reduce the amount of time they spend with their children even as they increase the amount of money they spend (for example, by hiring baby-sitters or sending children to camp), nonresident fathers who pay more child support also may spend less time with their children. This could occur if the child support contribution requires the father to increase his work hours or if he reallocates to child support money that he would otherwise have spent on travel to see his children.

More rigorous child support enforcement, particularly automatic withholding of child support, might also reduce fathers' contact with children because the mother no longer needs to trade time with the children for child support from the father. When child support is guaranteed, fathers lose the opportunity to insist on visitation in exchange for paying child support. As a result, increased child support enforcement, in the absence of policies to enforce visitation, may decrease nonresident fathers' contact with their children.

The empirical research thus far shows a positive association between paying child support and father's involvement (Furstenberg, Morgan, and Allison 1983; Seltzer, Schaeffer, and Charng 1989; Seltzer 1991; McLanahan et al. 1994; but see Veum 1993). This does not mean, however, that child support has a causal effect on visiting or that stricter child support enforcement will necessarily lead to more frequent contact between nonresident fathers and children in the future. The correlation between visiting and paying could be spurious; that is, it could be due to a third factor that is causing fathers both to pay support and to visit their children frequently. An obvious source of a spurious association between paying and visiting is a father's financial resources, which affect his ability to pay support and to absorb visitation expenses. Past studies have rarely controlled for differences in fathers' income or wealth. Another possible source of a spurious relationship is fathers' attachment to their children or parents' ability to cooperate. Fathers with strong attachments are more likely to pay child support; they are also more likely to maintain frequent contact with their children. Evidence of stability in family relationships before and after separation (Koch and Lowery 1984; Block, Block, and Gjerde 1988) is consistent with this argument. Unfortunately, attempts to evaluate sources of spurious association suffer from a lack of information regarding both the quality of family relationships before separation and fathers' economic resources.

Child Support and Conflict Between Parents

Enforcing child support responsibilities for families in which parents would otherwise avoid each other to limit disagreements is likely to increase children's exposure to conflict. As noted earlier, nonresident parents have an incentive to monitor how their child support dollars are spent, and therefore they may increase their visitation to make sure that the money is going to the children. Similarly, paying child support may make a father feel more justified in demanding more access to and influence over his child. In either case, greater father involvement increases the potential for parental conflict. This is especially true if the parents have strong negative feelings about each other, or if one parent feels angry or hurt about the other parent's decision to end their relationship.

Child support enforcement may also affect parental conflict directly. The new child support laws change the rules under which parents decide who will bear the financial costs of children after separation. Specifically, the new laws shift more of the costs of children from mothers to fathers. These changes are likely to increase parental conflict in the short run, as mothers become more assertive in seeking child support orders, as more reluctant fathers are brought into the system, and as order levels and enforcement of child support orders are increased. (Note, however, that mothers may be more satisfied with their orders and the payments they receive, which may reduce this particular source of conflict.) In the long run, a more universalistic system in which child support collections are handled as an administrative procedure through a court agency rather than as a private transfer between parents may actually reduce dissatisfaction and disagreement about financial matters, thereby reducing children's exposure to conflict. Parents' perceptions about the child support system are likely to change gradually, however, and thus we do not expect these more positive effects to occur immediately.

Research findings are inconsistent on the effect of child support on parental conflict. Using data from a national survey, Judith Seltzer (1990) found that conflict was actually lower in divorced families where the nonresident father paid child support, although she noted that this might be due to selection bias. Sara McLanahan and her colleagues (1994) also used national data to show that the relationships between child support and parental conflict may differ for divorced families and families of children born outside of marriage. They found that once selectivity is taken into account, increasing child support enforcement is likely to decrease conflict between divorced parents but may increase conflict between parents of children born outside of marriage. However, the effects on conflict of child support were not statistically significant, perhaps because the instruments used in their statistical analysis were weak.

Child Support Among Low-Income Fathers and Fathers of Children Born Out of Wedlock

The effects of stricter child support enforcement on parent-child contact may be different for low-income families and for parents who were never legally married to each other. For example, until the 1996 welfare reforms, if the mother and child receive AFDC (Aid to Families with Dependent Children), which most poor, never-married mothers do, the child support paid by the nonresident father does not go directly to the mother. Rather, it goes to the state to offset welfare costs. The state may "disregard" or "pass through" to the mother the first fifty dollars a month. Despite this state payment to the mother, neither parent is as likely to view paying child support as a signal of a "good father" as are parents in families where the money is going straight to the child (Waller 1997; see also chapter 9 in this volume). Indeed, since the money does not go to the child, poor fathers have a greater incentive than nonpoor fathers to move to a different county or state, to avoid paying child support.

The effects of child support enforcement on parental conflict also may be different for parents of children born out of marriage. Although child support laws treat all fathers the same, social norms regarding paternal responsibility are much weaker for fathers who were never married to the mothers of their children. To the extent that unwed fathers feel less obligated to support their children, stricter enforcement is likely to lead to more resentment, which, in turn, would intensify parental conflict. The AFDC-welfare system further exacerbates this problem. Until recently, most states have been slow to establish paternity for children born outside of marriage and to collect child support from poor, unwed fathers. Even today, poor mothers exercise considerable discretion on how much information about the father they disclose to the child support office. Ethnographic studies have shown that some mothers on welfare use the threat of "official" child support to force nonresident fathers to comply with their demands, including making informal contributions to their children (Edin 1995a, 1995b). In such an environment, stricter child support enforcement is likely to intensify parental conflict, at least in the short run.

ANALYTIC TECHNIQUES, DATA, AND MEASURES

Plans and Techniques of Analysis

We adopt two strategies to assess the effects of child support enforcement, exploiting the relative strengths of the cross-sectional and longitudinal samples available from the National Survey of Families and Households (NSFH). Using the cross-sectional data, we take advantage of state variation in policies and practices to examine the effects of stricter enforcement on fathers' contact with children and conflict between parents. This analysis progresses in three steps. In the first part of the cross-sectional analysis, we examine the reduced-form effects of state policies and practices on father involvement and parental conflict. This analysis tells us whether children in states with strong policies are more likely to see their fathers and more likely to be exposed to parental conflict than children in states with weak policies.

Next, we estimate the effects of individual child support payments on father's involvement and conflict, using mothers' reports about how much child support they received. We use two indicators of child support: whether the father paid something, and how much he paid. This analysis allows us to quantify the effects of child support dollars on father-child contact and parental conflict, but it ignores the fact that unmeasured characteristics may account for both child support and the outcomes—that is, contact and conflict. Finally, we use instrumental variables to estimate the effects of child support payments. The instrumental variables approach presumably purges the child support variables of the unmeasured characteristics that are associated with child support payment, fathers' involvement, and parental conflict. We assume that the instruments have no direct effect on father involvement and parental conflict, except via child support payments. Thus, the estimates from the instrumental variables analysis of the effects of child support on parental behavior should be unbiased by these factors. The cross-sectional analysis improves on our earlier work by using improved instruments for child support enforcement—including more varied measures of paternal involvement—and examining in more detail the experiences of low-income families and those whose children were born outside of marriage.

Our instruments for the child support variables (any payment and amount of payment) include two state practice variables—effectiveness and effort—and three state statutes—guidelines, paternity establishment to age eighteen, and central agency. These variables are described later. The results we report are from ordinary least squares (OLS) regressions, which include observed child support and residuals from predicted child support variables. Our evaluations of statistical significance are similar whether we use results from two-stage least squares (TSLS) regression, correcting the standard errors in the instrumental variables models, or the OLS-generated standard errors.[2]

Finally, we use new longitudinal data to estimate the effects of child support payments on father's involvement and parental conflict. The longitudinal data contain more detailed information on fathers' characteristics prior to separation and thus we are able to control directly for some of the preseparation characteristics that might be causing the association between child support, father involvement, and parental conflict. This complements the instrumental variables approach used in the analysis of the cross-sectional sample, because the prospective design enables us to investigate explicitly the effects of child support on fathers' involvement and conflict, taking account of important characteristics usually omitted from such analyses—father's income, father's attitudes about child-rearing responsibilities, and the quality of family relationships before separation. As in the cross-sectional analysis, we report OLS parameters, but these results are generally consistent with those from ordered logit and logistic regression. Only the cross-sectional data include a sufficient number of cases to allow separate analyses for low-income families and those in which the child was born out of wedlock.

Data and Sample

We use data from the first and second waves of the National Survey of Families and Households. The NSFH is a national probability sample of adults in U.S. households in 1987 and 1988. The original design included face-to-face interviews supplemented by responses to a self-administered questionnaire and a mail-back survey of the primary respondent's spouse or cohabiting partner (secondary respondent). The study oversampled adults in some types of families and some minority groups, including single-mother families and stepfamilies. The overall response rate at wave 1 (NSFH1) was approximately 74 percent (Sweet, Bumpass, and Call 1988). In the first wave, the survey asked a detailed series of questions about a randomly selected minor child in the respondent's household, including the relationship between the father and child.

The second wave, conducted from 1992 to 1994, attempted to reinterview all members of the original sample. The follow-up was conducted as a face-to-face, computer-assisted interview with self-administered questionnaires. The follow-up design (NSFH2) included interviews with the original spouse or partner, whether or not that person was still living with the primary respondent. The response rate for original respondents at the second wave was 82 percent. For original spouses or partners who separated from the primary respondent between surveys, the response rate was 71 percent (Sweet and Bumpass 1996).

We use two samples in our analysis: a cross-sectional sample and a longitudinal sample. The cross-sectional sample is taken from the 1987 survey and includes all families with a child eighteen or younger who is eligible for child support, approximately 1,300 families. The sample is restricted to families in which the random child is living with the mother. We use reports from mothers who were primary respondents. The longitudinal sample is families in which the parents were married (wave 1) and separated or divorced between 1992 and 1994.[3] The longitudinal sample is restricted to families in which the children were living with the mother during the year before the second interview, approximately 190 families with children under age seventeen.[4] The two samples complement each other. The cross-sectional sample includes children whose parents divorced as well as children born outside of marriage. A particular advantage of the NSFH data is that nonmarital children include both those born to never-married mothers and those born to mothers who have previously been married. The cross-sectional sample is also larger than the longitudinal sample. The longitudinal sample includes information about divorced families before and after separation to allow an investigation of whether fathers' income and the quality of family relationships before divorce explain any effect of child support on fathers' involvement and conflict after divorce.

In both samples, the unit of analysis is the family as represented by one parent's report. The cross-sectional analyses use information from resident mothers only. Because the cross-sectional data are from unmatched parents, resident mothers provide the limited information available about nonresident fathers. The longitudinal analyses use information from both mothers and fathers for measures of pre-separation family characteristics. However, the longitudinal analysis relies almost exclusively on resident mothers' reports about fathers' involvement at time 2. We include a small number of cases for which only the nonresident father's report is available. All longitudinal analyses control for whether the information for time 2 comes from the mother or nonresident father.

Measures

Weighted means and standard deviations for variables used in the analyses are reported in table 6A.1.

CHILD SUPPORT PAYMENTS   Child support paid was measured both as a dichotomous variable, indicating whether the resident mother received any child support in the year before the interview, and as a continuous variable indicating the total amount received per year. Child support includes transfers made as the result of a child support order as well as informal transfers. Parents with and without orders reported about informal transfers, including payments through a third party. For parents separated less than a full year, total payments were converted into annual payments. In both the cross-sectional and longitudinal samples, child support is reported in 1993 dollars.

In the cross-sectional sample, the average child support payment was $1,530 per year. About 45 percent of the mothers in this sample received some payment, and the mean payment for these mothers was $3,430. In the longitudinal sample, the average child support payment was $5,260. About four-fifths of the mothers received some child support, and the mean payment for these mothers was $6,510 (see table 6A.1). Differences in amounts of child support between the two samples can be attributed, in part, to the fact that the cross-sectional sample includes more low-income families than the longitudinal sample. The former includes more families with young children and more families of children born outside of marriage; the latter is restricted to families of older children in which parents were previously married to each other. The longitudinal sample may also underrepresent low-income families because of differential attrition at the second wave and higher item nonresponse among low-income families on the child support variables.

FATHERS' INVOLVEMENT WITH CHILDREN   Both the cross-sectional and longitudinal analyses use similar measures of nonresident fathers' involvement. The questions ask about involvement with a randomly selected child. At each time, nonresident fathers' contact with their children was measured by a closed-ended question asking how often the child saw his or her father during the twelve months before the interview. Responses were: "not at all," "about once a year," "several times a year," "one to three times a month," "about once a week," and "several times a week" (or "more than once a week," depending on the wave of the survey). Father's influence is measured by the question: "How much influence does (child's) father have in making major decisions about such things as education, religion, and health care?" We group the responses in three categories: "none," "some," or "a great deal of influence."[5]

In the cross-sectional sample, 71 percent of nonresident fathers had seen their children during the past year. The average father visited his child several times a year and reported having little or no influence on how the child was raised. In the longitudinal sample, approximately 90 percent of fathers had visited their child during the past year. The average father saw his child one to three times a month and reported having between no influence and some influence. We would expect fathers' involvement to be higher in the longitudinal sample than in the cross-sectional sample because parents in the first sample had been separated or divorced for a shorter period of time—an average of 3.3 years for families in the longitudinal sample and 7 years for those in the cross-section. Contact and influence decline over time, along with child support (Seltzer 1991). The cross-sectional sample also includes families in which the child was born outside of marriage; fathers' involvement is lower in these families than in divorced families (Seltzer 1991).

PARENTAL CONFLICT   Postseparation conflict between parents was measured by the question: "How much conflict do you have over . . . ," followed by six different aspects of child-rearing: where the child lives, how he or she is raised, how the resident parent spends money on the child, how the nonresident parent spends money on the child, the time and visits the nonresident parent spends with the child, and the nonresident parent's financial contribution to the child's support. Response categories differed between the two NSFH waves. At wave 1, response categories were: "none," "some," "a great deal." At wave 2, they were: "none," "a little," "some," "pretty much," or "a great deal." In the cross-sectional sample, about 48 percent of parents reported some conflict, and nearly one-quarter reported a great deal of conflict (high conflict) in at least one area. In the longitudinal sample, about 84 percent of parents reported some conflict, and about one-third reported high conflict.[6]

STATE POLICIES AND PRACTICES   To measure state policies and practices, we used data from the Office of Child Support Enforcement (OCSE) and a data file on state child support statues compiled by Irwin Garfinkel and his colleagues (1995). All variables are measured in 1985, a year or so before the reference period for the 1987 cross-sectional sample. *State effectiveness* was measured as the amount of child support collected per OCSE case (multiplied by 1,000). *State effort* was measured as OCSE expenditures per female-headed family in the state (multiplied by 1,000). In addition to these "state practice" variables, we also used information on state laws and policies to create dummy variables indicating whether particular laws had been enacted. *Guidelines* indicates whether a state used legislative guidelines as the presumption to set child support orders. *Paternity* indicates whether the state allowed paternity to be established up to age eighteen for any child born out of wedlock. *Central agency* identifies states in which a central agency was used to collect and distribute child support payments. For the cross-sectional sample, we used information on current state of residence because the data do not include information about where the family lived when the child was born or at divorce. We do not use state policy variables in the longitudinal analysis because the longitudinal sample is too small. However, both the cross-sectional and longitudinal analyses control for per capita income and unemployment rate for the respondent's current state of residence.

PARENT AND HOUSEHOLD CHARACTERISTICS We use a variety of measures of family characteristics to take account of potential sources of spurious associations between child support and father's contact with children and child support and conflict between parents. For the cross-sectional sample, we controlled for the mother's age, race or ethnicity, and education, whether the random child was born inside marriage, age and sex of the child, and number of children in the household. All of these variables are intended to measure family characteristics at the time of separation or divorce. We also controlled for time since separation (child's age for nonmarital families).

For the longitudinal sample, we had additional information on father's age and education, as well as important characteristics of the family before separation, including both parents' incomes, the quality of parents' relationship with each other, the quality of the father-child relationship, and father's attitudes about paternal responsibility. All of these characteristics were measured in 1987. The relationship between the father and child was measured by a self-administered item asking: "How would you describe your relationship with each of these children?" Responses range from "very poor" to "excellent" on a seven-point scale. We recoded responses on this highly skewed variable to a dichotomous variable indicating whether the father reported an excellent relationship with the random child at time 1. We also identified cases in which the father's report on this item was missing. Although these variables capture a limited number of aspects of fathers' attachment to children and commitment to child-rearing, the range of measures of paternal involvement before separation improves on most past work, which, at best, relies on retrospective reports on these characteristics.

The quality of the parents' relationship with each other at time 1 was measured in three ways. The first identifies couples who reported that open disagreements occurred at least several times a week during the previous year about: household tasks, money, spending time together, sex, having another child, in-laws, and the children. The second was a measure of aggressive conflict styles. This dichotomous variable was coded 1 if the parents reported that they "argue heatedly" very often or always, or if either parent reported that during the previous year he or she had engaged in physical violence, including throwing things at each other or other physical arguments. The third indicator of time 1 marital quality was the mean of both parents' responses to the question: "Taking things all together, how would you describe your marriage?" The response scale ranged from 1 ("very unhappy") to 7 ("very happy").[7]

Fathers' attitudes about paternal responsibility in 1987 were measured by two questions. The first question asked respondents whether they agreed with the statement: "It is much better for everyone if the man earns the main living and the woman takes care of the home and family." The average father responded in the middle—neither agreeing or disagreeing. The second question asked about agreement with the statement: "Parents ought to help their children with college expenses." Response categories ranged from "strongly disagree" to "strongly agree." We treat this as a dummy variable in which 1 equals "agree" or "strongly agree." Nearly 60 percent of nonresident fathers fell into this category.[8]

LOW-INCOME FAMILIES AND FAMILIES OF CHILDREN BORN OUT OF WEDLOCK   As noted earlier, only the cross-sectional sample can be used to examine separately low-income fathers and fathers of children born outside of marriage. We consider low-income families to be those in which the mother had no more than a high school education. Approximately 69 percent (weighted) of the cross-sectional sample is low-income by this definition. Note that the cross-sectional sample does not include father's income or education. Although we considered a more restrictive definition of potentially low-income families, such as families in which the mother did not complete high school, the resulting sample size would have been too small to support the statistical analyses we conduct. About half (weighted) of the sample are mothers of children born outside of marriage. Mothers of children born in nonmarital relationships are more likely to be low-income (78 percent) compared to divorced and maritally separated mothers (61 percent).

The next section reports the results for both the cross-sectional and longitudinal analyses.

RESULTS

Child Support, Father's Involvement, and Conflict: Zero-Order Associations

Table 6.1 reports zero-order associations between child support and measures of father involvement and parental conflict for the cross-sectional sample.

The table shows that fathers who paid child support during the past year were more likely to see their children than fathers who did not pay. In 1987 just over 50 percent of nonpayers saw their children at least once during the year, as compared with 86 to 95 percent of payers (column 1). Among fathers who paid something, the relationship between the amount paid and the likelihood of some contact was quite weak. Moreover, conditional on some contact, we found no association between payments and weekly contact between fathers and children (column 2). In contrast, the relationship between the amount paid and the level of father's influence was positive. The higher the payment, the more likely the father was to have a great deal of influence.

The results based on the longitudinal sample are similar to those based on the cross-sectional sample. Table 6.2 shows that fathers who paid child support were more likely to have seen their children during the past year than fathers who did not pay, but the amount paid was not strongly related to contact. The same pattern holds for weekly visits (column 2) as in the cross-sectional data. Conditional on some contact, the amount paid is not associated with weekly visits. Nor is there an association between child support and influence. Indeed, fathers who paid the least

TABLE 6.1 / Associations Between Child Support, Father's Involvement, and Conflict After Separation, 1987 Cross-Sectional Sample

	Any Visits (Percent)	Weekly Visits, If Any (Percent)	Father Has a Great Deal of Influence (Percent)	Percent of Total
Child support and visits				
Annual child support				
$0	54.8***	37.0	5.9***	55.4
$1–1,499	86.1	36.1	12.1	15.0
$1,500–3,499	93.3	41.5	18.8	16.9
$3,500+	94.9	41.2	21.1	12.7
All cases	71.1	38.5	10.9	100.0

	Any Conflict (Percent)	High Conflict, If Any Conflict (Percent)
Child support and conflict		
Annual child support		
$0	37.6***	59.7***
$1–1,499	62.5	53.5
$1,500–3,499	58.2	38.4
$3,500+	65.3	37.1
All cases	48.4	50.3

	Any Conflict (Percent)	High Conflict, If Any Conflict (Percent)	Percent of Total
Involvement and conflict			
Frequency of visits			
No visits	17.7***	68.4**	28.9
Between once a year and 1 to 3 times a month	59.9	45.7	43.7
Weekly or more	62.3	51.9	27.4
Father has a great deal of influence			
No	47.2*	50.9	89.5
Yes	58.0	46.1	10.5
All cases			100.0

Source: National Survey of Families and Households, wave 1.

Notes: Children who live with their mother and whose father is the nonresident parent. Data are reports from resident mothers. Distributions use weighted data. $N = 1,302$. F-test for differences among means significant at: *$p \leq .05$, **$p \leq .01$, ***$p \leq .001$.

TABLE 6.2 / Associations Between Child Support, Father's Involvement, and Conflict After Separation, 1987 to 1992 Longitudinal Sample

	Any Visits (Percent)	Weekly Visits, If Any (Percent)	Father Has a Great Deal of Influence (Percent)	Percent of Total
Child support and visits				
Annual child support				
$0	72.5***	36.1*	7.2	19.2
$1–1,499	85.5	66.6	15.0	11.5
$1,500–3,499	93.3	27.9	3.6	18.3
$3,500+	99.2	44.9	10.9	50.9
All cases	91.4	42.7	9.3	100.0

	Any Conflict (Percent)	High Conflict, If Any Conflict (Percent)
Child support and conflict		
Annual child support		
$0	79.0	70.1***
$1–1,499	92.4	40.5
$1,500–3,499	84.5	52.0
$3,500+	83.8	25.1
All cases	84.0	40.1

	Any Conflict (Percent)	High Conflict, If Any Conflict (Percent)	Percent of Total
Involvement and conflict			
Frequency of visits			
No visits	74.0	100.0***	8.6
Between once a year and 1 to 3 times a month	85.4	45.9	52.4
Weekly or more	84.3	20.7	39.0
All cases			100.0
Father has a great deal of influence			
No	84.4	43.6*	90.7
Yes	79.9	4.7	9.3
All cases			100.0

Source: NSFH, waves 1 and 2.

Notes: Children whose parents separated between waves, who live with their mother, and whose father is the nonresident parent. Distributions use weighted data. $N = 187$. Column totals may not equal 100 percent due to rounding. F-test for differences among means significant at: *$p \le .05$, **$p \le .01$, ***$p \le .001$.

amount of child support (but not zero) had about the same amount of contact with their children and marginally more influence in decisions about the children than fathers who paid the most. In sum, both the cross-sectional and longitudinal samples suggest that the critical factor in determining a nonresident father's involvement is *whether* he pays child support as opposed to *how much* he pays.

The second panel of table 6.1 shows the relationships between child support payments and parental conflict in the cross-sectional sample. As before, nonpayers were less likely to experience conflict than payers (column 1), an indication that some parents may avoid each other completely in order to limit conflict and disagreements. The association between payments and conflict also may occur because parents who see one another have more opportunity to disagree about how the child support money should be spent.

Conditional on some conflict, fathers who paid no child support were somewhat more likely to experience high conflict than fathers who paid something (column 2), but the amount paid was inversely related to the incidence of high conflict. The pattern was more or less similar for the longitudinal sample on the association between payments and "any" or "high" conflict (see table 6.2).

The last panel of table 6.1 provides some additional evidence that parents may avoid each other to minimize conflict. When fathers do not see their children, parents are much less likely to report conflict. However, among those who report some conflict, nonvisitors experience the most (columns 1 and 2). Notice that in the longitudinal sample (table 6.2), in which parents had been recently divorced or separated and were likely to be negotiating rights and responsibilities, the incidence of high conflict is inversely related to the frequency of visits.

The pattern in the zero-order associations suggest that the difference between fathers who pay child support and fathers who do not pay may be more important for conflict than the difference between fathers who pay a small amount and fathers who pay a lot. More universalistic child support orders and collection strategies are likely to increase the percentage of nonresident fathers who pay something, however modest. The effect of reforms on the percentage of nonresident fathers who pay large amounts of child support is more ambiguous, because amounts of child support orders depend on variation in guideline formulas, on the distribution of parents' incomes, and on whether the guidelines are actually implemented and enforced. Differences among nonresident fathers in amounts of support paid may reflect both differences in predivorce family relationships and variation in fathers' ability to pay support. The difference between paying even a very small amount and paying nothing is more likely to be the result of variation in fathers' predivorce relationships than in their financial resources.[9]

Child Support and Father's Involvement

Table 6.3 reports results from multivariate models using the 1987 cross-sectional sample. We begin by estimating reduced-form models that provide information about the effects of state policies and practices on fathers' involvement. The results

TABLE 6.3 / Effects of Child Support Practices and Payments on Nonresident Fathers' Behavior, 1987 Cross-Sectional Sample

	Any Visits		Frequency of Visits		Father's Influence	
	Coefficient	t	Coefficient	t	Coefficient	t
State practices, all fathers						
Effectiveness	.065	.22	2.07	1.73	1.17	2.48
Effectiveness squared	-.198	-.68	-2.04	-1.75	-1.13	-2.47
Effort	-.007	-.02	-1.11	-.76	-.592	-1.09
Guidelines	.012	.16	.603	2.01	—	—
Guidelines × child born in marriage	-.114	-1.18	-.339	-.88	—	—
Paternity	.058	.48	.679	1.41	.372	1.96
Paternity × child born in marriage	-.054	-.36	-.297	-.49	-.494	-2.05
Central agency	.018	.43	-.012	-.07	-.018	-.27
Central agency × child born in marriage	.020	.38	.054	.25	-.036	-.43
Observed child support						
All fathers						
Any child support (1 = yes)	.284	10.9	1.06	10.2	.355	8.52
Child support amount (thousands of dollars)	-.000	-.12	.026	2.22	.016	3.39
Nonmarital fathers						
Any child support	.262	4.74	1.08	5.09	.385	5.10
Child support amount	.019	1.14	.133	2.04	.021	.93
Low-income fathers						
Any child support	.296	9.16	1.15	8.94	.367	7.27
Child support amount	-.002	-.52	.006	.35	.014	2.03

(Table continues on p. 172.)

TABLE 6.3 / *Continued*

	Any Visits		Frequency of Visits		Father's Influence	
	Coefficient	*t*	Coefficient	*t*	Coefficient	*t*
Child support, instrumental variable						
All fathers						
Any child support	.118	.56	1.04	1.23	.947	2.69
Child support amount	−.010	−.43	.063	.67	−.023	−.48
Nonmarital fathers						
Any child support	.060	.16	1.36	.93	.824	1.54
Child support amount	−.024	−.10	−.414	−.46	.309	.87
Low-income fathers						
Any child support	−.052	−.12	.851	.50	1.84	2.60
Child support amount	−.007	−.08	−.054	−.16	−.284	−1.90

Source: NSFH, wave 1.

Notes: Children who live with their mother and whose father is the nonresident parent. Data are reports from resident mothers. Parameters are from OLS regressions. Other variables in the models are described in the text. Data are unweighted, $N = 1,302$ for all; 599 for nonmarital; 890 for low income. Dashes indicate variables excluded from model.

are reported in the first panel of table 6.3. Because some state policies and practices are expected to affect families differently, depending on parents' marital status at their child's birth, interaction terms were included to capture these different effects.

The first panel of table 6.3 shows the effects of state policies and practices on fathers' involvement, controlling for the family and state characteristics described earlier. The table shows that state policies and practices have some effect on fathers' involvement. None of the state variables is significantly related to "any visits"; two of the five policy/practice variables are significantly related to "frequency of visits," and another is nearly significant; and two affect "influence" (using one-tailed tests). Effectiveness of state collections, administrative guidelines, and paternity establishment to age eighteen increase frequency of visits. Both effectiveness of collections and paternity laws increase fathers' influence over children. Note that the interaction term shows that paternity laws increase the frequency of visits for fathers of children born outside of marriage but have essentially no effect on visits among divorced and separated fathers, as we would expect.

The next step in the analysis examines whether differences in child support payments at the individual level are associated with differences in fathers' behavior. The results are reported in the second panel of table 6.3. We provide separate estimates for all nonresident fathers, for fathers of children born out of wedlock, and for low-income fathers. The results, again reported net of other family characteristics, indicate that fathers who pay child support are more likely to visit their child, to see their child more frequently, and to influence how their child is raised than fathers who do not pay child support. The critical factor for maintaining contact is whether a father pays *any* child support rather than how much he pays. However, the amount of support paid is also positively associated with frequency of visits and influence.[10] The results for nonmarital fathers and low-income fathers are similar to those for all fathers, except that the coefficients for "amount paid" are not always statistically significant for these groups.

The results in the second panel could be interpreted as showing that stronger child support enforcement will increase fathers' involvement, but the results are also consistent with the claim that fathers who care about their children are more likely to both pay child support and stay involved with their children. It is important to distinguish between these two explanations because they have very different policy implications. If paying child support *causes* fathers to see their children more often and to have more influence over how they are raised, then stricter enforcement will increase the proportion of nonresident fathers who are involved with their children. If the relationship between payments and visits is due to some unmeasured characteristic—such as fathers' concern for their children—changes in child support policies and practices are unlikely to lead to increases in fathers' involvement.

To address this issue, we used instrumental variables to measure the effects of child support payments (whether they are made, and in what amount) on fathers' behavior. The instrumental variables are intended to purge the child support coefficients of unobserved characteristics of fathers and families and therefore to provide unbiased estimates of the "true" effect of stricter enforcement on parental involvement when the statistical model is properly specified. The third panel of table 6.3 reports the coefficients from the instrumental variables models. For the estimates for all nonresident fathers, we are reasonably confident that both sets of instruments—those for "any payment" and those for "amount of payment"—are adequate. We are also confident that the instruments are acceptable for "any payment" for the subsamples of nonmarital and low-income fathers, although the instruments are weaker for "any payment" among low-income fathers than among nonmarital fathers. The instruments for "amount of payment" are very weak for both of these subsamples.[11]

The coefficients in the third panel of table 6.3 indicate that stricter child support enforcement is likely to increase the amount of influence fathers have over their children. The results also suggest that enforcement may increase the frequency of visits, but the effect is not statistically significant. In contrast to the results in the second panel, what matters is whether a father pays support, not how much he pays.[12] The results for the effects on influence of paying any child support are similar for nonmarital fathers and all nonresident fathers, except that the coefficients are not statistically significant for nonmarital fathers. We ignore the coefficients on amount of child support for nonmarital and low-income fathers because the instruments for this variable are inadequate. The results for low-income fathers are similar to those for nonmarital fathers for frequency of visits, but the effect on influence of paying any child support attains statistical significance. This pattern suggests that some of the effects observed in the second panel are more likely to be causal than spurious and that stricter child support enforcement is likely to increase fathers' influence over their children.

Child Support and Parental Conflict

Table 6.4 reports the effects of child support payments on parental conflict, using the same sample that was used for table 6.3. We examine two indicators of parental conflict: whether the parents experience "any conflict," and whether they experience "high conflict."

Most of the state policy/practice variables are only weakly related to parental conflict. Just one of the policy variables—effectiveness (collection rate)—has a close to significant association with "any conflict," and only three variables—guidelines, paternity laws, and whether payments are made through a central agency—have moderate effects on "high conflict." The effect of collections through a central agency is positive for divorced parents but has no effect on those whose children were born out of wedlock.

The second panel of table 6.4 reports the net effects of child support payments on parental conflict, using individuals' reports. The coefficients in column 1 show that families in which the nonresident father pays child support are more likely to experience "some conflict" than families in which the father does not pay. The risk of conflict declines as payments go up, but the latter effect is not statistically significant at conventional levels. The results are similar for nonmarital and for low-income fathers.

TABLE 6.4 / Effects of Child Support Practices and Payments on Conflict Between Parents, 1987 Cross-Sectional Sample

	Any Conflict		High Conflict	
	Coefficient	t	Coefficient	t
State practices, all fathers				
Effectiveness	.332	.96	.341	1.12
Effectiveness squared	−.504	−1.49	−.331	−1.11
Effort	.000	.00	−.083	−.22
Guidelines	−.017	−.19	.029	.38
Guidelines × child born in marriage	−.047	−.42	.145	1.47
Paternity	.017	.12	−.193	−1.57
Paternity × child born in marriage	−.103	−.58	.208	1.34
Central agency	−.008	−.16	−.042	−.97
Central agency × child born in marriage	.025	.40	.107	1.94
Observed child support				
All fathers				
Any child support (1 = yes)	.225	7.24	.076	2.71
Child support amount (thousands of dollars)	−.005	−1.34	−.003	−.98
Nonmarital fathers				
Any child support	.256	4.34	.165	3.22
Child support amount	−.019	−1.04	−.020	−1.29
Low-income fathers				
Any child support	.237	6.27	.077	2.27
Child support amount	−.007	−1.35	−.010	−2.12
Child support, instrumental variable				
All fathers				
Any child support	−.193	−.55	−.155	−.69
Child support amount	.003	.10	.073	2.91
Nonmarital fathers				
Any child support	−.115	−.26	−.001	−.003
Child support amount	.396	1.84	.401	1.87
Low-income fathers				
Any child support	−.448	−.92	−.673	−1.52
Child support amount	.073	.98	.230	2.53

Source: NSFH, wave 1.

Notes: Children who live with their mother and whose father is the nonresident parent. Data are reports from resident mothers. Parameters are from OLS regressions. Other variables in the models are described in the text. Data are unweighted; N = 1,302 for all; 599 for nonmarital; 890 for low income.

These findings are not very surprising. We know that fathers who pay support are more likely to be involved with their children than fathers who do not pay support, and we would expect parents who have contact with their children (and with each other) to experience more disagreement than parents who have no contact. Furthermore, some disagreement may actually be good for children insofar as it indicates that both parents are actively engaged in raising their child. The more serious question, for children's well-being, is whether child support increases "high conflict." The results reported in the last two columns of the second panel suggest that it does. Families in which the nonresident father pays child support are more likely to experience high levels of parental conflict than families in which the father pays nothing. Conflict declines as payments increase, but this effect is fairly small and only statistically significant among low-income fathers.

The third panel reports the coefficients from the instrumental variables models that try to take account of unmeasured characteristics that affect both child support and conflict. Fathers' payment of child support decreases conflict between parents (both "any conflict" and "high conflict") for all of the subsamples, but the effects only approach statistical significance for low-income fathers. This is the opposite of the pattern in the second panel, suggesting that the results in that panel are due to other factors that explain both child support and conflict. The instrumental variables results in the last panel show that the effect on high conflict of the amount of child support is positive and statistically significant for the full sample of nonresident fathers. Higher child support payments increase the incidence of high conflict, net of other factors. The positive effect of the amount of child support payments on conflict supports concern that strict enforcement of child support may increase children's exposure to conflict between their parents. Note that because of the weakness of the instruments for child support payments for the nonmarital and low-income subsamples, we do not attempt to interpret variation across samples in the signs of the coefficients for child support amounts.

To provide a way to interpret the combined effects on conflict of the two child support variables, "any payment," and "amount of payment," we conducted a simple simulation based on the instrumental variables results. We assumed that all families had the characteristics of the average NSFH respondent, but that the amount of child support paid varies. If no one paid any child support, about 57 percent of the families would have some conflict between parents, and 20 percent would have high levels of conflict. If all nonresident fathers paid $2,000 a year in child support, conflict would be reduced: 38 percent of families would have "any conflict" between parents, and the incidence of "high conflict" would be approximately stable at 19 percent. Increasing child support collections to $3,000 a year for each family would have virtually no effect on the percentage of families who report at least some conflict, compared to $2,000 a year, but would increase the incidence of high conflict to about 26 percent. If child support payments rose to $5,000 a year, this would result in a very small increase in the incidence of any conflict (39 percent), but the higher payments would greatly increase the share of families with high levels of conflict, to nearly 41 percent. Recall that the mean annual payment for this sample is a little over

$1,500. Only about 7 percent of nonresident fathers in the weighted sample pay $5,000 or more a year in child support. However, under child support guidelines in some states, a nonresident father with two children and an annual income of $20,000, would be expected to pay 25 percent of his income in child support, or $5,000. Thus, an increase in child support collections to a level prescribed by state guidelines would increase dramatically the percentage who experience high conflict.

The finding that payments per se do not increase the risk of high conflict is inconsistent with the argument that fathers who do not pay are just "disagreeable men" who cannot get along with their former partners and that bringing these men into the system will inevitably lead to higher conflict. Rather, our findings are more consistent with the notion that fathers who pay child support will try to monitor how their money is spent, since we would expect monitoring efforts to increase as payments go up, and that the monitoring is likely to lead to conflict between parents.

Interestingly, the information from the previous table may provide a clue as to why increases in payments lead to increases in conflict. If fathers expect their influence to grow as their payments increase, and if mothers are correct that additional payments do *not* lead to additional influence (as shown in table 6.3, the third panel), then the gap between expectations and reality may be a source of conflict. Mothers may accept the fact that fathers who pay child support are entitled to some say in child-rearing decisions but resist attempts to exercise too much authority. Clearly much more research is needed on these questions, including studies of the sources and nature of interhousehold conflict between parents.

Child Support, Fathers' Involvement, and Conflict: Longitudinal Results

In the final section of the analysis, we use the longitudinal data to examine the effects of child support on fathers' involvement and parental conflict. The availability of detailed information on fathers' characteristics and family relationships prior to separation allows us to adjust for factors associated with child support and fathers' involvement. This complements the instrumental variables approach, in which we try to take account of these characteristics using statistical procedures, but without observing the characteristics directly. The longitudinal data provide another way to address the question of whether the effects of child support payments are spurious or causal. In our discussion of the results, we compare the results from the longitudinal data with results from the cross-sectional data, bearing in mind that the samples differ significantly in composition. (For example, there are formerly marrieds only in the longitudinal sample, but nonmarital as well as formerly married parents in the cross-sectional sample.)

The first column of table 6.5 shows the coefficients for the effects on contact and conflict of the child support variables for the baseline model. The child support effects take account of sociodemographic characteristics of the family, child's age

TABLE 6.5 / Effects of Child Support on Father-Child Contact and Conflict Between Separated Parents, 1987 to 1992 Longitudinal Sample and 1987 Cross-Sectional Sample

| | Longitudinal Sample | | | | Cross-Sectional Sample | | | |
| | (1) Baseline | | (2) Adjusted | | (3) Observed | | (4) Instrumental Variables | |
	Coefficient	t	Coefficient	t	Coefficient	t	Coefficient	t
Any visits								
Any support (1 = yes)	.175	3.13	.153	2.54	.284	10.9	.118	.56
Amount of support (thousands of dollars)	.002	.40	.003	.75	−.000	−.12	−.010	.43
Frequency of visits								
Any support	.800	2.81	.754	2.48	1.06	10.2	1.04	1.23
Amount of support	−.008	−.38	−.008	−.36	.026	2.22	.063	.67
Influence								
Any support	.465	3.51	.428	3.00	.385	8.52	.947	2.69
Amount of support	.003	.29	.006	.57	.016	3.39	−.023	−.48
Any conflict								
Any support	.172	2.08	.173	2.00	.225	7.24	−.193	−.55
Amount of support	−.006	−.92	−.004	−.61	−.005	−1.34	.003	.10
High conflict								
Any support	−.091	−.88	−.061	−.56	.076	2.71	−.155	−.69
Amount of support	−.015	−1.99	−.019	−2.42	−.003	−.98	.073	2.91

Source: The longitudinal sample is defined in table 6.2, N = 187. The cross-sectional sample is defined in table 6.1, N = 1,302.

Notes: Parameters are from OLS regressions. Column 1 shows net effects, excluding information on fathers' characteristics. Column 2 shows net effects taking account of fathers' characteristics, controlling for sociodemographic characteristics, attitudes toward parental responsibilities, and the quality of family relationships before separation. Column 3 repeats results for all fathers from the second sections of tables 6.3 and 6.4. Column 4 repeats results for all fathers from the third sections of tables 6.3 and 6.4.

and sex, and time separated. The second column presents coefficients from models that also control for fathers' characteristics prior to separation, including father's income and education, father's attachment to children, the quality of the parents' relationship with each other, and father's attitudes about parenting prior to separation or divorce. The logic of the comparison between these columns is analogous to that in the comparison between the observed effects of child support (the second panels in tables 6.3 and 6.4) and the instrumental variables effects (the third panels in tables 6.3 and 6.4). For convenience, we repeat the cross-sectional results in the last two columns of table 6.5. The major difference between the results in columns 1 and 3 is the sample of fathers: the longitudinal sample represents fathers who have been separated or divorced for up to seven years (just over three years on average), whereas the cross-sectional sample represents both nonmarital and divorced fathers who have been separated up to eighteen years (seven years on average).

What do the estimates from the longitudinal data tell us about the effects of child support on fathers' involvement? What do they tell us about causality? To what extent do the two samples present similar stories? With respect to the first two questions, the longitudinal estimates show that fathers who pay at least some child support are more likely to visit their child, to see their child more frequently, and to have more influence over how the child is raised than fathers who pay no support. The estimates suggest that it is whether or not a father pays support rather than the amount paid that determines his involvement. When we adjust for preseparation differences, the coefficients become only slightly smaller and remain statistically significant. The fact that positive effects persist even after controlling for preseparation characteristics lends support to the argument that the effects of child support on fathers' involvement are causal rather than spurious.

With respect to the third question—do the two samples tell similar stories about whether the effects on fathers' involvement of child support are causal or spurious?—the answer is mixed. In terms of fathers' involvement, the longitudinal estimates point to a causal effect for all three indicators of involvement (column 2, adjusted), whereas the estimates from the instrumental variables model point to causal effects for fathers' influence, a possible causal interpretation of the effects of paying support on frequency of visits, and no evidence of causation for whether the father has any visits (column 4, instrumental variables). The coefficients consistently show that amount of child support does not have a statistically significant effect on fathers' involvement for either the cross-sectional or longitudinal samples. We interpret the results as indicating that stronger child support enforcement, at least bringing more fathers into the child support system and collecting some child support from them, is likely to increase fathers' involvement with children in terms of their influence over their children and possibly in terms of visitation.

Looking next at conflict, we find that the longitudinal estimates show that whether the father pays any child support increases the incidence of "any conflict" but reduces the incidence of "high conflict." The effect of paying support on high conflict is not statistically significant, however. The amount of support paid reduces the incidence of any conflict and of high conflict. The coefficients for amount of child support are statistically significant for high conflict but not for whether there is any conflict. These effects persist even after controlling for all of the preseparation characteristics.

These results for "any conflict" are consistent with those from the cross-sectional analysis of observed child support but not with the results from the instrumental variables. The latter suggest that, if it has any effect at all, paying child support reduces the incidence of any conflict between parents. Amount of child support paid reduces the chance of any conflict in the longitudinal sample, but the coefficients are not statistically significant (columns 1 and 2). The effect of child support on high conflict is quite different for the longitudinal results and the instrumental variables results. The second column (adjusted) shows that the more child support the nonresident father pays, the less likely the parents are to have high levels of conflict, once the father's characteristics and the quality of the family relationships are taken into account. In contrast, the instrumental variables results summarized in column 4 show that higher payments increase the incidence of high conflict.

Because the two samples differ in important ways, including amount of time since separation, whether the parents were ever married to each other, and families' socioeconomic status, it is difficult to resolve the inconsistent findings between the longitudinal and cross-sectional samples. Differences between the two sets of results may be attributable to differences in the composition of the samples or to the fact that families in the longitudinal sample all separated under a more rigorous child support regime—that is, after passage of the Family Support Act of 1988—than the families in the cross-sectional sample, who were separated by 1987 or early 1988. To examine whether differences in sample composition account for the inconsistent results, we estimated the instrumental variables model restricting the cross-sectional sample to those whose children were born in marriage and who had been separated for six years or less. In this subsample, the effect on high conflict of the amount of child support paid remains positive, but the coefficient is smaller than in the full cross-sectional sample and is not statistically significant (not shown). Neither the longitudinal analysis, with its explicit controls for fathers' characteristics and the quality of family relationships, nor the instrumental variables approach, which takes account of these factors implicitly, provides the definitive answer to whether increasing child support payments will expose more children to high levels of conflict between parents. That the instrumental variables result shows a positive effect of amount of child support paid on the incidence of high conflict suggests that stricter child support enforcement may have costs as well as benefits for children. Concern about these costs is tempered, somewhat, by the inconsistency of our results between the cross-sectional and longitudinal samples.

SUMMARY AND CONCLUSIONS

We find that child support payments increase nonresident fathers' influence over children and may increase frequency of contact between fathers and children. Both the instrumental variables models in the cross-sectional analysis and the longitudinal analysis, in which we take account of fathers' income and many aspects of the quality of family relationships prior to separation, suggest that requiring fathers to pay at least some child support will increase their involvement with their children. The results are less consistent across the two samples and analytic strategies for whether requiring some child support will increase the percentage of fathers who see their children at all. In general, we find no effect of the amount of support paid on fathers' involvement, once we take into account whether the father pays any support at all. Our estimates of the effects on contact of child support probably represent an upper bound for the potential consequences of increased child support enforcement. Our analyses assume that the direction of causation is from child support to visitation and influence. However, spending time with their children may increase fathers' knowledge about the children's material needs and increase their incentive to pay child support. To the extent that visiting affects fathers' child support contributions, our findings may overstate the effects on contact of more rigorous child support enforcement. A dynamic interpretation of what might happen under a regime of strict enforcement would be that once a father begins to pay child support, his efforts to monitor how the child support money is spent may increase visitation, and by spending more time with his children, the nonresident father who can afford to do so may further increase his financial investment in his children.

Our findings about the potential effects of child support enforcement on children's exposure to conflict are less consistent and, to some extent, less optimistic. Our longitudinal results, in which we control for how well parents got along before separation, show that paying any child support increases the incidence of conflict between parents. That we observe this effect even after taking account of the quality of parents' relationships before divorce limits the possibility that the association between paying child support and conflict occurs because fathers are more likely to pay support when they have a good relationship with the mother of their children. Whether fathers pay any child support has no effect on the incidence of high conflict between parents in either the longitudinal or cross-sectional instrumental variables results. Although the longitudinal data suggest that for recently divorced parents the amount of support paid may slightly decrease the incidence of high conflict, these results differ substantially from those for the cross-sectional sample. There we find that the amount of child support has a strong positive effect. Our results imply that if all nonresident fathers were to pay $3,000 a year, more than a quarter of the families would experience serious conflict. Serious disagreements are especially damaging to children's adjustment. This finding suggests that an unintended consequence of child support reform may be to increase children's exposure to conflict between their parents. One way to minimize the risk of high conflict would be to place an upper limit on the amount of child support owed by a nonresident parent.

Such a limit would be consistent with child support policies in European countries where child support obligations are strictly enforced but order levels are relatively low. These other countries can afford to keep private child support obligations low because they provide more public benefits for all children, including children with nonresident parents. In the absence of substantial public support for child-rearing, parents in this country must bear more of the costs. In any case, the potential negative effects of conflict must be balanced against the improved economic security that child support enforcement provides children.

Our investigation of the effects of child support on fathers' involvement and conflict between parents for nonmarital fathers and for low-income fathers shows that more rigorous enforcement is likely to increase the fathers' influence, regardless of fathers' economic status or the parents' marital status at their child's birth. This is notable in light of the fact that low-income fathers are more likely than other fathers to make child support payments to the state welfare agency, with the mother receiving little of each payment. Even under these conditions, our findings are consistent with the idea that parents accord greater legitimacy to fathers' participation in child-rearing decisions when they pay support than when they do not pay support. Our finding that paying more support does not increase the amount of fathers' influence in child-rearing decisions points to a likely source of conflict between parents. However, our results derive from a comparison between different fathers who pay higher and lower amounts of support. Without longitudinal data on the effects on influence of increases (or decreases) over time in the same father's payments, we cannot determine whether a father can acquire more influence by increasing the amount of child support he pays (for example, by paying $3,000 a year instead of $2,000).

Our findings shed little light on the potential effects on conflict of increased child support enforcement for nonmarital and low-income fathers. Although the signs of the coefficients are usually similar to those for all fathers, the quality of the statistical instruments for child support amounts is much lower for the samples of nonmarital and low-income fathers than for the full sample. It is notable, however, that among low-income fathers, those who pay at least some support are less likely to experience high conflict than those who pay no support. This effect is larger in magnitude than for the full sample or the sample of nonmarital fathers. Although the effect of paying any support is not statistically significant, the ratio of the coefficient to its standard error is large enough to merit our attention. Taken with the (admittedly unstable) positive effect of amounts paid on conflict, these results suggest that the child support obligations of low-income fathers should be considered carefully. Low-income fathers' participation in the child support system may reduce conflict as long as these men are not required to pay much higher percentages of their incomes compared to the percentages paid by higher-income fathers (see chapters 1 and 3 in this volume).

The inconsistent findings for low-income fathers and all nonresident fathers, and between the longitudinal and cross-sectional samples we employ, point to the need for more information about fathers who differ in their treatment by the child support system. Our reliance on mothers' education as a substitute for information about fathers' potential economic resources limits our ability to examine the effects of child support enforcement on fathers with low incomes. Nevertheless, our findings suggest that there may be significant differences in the experiences of those who are poor and those who are not poor. Particularly because more rigorous enforcement may increase fathers' participation in child-rearing after separation, evidence that child support enforcement may also increase extreme conflict between parents is a warning to policy-makers to use caution in balancing the potential financial gains to children against their possible psychic costs.

APPENDIX

TABLE 6A.1 / Weighted Means and Standard Deviations for Analysis Samples

	1987 Cross-Sectional Sample		1987 to 1992 Longitudinal Sample	
	Mean	Standard Deviation	Mean	Standard Deviation
Child support				
Any child support received (1 = yes)	.45		.81	
Child support received (thousands of dollars)	1.53	3.87	5.26	6.14
Amount received (if any)	3.43	5.20	6.51	6.21
Father involvement				
Any visits (1 = yes)	.71		.91	
Frequency of visits (1–6)	3.16	1.79	4.06	1.50
Father's influence (1–3)	1.41	.68	1.68	.64
Parental conflict				
Any conflict (1 = yes)	.48		.84	
Any high conflict (1 = yes)	.24		.34	
Background characteristics				
Mother's age	32.6	7.94	29.7	6.08
Race/ethnicity				
White non-Hispanic	.58		.86[a]	
Black	.32		.09	
Mexican American	.06		.05	
Other	.04		—	
Mother's education[b]				
Less than high school	.23		.15	
High school	.46		.47	
Some college	.23		.18	
College degree or higher	.07		.19	
Duration eligible for child support	7.03	4.93	3.31	1.78
Eligible less than one year (1 = yes)	.09		.11	
Child born in marriage (1 = yes)	.53		—	
Number of children	1.78	.96	1.82	.91
Child's age	8.95	5.54	10.2	3.42
Female child (1 = yes)	.47		.53	
State per capita income (thousands of dollars)[c]	13.8	1.90	18.3	2.49
State unemployment[d]	7.49	1.85	5.46	1.21
Mother's income (tens of thousands of dollars)	—		1.37	2.33

(Table continues on p. 184.)

TABLE 6A.1 / *Continued*

	1987 Cross-Sectional Sample		1987 to 1992 Longitudinal Sample	
	Mean	Standard Deviation	Mean	Standard Deviation
State practices				
Effectiveness	.30	.19	—	
Effort	.14	.07	—	
Guidelines	.06		—	
Paternity	.02		—	
Central agency	.27		—	
Father's demographic characteristics				
Father's education[b]				
Less than high school	—		.09	
High school	—		.40	
Some college	—		.31	
College degree or higher	—		.19	
Father's income (tens of thousands of dollars	—		3.77	3.13
Father's age	—		32.4	6.48
Marital relations before separation				
High disagreement (1 = yes)	—		.39	
High aggression (1 = yes)	—		.51	
Marital happiness (1–7)	—		5.20	1.36
Father's relationship with child				
Excellent relationship (1 = yes)	—		.52	
Father's attitudes				
Traditional breadwinner role (1–5)	—		3.33	1.07
Help college expenses (1 = yes)	—		.59	
Number of cases	1,302		187	

Source: NSFH data on families in which children live with their mother and whose father is the nonresident parent.

Notes: Percentages may not equal 100 due to rounding.

[a] Includes two cases with other race/ethnic identification.

[b] Treated as a continuous variable in the longitudinal analysis.

[c] Measured for 1985 in the cross-sectional analysis, in 1990 in the longitudinal analysis.

[d] Measured for 1985 in the cross-sectional analysis, in 1989 in the longitudinal analysis.

TABLE 6A.2 / F-tests for Inclusion of Instruments in Reduced-Form Models

| | Dependent Variable | | | | | |
| | Any Visits | | Frequency of Visits | | Influence | |
	F, p	Instruments	F, p	Instruments	F, p	Instruments
All fathers						
Any child support	$5.00, p \leq .001$	1, 2, 6, 7	$5.00, p \leq .001$	1, 2, 6, 7	$5.00, p \leq .001$	1, 2, 6, 7
Amount of support	$2.87, p \leq .01$	1, 2, 3, 4, 5, 8, 9	$2.87, p \leq .01$	1, 2, 3, 4, 5, 8, 9	$2.56, p \leq .05$	1, 2, 3, 8, 9
Nonmarital fathers						
Any child support	$3.34, p \leq .05$	1, 2, 6	$3.34, p \leq .05$	1, 2, 6	$3.34, p \leq .05$	1, 2, 6
Amount of support	.50, N.S.	1, 2, 3, 4, 8	.50, N.S.	1, 2, 3, 4, 8	.53, N.S.	1, 2, 3, 8
Low-income fathers						
Any child support	$3.39, p \leq .01$	1, 2, 6, 7	$3.39, p \leq .01$	1, 2, 6, 7	$3.39, p \leq .01$	1, 2, 6, 7
Amount of support	.86, N.S.	1, 2, 3, 4, 5, 8, 9	.86, N.S.	1, 2, 3, 4, 5, 8, 9	1.14, N.S.	1, 2, 3, 8, 9

(Table continues on p. 186.)

TABLE 6A.2 / Continued

	Any Conflict		High Conflict	
	F, p	Instruments	F, p	Instruments
All fathers				
Any child support	3.06, $p \leq .05$	1, 6, 7	5.00, $p \leq .001$	1, 2, 6, 7
Amount of support	2.87, $p \leq .01$	1, 2, 3, 4, 5, 8, 9	2.87, $p \leq .01$	1, 2, 3, 4, 5, 8, 9
Nonmarital fathers				
Any child support	3.24, $p \leq .05$	1, 6	3.34, $p \leq .05$	1, 2, 6
Amount of support	.50, N.S.	1, 2, 3, 4, 8	.50, N.S.	1, 2, 3, 4, 8
Low-income fathers				
Any child support	2.50, $p \leq .10$	1, 6, 7	3.39, $p \leq .01$	1, 2, 6, 7
Amount of support	.86, N.S.	1, 2, 3, 4, 5, 8, 9	.86, N.S.	1, 2, 3, 4, 5, 8, 9

Notes: 1 = state effectiveness, 2 = state effectiveness squared, 3 = state effort, 4 = guidelines, 5 = guidelines × child born in marriage, 6 = paternity, 7 = paternity × child born in marriage, 8 = central agency, 9 = central agency × child born in marriage. See the text for definitions of variables. N.S. means not significant.

This chapter is based on a paper prepared for presentation at the conference "The Effects of Child Support Enforcement on Nonresident Fathers," Princeton University, September 14–16, 1995. The research was supported by grants from the National Institute of Child Health and Human Development (NICHHD) (HD–24571, HD–19375, and HD–29601). Support also came from the Center for Demography and Ecology at the University of Wisconsin, the Office of Population Research at Princeton University, and the Population Research Center at RAND. The National Survey of Families and Households (NSFH) was funded by the Center for Population Research of NICHHD and the National Institute on Aging. We thank Anne Case for advice on the statistical analysis, James Sweet, Diane Hansen, and other members of the NSFH research staff for help with the data, I-Fen Lin for able research assistance, and the conference participants and anonymous reviewers for helpful comments. Opinions expressed are our own.

NOTES

1. The 1992 reports from state Offices of Child Support Enforcement (OCSE) indicate that the percentage of all OCSE expenditures devoted to AFDC cases ranges from 85 percent in Oklahoma to 26 percent in Hawaii. The national average is 57 percent (U. S. Department of Health and Human Services 1992, table 26).

2. We report the IV estimates from OLS regression because this allows us to include both a dichotomous variable for whether any support was paid and a continuous variable for the amount of support paid in the same model. The TSLS results (not shown) include one child support variable at a time. We also used ordered logit or logistic regression to reestimate the OLS models for effects of observed child support on involvement and conflict, and the pattern of effects of the child support variables is generally the same.

3. We also include two cohabiting couples from wave 1 who formalized their union by marriage and then became separated or divorced by the second wave.

4. In the panel sample, more than 90 percent of children who spent most of the year in the mother's household spent at least two-thirds of the year with her. A similar percentage of children who spent most of the year with their father spent at least two-thirds of the year with him. These figures suggest that it is still uncommon for children whose parents have separated to spend large portions of the year with both parents.

5. For the cross-section, primary-respondent mothers who reported that they had not discussed the children with their father in the past year are all coded as "none" on the influence question because these mothers were not asked the influence question. At time 2 there were five response categories: "none," "a little," "some," "pretty much," and a "great deal of influence." We combined the three middle categories for consistency across the two samples.

6. Both waves of the NSFH asked about conflict between separated parents regardless of whether the parents talked to each other. This strategy was followed because parents may disagree about child support and related issues but still arrange to have nothing to do with each other. Stricter child support enforcement is likely to increase contact between parents in this type of highly conflicted family.

7. If one parent's report is missing, the happiness variable takes its value from the other parent's response. The three measures of relationship quality are correlated in the expected directions. For this sample, the correlation between disagreement and aggressive conflict style is .27, between disagreement and marital happiness is −.21, and between aggressive style and happiness is −.31.

8. We experimented in preliminary analyses with a third variable, whether the father said he wanted to be free of the responsibility of parenthood at time 1. Incorporating this additional measure of attitudes about paternal responsibility does not alter our conclusions.

9. Fathers' involvement with children and conflict between parents may also be a function of the amount of child support paid compared to the amount owed as part of a child support order. In this chapter, we consider child support payments only so that we can include both families with and without child support orders. Child support orders are less common among families of children born outside of marriage and low-income families, and an important aspect of this analysis is a consideration of how child support enforcement may affect these families.

10. When we examine the net effect on any contact of observed child support amounts using logistic regression, the coefficient for amount of support is positive and statistically significant.

11. F-tests for the statistical significance of the sets of instrumental variables in reduced-form models are reported in table 6A.2.

12. However, this result is sensitive to the treatment of outliers on the amount of child support paid. When nine cases are recoded to the ninety-ninth percentile on payments, the coefficient for the effect on frequency of visits of the amount of support paid becomes statistically significant in the instrumental variables model. The treatment of outliers has little effect on the pattern of statistical significance in other parts of the analysis for the full sample of fathers. All of the outliers occur in cases in which the parents were previously married. Just over half of them are families separated less than a full year. This illustrates the difficulty of obtaining good information about the flow of child support between very recently separated parents.

REFERENCES

Amato, Paul R., and Sandra J. Rezac. 1994. "Contact with Nonresident Parents, Interparental Conflict, and Children's Behavior." *Journal of Family Issues* 15(2): 191–207.

Arendell, Terry. 1992. "After Divorce: Investigations into Father Absence." *Gender and Society* 6(4): 562–86.

Block, Jack, Jeanne H. Block, and Per F. Gjerde. 1988. "Parental Functioning and the Home Environment in Families of Divorce: Prospective and Concurrent Analyses." *Journal of the American Academy of Child and Adolescent Psychiatry* 27(2): 207–13.

Braver, Sanford L., Sharlene A. Wolchik, Irwin N. Sandler, Virgil L. Sheets, Bruce Fogas, and R. Curtis Bay. 1993. "A Longitudinal Study of Noncustodial Parents: Parents Without Children." *Journal of Family Psychology* 7(1): 9–23.

Buchanan, Christy M., Eleanor E. Maccoby, and Sanford M. Dornbusch. 1991. "Caught Between Parents: Adolescents' Experience in Divorced Homes." *Child Development* 62(5): 1008–29.

Camara, Kathleen A., and Gary Resnick. 1988. "Interparental Conflict and Cooperation: Factors Moderating Children's Post-Divorce Adjustment." In *Impact of Divorce, Single Parenting and Stepparenting on Children,* edited by E. Mavis Hetherington and Josephine D. Aresteh. Hillsdale, N.J.: Erlbaum.

Cummings, E. Mark, and Jennifer L. Cummings. 1988. "A Process-Oriented Approach to Children's Coping with Adults' Angry Behavior." *Developmental Review* 8(3): 296–321.

Edin, Kathryne. 1995a. "Single Mothers and Child Support: Possibilities and Limits of Child Support Policy." *Child and Youth Services Review* 17(1/2): 203–30.

––––––. 1995b. "The Myths of Dependency and Self-Sufficiency: Women, Welfare, and Low-Wage Work." *Focus* 17(2): 1–9.

Emery, Robert E. 1982. "Interparental Conflict and the Children of Discord and Divorce." *Psychological Bulletin* 92(2): 310–30.

Furstenberg, Frank F., S. Philip Morgan, and Paul D. Allison. 1987. "Paternal Participation and Children's Well-Being." *American Sociological Review* 52(5): 695–701.

Furstenberg, Frank F., Christine Winquist Nord, James L. Peterson, and Nicholas Zill. 1983. "The Life Course of Children of Divorce." *American Sociological Review* 48(5): 695–701.

Garfinkel, Irwin, Cynthia Miller, Sara McLanahan, and Thomas L. Hanson. 1995. "Deadbeat Dads or Inept States? A Comparison of Child Support Enforcement Systems." Paper presented at the annual meeting of the Western Economics Association, San Diego, Calif. (July).

Hess, Robert D., and Kathleen A. Camara. 1979. "Post-Divorce Family Relationships as Mediating Factors in the Consequences of Divorce for Children." *Journal of Social Issues* 53(4): 79–96.

Hetherington, E. Mavis, Martha Cox, and Roger Cox. 1982. "Effects of Divorce on Parents and Children." In *Nontraditional Families: Parenting and Child Development,* edited by Michael E. Lamb. Hillsdale, N.J.: Erlbaum.

King, Valarie. 1994. "Nonresidential Father Involvement and Child Well-being: Can Dads Make a Difference?" *Journal of Family Issues* 15(1): 78–96.

Koch, Mary Ann P., and Carol R. Lowery. 1984. "Visitation and the Noncustodial Father." *Journal of Divorce* 8(2): 47–65.

Lund, Mary. 1987. "The Noncustodial Father: Common Challenges in Parenting After Divorce." In *Reassessing Fatherhood: New Observations on Fathers and the Modern Family,* edited by Charlie Lewis and Margaret O'Brien. London: Sage.

McLanahan, Sara, Judith A. Seltzer, Thomas L. Hanson, and Elizabeth Thomson. 1994. "Child Support Enforcement and Child Well-being: Greater Security or Greater Conflict?" In *Child Support and Child Well-being,* edited by Irwin Garfinkel, Sara McLanahan, and Philip K. Robins. Washington: Urban Institute Press.

Scoon-Rogers, Lydia, and Gordon H. Lester. 1995. "Child Support for Custodial Mothers and Fathers: 1991." *Current Population Report,* series P–60–187. Washington: U.S. Government Printing Office for the U.S. Bureau of the Census.

Seltzer, Judith A. 1990. "Child Support Reform and the Welfare of U.S. Children." NSFH Working Paper No. 34. Madison: University of Wisconsin, Center for Demography and Ecology, (http://ssc.wisc.edu/nsfh/home.htm).

––––––. 1991. "Relationships Between Fathers and Children Who Live Apart." *Journal of Marriage and the Family* 53(1): 79–101.

Seltzer, Judith A., Nora Cate Schaeffer, and Hong-wen Charng. 1989. "Family Ties After Divorce: The Relationship Between Visiting and Paying Child Support." *Journal of Marriage and the Family* 51(4): 1013–32.

Sen, Amartya K. 1990. "Gender and Cooperative Conflicts." In *Persistent Inequalities,* edited Irene Tinker. New York: Oxford University Press.

Sherwood, Kay E. 1992. "Child Support Obligations: What Fathers Say About Paying." In *What Fathers and Mothers Say About Child Support,* edited by Frank F. Furstenberg Jr., Kay E. Sherwood, and Mercer L. Sullivan. New York: Manpower Demonstration Research Corporation.

Sweet, James A., and Larry L. Bumpass. 1996. *The National Survey of Families and Households—Waves 1 and 2: Data Description and Documentation.* Madison: University of Wisconsin, Center for Demography and Ecology (http://ssc.wisc.edu/nsfh/home.htm).

Sweet, James, Larry Bumpass, and Vaughn Call. 1988. "The Design and Content of the National Survey of Families and Households." NSFH Working Paper No. 1. Madison: University of Wisconsin, Center for Demography and Ecology (http://ssc.wisc.edu/nsfh/home.htm).

U.S. Department of Health and Human Services, Office of Child Support Enforcement. 1992. *Child Support Enforcement: Seventeenth Annual Report to Congress.* Washington: U.S. Department of Health and Human Services.

Veum, Jonathan R. 1993. "The Relationship Between Child Support and Visitation: Evidence from Longitudinal Data." *Social Science Research* 22(3): 229–44.

Waller, Maureen R. 1997. "Redefining Fatherhood: Paternal Involvement, Masculinity, and Responsibility in the 'Other America.'" Ph.D. diss., Princeton University.

Wallerstein, Judith S., and Joan B. Kelly. 1980. "Effects of Divorce on the Visiting Father-Child Relationship." *American Journal of Psychiatry* 137(12): 1534–39.

Weiss, Yoram, and Robert J. Willis. 1985. "Children as Collective Goods and Divorce Settlements." *Journal of Labor Economics* 3(3): 268–92.

Chapter 7

The Effects of Stronger Child Support Enforcement on Nonmarital Fertility

Anne Case

T
he last twenty years have witnessed fundamental change in child support enforcement in the United States. The Child Support Enforcement (CSE) program, added as part D to Title IV of the Social Security Act in 1975, provided federal backing for state programs designed to locate absent parents, establish paternity and child support orders, and obtain payments.[1] The states' obligation to child support was increased with the passage of the 1984 CSE amendments, which required withholding of support payments from the paychecks and tax refunds of parents delinquent in their support, and which also required states to establish guidelines to be used in child support award determinations (see Dodson 1988). The 1984 amendments also permitted paternity to be established through a child's eighteenth birthday. The Family Support Act of 1988 again increased the role of the states, requiring them to establish presumptive guidelines (quantitative formula) to be used in setting child support levels.[2] There is an important, growing literature on the effect of the legislation on paternity establishment and award determination. Ann Nichols-Casebolt and Irwin Garfinkel (1991), for example, find an increase in child support awards that "appear[s] to be related to changes in policy and practice that have been implemented in recent years" (95).

The success of legislation may also be measured by its effect on the behavior of individuals whose incentives are altered by changes in child support policy and practice. Requiring absent parents to take greater financial responsibility for their children may reduce the desire to become a parent, for example, or to dissolve marriages when children are present. Differences in the timing of guideline adoption and in the generosity of awards over location has allowed researchers to correlate differences in behavior over time and location with differences in CSE policy. For example, Freya Sonenstein, Joseph Pleck, and Leighton Ku (1994) use differences between counties in their child support and paternity establishment programs to investigate whether young men's increased child support obligation has a significant effect on their contraceptive behavior. Their research finds "no path from child support program strength to perceived cost of pregnancy and pregnancy risk behavior" (12). Lucia Nixon (1997) uses cross-state variation in child support enforcement to investigate its impact on rates of marital dissolution and AFDC (Aid to Families with Dependent Children) participation. She finds that child support enforcement reduces both the probability that a woman will become a single parent through divorce and the probability of AFDC participation.

Differences between county- and state-level programs provide a potentially rich source of variation through which differences in behavior may be examined. However, the reasons for differences in states' policies must be well understood before this source of variation is exploited. States that frown on out-of-wedlock childbearing may have both lower rates of out-of-wedlock childbearing and more stringent child support enforcement policies, but the lower birth rates may be the outcome of the underlying ethos in the state, not of child support enforcement. Alternatively, states that have witnessed rapid growth in out-of-wedlock childbearing may be the first states to adopt tougher child support enforcement legislation, which might lead to a positive correlation between out-of-wedlock childbearing and adoption of child support enforcement policies. Estimation of the incidence of enforcement policies that treats them as exogenous may attribute to child support enforcement the effects of some other (possibly unobserved) forces at work. We address this potential problem head on by modeling the timing and generosity of state-level program changes. In doing so, we are able to speak to the political and economic conditions that affect the timing of adoption of stricter child support enforcement and to control directly for the potential endogeneity of state programs.[3]

We find that state child support policies respond both to changes in the states' economic and demographic conditions and to political forces at work within the state. Using the variations in state policies that are due to the sex composition of state legislatures, we find evidence that some state programs—genetic testing to establish paternity, establishment of paternity to age eighteen, and presumptive guidelines—are negatively and significantly correlated with future out-of-wedlock birth rates. Adoption of each of these policies appears to have reduced the rate of out-of-wedlock childbearing by one and a half to two percentage points.

In the next section, we discuss the effect of stricter child support enforcement on nonmarital parenting. In the succeeding section, we estimate policy choice and incidence.

CHILD SUPPORT ENFORCEMENT AND OUT-OF-WEDLOCK CHILDBEARING

Out-of-Wedlock Childbearing

We begin with a simple model of out-of-wedlock childbearing, to make clear the ways in which government programs influence the decision to become a parent. The model is based on two assumptions: (1) women and men calculate the expected benefits and costs of having children out-of-wedlock, and (2) both men and women have access to contraceptives and choose whether to become parents based on the expected costs and benefits. Children are born only if a bargain can be struck between prospective parents so that the expected benefits of parenthood outweigh the costs for both the prospective mother and father. Anything that increases the cost of fatherhood will reduce the probability that such a bargain can be struck and should, then, reduce the number of children born.[4]

We will focus here on the impact of changes in child support enforcement on the incentives of men who may choose, at some cost, to limit their parenting of children out of wedlock. (We have in mind financial and other costs associated with contraception.) Here, we hope to capture some of the important considerations to be included in the empirical analysis that follows.

The probability that a woman bears a child, p, depends in part on her actions and in part on the actions taken by her partner. We assume here that contraception is costly, and that we can describe these costs in monetary terms using a variable x. We assume the probability of childbearing falls with increases in expenditure on contraception, $p'(x) < 0$. We assume that a man's utility depends upon whether he becomes a father. Without a child, his indirect utility is given by

$$u(W - x),$$

where W represents his income. With a child, his utility is given by

$$v(W - x - c),$$

where c represents his child support obligations. (The variable c could also include any side payments made between a man and a woman related to parenthood.) Each man chooses his contraceptive "expenditure" x to maximize

$$(1 - p(x)) \, u(W - x) + p(x) \, v(W - x - c). \tag{7.1}$$

The level of contraceptive expenditure that maximizes equation (1), x^*, will depend upon the level of income (and economic conditions more broadly), the cost associated with contraception, the generosity of the child support guidelines adopted by the states, and the strictness with which they are enforced. It is straightforward to show, under a reasonable set of assumptions about the utility functions in both states of the world and the function $p(x)$, that the optimal amount of contraceptive expenditure will rise with increases in child support enforcement, c. We would expect then that increases in child support enforcement would lead to lower out-of-wedlock birth rates.

In the empirical work that follows, we model out-of-wedlock childbearing as a direct reflection of x^*, the contraceptive strategy chosen by young men. Specifically, we estimate equations of the form:

$$\text{Out-of-Wedlock Birth Rate} = f(W, c, S, T) + e, \tag{7.2}$$

where W is captured by state economic and demographic variables; S represents state indicator variables that help to control for unobservable, unchanging qualities of the state that may affect childbearing and that absorb state-specific contraceptive costs; T represents year indicator variables that absorb contraceptive and child-bearing costs that vary over time proportionately across states; and c represents measures of child support enforcement. We assume that unobservable variables that affect out-of-wedlock childbearing can be represented adequately by an additive error term, e.

We are primarily interested in estimating the effect of child support enforcement on out-of-wedlock birth rates. Care must be taken, however, in exploring this relationship. If there are determinants of child support enforcement that also affect out-of-wedlock birth rates directly and that are not captured in the variables included in equation (7.2), this will lead to bias in the effect of child support enforcement on out-of-wedlock birth rates. We turn now to determination of state policy and then to the reasons we might expect child support enforcement and out-of-wedlock childbearing to be jointly determined.

Determination of State Policy

State legislators, facing federally mandated changes in child support enforcement, must decide upon the timing of changes in state laws, the generosity of their child support guidelines, and the amount of state funding they are willing to provide to child support enforcement. These legislators must balance the preferences of families with an absent parent and of other citizens not directly involved in child support cases. The latter group, the majority of state residents, would appear to have two interests in child support. First, they underwrite state programs associated with child support enforcement and AFDC benefits, which are affected by the number of families with an absent parent. In addition, they may hold strong beliefs about what absent parents should pay in terms of child support and about the role of the state in enforcing such payments.

The generosity of states' AFDC policies and the rigor with which states pursue child support enforcement are likely to be jointly determined. States that choose to be more generous in their AFDC programs may find it is politically expedient to link AFDC benefits to more stringent child support enforcement policies. State residents may be more enthusiastic about increasing AFDC generosity if they believe that absent parents who can support their children are doing so. State residents may also believe that increased AFDC benefits, if enacted, would increase the rate of out-of-wedlock childbearing, all else held equal. Linking AFDC to child support enforcement may limit the extent to which increases in AFDC generosity distort childbearing behavior. The empirical link between AFDC generosity and child support enforcement is explored later in this chapter. In what follows, we model the impact of AFDC benefits and child support enforcement policies jointly.

The economic climate within a state may influence citizens' opinions on how much money should be spent on programs that affect children (AFDC and child support enforcement) and how that money should be divided between AFDC and child support enforcement. Those same economic conditions may also influence individuals' decisions on childbearing, as in equation (7.2). What would be helpful, if we hope to separate out the impact of child support enforcement legislation on individuals' behavior, would be to find some determinants of state policy that we believe do not systematically influence out-of-wedlock childbearing, except through the effect they have on policy. We could then use these variables as instruments for state policy. We propose, in what follows, to use the sex composition of the state legislature in just this way.

The Role of Female Legislators in Policy Determination

The presence of women in legislatures has a significant effect on state policy, according to recent studies conducted by the Center for the American Woman and Politics at Rutgers University. These studies demonstrated that "women were more likely to give priority to public policies related to their traditional roles as care givers in the family and society—e.g., policies dealing with children and families and health care" (Center for the American Woman and Politics 1991; see also Mills 1991). A case in point is provided by legislation in Florida, where the introduction of bills to expand child support guidelines was attributed in part to the election of a Democratic governor, in part to the Senate's first woman president, and in part to "women's advocates—from lobbyists to female legislators—[getting] together for the first time to hash out an agenda they could all agree on" (Marquez 1991, A18).

Sue Thomas (1994) reports the results of a recent survey she conducted of men and women in twelve state legislatures; she found significant differences in the legislative behavior of men and women. She notes: "Women and men were both interested in and introduced legislation on the full range of issues before the legislature. However, even allowing for wide-ranging interests by both sexes, we did find distinctive patterns. Women did give more time, energy, and effort to bills dealing with womens' and children's and family issues. This is reflected in the kinds of committees on which they sat, the chair positions they held, the types of accomplishments about which they displayed pride, as well as the bills they pursued" (75). Leadership on child support enforcement legislation in New Jersey, for example, was long provided by state Senator Wynona Lipman. Lipman sponsored child support enforcement legislation signed by Governors Brendan Byrne (1982) and Thomas Kean (1983), and cosponsored legislation passed by the New Jersey Senate in 1994 (Booth 1994).

The number of female legislators is a good instrument with which to measure the impact of child support enforcement legislation on out-of-wedlock childbearing. It is highly correlated with many enforcement procedures (see the discussion later in the chapter). At the same time, it does not appear that women are elected to strengthen child support enforcement procedures. A study of seven hundred women conducted by Sherrye Henry (1994) suggests that "when pollsters asked respondents if they would vote for a woman because she understands the problems other women face, 69% said no, the sex of a candidate made no difference" (48).

Timothy Besley and Anne Case (1997) model and discuss the conditions that must hold for the sex composition of the legislature to be useful as an instrument in incidence analysis. In general, this requires the election of women legislators to be uncorrelated with the unobservables that determine outcomes of interest (here, shocks to out-of-wedlock childbearing). This condition is met, for example, if women in politics affect policies through their work on party platforms, and if voting then takes place over parties' platforms (including child support issues), not over the sex of the candidate. The Henry study suggests that this condition does hold. We present over-identification tests, in our empirical work, of whether the number of women legislators belongs in the main (outcome) equations. These tests provide additional support for the Henry findings: women legislators appear to affect outcomes only through their impact on policies chosen.

In the empirical work presented later in the chapter, we model child support enforcement and AFDC benefits as a function of W, the economic and demographic variables that entered equation (2); state and year effects; and political variables, P, including the number of women legislators in both houses, those numbers squared, and the sizes of the state's lower and upper houses, and those numbers squared.

DATA

Out-of-wedlock birth rates are births to unmarried women relative to the total number of unwed women age fifteen to forty-four, expressed as a percentage. We examine the determinants of out-of-wedlock birth rates for the continental U.S. states by year from 1978 to 1991, the years in which many changes in state policies and programs were adopted. These data, drawn from the *Vital Statistics* bulletins, are summarized in table 7.1. Out-of-wedlock birth rates vary greatly between states, with the lowest rates found in New England (Vermont, New Hampshire, and Massachusetts) and the highest rates in the South (Louisiana, Georgia, and Mississippi). These rates increased substantially during the period studied here, rising nationally from 3.0 in 1978 to 6.4 in 1991. There is a lot of variation between states in the rate of growth: Mississippi had less than a 2 percent average annual growth rate in out-of-wedlock childbearing, and North Dakota and Delaware had greater than 10 percent average annual growth rates. Growth in the out-of-wedlock birth rates calculated for Delaware is due to a large decline in the reported number of unmarried women age fifteen to forty-four in the last two years in the sample period. All results reported here have been reestimated omitting observations for Delaware in 1990 and 1991. Results do not change in any meaningful way.

States with the lowest out-of-wedlock birth rates in 1978 tended to have the highest growth rates in nonmarital fertility. (See, for example, New Hampshire, North Dakota, Iowa, and Rhode Island.) The empirical analysis below controls for state fixed effects, which absorb differences between states in their mean levels of nonmarital parenthood. Our analysis thus focuses on deviations in states' nonmarital birth rates from state means and explores the extent to which these can be explained by changes in states' policies during this period.

Out-of-wedlock birth rates take as their denominator the number of unwed women age fifteen to forty-four. Changes in child support enforcement policies and

TABLE 7.1   /   Out-of-Wedlock Birth Rates

State	Out-of-Wedlock Birth Rate 1978	State	Growth in Out-of-Wedlock Birth Rate 1978 to 1991
VT	1.41	MS	.019
NH	1.55	AL	.020
MA	1.56	GA	.026
ND	1.56	SC	.027
IA	1.80	TX	.027
RI	1.86	LA	.029
WA	1.88	NJ	.032
CT	2.02	MD	.033
UT	2.04	IL	.036
WI	2.05	WY	.037
CO	2.19	VA	.038
ME	2.29	MI	.038
NV	2.34	AR	.038
ID	2.37	KY	.039
PA	2.39	FL	.041
WY	2.46	OK	.042
KS	2.53	MO	.044
WV	2.58	OH	.044
NM	2.62	NC	.044
MT	2.63	NY	.046
NJ	2.75	ID	.046
OR	2.76	SD	.046
IN	2.82	UT	.047
SD	2.84	TN	.048
VA	2.86	IN	.049
NY	3.02	VT	.050
MI	3.06	KS	.050
KY	3.12	CA	.050
DE	3.18	ME	.051
OK	3.30	OR	.054
MD	3.30	PA	.055
MO	3.31	CT	.056
OH	3.36	CO	.056
NC	3.39	AZ	.057
TX	3.39	WI	.058
AZ	3.60	MT	.058
IL	3.63	WA	.062
TN	3.69	MA	.064
FL	3.87	RI	.065

(Table continues on p. 198.)

TABLE 7.1 / *Continued*

State	Out-of-Wedlock Birth Rate 1978	State	Growth in Out-of-Wedlock Birth Rate 1978 to 1991
CA	3.93	WV	.069
SC	4.32	IA	.069
AR	4.47	NH	.072
AL	4.55	NV	.076
LA	5.04	NM	.077
GA	5.30	ND	.109
MS	6.00	DE	.152

Notes: Out of wedlock birth rates are births relative to the number of unmarried women in the state, age fifteen to forty-four, expressed as a percentage. The growth rates are state average growth rates for the period 1978 to 1991.

AFDC benefits may influence decisions to marry—as well as decisions to bear children out of wedlock—and the change in out-of-wedlock childbearing we estimate may be working through both behavioral responses. In auxiliary regressions (not shown), we regressed the number of unwed women age fifteen to forty-four on the same child support enforcement policies and AFDC benefit variables studied here, together with state economic and demographic variables and state and year indicators. We found no significant effects of CSE policies or AFDC benefits on the number of unwed women, in either ordinary least squares (OLS) or two-stage least squares (TSLS) specifications. We take this as some evidence that the policies appear to work primarily through their impact on out-of-wedlock births.

We investigate the effect of five CSE programs, with an eye toward those programs thought to be influential in the decisions made by young men. These include indicators that the state uses genetic testing to establish paternity, that the state has long-arm statutes to pursue men in other states, that paternity may be established to age eighteen, that withholding becomes mandatory when payments are in arrears,[5] and that the state has adopted presumptive child support guidelines. These data are summarized in table 7.2, which provides information on the year in which states established each policy. There is great variation between states in the timing of adoption of these measures. For example, sixteen states had adopted long-arm statutes before 1980, while by 1992 twenty states had not yet adopted such statutes. By 1986 most states had passed legislation to allow establishment of paternity to age eighteen. However, nine states (Arizona, Arkansas, Florida, Georgia, Missouri, North Carolina, South Carolina, Utah, and Virginia) had not passed such legislation by 1992. Table 7.2 also presents a measure of state AFDC benefits. The last column of the table presents the states' maximum monthly AFDC benefit in 1983 for a family of four (measured in 1982 prices). The variation between states is substantial, with lower benefits observed in the South ($115 per month in

TABLE 7.2 / Adoption of Child Support Policies

State	Genetic Testing to Establish Paternity	Long-arm Statutes	Paternity Established to Age Eighteen	Mandatory Withholding	Child Support Guidelines Are Presumptive	Maximum Real AFDC Benefits 1983[a]
AL	1986	—	1985	1982	—	141.21
AZ	1987	—	—	1979	1988	270.89
AR	1987	1985	—	1979	—	157.54
CA	1988	1976	1985	1980	1986	600.38
CO	1987	1979	1985	1981	1986	371.76
CT	1986	—	1985	1976	—	511.05
DE	1986	—	1985	1976	1988	299.71
FL	1987	1988	—	1978	1989	252.64
GA	1987	1980	—	1985	1989	228.63
ID	1987	1988	1986	1986	1989	330.45
IL	1987	1988	1985	1982	1985	353.51
IN	1987	—	1986	1982	—	303.55
IA	1987	1984	1985	1985	1989	402.50
KS	1986	1976	1985	1978	1986	369.84
KY	1984	1980	1986	1985	1990	225.74
LA	1987	—	1985	1982	1989	224.78
ME	1986	1977	1986	1968	1990	413.06
MD	1984	1980	1986	1976	—	341.02
MA	1987	—	1986	1983	—	427.47
MI	1984	—	1986	1980	—	449.57
MN	1987	1978	1985	1987	1986	560.04

(Table continues on p. 200.)

TABLE 7.2 / *Continued*

State	Genetic Testing to Establish Paternity	Long-arm Statutes	Paternity Established to Age Eighteen	Mandatory Withholding	Child Support Guidelines Are Presumptive	Maximum Real AFDC Benefits 1983[a]
MS	1987	—	1985	1985	1989	115.27
MO	1988	—	—	1976	—	292.99
MT	1987	1977	1986	1980	1989	408.26
NB	1984	—	1986	1976	1988	403.46
NV	1985	1979	1985	1977	1987	261.29
NH	1976	—	1985	1976	1988	393.85
NJ	1987	—	1985	1982	1988	397.69
NM	1986	—	1985	1979	1988	269.93
NY	1987	1986	1986	1977	1989	494.72
NC	1986	1979	—	1986	1989	212.30
ND	1987	1976	1985	1979	1989	419.79
OH	1987	—	1985	1986	1988	314.12

OK	1987	—	1986	1986	1988	335.25
OR	1987	1979	1985	1976	1989	415.95
PA	1982	—	1986	1986	—	385.21
RI	1987	1979	1985	1980	1987	404.42
SC	1976	1985	—	1985	—	167.15
SD	—	1978	1985	1981	1986	346.78
TN	1987	—	1984	1983	1989	147.93
TX	1988	1976	1985	1985	1989	135.45
UT	1987	1986	—	1977	1989	385.21
VT	1987	—	1985	1977	1986	545.63
WA	1987	1976	1985	1985	1988	522.57
WV	1986	—	1986	1986	1986	239.19
WI	1981	1979	1986	1977	1986	576.37
WY	1981	1978	1985	1986	1989	374.64

Notes: Observations are marked "1976" for states that adopted the policy in or before 1976. Observations marked "—" are for states that had not adopted a given policy by 1992.

[a] Maximum AFDC benefits for a family of four, in 1982 dollars.

Mississippi, $141 per month in Alabama) and higher benefits in New England ($511 in Connecticut, $546 in Vermont).

There is a strong empirical link between AFDC generosity and child support enforcement. Correlations between maximum state AFDC benefits for a family of four in 1983 and the years in which different child support enforcement policies were adopted are negative and substantial. Correlations between AFDC and long-arm statutes (−0.22), paternity establishment to age eighteen (−0.35), mandatory withholding of payments in arrears (−0.37), and presumptive guidelines (−0.24) demonstrate that states with higher AFDC benefits were the early adopters of child support enforcement policies.

The passage of legislation does not guarantee enforcement of child support policies within any given state. If we had reliable information on the determination with which policies were enforced, by state and year, we would include this in our analysis as well. Both sets of measures (laws and their enforcement) would be interesting to examine. Some potential fathers may change their behavior as the laws change, knowing that the laws may in the future be enforced. Some potential fathers may be more heavily influenced by the enforcement they observe. As we discuss later in the chapter, we find that the passage of child support policies appears to affect the behavior of potential fathers within a couple of years. This may be an underestimate of the ultimate impact of legislation, if states are slow in bringing their enforcement into line with the law and potential fathers are more heavily influenced by states' enforcement policies than by laws.

We explore the timing of changes in policy using data on recent state economic conditions, demographic makeup, and political climate. The economic and demographic variables that we analyze include state income per capita, state population, the employment-to-population ratio, the proportion of the state population that is elderly, and the proportion that is black. These data are drawn from the *Statistical Abstract of the United States.*

Political variables, which help to identify the timing of law changes, include the total number of legislators in both houses, and those numbers squared. These data are drawn from *The Book of the States* (Council on State Governments, various years). In addition, we use the number of women in each chamber of the state legislature, and these numbers squared, to explain the timing of policy changes. These data are drawn from *Women in State Legislatures: Fact Sheets* (Center for the American Woman and Politics, various years).

Summary measures of these variables are provided in table 7.3. There is substantial variation between states and within states over time in many of these variables. During this period, the number of women in state assemblies and senates grew dramatically, as can be seen in figures 7.1 and 7.2. With controls for state and year effects, it is the variation within states over time that identifies the effect of economic and political conditions on state policies and the effect of the economic and policy variables on out-of-wedlock childbearing. The year effects absorb phenomena that are common to all states at a point in time, and the state effects absorb state-specific forces that are unchanging over time.

TABLE 7.3 / Summary Statistics of the Economic, Demographic, and Political
Variables Used in the Analysis

	Mean	Standard Deviation	Minimum	Maximum
State income per capita[a] 1977 to 1990	11,496	1,927	7,705	19,002
Fraction employed[b] 1977 to 1990	.400	.045	.297	.547
State population (millions) 1977 to 1990	4.92	5.05	.406	29.8
Proportion elderly 1977 to 1990	.117	.019	.075	.188
Proportion black 1977 to 1990	.115	.090	.002	.368
Number of women, state upper house 1977 to 1990[c]	3.43	2.62	0	12
Number of members, state upper house 1977 to 1990	40.5	10.2	20	67
Number of women, state lower house 1977 to 1990	16.8	17.7	1	133
Number of members, state lower house 1977 to 1990	113.5	55.6	40	400
Out-of-wedlock birth rate[d] 1978 to 1991	4.25	1.96	1.41	35.1

Notes: Number of observations = 672. Observations are for all forty-eight continental U.S. states for fourteen years. Years reported vary between explanatory variables and out-of-wedlock birth rates, reflecting the fact that lags of explanatory variables are used in the analysis.

[a] State income is in per-person, constant 1982 dollars.

[b] Fraction employed is the employment-to-population ratio.

[c] Nebraska has a unicameral legislature and is assigned this number of legislators to both variables for the lower house and the upper house.

[d] The out-of-wedlock birth rate is the number of births to unmarried women divided by the number of unmarried women age fifteen to forty-four, expressed as a percentage. The highest rates are recorded in Delaware for the years 1989, 1990, and 1991. I have reestimated the results presented here without these three observations (in case they are outliers caused by measurement error). None of the results change in any meaningful way.

ESTIMATION RESULTS

The Determinants of Child Support Policies

The impacts of state economic, demographic, and political conditions on state AFDC benefits and child support policies are examined in table 7.4. We regress AFDC benefits and each of five child support enforcement policies—genetic testing, paternity establishment to age eighteen, long-arm statutes, presumptive guidelines, and mandatory withholding—on the number of women in the state upper house, that number squared, the number of women in the state lower house, that number squared, the number of legislators in each house, and those numbers

(Text continues on page 208.)

FIGURE 7.1 / Women Serving in State Lower Houses, 1975 to 1995

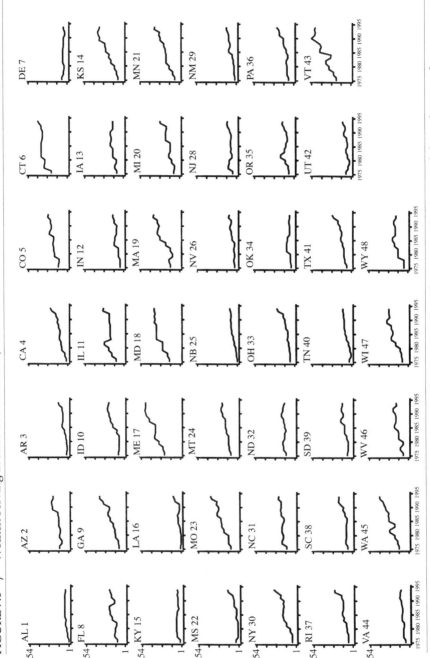

Notes: New Hampshire (27) not shown. Each graph shows the number of women serving in a state's lower house each year.

FIGURE 7.2 / Women Serving in State Upper Houses, 1975 to 1995

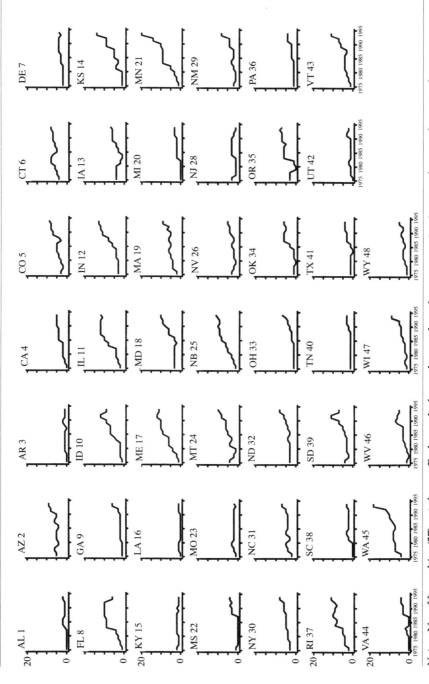

Notes: New Hampshire (27) not shown. Each graph shows the number of women serving in a state's upper house each year.

TABLE 7.4 / Determinants of States' Child Support Policies (Standard Errors in Parentheses)

Explanatory Variables	Paternity Established to Age Eighteen	Paternity Long-arm Statutes	Genetic Testing	Mandatory Withholding	Presumptive Guidelines	Maximum AFDC Benefits
Number of women in upper house	.0306	-.0489	-.0081	.0339	.0253	1.983
	(.0143)	(.0213)	(.0136)	(.0213)	(.0178)	(2.980)
Number of women in upper house (squared)	.0002	.0034	.0010	-.0049	-.0007	-.2276
	(.0013)	(.0019)	(.0011)	(.0018)	(.0020)	(.2524)
F-test: women in upper house and upper house (squared)[a]	10.72	2.94	0.54	5.50	3.22	0.52
	(.0000)	(.0536)	(.5857)	(.0040)	(.0405)	(.5971)
Number of women in lower house	.0020	.0023	.0078	.0039	.0032	.9315
	(.0033)	(.0043)	(.0037)	(.0051)	(.0037)	(.6289)
Number of women in lower house (squared)	.0001	-.0001	-.0001	-.0001	.00002	-.0102
	(.00002)	(.00003)	(.0000)	(.00003)	(.00003)	(.0043)
F-test: women in lower house and lower house (squared)	9.91	10.56	5.74	11.32	0.61	2.88
	(.0001)	(.0000)	(.0034)	(.0000)	(.5463)	(.0566)
Number of legislators in upper house	-.1904	.1959	.1315	.3115	.0565	30.02
	(.0844)	(.1266)	(.0784)	(.1536)	(.0997)	(13.66)
Number of legislators in upper house (squared)	.0022	-.0018	-.0017	-.0029	-.0006	-.4989
	(.0010)	(.0015)	(.0009)	(.0019)	(.0011)	(.1564)
Number of legislators in lower house	.0069	-.0158	.0029	-.0327	-.0319	1.216
	(.0062)	(.0101)	(.0059)	(.0104)	(.0124)	(1.254)
Number of legislators in lower house (squared)	-.00002	.00004	-.00001	.0001	.0001	-.0028
	(.00002)	(.00002)	(.00002)	(.0003)	(.00003)	(.0037)
F-test: all legislative variables[b]	6.26	7.26	2.42	7.13	3.26	6.12
	(.0000)	(.0000)	(.0139)	(.0000)	(.0012)	(.0000)

	(1)	(2)	(3)	(4)	(5)	(6)
State income per capita	.042	-.012	.003	-.049	-.0188	.493
	(.015)	(.023)	(.017)	(.027)	(.0296)	(3.39)
Employment/population	-4.52	1.45	-.191	.322	.6599	309.0
	(.725)	(.934)	(.875)	(1.16)	(1.195)	(142.5)
State population	-.047	-.024	-.021	.055	.0054	20.18
	(.025)	(.023)	(.022)	(.024)	(.0206)	(2.57)
Proportion elderly	7.65	-5.75	4.16	5.30	-3.856	-1726
	(2.94)	(3.86)	(3.20)	(4.08)	(3.122)	(433)
Proportion black	1.88	1.38	.609	1.78	-5.599	76.2
	(.938)	(.746)	(1.05)	(1.06)	(1.029)	(142.5)
F-test: economic variables[c]	11.59	2.61	1.19	2.03	7.61	32.27
	(.0000)	(.0236)	(.3114)	(.0728)	(.0000)	(.0000)
R^2	.8056	.7650	.8099	.6715	.6646	.9496

Sources: Dependent variable data sources columns 1 through 5: National Conference of State Legislatures, as reported in Garfinkel et al. 1995. Data provided by Sara McLanahan and Cynthia Miller. Explanatory variables data sources: Economic and demographic variables are from the *Statistical Abstract of the United States* (various years). Political variables are drawn from Council on State Governments, *The Book of the States* (various years) and *Center for the American Woman and Politics, The Impact of Women in Public Office: Findings at a Glance* (1991), and *Women in State Legislatures: Fact Sheets*, (various years).

Notes: OLS regressions with robust standard errors reported in parentheses. All regressions include state and year indicators. Observations available for continental U.S. states from 1975 to 1989 for real maximum AFDC benefits (column 6) and from 1976 to 1990 for all other dependent variables. Number of observations in each regression is 720 (48 state observations over 15 years).

[a] *F*-test of the joint significance of the number of women in the upper house, and that number squared. *P*-values provided in parentheses for all *F*-tests.

[b] *F*-test of the joint significance of the number of women in the upper house, that number squared, number of women in the lower house, that number squared, total number of legislators in state upper house, that number squared, and total number of legislators in state lower house, and that number squared. *P*-value provided in parentheses.

[c] *F*-test of the joint significance of state income per capita, fraction employed, state population, proportion elderly, and proportion black.

squared. We include in these regressions state income per capita, employment-to-population ratios, state population, the proportion of the state that is elderly (sixty-five or older), and the proportion that is black. State indicator variables and year indicator variables are also included in each regression (but are not reported in the table). For each regression, robust standard errors are estimated, allowing for an unspecified form of heteroskedasticity.

The legislative variables are significant determinants of state policies. Beginning with column 1, the number of women in a state's upper house has a large and significant effect on the probability that the state will adopt legislation to establish paternity to age eighteen. All else equal, a one-standard-deviation increase in the number of seats held by women in the state upper house (2.62 seats) is associated with a nine-percentage-point increase in the probability that the state will have in place legislation to establish paternity to age eighteen ($0.0306 \times 2.62 + 0.0002 \times (6.05^2 - 3.43^2)$), measured at the mean of the number of seats held by women (3.43 seats). An F-test of the joint significance of the number of women in the upper house and that number squared is provided under the estimates ($F = 10.72$) and suggests that the effect of the number of women in state upper houses is highly significant. The number of women in state lower houses also has a large and significant effect on the probability of legislation to establish paternity to age eighteen. All else equal, a one-standard-deviation increase in the number of seats held by women in the lower house (17.7 seats) is associated with a thirteen-percentage-point increase in the probability of legislation, measured at the mean number of seats held by women in the lower house (16.8 seats). These variables are also highly significant ($F = 9.91$). The number of women in the state upper house also has a positive and significant effect on the probability that the state will have passed legislation making support guidelines presumptive. All else equal, a one-standard-deviation increase in the number of women serving in the state upper house is associated with a 5 percent increase in the probability of presumptive guidelines, measured at the mean number of women serving in the state upper house. The number of women in the state lower house also has a positive and significant effect on the probability that the state will allow genetic testing to establish paternity. All else held equal, a one-standard-deviation increase in the number of seats held by women in the lower house (17.7 seats) is associated with a five-percentage-point increase in the probability that the state will have passed genetic testing legislation, measured at the mean number of women legislators during this period (16.8 seats). A one-standard-deviation increase in the number of women seated in the lower house (17.7 seats), all else equal, is also estimated to increase maximum AFDC benefits by roughly $7 per month, measured at the mean of the number of women legislators during this period (16.8 seats). This is 2 percent of the mean of maximum AFDC benefits received over this period ($368 per month).

The legislative environment is also determined by the number of legislators seated at any particular time. The ability to strike bargains may depend on the quality of negotiations between parties, which may depend in turn upon the number of legislators seated. For this reason, we also include the number of legislators in each house, and those numbers squared. The joint impact of the number of women and the number of legislators can be seen in the F-tests for the set of legislative variables (row 11). For each policy examined here, the legislative variables are jointly highly significant. Many specifications of the impact of women legislators were explored, and the results presented here are robust to functional form.

Recent economic and demographic changes within the state are also significant determinants of policy (F-statistics, row 17). The proportion of the state population that is elderly has a negative and significant effect on maximum AFDC payments, a finding that is complementary to those of James Poterba (1997), who finds evidence of intergenerational competition in public-sector resource allocation. The proportion of the state that is black has a positive and significant effect on the speed with which states adopt certain peices of legislation. Specifically, the proportion of the state population that is black is associated with faster adoption of genetic testing, paternity establishment to age eighteen, long-arm statutes, and mandatory withholding for nonresident parents in arrears. Larger states are significantly less likely to have passed legislation on paternity establishment to age eighteen and significantly more likely to have mandatory withholding. Together, the economic and demographic variables are significant determinants of AFDC benefits, paternity establishment to age eighteen, long-arm statutes, presumptive guidelines, and mandatory withholding. Given that we think all five of the economic and demographic variables examined here may have independent effects on out-of-wedlock childbearing, it is important to try to separate out their effects.

The Impact of Child Support Policies on Out-of-Wedlock Childbearing

We present estimates of the impact of child support enforcement policies on nonmarital fertility in table 7.5. We estimate the impact of policy measures on out-of-wedlock childbearing policy by policy. For each, we model out-of-wedlock childbearing in a given year as a function of a particular child support enforcement policy in place two years before that, of the demographic and economic variables discussed earlier (state income per capita, state population, the employment-to-population ratio, the proportion of the population that is black or elderly) and of state and year effects. We use one-year lags in the economic and demographic variables to reflect the time lag between conception and birth. Our interest is primarily in the impact of economic conditions in place at the time of conception. The two-year lag for child support enforcement policies was chosen to reflect the time it may take for information to reach young men making contraception decisions.

For each policy, we present two sets of estimates. The first set (columns 1 through 5) is based on an ordinary least squares (OLS) regression. The OLS estimates treat the child support policies and AFDC benefits as exogenous variables. The second set (columns 6 through 10) is based on two-stage least squares (TSLS) estimation of the effect of the policy on out-of-wedlock childbearing. Here, the policy variables have been instrumented using the set of legislative variables presented in table 7.4 (the number of women in each house, that number squared, the number of legislators in each house, and those numbers squared).

TABLE 7.5 / The Impact of Child Support Policies on Out-of-Wedlock Childbearing

Explanatory Variables	OLS: Child Support Enforcement Policies and AFDC Taken as Exogenous					TSLS[a]: Child Support Enforcement Policies and AFDC Instrumented on Gender Composition and Size of Legislature				
Genetic testing to establish paternity$_{t-2}$	.083 (.100)	—	—	—	—	-1.70 (1.19)	—	—	—	—
Paternity establishment to age eighteen$_{t-2}$	—	.376 (.170)	—	—	—	—	-2.10 (1.11)	—	—	—
Long-arm statutes$_{t-2}$	—	—	-.397 (.183)	—	—	—	—	-.092 (.690)	—	—
Presumptive guidelines$_{t-2}$	—	—	—	.625 (.385)	—	—	—	—	-1.47 (.740)	—
Mandatory withholding$_{t-2}$	—	—	—	—	-.480 (.249)	—	—	—	—	.002 (.451)
Maximum AFDC benefits$_{t-2}$	.003 (.001)	.003 (.001)	.003 (.001)	.003 (.002)	.003 (.002)	-.002 (.004)	-.012 (.006)	-.006 (.003)	-.006 (.004)	-.006 (.003)
State income per capita$_{t-1}$ (thousands of dollars)	-.402 (.172)	-.422 (.179)	-.412 (.175)	-.397 (.168)	-.437 (.186)	-.403 (.187)	-.250 (.150)	-.374 (.180)	-.386 (.182)	-.371 (.165)
Fraction employed$_{t-1}$	22.4 (8.49)	23.8 (9.00)	22.7 (8.58)	21.9 (8.17)	22.6 (8.46)	21.3 (8.34)	13.4 (7.38)	21.7 (8.83)	22.6 (9.24)	21.6 (8.41)

State population$_{t-1}$	.162	.176	.152	.156	.185	.220	.320	.336	.337	.340
	(.103)	(.107)	(.101)	(.102)	(.112)	(.119)	(.182)	(.141)	(.164)	(.165)
Proportion elderly$_{t-1}$	49.0	49.0	49.1	54.5	54.5	54.5	29.8	33.0	22.7	33.0
	(30.6)	(30.1)	(30.0)	(32.5)	(32.3)	(40.7)	(28.4)	(27.1)	(25.5)	(27.0)
Proportion black$_{t-1}$	2.23	1.96	2.94	5.34	3.42	5.52	7.17	4.42	−2.90	4.29
	(9.40)	(9.22)	(9.56)	(11.0)	(9.79)	(11.0)	(11.3)	(10.7)	(8.51)	(9.95)
F-test: Economic variables[b]	6.34	6.40	6.26	5.41	6.45	3.60	1.25	5.95	4.40	5.70
(p-value)	(.0000)	(.0000)	(.0000)	(.0001)	(.0000)	(.0033)	(.2854)	(.0000)	(.0006)	(.0000)
Over-id test for	—	—	—	—	—	9.21	6.51	11.3	7.97	11.30
instruments[c] (p-value)						(.1619)	(.3681)	(.0784)	(.2401)	(.0793)

Notes: All regressions include state indicator variables and year indicator variables. Observations are for each of the continental U.S. states for the period 1976 to 1989 (number of observations = 672). For information on variable definitions and sources, see notes to table 7.4. Dependent variable: out-of-wedlock births/unmarried women age fifteen to forty-four (expressed as a percent).

[a] In columns 6 through 10, one child support enforcement variable and state maximum AFDC for a family of four are instrumented on the number of women in the upper house, that number squared, number of women in the lower house, that number squared, total number of legislators in state upper house, that number squared, and total number of legislators in state lower house, and that number squared.

[b] F-test of the joint significance of state income per capita, employment/population, state population, proportion elderly, and proportion black (all lagged one period).

[c] Chi-square test statistic of the validity of excluding the legislative instruments from the main regression (degrees of freedom = 6).

Economic Influences

Before turning to the effect of the child support policies, we will briefly discuss the economic and demographic variables thought to affect out-of-wedlock childbearing. As discussed earlier (see equation [7.2]), we might expect state economic and demographic variables to affect nonmarital fertility, if only because they affect the well-being of potential parents in the state of the world in which they become parents relative to their well-being if they choose not to become parents. Increases in state income per capita, holding all else constant, are negatively and significantly correlated with the out-of-wedlock birth rates in the following year. This is true in both the OLS regressions and those in which child support enforcement policies are instrumented. We control for state-level fixed effects in each of these regressions, so that this is due to differences within states over time, not to differences between wealthier states and poorer states. The proportion of the population that is elderly is positively and significantly correlated with the out-of-wedlock birth rates in the next period in the OLS regressions. However, this variable becomes insignificant when we instrument for child support enforcement policies using the political variables discussed earlier. This is the result we would expect if child support enforcement policies were endogenous and the proportion of elderly were a determinant of such enforcement. In such a case, the simultaneity bias resulting from treating child support enforcement as a control variable would lead to significance in a variable correlated with the true effect of child support enforcement—in this case, the proportion of elderly.

F-tests of the joint significance of the economic and demographic variables (presented in the second-to-last row of the table) suggest that the economic variables are significant determinants of out-of-wedlock childbearing. The difference in the joint significance of these variables between the OLS and TSLS regressions is again of interest because it highlights the endogeneity of the policy variables.

We focus on the TSLS estimates because of the potential joint endogeneity of child support enforcement policies. We find significant effects for three child support policies in our TSLS estimation: genetic testing to establish paternity, paternity establishment to age eighteen, and presumptive guidelines. Genetic testing to establish paternity, which appeared to have a positive and insignificant effect on childbearing in the OLS estimation, has a negative and significant effect when instrumented on the legislative variables. Holding all else constant, the passage of genetic testing legislation is associated with a reduction in out-of-wedlock childbearing (two years later) of 1.7 percentage points. Paternity establishment to age eighteen appears to be positively and significantly correlated with out-of-wedlock childbearing when estimated by OLS (column 2). This perverse result appears also for presumptive guidelines (column 4). However, both of these results change when child support enforcement policies are instrumented on legislative variables. The TSLS estimates have purged that part of the correlation between out-of-wedlock childbearing and the endogenous policies that led to the positive and significant OLS result. Holding all else constant, the passage of paternity establishment to age eighteen is associated with a 2-percentage-point reduction in the rate of out-of-wedlock childbearing. Holding all else constant, the passage of presumptive guidelines is associated with a 1.5-percentage-point reduction in the rate of out-of-wedlock childbearing.

AFDC benefits appear to have a positive and significant effect on nonmarital fertility when OLS estimation is performed. However, instrumentation suggests that this result is due to the joint endogeneity of AFDC benefit generosity and out-of-wedlock childbearing. In TSLS estimation, the AFDC benefits have a negative and insignificant effect on out-of-wedlock childbearing.

Over-Identification Tests

One caveat to the use of political variables as instruments for child support enforcement policies is that these variables may directly determine out-of-wedlock childbearing. For example, women legislators may have been elected in response to a rise in out-of-wedlock birth rates, or women legislators may affect the adoption of other policies, not modeled here, that have a direct effect on nonmarital fertility. We perform over-identification tests to see whether women legislators should be included in the main regression, as direct determinants of out-of-wedlock childbearing. We present the results of these over-identification tests in the last row of table 7.5. For policies found to have significant effects on out-of-wedlock childbearing—genetic testing, paternity establishment to age eighteen, and presumptive guidelines—we pass the over-identification tests easily. Instrumenting only for AFDC benefits and long-arm statutes (column 8) or for AFDC benefits and mandatory withholding (column 10), we do not pass the over-identification tests. These result can be explained by the fact that the instruments affect genetic testing, paternity establishment to age eighteen, and presumptive guidelines, and these are shown here to affect nonmarital fertility.

CONCLUSIONS

We draw three conclusions from our results. First, we find that women legislators play a role in setting a state's policy agenda. Although women were never in the majority in either a state assembly or state senate during the years under examination here, they appear to speed adoption of child support enforcement policies significantly. More generally, the generosity and timing of a state's child support enforcement programs respond to the economic, demographic, and political conditions present in that state.

Second, omitted variables that are correlated with the rate of out-of-wedlock childbearing within the state also appear to play a role in state policy. It is necessary, therefore, to control for the potential endogeneity of state policy when estimating its effect. We find that estimates of policy impact change dramatically when we control for potential policy endogeneity.

Finally, some state policies—such as paternity establishment to age eighteen, genetic testing to establish paternity, and presumptive guidelines—may act to limit nonmarital fertility significantly. Better instruments would be welcome, as they may lead to more precise estimates of policy impact, an observation that suggests an avenue for future work.

I am grateful to Angus Deaton, Irv Garfinkel, Sara McLanahan, Robert Moffitt, Judy Seltzer, Freya Sonenstein, seminar participants, and two referees for useful discussions and comments on an earlier draft of this chapter. I also thank Sara McLanahan, Cynthia Miller, and Linda Phillips for providing me with data.

NOTES

1. For discussion of the history of child support legislation, see Garfinkel, McLanahan, and Robins (1994).

2. "Presumptive guidelines are a standard method for setting child support orders based on the income of the parent(s) and other factors. Child support orders set according to the guidelines are presumed to be correct. Judges and others must use the state guidelines or demonstrate that the application of the guidelines would be unjust or inappropriate in a particular case" (GAO 1994, 63; see also Erickson 1993).

3. The potential endogeneity of child support enforcement programs is mentioned by Sonenstein, Pleck, and Ku (1994). Noting that "stronger programs may also signal and reinforce shared community expectations that non-marital childbearing should be discouraged" (5), they add to their analysis information available on the "ethic of good citizenship" within counties—the proportion of registered voters voting in the last election in the county and the county's crime rate. It is not clear how well these variables capture the county's attitude toward out-of-wedlock childbearing.

4. We are not assuming that this is the only force at work in men's decisions on contraception, or even the most important. But in any framework within which unmarried men are making contraceptive decisions, an increase in the cost of child support would be a force compelling men to follow a more conservative strategy.

5. These variables are drawn from Garfinkel et al. (1995) and were provided by Sara McLanahan and Cynthia Miller.

REFERENCES

Besley, Timothy, and Anne Case. 1997. "Women in Politics: Finding Instruments for Incidence Analysis." Princeton University. Unpublished paper.

Booth, Michael. 1994. "Child Support Sanctions for Lawyers." *New Jersey Law Journal* (November 28, 1994): 4.

Center for the American Woman and Politics. 1991. *The Impact of Women in Public Office: Findings at a Glance.* New Brunswick, N.J.: Eagleton Institute of Politics, Rutgers University.

————. Various years. *Women in State Legislatures: Fact Sheets.* New Brunswick, N.J.: Eagleton Institute of Politics, Rutgers University.

Council on State Governments. Various years. *State Elective Officials and the Legislatures.* Supplement 1 to *The Book of the States.* Lexington, Ky.: Council on State Governments

Dodson, Diane. 1988. "A Guide to the Guidelines: New Child Support Rules Are Helping Custodial Parents Bridge the Financial Gap." *Family Advocate* 10(4): 81–87.

Erickson, Nancy S. 1993. "Child Support Guidelines: A Primer." *Clearinghouse Review* 27(7): 734–40.

Garfinkel, Irwin, Cynthia Miller, Sara McLanahan, and Thomas L. Hanson. 1995. "Deadbeat Dads or Inept States? A Comparison of Child Support Enforcement Systems." Princeton University. Unpublished paper (May).

Garfinkel, Irwin, Sara S. McLanahan, and Philip K. Robins, eds. 1994. *Child Support and Child Well-being.* Washington: Urban Institute Press.

Government Accounting Office. 1994. "Child Support Enforcement—Families Could Benefit from Stronger Enforcement Program." GAO Report No. GAO/HEHS–95–24 (December 27).

Henry, Sherrye. 1994. "Why Women Don't Vote for Women—and Why They Should!" *Working Woman* 19(6): 48.

Marquez, Myriam. 1991. "Legislature Is Learning 'Women's Issues' Are Everybody's Issues." *Orlando Sentinel Tribune,* May 17, 1991, p. A18.

Mills, Kay. 1991. "The Latest Pressure Group in the Redistricting Battle; Politics: Women Are Learning That They, Too, Have a Stake in Reapportionment—The Keys to Political Kingdom and More." *Los Angeles Times,* December 29, 1991, p. M2.

Nichols-Casebolt, Ann, and Irwin Garfinkel. 1991. "Trends in Paternity Adjudications and Child Support Awards." *Social Science Quarterly* 72(1): 83–97.

Nixon, Lucia A. 1997. "The Effect of Child Support Enforcement on Marital Dissolution." *Journal of Human Resources* 32(1): 159–81.

Poterba, James M. 1997. "Demographic Structure and the Political Economy of Public Education." *Journal of Policy Analysis and Management* 16(1): 48–66.

Sonenstein, Freya L., Joseph Pleck, and Leighton Ku. 1994. "Child Support Obligations and Young Men's Contraceptive Behavior: What Do Young Men Know? Does It Matter?" Washington, DC: The Urban Institute.

Thomas, Sue. 1994. *How Women Legislate.* New York: Oxford University Press.

U.S. Bureau of the Census. Various years. *Statistical Abstract of the United States.* Washington: U.S. Government Printing Office for U.S. Bureau of the Census.

Part III

Should We Do More to Help Fathers?

The final chapters address the question of whether we should be doing more to help fathers meet their obligations. Two chapters focus on specific demonstrations designed to help fathers who are denied access to their children and to help poor fathers meet their child support obligations. The last chapter takes a step back and uses political and legal theory to assess our current policies toward poor fathers and fathers with second families.

In chapter 8, Jessica Pearson and Nancy Thoennes describe the results of two studies of programs designed to improve nonresident parents' access to their children. The first study examines court-based programs in five different states, and the second evaluates the Child Access Demonstration Projects funded by the Office of Child Support Enforcement in 1990 and 1991. Most of the sites in the OCSE demonstration projects used random assignment.

Parents were eligible for the programs if they had disputes (or were at risk of having a dispute) related to visitation, custody, or, sometimes, child support. The majority of children whose parents were in the access studies—between 70 and 80 percent—lived with their mothers. Families who participated in the intervention programs had much higher rates of serious conflict and allegations of domestic violence and substance abuse than parents in the general population.

Nonresident parents (usually fathers) and resident parents (usually mothers) were equally likely to report visitation problems. Both reported problems related to unclear visitation plans, disagreements about scheduling visitation, arguments that broke out when children were picked up or dropped off, and problems caused by new relationships. High percentages of nonresident fathers and resident mothers were also concerned about their child's safety in the other parent's home, but resident parents were more likely to report these concerns.

Pearson and Thoennes find that mediation and short-term counseling are effective ways to resolve conflicts over scheduling visits. The effectiveness of the programs depended in part on the seriousness of the problems between the parents. Among families with the most problems—if the nonresident father felt cut out of the child's life, for example, or if there was a history of continued fighting between parents or domestic violence—the majority of parents did not report improvements in their relationship. Patterns of continued hostility and anger were evident for both the treatment and control groups, suggesting that the passage of time rather than intervention accounts for the small improvements in parents' relationships.

The effects of program participation appear slightly more positive when success is measured by the amount of post-intervention contact between children and non-resident parents. Among families with less entrenched conflict who participated in mediation, nonresident fathers reported an increase in their time with children. Fathers in the control group did not experience this increase. However, among high-conflict families, there were no differences in subsequent contact for those who participated in the intervention relative to those who did not. Program participation resulted, at best, in a small improvement in compliance with child support orders. Finally, Pearson and Thoennes argue that participation in counseling and education programs at the early stages of separation and divorce are likely to be more successful in resolving access problems than participating in programs designed to intervene only after serious disputes develop. Although the vast majority of separating and divorcing parents do not report major problems with visitation or access, it is possible that more aggressive attempts to establish paternity for children born outside of marriage will lead to greater numbers of nonresident fathers needing help to gain access to their children.

In chapter 9, Earl Johnson and Fred Doolittle describe the Parents' Fair Share (PFS) demonstration, a program designed to increase nonresident parents' ability to pay child support to families of children on welfare. PFS is aimed at assisting nonresident parents who are under- or unemployed and have been unable to pay child support. Nonresident parents, almost always fathers, enter the program through the court system. PFS provides employment and training services, and it helps the fathers obtain temporary reductions in their child support obligation to enable them to complete the program. In addition, the program provides peer support groups, counseling, assistance in establishing paternity and child support orders, and, if necessary, help in arranging formal mediation between the father and the children's mother.

The authors draw on in-depth interviews and informal conversations with approximately thirty nonresident fathers, about two-thirds of whom are African American, to explore the family circumstances and attitudes of men in the program. Although most fathers in this sample have worked full-time in the past, they are sporadically employed, if employed at all, when they enter PFS. Because of their unstable income, they may owe much more child support each month than they earn. The fathers accrue large arrearages, which they do not expect ever to be able to pay. A substantial minority of the fathers do not have a stable residence; they move between friends' and relatives' homes, sleeping on couches or in cars. Johnson and Doolittle report that many of these fathers, despite their unstable living arrangements, manage to maintain some contact with their children. The father's mother—the children's grandmother—may be an important link between the father and his children.

The nonresident fathers in PFS believe that their lack of a good job and steady employment makes it impossible for them to be good fathers. Their experiences in the child support system teach them that informal or in-kind payments to their children's mother mean nothing to the family courts. Because both the fathers and the children's mothers consider child support payments part of a trade for access to children, fathers without stable incomes have less time with their children. Fathers also limit their time with children out of shame about their lack of employment and low status. Fathers who are unable to make regular, formal child support payments realistically believe that they may be jailed for failure to pay support. When the mothers receive AFDC, men's willingness to pay support is further discouraged by the knowledge that any payments will go to the state, not directly to their children. The fathers also feel obligated to contribute whatever money they can to support the household and children with whom they are living instead of the children from past relationships.

At this point, it is too early to judge the effectiveness of the Parents' Fair Share demonstrations. At its most promising, the combination of an employment and training program, the Responsible Fatherhood curriculum, peer support, and temporarily lowered child support orders offers fathers the potential to change their lives. But clearly, the challenge is daunting. Whether the employment and training component of PFS will be any more successful than previous job training programs, such as the National Job Training Partnership Act (JTPA) and JOBSTART, remains to be seen. The holistic approach of providing both economic and emotional support to low-income nonresident fathers may or may not reduce their frustration and feelings of powerlessness.

In chapter 10, Martha Minow, a legal theorist, addresses two frequently heard concerns—whether indigent nonresident fathers should have small or no child support obligations, and whether nonresident fathers should be able to reduce their child support orders if they support other children. Minow considers low-income fathers and children in second families in the context of other value judgments inherent in state policies addressing the support of children, such as the state's obligation to guarantee all children a minimum standard of living.

Minow ties parents' obligation to support children to their responsibility for bringing children into the world. Yet this rationale provides no insight into the amount of support beyond basic subsistence owed to children; nor does it provide a rationale for reducing the obligations of parents who decide to have more children in a new relationship. Historically, the state has been reluctant to intervene in parental support, except in cases of nonmarital childbearing or marital dissolution. In these instances, enforcement of child support obligations has been motivated by political concern about dependence on public aid. The goal of reducing dependence provides a framework for exploring questions about how the child support system should treat poor parents and children in second families. There is a second principle to apply to these contested issues: parents should share their incomes with their children to a degree that enables the children to achieve the same standard of living that they would enjoy if their parents lived together.

To resolve the question of child support obligations of poor parents and parents of second families, Minow reviews five normative theories: utilitarianism, Kantian theories of rights and duties, virtue ethics, ethics of care and relationships, and expressive models of law. She concludes that all of the theories are consistent with at least modest child support responsibilities of poor nonresident parents, although the ethics of care approach is more equivocal on this point than the other theories. Minow also argues that normative theories offer conflicting guidance on whether to modify child support responsibilities when a nonresident parent has children in a new family. In her view, however, the conflicting guidance does not justify allowing judges to use discretion in difficult cases. She points out that discretion can lead to inconsistent treatment of similar cases, obscure the message about the importance of providing for children, and lead to judgments that reflect the biases of individual judges.

As a result of her analysis, Minow recommends that poor nonresident parents be required to pay at least a token amount of child support. She cautions that establishing an obligation that is impossible for a parent to pay would be counterproductive, in ways similar to those identified by fathers participating in the Parents' Fair Share demonstration. Minow especially notes the importance of having some of the nonresident parent's child support go directly to the child instead of to the state to offset the cost of public support.

On balance, Minow also believes that child support obligations to children from a first relationship should not be forgiven if a nonresident parent has children in a subsequent relationship. She points to the complexity of the issues involved in deciding whether support obligations to children from the first relationship should be reduced somewhat to take account of the nonresident parent's new responsibilities. Her discussion of the responsibilities of low-income parents and obligations to second families argues for more information about public attitudes, beliefs, and family behavior to inform debate on how the law should handle children's needs and parents' competing interests.

The three chapters in this section all address the question of whether we should do more for nonresident fathers. While the authors use very different approaches (chapter 8 uses quantitative analysis, chapter 9 qualitative analysis, and chapter 10 normative analysis), all three chapters provide fresh insights into the particular problems and challenges faced by fathers and suggest ways that society might respond. This is a topic we consider more extensively in the concluding chapter.

Programs to Increase Fathers' Access to Their Children

Jessica Pearson and Nancy Thoennes

The 1984 Child Support Enforcement amendments, the Family Support Act (FSA) of 1988, and the Personal Responsibility and Work Opportunity Reconciliation Act (PRWORA) of 1996 have vastly increased the attention being paid to the issue of child support and the enhancement of the financial well-being of children. Under the new legislation, courts and child support agencies are required to use aggressive techniques to establish paternity, establish and update orders using guidelines that more accurately reflect the costs of raising children, and enforce child support orders using automatic wage-withholding procedures and other mass case-processing techniques like tax intercepts, driver's license suspensions, and reporting delinquent obligors to credit bureau reporting agencies.

Less attention, however, has been directed toward the issue of visitation, which many people see as closely connected to support issues. According to advocates of father's rights, children have the right to financial support from both parents as well as the right to a continuing relationship with both parents. Similarly, while parents have a responsibility to support their children, they also have a right to their company and companionship.

Noncustodial parent groups claim that the increasingly aggressive enforcement of child support obligations has not been matched by an equally aggressive enforcement of visitation rights, and that this imbalance has only exacerbated the already competitive behavior between parents following separation and divorce. Advocates argue that custodial parents frequently deny the noncustodial parent access because of hostility stemming from the breakup of the parental relationship. As a result, children suffer because they do not have sufficient contact with both parents. Frustrated by their lack of access, fathers attempt to exercise control by withholding child support payments. If programs existed to help noncustodial parents resolve their problems with access, the argument goes, they would be more likely to comply with court-ordered child support and maintain contact with their children.

In response to these contentions, Congress has urged state and local governments, in the words of the 1984 CSE amendments, to "focus on the vital issues of child support, child custody [and] visitation rights." The 1988 FSA authorized state demonstration projects to "develop, improve or expand activities designed to increase compliance with child access provisions of court orders," and to promote improvements in existing procedures or the development of new methods and techniques to resolve child access and visitation problems. More recently, the PRWORA included funding for every state to support programs that enhance access.

This chapter explores the range of programs that have been devised to increase fathers' access to their children following separation and divorce. We present a portrait of the interventions, the types of clients they serve, the problems that parents bring to the programs, and the outcomes they experience as a result of program participation.

THE PROBLEM

There is little disagreement that visitation following separation and divorce is a serious problem for many families. National probability samples find that approximately one-third (Seltzer 1991) to one-half (Furstenberg 1988) of children living apart from one parent had no direct contact with their nonresidential parent in the previous year; on average, only about one-sixth saw their fathers as often as once a week.

What is more controversial is the cause and nature of the access problem. Advocates for noncustodial parents contend that the root of the problem is interference by the residential parent and that millions of children are denied visitation because custodial parents: (1) are unsupportive of access, (2) are uncooperative in arranging visits, (3) are inflexible in altering visitation schedules, and (4) discourage children from visiting. The National Council for Children's Rights estimates that the residential parent interferes with access in 37 percent of divorce cases (NCRR 1991); lack of access is claimed to be a major factor in fathers' failure to pay child support (Bertoia and Drakich 1993; Coltrane and Hickman 1992). Advocates for custodial parents contend that most residential parents would welcome more access by the noncustodial parent and attribute visitation conflicts to noncustodial parents who miss or are late for visits, constantly change the visitation schedule, and/or do not provide safe visiting conditions.

The debate is hard to resolve. Self-reported behavior by mothers and fathers on visitation, child support, and child adjustment are frequently at odds and distorted in socially desirable directions (Braver, Fitzpatrick, and Bay 1991; Veum 1993; Petronio 1988; Thoennes et al. 1996; Pearson and Anhalt 1992). Although there has been no national, representative study of visitation denial, and measurement problems abound, the limited research available suggests that there is a certain amount of truth to both points of view. Several studies indicate that one-fifth to one-third of custodial parents have denied the noncustodial parent visitation privileges at least once (Haskins et al. 1985; Braver et al. 1991; Pearson and Thoennes 1988a; Wallerstein and Kelly 1980), with the higher estimate coming from reports by noncustodial parents and the lower estimate from custodial parents. Research also suggests that noncustodial father-child contact is most frequent when custodial mothers allow and encourage access without excessive hostility (Ahrons and Miller 1993; Koch and Lowery 1984; Kurdek 1988).

On the other hand, the National Survey of Children (Furstenberg 1988) and the Colorado Household Survey on Child Support (Pearson, Anhalt, and Thoennes 1991) indicate that the majority of custodial mothers would welcome the father playing a larger role in the children's upbringing and assuming more child-rearing responsibility. Several studies have also concluded that custodial parents (of both sexes) commonly report concerns about the child's safety, rather than anger with the other parent, when they refuse to cooperate with the visitation order (Braver et al. 1991; Pearson and Anhalt 1993).

The Public Response

Public policy in recent years has begun to reflect the complex nature of the access problem. In the wake of pressure by advocacy groups representing noncustodial parents, courts and legislative bodies have begun to recognize the importance of fathers' access to their children. At the same time, advocates for battered women and groups representing custodial parents have lobbied for measures that address their concerns. As a result, recent legislative and policy changes try to respond to pressure for more noncustodial access as well as more attention to child safety.

THE SPREAD OF JOINT CUSTODY   Since 1975 the number of states explicitly authorizing joint custody increased from one (North Carolina) to forty-three. Although most legislatures have adopted measures that stress voluntary joint custody and have rejected mandated or presumptive joint custody, this legislative trend represents a dramatic change in custody standards that until recently favored mothers.

STATUTORY PROVISIONS STRESSING ACCESS   Eleven states have "friendly parent" amendments that instruct courts to give preference in awarding custody to the parent who is more likely to allow frequent and continuing contact with the noncustodial parent. Welfare reform legislation enacted in 1996 awarded grants to states for services to increase fathers' access to their children.

THE GROWTH OF DIVORCE MEDIATION   During the past twenty years, divorce mediation has developed from a single experimental pilot in the Los Angeles Conciliation Court to a common feature in many domestic relations settings. The National Center for State Courts estimates that there are currently about 205 programs offering court-based or court-annexed services for divorce disputes, of which 75 mandate participation categorically. Initially motivated by pressures to relieve case backlogs in courts and concerns about the well-being of children who are the focus of protracted custody and visitation disputes, divorce mediation also affords parents an opportunity to negotiate post-decree access arrangements for their children that frequently call for more joint custody and more contact with the noncustodial parent than is typically the case in lawyer-negotiated and adjudicated divorce orders (Pearson 1994; Kelly 1990, 1996).

PROVIDING FOR ACCESS WHEN THERE ARE CONCERNS ABOUT SAFETY   Although legislation has been adopted in thirty-six states specifying that domestic violence and allegations of abuse or neglect be taken into account in the award of custody, courts are generally prohibited from denying a noncustodial parent access to his children unless there is evidence of imminent danger (*Harvard Law Review* 1993). One response to the rising incidence of allegations of domestic violence, child abuse, substance abuse, and other safety problems has been the creation of a new social service: supervised visitation. These programs offer supervised exchanges of children at neutral drop-off and pickup sites and monitored visits of non-custodial parents with their children. The Supervised Visitation Network, a national membership association, lists fifty-nine participating programs in seventeen states that provide supervised visitation services (Strauss and Alda 1994). Domestic relations judges maintain that supervised visitation has become an indispensable resource for family courts when safety allegations are made (New York City Bar Association 1994).

THE GROWTH OF THE FATHERS' RIGHTS MOVEMENT   A comprehensive directory compiled by Fathers for Equal Rights, Inc., of Des Moines, Iowa, identifies 282 fathers' rights organizations throughout the United States. Virtually all have been established since 1981 to provide direct services for fathers seeking to strengthen their ties with their children. Fathers' rights organizations have also lobbied for joint custody legislation and federal acknowledgment of custody and visitation issues. In addition to these organizations, many of the organizations that have evolved in the burgeoning "responsible fatherhood" and children's rights movement (Levine and Pitt 1995) also champion paternal contact and access.

THE NEW EMPHASIS ON PATERNITY ESTABLISHMENT   With approximately 31 percent of all births in the United States occurring out of wedlock (Moore 1995) and paternity being ultimately established for less than half of these births (OCSE 1996), a substantial amount of legislative activity has been aimed at enhancing paternity establishment, including aspects of the Family Support Act of 1988, the Budget Reconciliation Act of 1993, and the PRWORA of 1996. While the primary motive for paternity establishment is financial, access issues are far from irrelevant. Currently, there are several large-scale, multi-state demonstration projects winding down or starting up that aim to promote paternity establishment, financial responsibility, and access for unmarried fathers (Bloom and Sherwood 1994; Watson 1992; OCSE 1997, Johnson and Pouncy n.d.); hospitals in many states are required to make paternity acknowledgment procedures available to interested unmarried parents on a regular basis (Pearson and Thoennes 1995, 1996; Williams et al. 1995); and several juris-dictions have initiated mediation programs to address access problems among unmarried parents in adjudicated paternity cases (Manville 1995).

THE SPREAD OF PARENT EDUCATION PROGRAMS   Perhaps the newest trend is court-affiliated education programs for separated and divorcing parents. According to a recent survey, such programs are in operation in 541 counties throughout the United States (Blaisure and Geasler 1996). Most programs have some form of mandatory attendance, and in four states (Connecticut, Utah, Vermont, and Arizona) all divorcing parents with minor children are required to attend unless a waiver is granted. While parent education programs differ with respect to attendance policies, format, program content, fee structure, and management, they all stress the harmful effects of parental conflict on children and the benefits of contact with both parents following separation and divorce (Thoennes and Pearson 1998).

VISITATION ENFORCEMENT PROGRAMS   Pursuant to the 1984 Child Support Enforcement amendments, every state created a commission to examine other child support items, including issues pertaining to child access, and a handful of states enacted legislation calling for court-sponsored efforts to enforce visitation rights. In response to complaints that child support and visitation were not being treated in an even-handed manner in federal legislation and the courts, section 504 of the Family Support Act of 1988 authorized the U.S. Department of Health and Human Services to fund demonstration projects that test methods and techniques to resolve child access and visitation problems.

RESEARCH ON VISITATION ENFORCEMENT PROGRAMS

This chapter presents findings from several evaluations of visitation enforcement programs that we have conducted. One set of evaluations initiated in 1990, and funded by the State Justice Institute (SJI), involved five court-based programs in jurisdictions located in Michigan, Arizona, Florida, Kansas, and Los Angeles.[1] Another set of studies that we conducted jointly with Policy Studies, Inc., was the evaluation of the Child Access Demonstration Projects, which consisted of awards by OCSE in 1990 to the states of Florida, Idaho, and Indiana (OCSE-wave 1) and awards in 1991 to Arizona, Idaho, Iowa, and Massachusetts (OCSE-wave 2) for court, child support agency, and community-based interventions aimed at resolving disputes about access.[2]

In both sets of studies, we visited the program sites, observed the access interventions, and interviewed key program staff and the relevant judges and lawyers. For the SJI project, we collected information from program files maintained by visitation enforcement programs on 1,164 parents (678 couples) who were served in 1989. In 1990 we conducted telephone interviews with 394 parents about their experiences with the program and its more lasting effects. This represented a response rate of 34 percent. Refusal rates in the study were low (11 percent); we were simply unable to locate most program participants using the outdated location information in the files.

For the OCSE Child Access Demonstration Projects, we randomly assigned divorcing or previously divorced litigants to an experimental group and a non-treatment comparison group. Parents completed questionnaires when they were first identified as having an access dispute. They were recontacted approximately six months later for cases in the first set of OCSE projects and twelve months later for cases in the second set. Court files and child support agency records were reviewed for all project cases.

At least one parent completed a baseline questionnaire for 1,122 cases in the first set of OCSE projects, and 1,314 cases in the second set. At the follow-up time, the response rate for completed project questionnaires was 57 percent for the first set of OCSE projects and 65 percent for the second. At all project sites, the biggest reason for sample attrition was parental mobility and the absence of a valid telephone number when a follow-up contact was attempted (see table 8.1).

Description of the Interventions

The programs evaluated in the SJI and OCSE-funded research projects fall into four categories: (1) mediation interventions; (2) educational interventions; (3) conference or counseling interventions; and (4) monitoring interventions. In actual practice, jurisdictions may adopt hybrids that incorporate one or more of these types of

TABLE 8.1 / Response and Retention Rates in the Evaluation of Access Interventions

	SJI Sites		
Site	Number of Potential Respondents	Number of Completed Interviews	Response Rate (Percentage)
Arizona	393	131	33
Michigan	269	80	30
Kansas	231	71	31
Florida	184	63	34
California	87	49	56
Total SJI sites	1,164	394	34

	OCSE Sites		
	Baseline Cases	Follow-up Cases	Retention Rate (Percentage)
Wave 1			
Florida	182	135	74
Lake County, Indiana	222	98	44
Marion County, Indiana	391	186	48
Idaho	327	225	69
Total wave 1	1,122	644	57
Wave 2			
Arizona	551	414	75
Idaho	228	163	72
Iowa	307	119	39
Massachusetts	228	151	66
Total wave 2	1,314	847	65

interventions. Table 8.2 provides a summary of these programs. In all sites with both experimental and control groups, parents with access problems were randomly assigned to experimental and control groups following their referral to the project.

MEDIATION INTERVENTIONS   Several of the programs we studied rely heavily on mediation with parents who have access disputes. These programs include those in Lee and Leon Counties, Florida; Ada County, Idaho; and Lake and Marion Counties, Indiana. Those who are unable to reach agreements in mediation proceed to have hearings with referees and judges. In the Florida and Idaho programs, new divorces or modification cases with visitation disputes are ordered into mediation by the judge. In Indiana, child support workers refer all obligors they see who mention visitation problems to mediation, but participation is voluntary. In the event of the parties' failure to reach an agreement in mediation, and in all control group cases, the case is sent to a judge, who may also send the parties for a custody evaluation before a judicial decision.

EDUCATIONAL INTERVENTIONS   Another approach to the resolution of access disputes is the provision of educational services to parents with disputes or at risk of dispute. These programs include the Pre-Contemptors/Contemptors Group in California, which was created in 1988 by mediators at the Family Mediation and Counseling Service of the Los Angeles District Court. It is a mandated education program for those who are found in contempt of custody or visitation orders, are about to be found in contempt, or are engaging in behavior that judges determine is producing continuing litigation due to noncompliance with previous court orders. The six hours of classes for groups of parents who fall into this category provide information about the law concerning custody and visitation, the effects of parental conflict and litigation behavior on children, the developmental needs of children, and techniques to improve communication and develop problem-solving skills.

The project in Massachusetts, conducted by the University of Massachusetts in collaboration with the Family Service Clinic of the Middlesex County Division of the Probate and Family Court, provided an experimental intervention of three educational sessions aimed at sensitizing parents to the other parent's point of view. Participants included all newly divorcing couples and relitigating ex-spouses identified by project staff as having a visitation dispute. Parents were ordered into the project by the court and randomly assigned to the intervention or the control group.

The second project in Idaho, conducted by Boise State University in collaboration with the domestic relations court and private mediators in the community, provided all divorcing parents with minor children (or previously divorced parents filing for modification of the custody or visitation order) with an orientation program dealing with the divorce process and the deleterious effects of disputes about custody and visitation on children. At the end of the orientation, parents were asked to produce a detailed plan specifying how access was to take place. Parents who were unable to produce a plan were assigned to a four-session class on communication skills. At the conclusion of the sessions, parents were once again given an opportunity to develop a detailed parenting plan. Parents who failed to

TABLE 8.2 / Access Project Sites: Cases, Interventions, and Implementing Agencies

Site	Cases	SJI Evaluation Primary Intervention	Implementing Agency
California	Cases with continued litigation concerning custody or visitation. Referred by the court.	Education/classes and interactive support group for parents at risk of contempt of court proceedings.	Family and mediation conciliation court services of the Los Angeles County Superior Court.
Florida	Cases with a court order seeking to enforce child support and/or visitation terms where parents request assistance. Referred by the court.	Mediation and pretrial hearings with nonjudicial personnel followed by a hearing with a judge if no resolution reached.	Support and Visitation Enforcement (SAVE) program of the Lee County Family Law Division of the Twentieth Judicial Circuit.
Kansas	Divorce cases with a court order concerning visitation and continued legal filings. Referred by the court.	Case management whereby the court designates a court intermediary to work out ongoing disputes between the parents concerning custody or visitation using telephone contacts or face-to-face meetings.	Court Services of the Twenty-ninth Judicial District of Kansas (Wyandotte County).
Arizona	Cases with enforceable court orders concerning visitation where a parent files a request for enforcement services.	Telephone monitoring after visitation is supposed to occur.	Expedited Visitation Services (EVS), Maricopa County Clerk's Office.
Michigan	All paternity and divorce cases with continued access difficulties where parent files a pro se complaint form.	Court complaint filings; letters of notification; telephone or in-person conferences; mediation sessions; and court hearings.	Wayne County Family Counseling and Mediation Division, Friend of the Court, Third Judicial Circuit Court, Detroit, Michigan.

(Table continues on p. 228.)

TABLE 8.2 / *Continued*

| | OCSE Child Access Demonstration Sites | | |
Site	Cases	Primary Intervention	Implementing Agency
Wave 1			
Florida	New divorce cases with conflicting written claims; cases seeking legal modifications of custody and visitation orders. Ordered by court.	Mediation provided at the court by court-approved independent mediators.	Second Judicial District (Leon County), Florida State Court.
Idaho	New divorce cases with a request for hearing; cases seeking legal modifications; all pro se cases with minor children with no written parenting plan. Ordered by court.	Mediation provided by independent mediators in their private offices; services contracted through Boise State University.	Boise State University and Fourth Judicial District Court, Ada County, Idaho.
Lake County, Indiana	IV-D cases (mainly prior order cases) with an access dispute as indicated by client. Referred by IV-D agency.	Mediation provided at the IV-D office (Prosecuting Attorney's Office) by an independent mediator.	Lake County Prosecuting Attorney's Office.
Marion County, Indiana	IV-D cases (mainly prior order cases) with an access dispute as indicated by client. Referred by IV-D agency.	Mediation provided by court mediators at the Domestic Relations Counseling Bureau.	Marion County Prosecuting Attorney's Office and Domestic Relations Court.

Wave 2

Arizona See SJI Section

Idaho	New divorce cases, those seeking legal modifications of custody and visitation orders, and pro se clients with no parenting plan.	Family skills program for parents and children; mediation for some cases.	Boise State University and Fourth Judicial District Court, Ada County, Idaho.
Iowa	Parents who call Fathers for Equal Rights, Inc., requesting assistance with child access problems.	Access counseling, mainly for non-custodial parents.	Fathers for Equal Rights, Inc., Des Moines, Iowa.
Massachusetts	New divorce and modification cases with conflicting written claims indicating a relevant access dispute. Mandated by court to attend.	Parent education for some cases; clinical assessment and planning for others.	Family Service Clinic, Middlesex County Probate and Family Court.

produce such a plan were referred to private mediators for individual sessions. Those failing to produce an agreement in mediation were referred to court for a judicial hearing. All parents identified by project staff as having a dispute were ordered by the court to participate in the project.

CONFERENCE OR COUNSELING INTERVENTIONS   A third commonly utilized approach to solving access problems is to have disputing parents meet with counselors to discuss how they might restructure visitation or otherwise eliminate their access disputes. In most systems, parents who file visitation complaints are seen by judges or other hearing officers. The Visitation Intake Program in Wayne County, Michigan, was established in 1987 by the Counseling and Mediation Division of the Friend of the Court. It permits custodial and noncustodial parents with a court order for visitation to file a complaint alleging visitation denial. Upon filing, program personnel investigate the matter and attempt to resolve the problem, primarily through the use of a telephone or in-person conference with the parents. Following the conference, the parents may be referred for other types of interventions, such as mediation, treatment for drug or alcohol problems, and civil contempt procedures. Among the remedies for visitation denial available under Michigan law are makeup visitation provisions. The program is directly accessed by complaining parents.

Parents served in the OCSE demonstration project in Massachusetts were randomly assigned either to parent education or to a counseling intervention. Parents in the latter group met with court counselors to discuss their options and to work out a mutually acceptable access plan. Unlike mediators, counselors were free to develop recommendations that were provided to the court if the parents could not reach a settlement.

The OCSE demonstration project in Iowa was operated through Fathers for Equal Rights, Inc., a community-based advocacy group that has provided services to never-married, divorcing, and divorced parents since 1983. The main interventions it uses are a counseling session with the noncustodial parent ("access counseling") and referral to community services. Following the access counseling session, most noncustodial parents report that they have started keeping a journal of their visitation experiences, communicated with their child's school, communicated with the other parent in writing, retained a lawyer, and pursued a judicial hearing. Among the services that parents are offered but generally do not utilize are supervised drop-off and pickup services, anger management classes, and mediation. Noncustodial parents self-identify as having a dispute about access and participate in access counseling on a voluntary basis.

Court Services in Wyandotte County, Kansas, also provides case management for couples who have continuing problems with visitation. Designed to deal with "petty grievances" and to head off more serious parenting disagreements and communication blocks, case management may include telephone contacts by court workers with one or both parents, in-person meetings, and recommendations to the court. The process may also lead to referrals for various services, including mental health treatment and supervised visitation. All program participants are referred by the judiciary.

MONITORING INTERVENTIONS   A final approach to the resolution of access problems is to have court personnel involved in monitoring visitation to determine whether it occurs as ordered. Monitoring is usually performed along with other interventions, such as counseling or mediation. Expedited Visitation Services of Maricopa County, Arizona, is a court-based program established in 1988 to comply with an Arizona statute requiring expedited procedures for petitions regarding alleged noncompliance with an existing visitation order. When a request to enforce the terms of a custody or visitation order is filed, usually by the noncustodial parent, a conference is set up within seven days and the other parent is notified. The conference officer attempts to help the parents resolve their problems; the officer may also evaluate the situation and make recommendations to the court. Parents who file for visitation enforcement are monitored by program personnel for at least six months. The monitoring process typically involves telephone calls with each parent following each scheduled visitation episode. Parents may also be ordered to obtain services for supervised visitation and supervised exchanges or counseling. Complaining parents have direct access to the program or the court may order them to attend.

Characteristics of the Families Served

Table 8.3 provides summary information about the parents served in each of the visitation enforcement programs considered in this chapter. With the exception of cases recruited from the child support enforcement agencies in Indiana and Michigan, parents who utilize visitation enforcement services tend to be employed and educated at the high school level or with some college. They also have very modest incomes. Individual gross incomes reported by participating mothers at the SSI sites range from $6,648 to $15,324. Incomes for fathers range from $13,356 to $27,996.

Clients had been married on average for seven years and typically had one or two children. However, the programs also served never-married parents. Approximately 10 to 30 percent of the parents at each site had not been married, and many of these parents had never lived together. Interestingly, however, most patterns dealing with custody, access, and program outcome were identical for ever-married and never-married parents. As a result, in this chapter we merge these two groups of parents and contrast the experiences of noncustodial fathers and custodial mothers, without controlling for their marital status.

Among those divorced at project entry, the average amount of time that had elapsed between the date the divorce was final and the date they entered the project was about three years. The average age of the children whose parents were served ranged from 5.7 to 7.3 years.

At project entry, most children (68 to 93 percent) lived primarily with their mothers. The proportion of children in paternal residential arrangements ranged from 8 to 18 percent across the sites. Cases in which children divided their time between their mother's and father's residence on a roughly equal basis were rare.

Many of the parents at the project sites had unspecified visitation orders. For example, among the parents served at the sites studied with SJI funding, 41 percent

TABLE 8.3 / Selected Indicators of Demographic, Economic, and Family Status for Cases in the SJI Child Access Demonstration Projects

	OCSE Wave I				OCSE Wave II				SJI Sites				
	Florida	Idaho	Lake County, Indiana	Marion County, Indiana	Arizona	Idaho	Iowa	Massa-chusetts	Arizona	Michigan	Florida	Kansas	California
College graduate (percentage)													
Fathers	24	21	8	8	18	25	14	20	20	16	12	23	19
Mothers	19	12	4	6	13	14	—	22	24	17	10	12	48
Anglo	61	95	35	51	77	94	96	91	84	39	94	88	62
Employed													
Fathers	84	85	61	63	87	88	84	77	89	81	88	100	88
Mothers	69	77	28	41	71	73	67	52	87	71	59	96	86
Income													
Fathers	33,037	29,882	17,984	17,315	23,348	24,175	19,392	26,698	17,856	15,444	13,356	NA	27,996
Mothers	30,221	27,624	16,346	15,727	13,512	12,723	11,979	14,148	12,504	6,648	11,316	10,200	15,324

Marital status													
Never married	6	1	20	27	13	10	19	32	6	7	7	10	15
Divorced/divorcing	94	99	80	73	87	90	81	68	94	93	93	90	85
Average age of children	6	6	5	5	6.7	6.7	7.1	5.7	6.7	8.5	7.2	6.7	7.1
Mother primary custodian (percentage)	74	69	93	90	73	68	85	88	77	82	84	76	73
Average days per month with non-custodial fathers[a]	6.2	5.7	2.3	2.4	4.5	4.5	3.3	6	—	—	—	—	—
Number of cases													
Fathers	109	209	112	173	478	206	267	167	54	32	25	30	16
Mothers	117	220	162	266	485	197	94	180	55	42	29	25	21

[a] Includes all cases where father is noncustodian.

entered the project with unspecified, "reasonable" visitation orders. Those with specific orders were equally apt to have orders calling for one to four days of contact per month, or five to eight days. Less than 10 percent called for nine or more days of contact per month.

There were, however, some differences by site in the type of families served. These differences undoubtedly reflect the stage in the dispute at which the intervention occurred and the nature of the agency providing services. For example, families served in the court-based mediation and education projects at several of the OCSE sites tended to be newly separated couples who had not participated in prior dispute resolution interventions. These parents reported the highest levels of parental cooperation and trust when they were first surveyed.

Relitigating parents, such as those in many of the counseling and monitoring interventions in the SJI and OCSE-wave 2 sites, often reported high-conflict relationships, fraught with anger, distrust, and extreme communication deficiencies (see tables 8.4 and 8.5).

Where the information was available, it appeared that domestic violence was a factor for many families. For example, approximately 50 percent of the mothers in the second set of OCSE projects reported frequent incidents of violence.

Nature of Access Disputes

Parents were asked to review a long list of problems related to visitation and access and to check those that applied to them. Based on an analysis of their responses, we drew several conclusions about the nature of their access problems.

BOTH PARENTS HAVE ACCESS PROBLEMS   Noncustodial and custodial parents were equally likely to report problems with visitation. Noncustodial and custodial parents in the OCSE projects cited approximately four to six problems with visitation. In general, parents with post-decree disputes reported more problems than their recently separated counterparts. While this might suggest that visitation problems increase with the time since separation, it is equally possible that parents who continue to dispute long after their separation are simply the most contentious of all parents.

BOTH PARENTS CITE MANY OF THE SAME PROBLEMS   Although certain access problems were clearly more pronounced for noncustodial versus custodial parents, or were more apt to be cited by fathers versus mothers, every group of parents mentioned having some of the same problems with visitation. High and equal proportions of both noncustodial and custodial parents reported problems with unclear visitation plans, disagreements in scheduling visitation, fights during drop-off and pickup, and problems caused by new relationships.

ENFORCEMENT PROGRAMS TEND TO SEE LONG-STANDING ACCESS PROBLEMS   On average, parents who were already divorced when they entered OCSE-funded visitation enforcement projects reported that their access problems had begun twenty-nine months earlier. Never-married parents reported their problems had developed

TABLE 8.4 / Selected Relationship Characteristics Reported by Parents at the OCSE Project Sites Prior to Intervention

	Wave 1					Wave 2			
Percent Agreeing	Florida	Idaho	Lake County Indiana	Marion County Indiana	Arizona	Idaho	Iowa	Massachusetts
"I trust the other parent"								
Fathers	40	39	14	28	19	28	20	23
Mothers	27	29	11	19	16	20	34	20
"I can reason with the other parent"								
Fathers	31	35	19	27	20	25	18	22
Mothers	32	32	17	16	14	22	32	20
"The other parent and I cooperate well"								
Fathers	34	40	12	18	3	17	8	13
Mothers	34	40	12	16	5	17	23	12
"I am angry with the other parent"								
Fathers	32	39	41	39	46	54	64	56
Mothers	42	42	53	48	52	58	72	68

(Table continues on p. 236.)

TABLE 8.4 / *Continued*

	Wave 1				Wave 2			
Percent Agreeing	Florida	Idaho	Lake County Indiana	Marion County Indiana	Arizona	Idaho	Iowa	Massachusetts
"It is important for the children to see each of us frequently"								
Fathers	—	—	—	—	91	93	94	93
Mothers	—	—	—	—	77	83	80	77
"There have been several or frequent incidents of violence during the relationship"								
Mothers	—	—	—	—	53	43	49	52
"I am concerned about the child's safety when with the other parent"								
Fathers	25	23	31	24	31	32	37	39
Mothers	38	45	64	58	47	32	16	34
Sample size								
Fathers	109	209	112	173	501	205	268	167
Mothers	117	220	162	266	499	201	96	181

Note: Respondents are individual mothers and fathers, not couples.

TABLE 8.5 / Percent of Parents Agreeing with Various Statements About the Other Parent Prior to Participation in the OCSE Wave 2 Intervention

"The other parent is trying to cut me out of the child's life"	
Fathers (N = 860)	78
"The other parent is a bad influence"	
Fathers (N = 837)	42
Mothers (N = 633)	54
"The other parent is sick/immoral"	
Fathers (N = 835)	39
Mothers (N = 633)	44
"The other parent should see the child"	
More (mothers) (N = 624)	28
Less (mothers) (N = 692)	33

Notes: Respondents are individual mothers and fathers, not couples.

twenty-two to twenty-six months earlier. Even newly divorcing parents reported that their problems began sixteen months before they entered the project. In sites evaluated with SJI funding, half of the parents reported that problems had developed at separation, and one-third said they had developed within the first year following separation. These parents had been divorced for two to six years at project entry.

LACK OF ACCESS IS ONLY ONE OF MANY PROBLEMS OF NONCUSTODIAL PARENTS Much of the debate about access has centered on what has been termed "visitation denial," and at least half the noncustodial fathers at every OCSE project site, and 71 percent at the SJI-evaluated sites, complained about not getting enough time with their child. However, issues other than the amount of contact were at least as important, if not more important, to many parents. At least half of the noncustodial parents in the OCSE-funded projects mentioned problems with scheduling visitation or exchanging the children and problems with the other parent not being supportive of them as parents or denigrating them in front of the children.

EVEN IMPROVED ACCESS DOES NOT HELP NONCUSTODIAL PARENTS STOP FEELING CUT OUT OF THEIR CHILDREN'S LIVES Approximately 80 percent of noncustodial fathers in the second set of OCSE projects felt as though the custodial parent was trying to cut them out of their child's life. Fortunately, the proportion feeling cut out was significantly lower for those who reported regular and frequent contact. Nevertheless, this was a problem for 65 percent of noncustodial fathers who reported that visitation had been at least "fairly" regular, and for 38 percent of noncustodial fathers who saw their children nine days a month or more. Clearly, for many noncustodial parents even frequent access is no substitute for day-to-day residence and the level of involvement it permits. That more than half of the noncustodial fathers reported rarely attending a school event, and 45 percent reported infrequent telephone contact, suggests how hard it is for the noncustodial parent to stay in touch with the child's daily life. However, it is not clear whether one, both, or neither parent is responsible for this situation. While noncustodial parents often blame the custodial parent, the reverse is also true. Nearly one-third (28 percent) of custodial mothers agreed with the statement, "The other parent sees the children infrequently and they really need to have more contact with him."

CUSTODIAL PARENTS ARE CONCERNED ABOUT THE SAFETY AND SUPERVISION OF THE CHILDREN WHILE WITH THE OTHER PARENT   Both custodial and noncustodial parents express concerns about the well-being and safety of the child while in the other parent's care. However, custodial parents of both sexes express more concerns than noncustodial parents. At the SJI sites, 44 percent of the custodial mothers and an even higher percentage of the custodial fathers voiced safety-related concerns, ranging from alleged use of drugs and alcohol to violence, abuse, and neglect. While these allegations were noted in program files and court records, there was no information available to refute or substantiate them.

ACCESS DISPUTES HAVE MORE TO DO WITH THE RELATIONSHIP BETWEEN THE PARENTS THAN WITH FINANCIAL MATTERS   Many cases in visitation enforcement programs involve child support arrearages. Although child support and visitation problems are clearly interconnected, there is ample evidence that visitation problems go beyond economics. Fighting during pickup and drop-off of the children, complaints about the other parent being unsupportive, and feeling left out of the children's lives often reflect anger and communication problems between the parents. Indeed, at all four programs funded during the second round of OCSE awards, parents registered the highest levels of conflict on issues pertaining to parental communication rather than on the standard divorce issues of custody, visitation, or child support. They felt most passionately about the other parent not listening to what they had to say about the children, not sharing information about the children, and failing to communicate directly. Although half the fathers and one-third of the mothers at SJI sites indicated that they had disagreements about child support, fewer than one-fifth of either mothers (14 percent) or fathers (18 percent) at the OCSE projects said that their visitation problems were due to problems with child support.

Resolving Access Problems

The ability of parents to resolve their visitation disputes in the programs we studied varied according to the nature of their problems and the quality of their relationship. Certain problems, like scheduling difficulties, were very amenable to resolution in brief interventions like mediation and short-term counseling. For example, between one-third and one-half of the parents with "reasonable" visitation orders at every site evaluated under the SJI grant received specific orders as a result of the intervention.

However, many of the parents came to the programs with more deeply rooted problems that could not be easily negotiated. It is harder to resolve problems that stem from feeling cut out of the children's lives or unsupported by the other parent, continual parental fighting, or concerns about the children's safety and supervision while with the other parent. Indeed, half of the noncustodial fathers who participated in the second set of OCSE demonstration projects began the interventions with entrenched disputes that had already eluded settlement in several earlier dispute resolution efforts.

An indicator of the deep-rooted nature of parental animosity comes from surveys with parents administered both before and after participation in the access intervention. Parents in the second set of OCSE projects demonstrated no significant decline in anger levels following their participation in the program. About half of the parents continued to characterize their relationship with the other parent as extremely negative, hostile, and distrustful. Following participation in the programs evaluated with SJI funding, half the mothers still believed that the fathers had filed a visitation complaint only because of anger about child support, and more than one-third of the mothers at every site agreed that the children would be better off "not visiting with the other parent."

Thus, participants' degree of "success" in the visitation program depended in large measure on the initial quality of the parental relationship and the severity of the dispute. With their new divorce cases and relatively "young" disputes, 65 to 70 percent of participants in the first round of OCSE projects reached agreements in mediation, and limited evidence suggested that the mediation interventions resolved access conflicts, at least from the perspective of the noncustodial parent. Across these project sites, 46 to 68 percent of fathers reported experiencing no problems at all with visitation or access. Similarly, at the sites studied under SJI funding, cases with problems stemming from vague visitation orders were most likely to reach successful conclusions.

With their higher levels of conflict, previous failed efforts at dispute resolution, and lengthier, entrenched disputes, the families in the second set of OCSE projects generally failed to experience improvements in their access situations. At these sites, 60 to 84 percent of fathers in the experimental group reported ongoing problems with access when they were interviewed twelve months following their participation in the access intervention.

Table 8.6 provides a summary of the outcomes related to visitation.

Post-Intervention Contact with Children

One hypothesized outcome of the project interventions is an increase in the amount of time that noncustodial parents spend with their children. At least half of noncustodial fathers at every project site complained about not getting enough time with their children. One difficulty in determining whether the projects improved access is that mothers and fathers routinely give contradictory reports about the frequency and regularity of visitation. Fathers typically report either more visits with their children or more visitation denial than is reported by mothers (Braver et al. 1991; Petronio 1988; Veum 1993; Thoennes et al. 1996; Pearson and Anhalt 1992).

TABLE 8.6 / Selected Outcomes Following Program Participation

		SJI Sites				
		Arizona	Michigan	Florida	Kansas	California
Percent reaching agreement on visitation dispute		—	50	57	—	—
Percent of "Reasonable Visitation Orders" made specific		44	26	44	—	—
Percent noncustodial fathers reporting visitation situation better than a year ago	E C	69 —	45 —	54 —	76 —	62 —
Percent noncustodial fathers reporting problems with access in last few months	E C	52 —	79 —	55 —	35 —	50 —
Percent noncustodial fathers reporting increase in monthly access	E C	35 —	29 —	30 —	31 —	27 —
Average days per month noncustodial father reports seeing children	E C	— —	— —	— —	— —	— —
Percent mothers reporting safety concerns when child with other parent	E C	39 —	46 —	34 —	56 —	53 —
Percent fathers reporting no contact with child at follow-up	E C	— —	— —	— —	— —	— —
Number of cases	E C	158 —	94 —	83 —	107 —	53 —

Notes: E = experimental; C = control. With few exceptions there were no statistically significant differences between the experimental and control groups at the various project sites. The exceptions were that fathers in the experimental group in Massachusetts were less apt than their control group counterparts to report that their ex-spouse made negative comments about them to the children, that their ex-spouse was not responsive to the child's emotional needs, that the mother's

| OCSE Wave 1 | | | OCSE Wave 2 | | | | |
Florida	Idaho	Lake County, Indiana	Marion County, Indiana	Arizona	Idaho	Iowa	Massachusetts
67	70	68	65	—	25	—	40
—	—	—	—	—	—	—	—
—	—	—	—	47	32	28	45
—	—	—	—	52	—	24	54
47	32	56	54	81	60	78	84
71	56	74	73	81	—	63	100
50	36	57	48	36	40	26	19
23	38	13	42	36	—	28	39
3.4	3.8	6.3	5.2	4.8	6.6	3.9	4.6
4.9	2.0	8.1	4.4	4.5	—	3.7	5.1
22	20	12	46	42	35	—	36
17	21	34	45	34	—	5	14
15	15	34	39	17	10	32	25
—	—	—	—	18	—	32	14
72	195	103	172	163	60	42	101
85	148	35	64	82	—	18	21

new partner was interfering with access, and that they had problems scheduling visitation. Custo-dial parents in the experimental groups in Arizona and Massachusetts were less apt than their control group counterparts to complain that the children were upset at drop-off and pick-up times, that the children's father was unsupportive of their maternal role, and that there were still disagreements about custody.

Based on noncustodial parent accounts, there was some evidence that parents who participated in mediation and produced parenting agreements in the first round of OCSE projects experienced an improvement in the amount and regularity of contact. Noncustodial parents who reached settlements in mediation were more likely than control group parents to report contact with their children at the follow-up interview six months later. At three of the four sites, noncustodial parents who reached agreements in mediation reported an increase in the average days of visitation each month. Fathers in the control group did not report an equivalent gain.

With their more highly entrenched disputes and conflict-ridden relationships, parents who participated in the second round of OCSE projects did not report increased contact with their children following the project intervention. Comparable proportions of fathers in the experimental and control groups at the sites reported increases in monthly access; there were no significant differences in the average number of days of reported contact per month. Across the four OCSE sites, identical proportions of fathers in the experimental and control groups reported their access situation to be "better," "the same," or "worse," with 42, 34, and 24 percent of fathers proffering these ratings, respectively.

Compliance with Child Support Orders

All assessments of the effects of visitation enforcement programs on child support payment are hampered by contradictory reports by mothers and fathers and the lack of objective payment data for all cases. While some comparisons of parental reports with objective payment records suggest that mothers' reports are more accurate (Schaeffer, Seltzer, and Klawitter 1991), other comparisons find that both parents' reports are biased in self-serving ways (Braver et al. 1991; Petronio 1988; Veum 1993, Pearson and Anhalt 1992; Thoennes et al. 1996).

However, given these limitations, a review of custodial mothers' reports of child support payment patterns at the SJI and OCSE sites suggests modest but statistically insignificant improvements following program participation. For example, at four of the five SJI project sites, the percentage of obligors reported to have become current on their payments after project participation was greater than the percentage of obligors reported to have fallen behind, although most obligors did not reportedly change their payment behavior and remained consistently "current" or "behind." Across the five SJI project sites, 31 percent of current and delinquent obligors kept this payment status, respectively, while 26 percent of delinquent obligors became current and 12 percent of current obligors fell behind.

In the first set of OCSE projects, custodial and noncustodial parents in the experimental group reported better compliance with child support orders as compared with their counterparts in the control group. While these differences were not significant, they appeared across all four sites, with reported increases in compliance ranging from 5 to 28 percent for cases in the experimental group.

A review of parent reports of child support payment behavior for the second set of OCSE projects also fails to reveal statistically significant differences between the experimental and control groups. At the follow-up interview, 76 percent of all obligor fathers in the control group reported making full payments, compared to 81 percent in the experimental group. Similarly, at the follow-up interview, 50 percent of the obligee mothers in the control group reported receiving full payment, compared to 55 percent of the obligee mothers in the experimental group. Like fathers in other studies of child support compliance (Haskins 1988; Braver et al. 1991; Pearson and Thoennes 1988b), fathers in the OCSE projects tended to cite economic factors to explain their nonpayment, including income deficiencies and employment instability. Figure 8.1 provides a comparison of post-intervention payment patterns for the SJI and OCSE projects.

While the programs did not have a uniform positive impact on payment behavior, the data from all the sites do serve to confirm that access and payment are correlated. For example, 63 percent of parents at the SJI sites with visitation enforcement cases also had child support arrearages. In a similar vein, 41 percent of parents at these project sites had a history of prior litigation about child support; in one-third of the cases, at least one of the two litigation episodes they were engaged in immediately prior to filing the visitation complaint was a child support action. Typically, this consisted of a contempt proceeding regarding child support, a motion to modify a child support order, or an order to show cause regarding nonpayment of child support.

Visiting fathers at the SJI project sites were best helped with their access problems if they were current in their child support payments, while those who were behind in payments were apt to see their access deteriorate following program participation. Child support agency files for fathers in the second set of OCSE projects indicate that those who reported no visitation paid approximately 45 percent of the amount due, while fathers who reported at least some visitation paid close to 70 percent. And although not statistically significant, payment improved when fathers reported that the visitation situation had improved. Fathers who said that visitation was better at the follow-up interview paid 80 percent of what they owed, compared to the 72 percent paid by fathers who said that visitation was the "same as at baseline" and the 64 percent paid by fathers who said that visitation was "worse."

Parent Reactions to the Programs

While parents who participated in the visitation enforcement programs did not consistently report significant increases in parent-child contact, reduced parental anger levels, or the alleviation of ongoing visitation problems, the programs still garnered substantial levels of user satisfaction. For example, at least half the non-custodial parents who participated in mediation interventions at the OCSE projects in Florida and Idaho agreed that the mediator let them tell their side of the story (64

FIGURE 8.1 / Reported Child Support Payment Patterns Following Program Participation

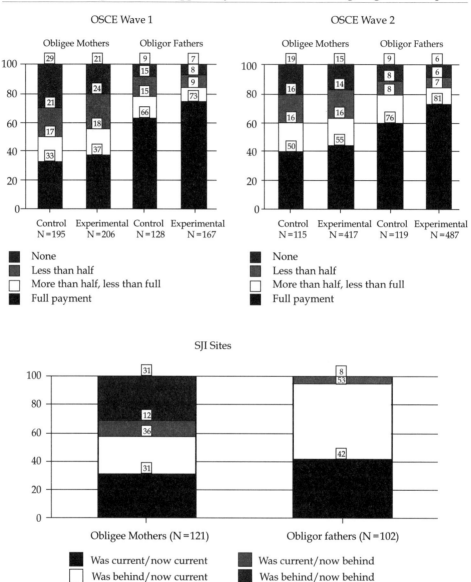

to 85 percent), kept the discussion on track (52 to 83 percent), and focused on the welfare of the children (58 to 73 percent). This is consistent with approval ratings reported in other investigations of divorce mediation (Pearson 1994).

Even parents with more protracted disputes about access also reacted positively to the various interventions to which they were exposed. Approximately half of the fathers and mothers at each site in the second round of OCSE projects reported that the education and the telephone monitoring and counseling interventions they had experienced had been either "somewhat" or "very" helpful. Fathers who began the program with no contact with their children were the most likely to describe the interventions as helpful; those who began with substantial levels of contact were less apt to perceive benefits. Mothers who reported the greatest program benefits were more apt to characterize the children's father as someone who could be trusted at the start of the program.

Some parents even felt optimistic about the program leading to tangible improvement in the behavior of the other parent, the regular payment of child support, or the ability to exercise visitation. Thus, about one-third of the fathers and one-quarter of the mothers at the SJI project sites agreed that the visitation program had "really made the other parent shape up," although two-thirds of fathers and three-quarters of mothers agreed that the "other parent was uncooperative and we accomplished little" in the program intervention.

The intervention that received the highest approval rating was access counseling conducted by the fathers' rights advocacy organization in Iowa. Fully 81 percent of the fathers who used this program characterized it as helpful. Iowa was the only site in our studies to provide services to interested parents on a voluntary basis, typically serving only fathers and rarely involving custodial mothers. It was also the only site to explore legal remedies with clients, including advising fathers about their legal rights and about their low- and high-level litigation options, as well as providing them with attorney referrals. Indeed, following access counseling, the most common actions taken by fathers were to retain an attorney (44 percent), begin keeping a journal or other written record of their interaction with the other parent (43 percent), and/or file a court action (23 percent).

We get another reading on the attractiveness of legal remedies to fathers from their assessments of what might have helped them to solve their access problems. The interventions favored by at least half of the fathers at all of the nine sites for which we have data were free legal assistance, so as to enter a visitation schedule as a court order, and changes in custody. At eight of the nine sites, at least half the fathers expressed support for making visitation orders more detailed and specific. More than half of the fathers at five of the nine sites with data were also supportive of imposing fines and makeup visitation arrangements, and more than half at six sites favored talking with court workers or mediators. Not surprisingly, there was little paternal support for supervised visitation, neutral sites at which to exchange the children, attending education programs, and monitoring calls by court workers following scheduled visitation episodes.

With their view that visitation problems are rooted in the personality of their children's fathers, mothers tended to be relatively unenthusiastic about all approaches to solving access problems, although a majority of the mothers expressed support for legal assistance with court hearings and one-on-one interventions with court workers or mediators. At least half of the mothers at sites with data also approved of making visitation orders more specific and de-

TABLE 8.7 / Percent Satisfied with the Access Intervention

Site	Fathers	Mothers
SJI		
Arizona	63 (50)	43 (51)
Michigan	48 (22)	58 (32)
Florida	65 (22)	68 (26)
Kansas	57 (20)	50 (25)
California	69 (16)	65 (17)
OCSE Wave 1		
Florida	64 (58)	73 (77)
Idaho	68 (106)	68 (119)
Lake County, Indiana	58 (36)	44 (62)
Marion County, Indiana	46 (63)	65 (123)
OCSE Wave 2		
Arizona	60 (216)	62 (205)
Idaho	42 (129)	46 (114)
Iowa	81 (70)	—
Massachusetts—Education	50 (42)	61 (50)
Massachusetts—Counseling	46 (31)	44 (30)

tailed. Not surprisingly, mothers were also more likely than fathers to recommend the use of supervised visitation services and neutral exchange sites (see table 8.7).

CONCLUSIONS

Public policy is changing in the child support arena from an exclusive focus on financial collections to an acknowledgment of the relevance of visitation. Evaluations of a number of visitation enforcement programs suggest that satisfactory, regular visitation, like the satisfactory, regular payment of child support, will not be easily accomplished, at least not for all parents. Like nonpayment of child support, nonvisitation is complex, with many causes and extenuating circumstances. Like child support disputes, access problems are often rooted in basic relationship disputes that are not easily addressed in brief problem-solving interventions.

These disputes are also complex and defy simple judgments or pronouncements of blame. Typically, they involve a web of contradictory allegations and counter-allegations that are difficult to unravel and appear to be supported by at least some empirical evidence.

Some problems are clearly more amenable to prevention or resolution in access interventions than others. For example, newly separating couples with minor children can benefit from information about their custody and visitation options, the dangers of parental conflict, and the availability of relevant community services. Newly separating couples who lack a visitation plan, divorced parents with vague visitation orders that call for "reasonable visitation," or divorced parents seeking modification of prior custody and visitation orders can often be readily helped in mediation and brief counseling interventions aimed at producing a parenting plan. Like many other research studies, however, these evaluations show that the typical mediation forum does not revolutionize communication and behavior patterns in dysfunctional families. Many high-conflict parents with a lengthy dispute history and prior episodes of failed problem-solving and litigation are not helped in short-term interventions that stress education, brief counseling, mediation, and case management using mail and telephone techniques. While some of these parents report relief and satisfaction with their program experiences, others need lengthier and more therapeutic interventions, such as impasse-directed mediation (Johnston and Campbell 1988; Johnston 1994), that go beyond the resources available in most public-sector programs. Moreover, most want free legal assistance and court hearings to pursue punitive remedies like fines, custody changes, and other enforcement actions that run counter to current judicial policy and the recommendations of mental health professionals and most family law attorneys.

Fortunately, most separating and divorcing couples do not require intensive and costly interventions. Indeed, the vast majority of them experience no significant access problems or only occasional problems that they solve on their own (Maccoby and Mnookin 1992).

As with child support enforcement, however, we need a variety of remedies for those with more persistent access problems. As in all areas of public policy, it will be a challenge to determine how to address the more costly and extensive needs of this troubled minority. It is important to note that the federal Office of Child Support Enforcement has made annual awards of $10 million in 1997 and 1998 to states to provide services that promote access between noncustodial parents and their children, some of which will presumably be devoted to serving high-conflict families.

Finally, the research on visitation problems underscores the need to develop community resources that address the underlying problems that some separating and divorced families face. For example, to enhance safety, neutral exchange sites and supervised visitation services are needed so that parents who should be kept apart may exchange their children in a nonthreatening setting and parent-child contact may occur when allegations concerning safety are made or parents who have been absent for long periods of time are reintroduced into a child's life. In a similar vein, communities need an array of relevant investigation, counseling, drug treatment, and support services to which parents may be referred. And to the extent that unemployment, job instability, and other financial factors contribute to nonvisitation and nonpayment of child support, the long-term solution to access problems for many families may require more basic economic reform.

Indeed, enhancing the employment and earning status of men at lower education and skill levels may be the only way to encourage poor fathers to assume more parental responsibilities. Black single men who are stably employed are twice as likely to marry the mother of the children they conceive out of wedlock (Testa and Krogh 1995). In a similar vein, a study of 289 single, teen-mother families on AFDC in Wisconsin finds father's work experience the strongest predictor of remaining involved in the child's life (Danzinger and Radin 1990).

In light of these findings, it is encouraging that child support policies are finally beginning to address the employment problems that many noncustodial parents face. For example, PRWORA gives states the capacity to order noncustodial parents who are delinquent in child support into work activities if their children are receiving public assistance (Sorensen 1997). In 1997, OCSE granted Washington State a waiver permitting the use of federal funds normally restricted to child support enforcement to support programs to help noncustodial parents. In 1997, OCSE also made multi-year awards to eight states to conduct demonstration projects that provide employment and support services to noncustodial parents. And in 1998, with the support of the Ford Foundation, the National Center for Strategic Nonprofit Planning and Community Leadership made awards to twelve states to plan demonstration projects in which child support agencies and community-based organizations will collaborate to recruit and assist poor nonresident parents for the purpose of promoting employment, paternal contact, and child support payment.

Although the impact of responsible fatherhood programs has not yet been assessed (The Lewin Group 1997) and the results of the Parents' Fair Share Demonstration, the pioneering project offering employment and support services to noncustodial parents, are not yet in, these developments suggest that we may be moving to an era when child support policies will be coupled with offers of assistance with employment and access to underemployed, unemployed, and low-earning fathers. If so, and if the offers are backed up with meaningful forms of help, we may have a viable strategy to meet the paternity acknowledgement and child support goals contained in the welfare reform law.

Data collection was supported by a grant from the State Justice Institute (grant no.: 89M–E–021, program officer: Philip Toelkes) and by contracts between the Office of Child Support Enforcement (OCSE) and Policy Studies, Inc., of Denver, Colorado, with subcontracts to the Center for Policy Research of Denver (1990–95). We conducted the OCSE-funded evaluations of the Child Access Demonstration Projects with David Price and Robert Williams of Policy Studies. The OCSE program officer for the Child Access Demonstration Projects and their evaluation was David Arnaudo. The points of view expressed here are those of the authors and do not necessarily represent the official position or policies of the agencies that funded the research.

NOTES

1. For further information, see Pearson and Anhalt (1992). See also Pearson and Anhalt (1994a, 1994b).

2. For further information, see Price et al. (1994), Thoennes et al. (1996), Pearson and Theoennes (1996), and Pearson and Thoennes (1997).

REFERENCES

Ahrons, Constance, and Richard Miller. 1993. "The Effect of the Post-Divorce Relationship on Paternal Involvement: A Longitudinal Analysis." *American Journal of Orthopsychiatry* 63(3): 441–61.

Bertoia, Carl, and Janice Drakich. 1993. "The Father's Rights Movement: Contradictions in Rhetoric and Practice." *Journal of Family Issues* 14(4): 592–615.

Blaisure, Karen, and M. Geasler. 1996. "Results of a Survey of Court-Connected Parent Education Programs in U.S. Counties." *Family and Conciliation Courts Review* 34(1):23–40.

Bloom, David, and Kay Sherwood. 1994. *Matching Opportunities to Obligations: Lessons for Child Support Reform from the Parents' Fair Share Pilot Phase.* New York: Manpower Demonstration Research Corporation (April).

Braver, Sanford, Pamela Fitzpatrick, and R. Curtis Bay. 1991. "Noncustodial Parent's Report of Child Support Payments." *Family Relations* (40): 180–85.

Braver, Sanford, Sharlene Wolchik, Irwin Sandler, Bruce Fogas, and Daria Zvetina. 1991. "Frequency of Visitation by Divorced Fathers: Differences in Reports by Fathers and Mothers." *American Journal of Orthopsychiatry* 61(3): 448–54.

Center for Policy Research and Policy Studies, Inc. 1996. "Evaluation of Child Access Demonstration Projects." Report to Congress. Denver: Center for Policy Research and Policy Studies, Inc.

Coltrane, Scott, and Neal Hickman. 1992. "The Rhetoric of Rights and Needs: Moral Discourse in the Reform of Child Custody and Child Support Laws." *Social Problems* 39(4): 400–20.

Danzinger, Sheldon K., and Norma Radin. 1990. "Absent Does Not Equal Uninvolved: Predictors of Fathering in Teen Mother Families." *Journal of Marriage and the Family* 54(4): 837–45.

Furstenberg, Frank. 1988. "Marital Disruptions, Child Custody, and Visitation." In *Child Support: From Debt Collection to Social Policy,* edited by Alfred Kahn and Sheila Kammerman. Beverly Hills, Calif.: Sage Publications.

Harvard Law Review. 1993. "Developments in the Law: Legal Responses to Domestic Violence: Battered Women and Child Custody Decision-making." *Harvard Law Review* 106(1597): 1498–1620.

Haskins, Ronald 1988. "Child Support: A Father's View." In *Child Support: From Debt Collection to Social Policy,* edited by Sheila Kamerman and A. Kahn. Beverly Hills, Calif.: Sage Publications.

Haskins, Ronald, et al. 1985. *Estimates of National Child Support Collections Potential and the Income Security of Female-Headed Families.* Report to the Office of Child Support Enforcement by the Bush Institute for Child and Family Policy, University of North Carolina at Chapel Hill (April).

Johnson, Earl, and Fred Doolittle. 1995. "Low-Income Parents and the Parent's Fair Share Program: An Early Qualitative Look at Low-Income Noncustodial Parents (NCPs) and How One Policy Initiative has attempted to Improve their Ability and Desire to Pay Child Support." Paper presented at the Effects of Child Support Enforcement and Nonresident Fathers Conference, Princeton, NJ (September 1995).

Johnson, Jeffrey Marvin, and Hillard Pouncy. no date. "Developing Creative Ways to Address the Needs of Fathers and Fragile Families: A View from the Field." Unpublished manuscript. Philadelphia, Penn.: The National Center for Strategic Nonprofit Planning and Community Leadership/University of Pennsylvania.

Johnston, Janet R. 1994. "High Conflict Divorce." *Future of Children* 4(1), *Children and Divorce*: 165–82.

Johnston, Janet R., and Linda E. G. Campbell. 1988. *Impasses of Divorce: The Dynamics and Resolution of Family Conflict.* New York: Free Press.

Kelly, J. 1990. *Mediated and Adversarial Divorce Resolution Processes: An Analysis of Post-Divorce Outcomes.* Final report prepared for the Fund for Research in Dispute Resolution.

———. 1996. "A Decade of Divorce Mediation Research: Some Answers and Questions." *Family and Conciliation Courts Review* 30(3): 373–85.

Koch, Mary Ann, and Carol Lowery. 1984. "Visitation and Noncustodial Fathers." *Journal of Divorce* 8: 47–65.

Kurdek, Lawrence. 1988. "Custodial Mothers' Perceptions of Visitation and Payments of Child Support by Noncustodial Fathers in Families with Low and High Levels of Pre-separation Interparent Conflict." *Journal of Applied Developmental Psychology* (9): 315–28.

Levine, James, and Edward W. Pitt. 1995. *New Expectations: Community Strategies for Responsible Fatherhood.* New York: Families and Work Institute.

Lewin Group, Inc. 1997. "An Evaluability Assessment of Responsible Fatherhood Programs." Report prepared for the Department of Health and Human Services and the Ford Foundation. Fairfax, VA: Lewin Group.

Maccoby, Eleanor, and Robert Mnookin. 1992. *Driving the Child: Social and Legal Dilemmas of Custody.* Cambridge, Mass: Harvard University Press.

Manville, D. 1995. "Information on Third Judicial Circuit Court's Paternity Visitation Program." Paper prepared for "Programs and Policies for Unmarried Families," annual conference of the Association of Family and Conciliation Courts, Montreal, Canada (May 18).

Moore, Kristin A. 1995. "Nonmarital Childbearing in the United States." Report to Congress On Out-of-Wedlock Childbearing Prepared for U.S. Department of Health and Human Services. Washington: U.S. Government Printing Office.

National Council for Children's Rights, Inc. 1991. "100 People Hear Message from President Bush at Candlelight Vigil." In *Speak out for Children*, NCCR, Washington (Fall 1991).

New York City Bar Association, Committee on Family Court and Family Law. 1994. "Court-Ordered Supervised Visitation: Documenting an Unmet Need." (November).

Office of Child Support Enforcement. 1996. *FY 1995: Preliminary Data Report.* Washington: Department of Health and Human Services, Administration for Children and Families (May).

———. 1997. "Request for Applications from State Child Support Enforcement Agencies, Priority Area 4.01: Noncustodial Parents and Their Relationship to the Child Support Enforcement System." (April 30).

Pearson, Jessica. 1994. "Family Mediation." In *National Symposium on Court-Connected Dispute Resolution Research,* edited by Susan Keilitz. Alexandria, Va: National Center for State Courts.

Pearson, Jessica, and Jean Anhalt. 1992. *Visitation Enforcement Program: Impact on Child Access and Child Support: Final Report to the State Justice Institute.* Denver: Center for Policy Research.

———. 1993. "When Parents Complain About Visitation." *Mediation Quarterly* 11(1):139–56.

———. 1994a. "Examining the Connection Between Child Access and Child Support." *Family and Conciliation Courts Review* 32(1):93–109.

———. 1994b. "Enforcing Visitation Rights: Innovative Programs in Five State Courts May Provide Answers to This Difficult Problem." *Judges' Journal* 33(2).

Pearson, Jessica, Jean Anhalt, and Nancy Thoennes. 1991. *Child Support in Colorado: The Results of a 1990 Household Survey.* Denver: Center for Policy Research.

Pearson, Jessica, and Nancy Thoennes. 1988a. "The Denial of Visitation Rights: A Preliminary Look at Its Incidence, Correlates, Antecedents, and Consequences." *Law and Policy* 10(4): 363–80.

———. 1988b. "Supporting Children After Divorce: The Influence of Custody on Support Levels and Payments." *Family Law Quarterly* 22(3): 319–39.

———. 1995. *The Child Support Improvement Project: Paternity Establishment: Final Report to the Federal Office of Child Support Enforcement.* Denver: Center for Policy Research (September 30).

———. 1996. "Acknowledging Paternity in Hospital Settings." *Public Welfare* 54(3): 44–52.

———. 1997. "Resolving Issues of Access: Noncustodial Parents and Visitation Rights." *Public Welfare* 55(4).

Petronio, Sandra. 1988. "Communication and the Visiting Parent." *Journal of Divorce* (11): 103–10.

Price, D., R. Williams, Jessia Pearson, and Nancy Thoennes. 1994. *Child Access Demonstration Projects: Final Wave I Report.* Denver: Policy Studies, Inc., and Center for Policy Research (September).

Schaeffer, Nora, Judith Seltzer, and Marieka Klawitter. 1991. "Estimating Nonresponse and Response Bias: Resident and Nonresident Parents' Reports About Child Support." *Sociological Methods and Research* 20(1): 30–59.

Seltzer, Judith 1991. "Relationships Between Fathers and Children Who Live Apart: The Father's Role After Separation." *Journal of Marriage and the Family* 53: 79–101.

Sorensen, Elaine. 1997. "States Move to Put Low Income Noncustodial Parents in Work Activities." *Public Welfare* (Winter).

Strauss, R., and E. Alda. 1994. "Supervised Child Access: The Evolution of a Social Service." *Family and Conciliation Courts Review* 32(2): 230–46.

Testa, Mark, and Marilyn Krogh. 1995. "The Effect of Employment on Marriage Among Black Males in Inner City Chicago." In *The Decline in Marriage Among African Americans: Causes, Consequences, and Policy Implications,* edited by M. Belina Tucker and Claudia Mitchell-Kernan. New York: Russell Sage Foundation.

Theonnes, Nancy, and Jessica Pearson. 1998. "Parent Education Programs in Domestic Relations." Final Report to the State Justice Institute. Denver, Colo.: Center for Policy Research.

Thoennes, Nancy, Jessica Pearson, D. Price, and R. Williams. 1996. *Child Access Projects: An Evaluation of Four Child Access Demonstration Projects Funded by the Federal Office of Child Support Enforcement.* Denver: Center for Policy Research and Policy Studies, Inc. (April).

Veum, Jonathan R. 1993. "The Relationship Between Child Support and Visitation: Evidence from Longitudinal Data." *Social Science Research* 22: 229–44.

Wallerstein, Judith, and Joan Kelly. 1980. *Surviving the Breakup: How Children and Parents Cope with Divorce.* New York: Basic Books.

Watson, B. 1992. *The Young Unwed Fathers Project.* Philadelphia: Public/Private Ventures.

Williams, R., et al. 1995. *Massachusetts Paternity Acknowledgment Program: Implementation Analysis and Program Results.* Report to the Child Support Enforcement Division, Massachusetts Department of Revenue. Denver: Policy Studies, Inc. (May).

Chapter 9

Low-Income Parents and the Parents' Fair Share Program

An Early Qualitative Look at Improving the Ability and Desire of Low-Income Noncustodial Parents to Pay Child Support

Earl S. Johnson and Fred Doolittle

I n recent years, there has been a growing recognition of the failure of many non-custodial parents to meet their parental obligations and a steady effort to tighten child support enforcement. This trend has continued into the current debate on welfare, where there is a surprising political consensus about the importance of the issue. Exemplifying this consensus, the *New York Times* reported on June 18, 1995, that "Eleanor Holmes Norton, a liberal female, and Pete Wilson, a conservative male, both stood up and said that fatherlessness is the [number] one problem in the United States of America."

In this context, the timeliness of the Parents' Fair Share (PFS) demonstration, a test of a program for the noncustodial parents of children receiving welfare, becomes even more pronounced. This chapter discusses how the PFS program tries to help noncustodial parents (primarily fathers) become both economically and socially connected to their children, describes the views and attitudes of a sample of fathers participating in the program, and discusses how the program has responded to the challenge of serving these men.

BACKGROUND AND PURPOSE OF THE PARENTS' FAIR SHARE DEMONSTRATION

In 1988 Congress took what appeared at that time to be a major step in reforming the Aid to Families with Dependent Children (AFDC) program with the passage of the Family Support Act. This legislation, which continued a fourteen-year trend toward greater emphasis on parental obligations and child support enforcement, included a provision (section 482[d][3] of the Social Security Act) that authorizes the secretary of Health and Human Services to allow up to five states to provide services under the Jobs Opportunity and Basic Skills (JOBS) program of the Family Support Act of 1988 to noncustodial parents (NCPs) of children receiving welfare.[1] The demonstration services were limited to noncustodial parents "who are unemployed and unable to meet their child support obligation" to their children receiving welfare (*Federal Register*, October 1988). The legislation further stated that any services provided to NCPs had to be evaluated. As a result of this legislation, the Parents' Fair Share demonstration was conceived and implemented in 1992.[2] PFS was designed to explore methods that would increase the NCPs' ability to pay child support and possibly help them establish or reestablish contact with their children.[3] Parents' Fair Share is available in the demonstration sites for unemployed and underemployed NCPs who are not paying their current child support or are in arrears to the state.

The seven sites in this study are Grand Rapids, Michigan; Jacksonville, Florida; Memphis, Tennessee; Springfield, Massachusetts; Dayton, Ohio; Trenton, New Jersey; and Los Angeles, California.[4] Six of the sites are located in a predominantly urban community with a population of between three hundred thousand and one million. The Los Angeles site is in one of the nation's largest metropolitan areas. All of these sites were affected by the economic slowdown of the early 1990s, but in several there is currently a relatively strong labor market, and many employers are actively recruiting new workers. Table 9.1 lists the unemployment rates in each of the sites, showing a high of nearly 9 percent in Los Angeles and a low of slightly over 4 percent in Dayton and Memphis. The minority populations, especially in low-income neighborhoods, in each of these sites have had unemployment rates two to three times as high as the official aggregate unemployment rate. Furthermore, in each of these sites minority parents seem to be disproportionately overrepresented in the AFDC population. Not surprisingly, PFS program staff report

TABLE 9.1 / Unemployment Rates in Parents' Fair Share Sites, January 1992 to January 1995 (Not Seasonally Adjusted)

Sites	January 1992	January 1993	January 1994	January 1995	Change 1994 to 1995
California—Los Angeles	8.6	10.4	11.0	9.0	−2.1
Florida—Jacksonville	7.7	6.5	6.5	5.3	−1.2
Massachusetts—Springfield	8.8	NA	8.6	7.2	−1.4
Michigan—Grand Rapids	7.5	6.6	6.7	5.0	−1.7
New Jersey—Trenton	6.4	6.3	5.9	6.4	0.5
Ohio—Dayton	6.9	7.0	6.0	4.3	−1.7
Tennessee—Memphis	6.7	6.0	5.5	4.4	−1.1

Sources: U.S. Department of Labor (various years). Employment and Earnings for years 1992 to 1995.

that as unemployment rates decline, those referred to the program tend to have more employment barriers.

The child support enforcement (CSE) system is a second important aspect of the context of PFS because referrals to the program are made through this system. All of the sites in the PFS demonstration are operating court-based—as opposed to administrative—child support enforcement systems. As table 9.2 shows, the agency identifying potential PFS cases varies among the sites, with regional offices of state CSE agencies, court or court-related agencies, the county district attorney's office, and the county department of social services and probation all involved. Most NCPs referred to PFS have been in arrears on an existing child support order, though some have been referred to the program at the point of paternity establishment. In four of the sites, civil contempt or a similar procedure is used to enforce the child support obligation. In three sites, NCPs found in contempt are fairly frequently sent to jail.

An NCP enters the PFS program through the court system, usually through the court that handles child support cases. At court, child support and court officials determine whether an NCP meets the eligibility criteria; if he is deemed eligible, he is then randomly assigned to either the program group or the control group.[5] If he is assigned to the control group, the NCP is told he is ineligible for PFS but subject to the normal enforcement procedures. If an NCP is assigned to the program group, he receives a brief orientation about the program and is told what he must do to meet the requirements of the program. In most sites, NCPs randomly assigned to the program go before a judge or hearing officer and are ordered into the program; in a few sites, they are given instructions on the next steps, asked to sign a stipulation that they agree to meet program requirements, and told to appear at the program on a designated date.

Once at the program, the NCP is required to participate in peer support groups in which the participants and facilitators discuss parenting, relationships, communication, racism, and other themes. The program provides a menu of employment and training services (including job search assistance, on-the-job training, education, and skills training), opportunities for formal mediation of disputes between the parents, and enhanced child support enforcement. This enhanced child support includes temporary reduction or modification of the NCP's child support order during participation in PFS activities so that his ongoing support obligation—which could force him to seek immediate employment—will not be an obstacle to successful completion of the program. It also involves lower caseloads for designated enforcement staff and closer monitoring so the child support agency can aggressively pursue child support payments from NCPs who have found employment or stopped meeting program requirements.

Components and Purposes of Parents' Fair Share Services

The four components of Parents' Fair Share are (1) enhanced child support enforcement; (2) peer support (NCP group interactions); (3) employment and training; and (4) mediation when necessary or requested. (See appendix 9.1 for a definition of

TABLE 9.2 / Key Characteristics of Child Support Enforcement in Parents' Fair Share Sites

Characteristics	Los Angeles County, California	Duval County, Florida	Hampden County, Massachusetts	Kent County, Michigan	Mercer County, New Jersey	Montgomery County, Ohio	Shelby County, Tennessee
Agency identifying PFS cases	County district attorney's office	State Office of Child Support Enforcement regional office	State Office of Child Support Enforcement regional office	Kent County Friend of the Court	Mercer County Board of Social Services and Probation Division	Montgomery County Child Support Enforcement Agency and prosecutor's office	Shelby County Juvenile Court
Sources of PFS cases	(1) List of open AFDC cases with child support orders in which the noncustodial parent has not made a recent payment, and (2) regularly scheduled hearings for paternity establishment and order modification	Paternity establishment and contempt cases for nonpayment on an existing order	Paternity establishment and contempt cases for nonpayment on an existing order	Paternity establishment and contempt cases for nonpayment on an existing order	Paternity establishment and contempt cases for nonpayment on an existing order	(1) List of open AFDC cases with child support orders in which the noncustodial parent has not made a recent payment, and (2) regularly scheduled hearings for paternity establishment, order modification, and contempt for nonpayment	(1) List of open AFDC cases with child support orders in which the noncustodial parent has not made a recent payment, (2) new AFDC cases referred to the child support enforcement office, (3) custodial parents' complaints,

	Col 1	Col 2	Col 3	Col 4	Col 5	Col 6	Col 7
Defining Eligibility for PFS							and (4) regularly scheduled hearings for paternity establishment and contempt for nonpayment
Use of civil contempt hearings to enforce child support obligations	Rarely used; agency uses administrative remedies primarily, such as tax intercepts	Used	Rarely used; agency uses administrative remedies	Used	Action similar to civil contempt is used	Used as last resort; agency emphasizes administrative remedies	Used
Use of jail when nonpayment	In certain egregious cases, the noncustodial parent will be criminally prosecuted and jail can result	Frequency of use depends on the judge	Rarely used	Used, depending on availability of jail space	Rarely used	Rarely used because of jail overcrowding	Frequently used

these four PFS processes.) In each of these components of Parents' Fair Share, tenets of socializing and resocializing are embedded to change the behavior of the NCP.

The message that comes from the enhanced child support component is clear and simple. In the eyes of the law, if you have children, you must be financially responsible for them. For some NCPs in the program, this responsibility is the one that they readily accept. Many of the men in the program state that they are already taking care of their children and their obligations through informal contributions and in-kind assistance. Others dispute the notion that paying support through the formal system will help their children since much of (or, in the view of many NCPs, all of) the money goes to the state to repay welfare costs, not to their children. More-over, some NCPs argue that they cannot pay their child support obligation and still meet their subsistence needs. Stories surface in peer support groups of NCPs' pay-checks amounting to zero or near zero owing to the child support deductions garnished from their paychecks. In an extreme case in Trenton, New Jersey, a par-ticipant told how at one point he had been working for over three years at a job. When child support officials started to garnish his wages, he had nothing left after child support was taken out. After a few such paychecks, he told the group, he quit his job and had been officially unemployed for the three years prior to entering PFS.

The enforcement mechanism of the enhanced child support serves as a means to change actions. Many of these men express a strong desire to avoid jail (for many, a return visit) because they do not want to set that example for their children. So the incentives and disincentives of the enhanced child support system serve as motivating factors for participation in peer support and the other services.

For some men, however, there is a breakthrough; the idea that they have a responsibility for and obligation to their children may resonate, causing them to change their attitudes or behavior toward their children and/or the custodial par-ent. Through the peer support sessions, the NCPs learn about and discuss their importance in the development and upbringing of their children. Sometimes these lessons help the men find the confidence to be more involved with their children.

The peer support groups are clearly and definitely designed to effect change in the behavior of NCPs who are delinquent or not paying the child support. This activity, which has sometimes been called the "glue" of PFS, serves to inculcate the participants with some methods and strategies for becoming responsible fathers.[6] For some of the participants this activity has great benefits, and for others it is a stepping-stone toward another goal—getting training or an actual job.

The employment and training component of the program operates in some sites concurrently with the peer support groups, and in others these activities become available after an NCP has successfully completed the peer support group and been formally assessed for job readiness.[7] For most of the participants in PFS, the employment and training portion of the program is the reward or the objective for their prior efforts. The NCPs often come into this program hoping that they are going to be able to find a job that is better than what they would have found on their own. Ultimately, access to better-paying jobs and benefits is their primary objec-tive. In the employment and training component of PFS, the socializing process discreetly conveys the message: get a good job and keep it, no matter what the obstacles are. Many of the NCPs have had jobs or have had some experience with the labor market, but most feel that "good jobs" are hard to come by. Most have faced many obstacles and barriers that have led them to walk off their jobs, to not show up regularly, or to quit. Some of the obstacles are grounded in racism. Many of the minority men (black and Latino) have spoken about how they have had to deal with racism and bigotry on the job. Other obstacles that the men have faced include the inability to communicate with supervisors, drug and substance abuse issues, and personal issues such as being unable to deal with authority and showing disrespect for their bosses. General anger at a system that they perceive as repressive and hostile is another personal obstacle that some of the men say has caused them to leave their jobs. These and many other barriers have kept many of the NCPs from holding on to their jobs. Some of these barriers are self-created, and some have the appearance of being self-imposed but are based in a system that is somewhat unforgiving to these men. We are learning that often these men are not given the second and third chances that other types of employees are given. For NCPs, learning to cope with and handle various difficult work situations is integral to their later success.

LINKS TO OTHER RESEARCH

The operations of and research on the Parents' Fair Share program are linked to four other lines of ongoing research: on child support payments from noncustodial parents; on the fatherhood role in low-income, single-parent families; on socialization through social program interventions; and on social and economic support networks in low-income, African American communities.

Research on Child Support from Noncustodial Parents

A substantial body of literature indicates that, at its current levels, child support as an income transfer does not dramatically change child well-being (Marsiglio 1995; McLanahan 1994). At the same time, within the same body of literature there are hints that increased child support enforcement and collection would improve the lives of poor children whose custodial parents are receiving public assistance from the AFDC program. The first and most critical question for this research is: Does assisting NCPs with economic and emotional barriers, along with an increase in child support enforcement and collection efforts, improve the lives of those on public assistance or those who have received such assistance in the past? According to some researchers, a potential $35 billion could be collected in unpaid child support (Ellwood 1988, 1992; Sorensen 1994; McLanahan and Sandefur 1995, 150), though most researchers recognize that the bulk of this amount would not be linked to custodial parents receiving welfare. Nevertheless, child support collection by agencies from NCPs has become a focal point of the welfare reform debate. It is estimated that by vigorously collecting child support, poverty would be reduced and the current number of AFDC caseloads would be lowered (Ellwood 1992).

The Parents' Fair Share demonstration makes several contributions to this line of research. First, it seeks to understand more about the target group for the program, a largely unstudied group. This chapter focuses on the characteristics and attitudes of the noncustodial parents who have ventured into the Parents' Fair Share program.[8] By studying NCPs, the research also addresses the question of what it would take for them to become regular payers of child support. This chapter also discusses the reasons for paying or not paying child support through the formal child support system that have been expressed by the noncustodial parents of children on AFDC. It also explores the idea of fatherlessness from the perspective of the noncustodial parent with the intention of displaying how the usual definitions of fatherlessness and "absent fathers" oversimplify the *father* relations that these NCPs have with their children. Furthermore, the themes that have developed out of the research enable us to highlight some of the obstacles for these NCPs in their efforts to be "present" fathers.

Research on the Father's Role in Low-Income, Single-Parent Families

There is little in the vast welfare literature that actually describes or discusses the noncustodial parent in any context other than that of their child support obligation. While it is important to acknowledge at least officially that these individuals are not meeting their financial obligations, there may be more to their stories. Research by Sullivan (1989, 1990) has shown that while some low-income, noncustodial parents do not pay child support, they do make other contributions to their children's or the custodial parent's livelihood in lieu of cash.

In addition to the low-income, welfare-recipient literature, there is a growing literature on the role of fathering (Marsiglio 1995; Seltzer and Brandreth 1995; Daly 1995). This research makes it apparent that "fathering" is very difficult to understand and that the techniques and models of parenting vary along many different dimensions. Others have discussed family relations and the ways in which poor families negotiate within various social and economic contexts (Jarrett 1994; Burton, Furstenberg, and Harris 1993; Seltzer and Brandreth 1995). The literature is shallow in one particular area, however. There is a dearth of information on low-income, nonresident, noncustodial African American males.

While this chapter does not solely focus on African American males, the sample population is predominantly African American. Thus, our efforts here are focused on understanding how the life courses and experiences of these NCPs have led them to the PFS program, and what the program has done (or not done) to improve their opportunities to achieve a better economic and social position. Information on low-income or non-income, noncustodial minority fathers is very limited (Perkins, 1995), with the exception of a few works (Sullivan 1993, 1989; Anderson 1990, 1993, 1994; Gibbs 1988; Joint Center for Political and Economic Studies 1994). Much of the popular literature ignores this population in discussing the mainstream of everyday life, making it extremely difficult to design research questions (and program services) for them. Efforts by Ron Haskins and his colleagues (1985) indicate that it takes a great deal of effort and time to locate and track this group of men. William Perkins (1995) concurs with this sentiment and suggests that greater resources and effort should be placed in this area in order to gain a better understanding of what fathering means and entails for low-income minority men.

Most of the current research on the "absent parent" is limited to the discussion of obligations left unfulfilled by the noncustodial parent. Presumably, this is part of the origin of the term "deadbeat dad." Economics notwithstanding, the point here is to describe. The research of Carol Stack (1974) and Robin Jarrett (1994) offers an inside view of the mechanisms and strategies that low-income, African American women use to survive and build a life in "high poverty economically transitional neighborhoods" in the major cities. Their work indicates that these women have developed intricate coping strategies that allow them to maintain households, friendships, and relationships. Jarrett's work, in particular, indicates that the networks that these African American women form increase their ability to survive the economic and social turmoil of their environments. The research of William Julius Wilson (1987) and of Douglas Massey and Nancy Denton (1993) gives a macro version of the complexities and intricacies of the dynamic social and economic situations in these communities. All of the authors present a community that is both economically and socially isolated from the "mainstream."

PFS's contribution to this literature is to introduce into the story the women's counterpart: the unemployed or underemployed African American male. Throughout the work of Jarrett, and to a lesser extent in that of Stack, the male role in the women's social network is often marginal and predicated on the men's ability to fulfill the role of provider. The role of provider heavily emphasizes the ability to provide financially within the community. According to Jarrett (1992, 1995) and Elijah Anderson (1994), male participation and utility within the social network that these women construct is limited and transitory. One has to ask the question: Why are the men not able to be more integrated into the social network that the women have devised as a coping device?

Our research indicated that the existing social network for this community is tolerant of the men and their situations. However, it also indicates that the men in our study, at this point, are so financially vulnerable and inexperienced or not trusted in child-raising that they have less to offer the network. On the other side of this situation, the men look at and question the very idea of participating in this network because it doesn't provide them with cash—the one thing they need to be active and respected participants in the network and to meet their child support obligations. Their in-kind contributions within the social dynamic of the community are often well received (baby-sitting, protection, friendship, and many other odd jobs). But because the community lacks the resources to pay the men for these services, the men place little importance on their contributions, and as a result, these contributions may be made infrequently. However, this does not mean that they are unwilling to contribute these social services when they are asked to. It is just that the community infrequently calls upon them. Because of his irregular participation in the survival system, the male's access to its network becomes more limited, and he finds himself on the fringe of the community.

SAMPLE, DATA, AND RESEARCH METHODOLOGY

The qualitative research findings presented in this chapter come from a sample of thirty-two noncustodial parents who have been randomly assigned to participate in the Parents' Fair Share program since April 1994. All those interviewed have had at least one post-random assignment contact with program services. This population was chosen because it provided a chance to learn more about why individuals would choose to utilize an intervention such as Parents' Fair Share and to understand what aspects of the intervention resonated with the participants to induce changes in behavior.

The Sample

The PFS sample can be compared to other studies of employment and training programs for men. Table 9.3 lists selected characteristics for the early PFS sample and males included in the national Job Training Partnership Act (JTPA) study (operated in sixteen sites) and the JOBSTART Demonstration (operated in thirteen sites). One of the most important characteristics is the age distribution of the sample since studies of employment and training programs (including the national JTPA study and JOBSTART) have repeatedly found minimal employment effects for male, out-of-school youth and positive impacts for adult males.[9] Importantly, PFS has enrolled a fairly broad age range of men, in contrast to JOBSTART, which by definition involved only youth. In the national JTPA study, both youth and adults were included (as is the case in PFS), but program impacts on employment and earnings were positive for adults twenty-two years of age and older and zero or possibly even negative for the youth.

The early PFS sample includes a larger percentage of black men than either the national JTPA study or JOBSTART and a lower percentage of whites. A smaller percentage of the PFS men have been married than was the case with the national JTPA study adult males, but still fewer JOBSTART males had been married, as would be expected for these younger men. PFS sample members had somewhat lower educational attainment than the adult males in the JTPA study, but higher than the male youth in that study. (The JOBSTART youth were selected because they had neither a high school diploma nor a GED.) Relatively small percentages of men in both the national JTPA study and JOBSTART were receiving cash public assistance. The sample of noncustodial parents of poor children included in this study is not a random sample of all such parents, and it is important to understand the steps that occurred prior to their selection for this study to put our findings in their proper

TABLE 9.3   /   Characteristics of Sample in the Parents' Fair Share Program and Other Studies of Employment Services for Men

Characteristics	PFS[a]	National JTPA Study— Adult Males	National JTPA Study— Young Adults	JOBSTART Demonstration— Males
Age distribution (percentage)				
Sixteen to nineteen	—	—	62	74
Under twenty	4	—	—	—
Twenty to twenty-one	—	—	38	26
Twenty to twenty-nine	47	—	—	—
Twenty-two to twenty-nine	—	44	—	—
Thirty to thirty-nine	35	—	—	—
Thirty to forty-four	—	44	—	—
Forty to forty-nine	13	—	—	—
Forty-five to fifty-four	—	8	—	—
Over fifty	5	—	—	—
Over fifty-four	—	4	—	—
Race/ethnicity				
White	17	57	54	8
Black	64	29	30	44
Hispanic	17	10	15	44
Other	2	5	2	5
Marital status				
Never married	63	42	—	90
Ever married	—	—	—	10
Divorced	15	—	—	—
Widowed, divorced, or separated	—	19	—	—
Married, living with spouse	10	34	—	—
Married, not living with spouse	—	5	—	—
Other	13	—	—	—
Education: no high school diploma or GED	52	31	59	100
Public assistance				
Receiving AFDC or other cash assistance	—	16	12	—
Own AFDC or general assistance case	—	—	—	12

Sources: Cave et al. (1993), Bloom (1991), and Kemple, Doolittle, and Wallace (1993).

[a] Parents' Fair Share 1998 report forthcoming.

context. Figure 9.1 presents the steps in the child support enforcement process that occurred prior to the point at which the sample was drawn.

The starting point is the pool of NCPs of children receiving AFDC in each PFS site who are not paying or are underpaying their child support. These parents have had paternity established and a child support order put in place; many have substantial support arrearages. Typically, child support administrators can find evidence of employment for some in this group (through automated records matches, tips from individuals, and so on), but for most there is no evidence they are working. For those with evidence of employment, child support enforcement staff would move to put an income deduction order in place.

When there is no evidence of employment, child support enforcement staff would then seek to bring the NCP into court or the administrative agency for a hearing or review on their nonpayment of support. The first step would be locating and serving the NCP with legal notice; depending on the PFS site, up to half the NCPs could be lost because child support staff could not achieve legal notice of the hearing.[10] Experience over the early stages of the demonstration showed that the addresses for NCPs in official records could be outdated, the NCP could be difficult to serve because he was moving frequently, or relatives and friends did not provide information on his whereabouts. Not all those actually served for a hearing appear or contact child support enforcement staff; there is considerable variation among the PFS sites in the appearance or contact rate.

A substantial proportion of those who appear or contact the child support agency provide information on previously unreported employment, and staff move to put in place an income deduction order. A smaller percentage provide evidence that they are disabled, reunited with the other parent, or otherwise ineligible for PFS. Others, however, can produce neither evidence of employment nor any substantial cash payment to reduce or eliminate their accumulated support arrearages. These NCPs are eligible for PFS and go through a lottery to be randomly assigned to a program group (almost all of whom are ordered by the court to participate in the PFS program) or to a control group subject to normal enforcement practices. In the program group, some NCPs choose not to participate in program services (possibly because they have an unreported job and cannot attend program services), but about two-thirds have participated in some PFS activities. The sample for this study is drawn from these program participants.

This group is appropriate for studying the issues arising in implementing a program like PFS. Nevertheless, the enforcement steps taken prior to the selection of the sample result in a group that is likely to be more disadvantaged (and probably more interested in the program) than the average NCP at the prior steps in the "flow" toward PFS. Some NCPs who were working in jobs previously unknown to the child support enforcement system are "smoked out" at some of the prior steps in the intake process (Doolittle and Lynn 1998). Others choose to keep avoiding the enforcement process, possibly by going further outside the mainstream economy. Thus, while it is interesting to compare the findings reported in this chapter to other work on NCPs, it is important to keep in mind the purpose of this work and the specific way in which this sample was drawn.

FIGURE 9.1 / Steps in the Child Support Enforcement Process Prior to Entry into Parents' Fair Share

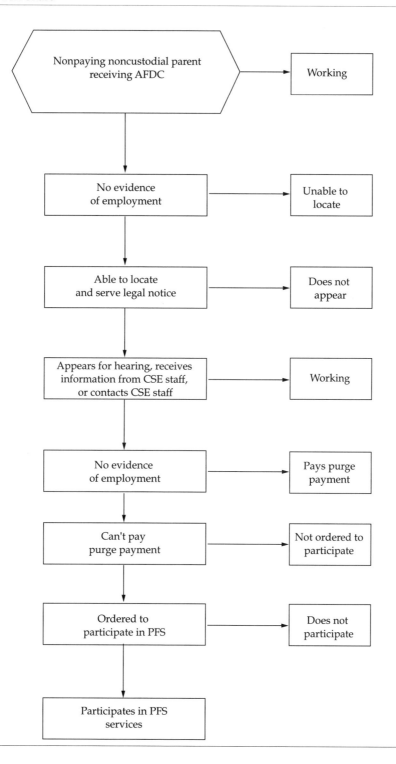

In developing our sample, we have made contact with NCPs coming through the intake process during our periodic site visits. Some of these initial contacts were made at either the various courts that handle PFS cases or the PFS program site. The second contact with PFS participants has typically been made at the program's services location after their admittance to the program. Other participants have been referred to us by past participants or staff members from the PFS program. As discussed later in this section, our qualitative research sample and the overall PFS sample are quite similar in basic demographic characteristics, family history, and work experience (see table 9.4).[11]

A summary of the characteristics of the thirty-two NCPs in our sample (men only) are shown in table 9.4. Their median age is thirty-two. Almost two-thirds of the sample are African American. Twenty-four percent are white, and the remainder of the sample are Latino. Nearly 90 percent have worked in a full-time job. Most report having been unemployed (that is, jobless but looking for work) for at least eight months within the last year. While they say that they are unemployed, many have been doing odd jobs or some type of "hustle" on the side. A good portion (81 percent) of the men have not worked steadily or at all over the past two years. Their level of education ranges from completing eighth grade to having graduated from college.[12] The average number of children that these men report having is two. Many claim to have at least some contact with their children, where contact is defined as having seen at least one of their children once over the past month. A large portion of these men have had encounters with the law that led to incarceration.

Tables 9.5 and 9.6 represent a snapshot of the income and expenditures of the participants in the qualitative research sample of the Parents' Fair Share program. Table 9.5 displays an aggregate picture of the income that people in these five PFS sites bring in during a month. It should be noted that the income streams for these individuals are constantly changing. This table gives the general ranges that the men in this sample made during a month in the fall of 1995. Generally, table 9.5 shows that the monthly income for these men is very low, primarily because the jobs they held were not full-time jobs. On average, the men were lucky to work twenty hours a week occasionally, with the usual total being ten to fifteen hours a week. The use of public assistance varies by site and individual. All of the sites in the PFS demonstration told participants, at orientation that they were potentially eligible for food stamps and, if there was a program in the county, general relief or general assistance. The food stamp source of income is officially noted as $119 per month in table 9.5 for those getting only food stamps with no other income. Yet the real value of the food stamp allocation may be less because they may be sold for currency on the street. Usually, food stamps traded on the street will bring around 75 to 80 percent of their value. These men need this income not only to buy food but to help them survive on a day-to-day basis by covering other expenses. The four men in table 9.6 depict the range of income and expenditures of nonresident fathers in this sample.

From table 9.5, it is apparent that the expenditures that these men make are closely linked to their low-income salaries. Their child support is a regular obligation. However, the payment of the child support debt (past and present) can change

TABLE 9.4 / Demographic Characteristics of Parents' Fair Share Participants at Entry into Program

Characteristics	Pilot Phase	Demonstration[a]	Qualitative Research[b]	NSFH[c]	JOBSTART Demonstration— Males[d]
Average age of participants	29.1	31.1	32.0	35.2	18.5
Average number of own children	2.4	2.4	2.0	2.1	—
Current marital status (percentage)					
Never married	58.6	62.4	56.3	13.6	93.0
Married, living with significant other	9.1	9.1	12.5	53.7	—
Divorced	18.3	15.4	25.0	32.7	—
Other	14.0	13.1	6.2	—	—
Living arrangements					
Living with relative	—	58.9	43.7	25.6	—
Living with girlfriend/spouse	22.8	22.4	21.9	50.8	—
Living alone	11.5	9.3	34.4	16.3	—
Other nonfamily households	8.7	9.4	7.2	—	—
Ethnicity/race					
Black	63.7	64.0	62.0	29.0	44.8
White	29.1	17.0	23.8	59.2	7.0
Latino/Hispanic[e]	5.9	17.2	14.2	10.7	45.5
Other	1.3	1.8	—	1.0	2.7
Received high school diploma or GED[f]	50.2	52.3	61.0	78.5	0.0

(Table continues on p. 268.)

TABLE 9.4 / Continued

Characteristics	Pilot Phase	Demonstration[a]	Qualitative Research[b]	NSFH[c]	JOBSTART Demonstration—Males[d]
Income					
Receiving public assistance	—	—	25.0	5.2	49.5
Ever employed	99.0	97.1	93.3	98.4	—
Currently employed[g]	13.1	17.3	18.7	82.2	—
Sample size	2,404	2,641	32	501[h]	473

Source: Manpower Demonstration Research Corporation Parents' Fair Share MIS system.

[a] Sample as of July 1995.

[b] Sample as of July 1995.

[c] These means (proportions) are based on weighted data that adjust for underrepresentation of nonresident fathers as well as underreporting of paternity status. To correct for underreporting, we use weights that assume that fathers who deny paternity status are similar to other nonresident fathers of similar age, education, race/ethnicity, and marital status at a child's birth who do not pay child support.

[d] JOBSTART 1989 report sample of participants.

[e] The category of Latino/Hispanic is not actually exclusive of the categories of black/white. As a result, table can be greater than 100 percent for the pilot sample.

[f] Refers to the educated status of the participant at the beginning of his initial contact.

[g] "Currently employed" refers to work status at the time of the participant's initial contact with the program.

[h] This sample size represents a subsample of an unweighted sample of 9,576,981.

TABLE 9.5 / Monthly Income and Expenditures of Participants in the Parents' Fair Share Program—from the Qualitative Research Sample

Sites	Income			Expenses			
	Reported Income from Work[a]	Other Sources	Public Assistance[b]	Rent	Food	Child Support	Other[c]
California—Los Angeles	$150–1,000	$100	$0–338	$100–650	$100–400	$50	$100–400
Michigan—Grand Rapids	360–760	100–500	0–119	200–450	150–500	56	300–400
New Jersey—Trenton	50–800	150	0–338	0–450	300–400	0	300–500
Ohio—Dayton	500	100	0–119	0–400	100–350	100	100–250
Tennessee—Memphis	390–1,000[d]	0	0–119	0–450	90–400	50	100–320

Source: Data based on reported income and expenditures from the month of November 1995.

[a] Income from employment where income is reported.

[b] Public assistance income includes either food stamps and/or general assistance or general relief, depending on the location of the participant.

[c] Some of these items are personal items such as toiletries, support for relatives and other family members, utilities, transportation costs (public transit and personal car expenses), expenses for children that come outside the realm of child support, fines, personally accrued debts, recreation (cigarettes, alcohol, movies, videos), and medical and other emergency expenditures.

[d] Based on an hourly wage of $6.50 working part-time at fifteen hours a week. This estimate is based on the pay reported by the men of Memphis for warehouse, maintenance, general, and convenience store work. Many of the full-time jobs in Memphis are not given right away to these men. They have to work part-time for anywhere from a month to four months before they may become eligible for a full-time position.

TABLE 9.6 / Actual Income and Expenditures for Four Participants in the Parents' Fair Share Program

		Income						Expenses			
			Assistance								Long-term Debt:
Name	Site	Reported/ Unreported Income[a]	General Assistance/ General Relief	Food Stamps Program	Unemployment Insurance	Housing	Other Sources	Rent	Food and Other Expenses	Child Support Owed[b]	Child Support Arrearages
Viceroy	Grand Rapids, Michigan	$760	No	No	$300[c]	Yes	Some from father	$300	$420	$500	$500–1,000
Fila-G	Memphis, Tennessee	400–800	No	119	No	No	No	0[d]	600	600	35,000
Jah	Trenton, New Jersey	No	100	119	No	Yes	Small amount	450	No[e]	108	10,000
Arron	Los Angeles, California	220[f]	No	No	No	No	No	350	450–500	400	5,000

Source: Data based on reported income and expenditures from the month of November 1995.

a Reported and unreported income are calculated as monthly amounts.

b Child support payments owed are calculated as monthly amounts.

c Receives this amount of unemployment insurance benefit after $125 is taken out for child support.

d Lives rent-free.

e No reported food or other expenses for this particular month due to incarceration.

f Receives this amount when working as a temporary employee.

from month to month depending on how much the participant has available to pay. They do try to pay the monthly or weekly amount that the courts have obligated them to pay. Yet, when they are unable to make their full child support payments, their child support debt accumulates into an arrearage, which they view as an obligation they are unlikely to ever pay off. These men also have a substantial number of personal expenses given their limited sources of income. For some, their utility bill alone may be more than their income for a given month. Each month these and other personal expenses are juggled so as not to lose utility services. Sometimes this juggling act becomes too complicated, bills go unpaid, and ultimately they lose the utility services. Usually the first utility lost is the telephone, followed by gas and electricity. Sometimes, in an effort to keep these utilities, the men cash in their food stamps to get money to pay bills.

Table 9.6 gives a snapshot of the income and expenditures of four sample members. As the table indicates, these men have very limited resources. None were working full-time during this period. Their income was from part-time work (on or off the book) or from unemployment insurance. They were generally making about six dollars an hour if they worked. All but one of the men was living with the mother of one of their children, so they were getting help with the rent. Either the rent was subsidized or the mother was working and paying a portion of the rent while the NCP watched the children. The one person who lived on his own lived in his grandmother's home. He was expected to keep the utility bills paid and to cover other expenses when they arose. He had had a great deal of trouble meeting this obligation, but his grandmother had allowed him to stay in the home despite his inability to cover the household debts.

The men make child support payments when they can, which is infrequently. Viceroy, from Grand Rapids, was meeting his obligation during this period because his child support payments were being taken directly out of his unemployment insurance check. Otherwise, these men rarely could make official child support payments voluntarily. The men cited several reasons, including their need for income to survive, their alternative payment of money directly to the mothers of their children, and their need to spend what little money they had on maintaining their current household.

These men receive a very limited amount of help from others. Column 6 in table 9.6, "Other Sources (of Assistance)," indicates the limited amount of help that these men and their families receive from outside sources. For example, Viceroy receives sporadic gifts of $150 a month from his father, in Mississippi, for his girlfriend and baby girl. Fila-G recently spent thirty days in jail because no one would pay his bail. In fact, he stated that during his time in jail (for failure to pay child support), not one person came to visit him. When he got out of jail, there were notices to shut off his electricity and gas. Some of the men receive in-kind assistance from relatives or parents when the relative or parent has some cash available. Arron's mother takes clothes and other items to his son's mother because she knows that Arron doesn't have any money. She recognizes that the money he makes when he works sporadically, for temporary agencies or while pursuing an entertainment career, has to go to the family that he is living with. Arron's mother is also living on a tight budget and can give presents to the baby only infrequently, but they serve as tokens that allow her access to her grandchild. Otherwise, Arron wouldn't know what is happening with his child.

Finally, when these men do have money to support their child, or others in their family provide support, they get something in return: they are able to see their children and are able to stay over at the mother's house. Further, through outside contributions given directly to the mothers of the NCPs' children, the men sometimes gain a sense of assurance that their children are being cared for despite their absence. While not a perfect solution, the NCPs settle for these arrangements. As a result of the NCPs' financial situation, leaving any money means more access to their children and their social community.

Many of these NCPs have tenuous living arrangements. Over 40 percent of our sample are living with a relative (grandmother, mother, son, sister, and so on). Thirty-four percent of the sample are living by themselves. For about half of those who live alone, this translates into being homeless or sleeping on a couch or in a car. Among the other half, some have lived in their own apartment or house in a relatively stable way, and others have "bounced around" between living on their own and living with friends or a girlfriend and are currently living by themselves. Another 22 percent of the sample are living with their girlfriend, ex-spouse, or spouse.

In the following passage, Geraldo explains his precarious living situation and how he manages to find shelter. Elements of his story appear in those of others in the sample:

GERALDO: I try to deal with life.
INTERVIEWER: Uh-huh. You need to get away?
GERALDO: I need to get away, I mean, I've had enough of this, of bouncing around, here, there, not knowing where to stay—it got hectic.
INTERVIEWER: Were you literally homeless for a while?
GERALDO: Yes, yes.
INTERVIEWER: I'm sorry.
GERALDO: Well, actually the day, the day I left here, I was in that condition. The day I was thrown out of that place.
INTERVIEWER: Out of the … out of your—
GERALDO: The house I was staying in. He's still there.
INTERVIEWER: That was the … yeah. So how long were you homeless for?
GERALDO: Oh, about a week.
INTERVIEWER: Yeah? And then you—how, how did you find your bud—your friend?
GERALDO: Actually, I still am, you know. I stay here, I stay there, you know, but I really have no home.
INTERVIEWER: Yeah.
GERALDO: I mean, in the places I stay, I—they're friends, or, you know, they're mostly friends, or my sons, but I, I really can't stay here, not under the landlord's— uh, rules.
INTERVIEWER: Right. Exactly. Yeah, I remember, that was the problem last time.

GERALDO: Right. So basically, I still am, you know. I mean, I have shelter, but not a place I can really go home.

Data and Research Methods

Every participant in the qualitative research sample has been interviewed at least twice over the last year. Most of the conversations and interviews are tape-recorded and transcribed verbatim. Many formal interviews lasted nearly one and a half hours, and informal interviews and conversations have lasted from five minutes to three hours. Among the questions participants are asked are: "Why did you go to court?" "What was your past relationship with your 'ex' like?" and, "What is your relationship with your children right now?" The formal interview has an open-ended approach to it to allow the interviewee to relax, but the questions have been prepared in advance (see table 9A.1 for questions). Many times during less formal interactions with participants, formal questions are asked as a form of cross-reference and validation. Also, a number of questions are asked whenever a conversation or interview occurs—for example, "Have you seen or spoken with your children lately?" "What have you been doing since we last spoke?" "Have you worked since we last spoke?" or, "How are you doing?" These questions relate to interactions with the NCP's children, the custodial parent, and the NCP's current status in the program. Most of the data come from the conversations and program activities with the NCP, but field notes from past observations and conversations with participants also serve as a source of data to see whether the intervention of PFS has had any lasting effect on the program participant as well as to gauge whether and how his story has changed since the previous interaction.

Conducting the conversations in a semistructured manner that gives the participant some control over the pace and depth of the conversation seems to be an effective mechanism for maintaining contact with these men over a period of time. Their sense that they have ownership of the research has added to our ability to follow them over time. As a result, they have been more willing to open up and share their lives with the researchers.

In addition, we have tried to get a bit further into their lives by offering them disposable cameras to take pictures of their world (for example, their families, girlfriends, jobs, buildings). Currently, twelve NCPs have cameras and are taking photographs, which are used as a resource to gain more insight into their lives.[13] The purpose of the photographs is to get the participants to think about their lives and community and to capture images of what is interesting or significant to them. This is done with the explicit purpose of sharing the information with the researcher. In addition, the photos serve as another source of future questions into the lives of these men.

To complement the qualitative data, data from the baseline information is collected at random assignment from each person in the impact research sample. This information demonstrates the general characteristics of the PFS population (see table 9.4). Another source of data is PFS program participation data, completed monthly by each site for each person who has been randomly assigned to the program group. These data, along with our interview or conversational data, show us to what degree the program's socialization process is taking hold. Our assumption is that the more contact the NCP has with the program, the more he can take from it.

The qualitative research in PFS has gone through several phases, each of which has provided a somewhat different insight. The project began with early focus groups with NCPs. These focus groups informed the program design of PFS and have been integral in carrying out the current phase of more in-depth qualitative research. At the start of this project, there was a great deal of doubt that men—especially low-income or non-income minority men—would be interested in participating on a regular basis in a program that made them sit in groups to discuss issues of fatherhood, parenting, relationships, and societal views.[14] In an attempt to reduce our uncertainty about this group of men, as well as our dependence on stereotypes, we used focus groups to uncover some of the issues that these men identified as having an impact on their lives and to explore the feasibility of having low-income, minority men come together and discuss issues of parenting and fatherhood.[15]

These early focus groups led to some false starts in developing questions and the observation focus for the later qualitative research on program participants because the noncustodial parents included in the groups tended to have higher employment rates and more income (albeit often unreported) than those NCPs later participating in PFS.[16] Further, since some of these men had not even had paternity established, as a group they tended to have less of a relationship and fewer interactions with their children than has been the case for the sample in this study. In summary, some in the focus groups came from further up the flow in figure 9.1 than the eventual sample for this work. This emerging difference between the earlier focus group participants and those in our current sample highlighted for us the importance of understanding where in the child support enforcement process individuals are identified.

The next section discusses the early findings and themes that emerged from contacts with the participants in Parents' Fair Share.

EMERGING THEMES CONCERNING THE LIVES OF PARTICIPANTS

At this point, three themes dominate the description of the lives of participants, in and out of the Parents' Fair Share program.[17] The first theme is opportunity. The PFS participants generally are looking—often desperately—for an opportunity to find work that gives them some stability in their lives. Many see such jobs as what will give them the confidence and courage to pursue things that they have either avoided or never considered. Because of the urgency of their search for new opportunities, they have little tolerance for bureaucratic delays, inconsistencies, and mistakes.

The second major theme is powerlessness: many NCPs believe they lack the ability to advocate on their own behalf or to receive the respect and assistance they might need to be a parent, father, and contributing member of society. This feeling often focuses on their experiences on the job and in dealings with the courts. The NCPs also talk about how powerless they feel to create opportunities to be with their children. Many of them have limited contact with their children, in part because they do not feel they possess the "power" to change their situation. Some of these men look to the program and other sources to help them gain power in order to participate in their children's lives.

The third theme is social and economic isolation. This theme seems to be emerging because of the two previous themes. The theme of isolation indicates that these men are socially and economically barred from many of the better opportunities and safeguards that society offers to others with more economic and social capital.

Perceptions of Opportunity

Though PFS is a mandatory program, there are a number of ways in which NCPs can choose not to cooperate and avoid participating in it (for example, never responding to court mailings, claiming to be employed, or never showing up for program activities). The NCPs in our sample have chosen to show up (at several stages along the way to PFS) and utilize the services that are available to them. This does not mean that every person who enters the PFS program door has the same high level of motivation or range of life experience. What it does indicate is that for some reason (opportunity, perceived obligation, curiosity) these participants are looking to change their situation.

These participating noncustodial parents share something else: for some time they have not met their child support obligation, and they are currently unemployed or underemployed.[18] We have observed that during the peer support groups, especially at the first group meeting, one of the major unifying comments that usually comes from the peer support facilitator is, "You are all in the program because of one reason and one reason only—you haven't paid child support." This usually produces a few dropped heads and results in an instant discussion of the child support enforcement system. The facilitators generally follow with, "This program is about giving you the opportunity to become a child support–paying father."

One of the first questions asked during conversations with the NCPs in our sample is usually, "Why have you come to this program?" or, "What made you come to the [PFS site]?" Asking this question gives the NCP a chance to explain how he is feeling at the moment and to articulate his expectations for the program. Often this question is raised by peer support facilitators in the first two sessions of peer support. The facilitators use this question to gauge interest, anxiety, and aspirations among the NCP group.

From site to site the responses to this question vary somewhat, but the NCPs' primary focus is on one objective: finding a job. Often in the same breath, however, he will say he has come to the program because it was a chance to get "straight." Mack's comments exemplify why the majority of the NCPs in this sample said they gave the PFS program a chance: "I don't know. I just went to clear the smoke really, because I knew I couldn't run and hide from them all my life, so I say I might as well go."

To further understand what the NCP is looking to get out of the program, general probe questions are asked. From these questions other telling comments emerge. Some of the comments from peer support groups in New Jersey and California are:

"Survival."

"To get a job so I can kick it."

"Getting a job."

"To get a job so I can support my kids."

"I've always supported my kids."

"I had to come or go to jail."

The participants are not naive, however, about the origins and policy purpose of the program and clearly recognize that its goal is to increase child support payments. Jah, a twenty-nine-year-old father of a newborn, articulated what it meant for him to come into the program and described his frustration, conflicting feelings, and disappointment with the program.

> What [do] I think the purpose of the program is? The purpose of the program is to find you a job so you can be a better father to your kid, so you can be able to pay this child support. I figure it like that because you can come into this program through the courts, right? And when the courts allow you, when you get into this program, the courts are trying to say they want you to pay this support, they don't care how much money you make, and to take care of your family or nothing, that's irrelevant. What they're trying to do is to get you a better job so you can pay this child support. So that's what I think this program is based on, is to help you to find a better job for you to pay child support, and they say have a little extra money for yourself.

Occasionally unique statements are made that highlight an NCP's willingness to be affiliated with the program and utilize and benefit from what it has to offer. In a peer support group in California, a participant named G-man responded to a question about goals and objectives by stating that he was participating in the program "to pass on my heritage." G-man went on to say that he had worked for many years and supported his kids during those years: "I was with my girlfriend the whole time. We stayed together ten years. I was taking care of my kids the whole time."

Even though he attempted to stay close to his children, G-man's story became more complex and complicated as he tried to navigate through the child support and welfare systems and PFS in an attempt to pass on his heritage. He reports that he accumulated a substantial arrearage owed the state because he was living with his girlfriend and children while she was receiving welfare.

[I] owed $28,000 [in arrearage]. When they first started garnishing my wages, they're telling me, they don't care nothing about why you owe them, it's just that they've been paying your kids and paying your ex-girlfriend for your kids, or whatever. Especially everybody in here [referring to the peer support group] is paying welfare. Nobody in this program that's ordered to pay their wife; it's just that the welfare is taking care of the kids in my situation, the check was in her name.

Even though G-man wants to pass on his heritage and he does have contact with all but one of his children, he is faced with a child support payment situation that is not dissimilar from that of the other members of his peer support group or other noncustodial parents at other sites. High arrearages, no job, and no opportunities in sight made even the reluctant G-man participate in and the program and take it seriously. G-man has filled out dozens of job applications on his own, and nothing has panned out.

It is usually from this point on (the realization that he is not alone in his struggle to pay child support) that the participant in Parents' Fair Share takes over, aids, or directs the discussions and agenda of the "Responsible Fatherhood" curriculum within the peer support group. This sense of ownership in the peer support group process also serves as a source of empowerment and an opportunity for validation of self-worth. In response to the question, "Why did you choose to participate?" many of the NCPs have also said that they were "tired of running" from the local CSE agency and that "this looked like a chance to do something different."

Some of the NCPs perceived that just participating in the program presented certain opportunities. A participant named Kenny observed that

since I've been here it's kind of fixed patterns, it gave me a motivation, something to do with myself during the day. It keeps me out of trouble, it's basically helping me foster my future with a career, job, and all the good things in life like you said, to pay my child support and to go on with my life. It's helped me a lot. It's been a good experience in my life, you know what I'm saying…. I've never been to nothing like this.

For some of the participants in PFS, the opportunities they are seeking (regular visitation, a job, training, getting the system off their backs) do not come as quickly or as thoroughly as they perceive that they should. When this feeling starts, NCPs discuss their frustrations and disappointment with the program and the things that are not getting resolved even though they are doing what they are supposed to be doing. One such incident that occurs over and over, according to participants and staff members, is the resolution of visitation issues. The noncustodial parent in the program starts internally incorporating the messages of the peer support group and decides that he would like to see his children, or see them more regularly. Now willing to participate in visitation, the NCP feels frustrated and angry when the program is unable to get the custodial parent to cooperate in the process. Thus, the feeling of injustice and betrayal heightens.

The greatest frustration, however, and probably the issue that makes NCPs feel that the program is not keeping its side of the bargain, is related to work and working. After a few weeks of peer support sessions, the men become frustrated if they are not moving into better jobs than they had before or into skill training that will help them become more employable. The frustration sets in when, after a month or so in peer support, they are sent out on an interview for a warehouse job for five dollars an hour when they were expecting to get job leads for positions with a future.[19] Meanwhile, the NCP is still being held responsible for paying his child support, even though it's reduced, and making sure that he can live on his own. A number of participants at this point have become homeless. Others have had to move frequently to maintain shelter or had their telephone and electricity turned off. Participants have informed us of how they have lost, regained, and again lost public assistance benefits (mostly general assistance, which is now being eliminated in more sites), and how the program was unable to resolve the problem. Needless to say, the anger that a person feels when he is not given the services that he wants or feels he has earned is very real. But when those services are so closely linked to survival and subsistence, the anger, frustration, and disappointment begin to shroud all other efforts he has made up to that point. Survival becomes tantamount. One participant expresses an extreme sense of unfulfilled promises that has colored his experience in PFS.

> So what's, what's, what's the program seem to be doing, man, because—eh, if I don't call nobody, they don't call me, man. You know, they said I was supposed to stay in touch with you and the program. All I'm getting is just letters. . . . Nobody call, man. Man, it's a dog-eat-dog world out there, man. I ain't—you know, I am very sorry I turned myself in, man. I'm very sorry, because it's not only cramped my style, but you know, people—I'm going to tell you another thing, man. Um, when you go to these places and tell these people that you have a child support problem, they don't hire you.

In the following statement, Fila-G aptly summarizes his frustration and disappointment with his situation and with the program:

FILA-G: I've been seeing them weekly now, all this here, they ain't found me no job, you know, I got paperwork down there, where I been looking for jobs and stuff like that, you know.
INTERVIEWER: Right.
FILA-G: So, huh, you know. Like I say, I'm in the same old boat, uh, you know, that I was the day they picked me out of juvenile court, the only thing different, I ain't down in court right now.
INTERVIEWER: Right.
FILA-G: You know, I was unemployed then, and I'm unemployed now, so, you know. No cash flow, I was on stamps then, and I'm on stamps now.

Feelings of Powerlessness

Throughout the discussions with the NCPs in our sample and through observations and conversations with other PFS participants, there is a constant, sometimes subtle, reference to powerlessness. This shows up on the job, in their dealings with the courts, and in their dealings with the custodial parent.

FEELINGS OF RACISM ON THE JOB   Many of the men, especially the African American men, express some of this powerlessness in racial terms; statements such as, "Being a black man in this city, you don't have a chance," are echoed from one site to another. In every city, some of the men discuss the obstacles that race presents in pursuing their goals and objectives.

Even working does not reduce or remove all of the powerlessness that many of the participants express. In a conversation with a young African American male from Dayton named Bob, we explored his feeling of powerlessness in challenging the racist practices of the liquor store owner for whom he worked. Bob eventually grew tired of what he perceived as mistreatment and quit. For him, this was his only option. PFS staff attempted to speak with him and his employer. They urged Bob to work a little harder at pleasing the owner. Bob found this solution unacceptable. He believed there was no way to change the way the "white people" in the liquor store felt about him and his friends, and he refused to return.

Other African American NCPs in our sample have experienced similar feelings as they try to enter the mainstream labor force. They are led to lower-paying jobs. Often they feel tension and animosity while working with whites. This feeling is often compounded by the fact that the jobs are usually located in unfamiliar environments. The participants have told us that they feel they put up with many indignities and sooner or later they do something wrong and are fired or let go. Usually there is no one to back them up or lobby on their behalf. From Bob's perspective, PFS staff checked out his work situation because they may have been more interested in saving the job for another participant than in challenging the proprietor's treatment of African American males.[20] On the whole, the participants see that the program is trying but that it cannot change employers' behavior. Bob has stated that he will probably go back on the streets again. There, he'll be able to be economically independent (he'll be making money on the streets) and have some control over what he's doing. As long as he pays his child support, he'll have no problems from the custodial parent of his children or from the courts.

INTERACTIONS WITH THE COURT   For the men of PFS, one of the primary sources of their feelings of powerlessness is the court system. From their perspective, especially that of African American males, being called into court is the first step in being sent to jail. Their cynicism about court and about appearing before judges is so great that when sites have sent them letters asking them to come to court voluntarily to look into their eligibility for PFS, they have wondered whether it is really a "sting operation." Their relief when they find out that it is not is often accompanied by surprise and disbelief.

Nonetheless, once an NCP goes before the judge or referee, the reality strikes him again that this system is not interested in *why* he is not paying child support. Most of the reasons that NCPs would offer for their nonpayment of support are, from a legal perspective, irrelevant to the findings of what they owe (although they may be relevant to whether his nonpayment was willful contempt of the court order and thus grounds for jailing). Many a participant has told us that the judge did not listen to him when he was telling his side of the story. Judges have ordered many men in our sample to make payments directly to the court or to an agency that handles the collection of funds for child support. In several of the PFS sites, making in-kind payments or direct payments to the custodial parent on welfare without making child support payments through the formal system could get a noncustodial parent "locked down" for an indefinite period until he makes a purge payment. From the perspective of many men who find themselves in this situation, there is nothing they can do but have some money available when they come to court or risk being sent to jail. The perceived importance and likelihood of jail often is greater than would be statistically justified.

The court proceedings themselves reinforce the feelings of vulnerability that come with being a low-income or non-income, noncustodial parent. Very rarely do these men appear before the court with any legal representation. They usually stand alone before the judge and bailiffs, opposite an attorney for the state (who in the NCP's eyes is representing the custodial parent, who may or may not be present). From the very start, he is on the defensive unless there has been a mistake in the payment records or some technicality has been overlooked. The proceedings are brief (usually about five minutes), and the discussion of evidence is quite cursory; as a result, the NCPs often do not feel that they "had their day in court."[21] In many of the PFS sites, the majority of low-income or non-income NCPs who come before judges are found in contempt and ordered to do something (pay, get a job and pay, or go to jail until a purge payment is made).

For the NCPs about to be referred to PFS, the experience before the judge or referee is a little less ominous, because they know beforehand that there will be a recommendation that they go to the program. However, the judges or referees are still firm with these men, and many will quite candidly pose the threat of jail if the NCPs do not meet the guidelines of the program. For some of the NCPs, PFS is a momentary reprieve from the judicial system and jail, and many of the NCPs appreciate this opportunity. Others are angry that they have to participate yet feel powerless to do anything else considering the increasing likelihood of incarceration.

Many of the complaints heard from higher-income NCPs (whose children live with a custodial parent who is not on welfare) also appear among the NCPs in PFS. Quite a few men feel that the court system is so one-sided that they do not have a chance, no matter what they do. These men feel that the custodial parents (the women) receive a great deal of the benefits from the courts and the welfare system with few strings (behavioral requirements) attached, and that they get nothing. Some state that they do not even get to see their children when they have established visitation; others allege that the custodial parent is not taking proper care of the children or not using the support she does receive properly. Usually the NCP is told that another agency or court handles such problems; then the NCP is either dismissed or taken to jail. G-man, an African American male in his late twenties, expressed his sense of powerlessness and discontent with the system:

> Well, the program, that's the way it seems so far. They send a guy on a five-dollar-an-hour job at the EDD [Employment Development Department] office, I'm like—all they want is their money. They don't care how you live, as long as you sign this paper. If you don't, you go to jail. If there's an opening you don't go on it, you go to jail. If there's an opening you don't go to it, you go to jail—simple as that.

From our interactions with the NCPs in our sample, the notion of powerlessness is inextricably linked to respect, control, and autonomy. Many of the NCPs, especially those in their late twenties and older, have had some experience with respect, control, and autonomy. But what seems to have happened is that little by little they lost control over the various elements in their lives that grounded them and gave them their stability, such as their "hustles," their children, and their confidence in themselves. As these things started to spiral away from them, the NCPs spiraled down as well. Unfortunately, they see very few avenues to pursue during this time. As a result, they hit a level of personal discomfort that makes an opportunity like PFS look enticing.

This is not to say that some of the men in this program do not have the resources to get their lives on course without PFS. But putting those resources together consistently over time appears to many of the men to be too great a challenge. For example, the experience of applying over and over again for jobs and never even getting an interview has drained many of these men of their self-respect. Not having a job and not having custody of their children, according to some of the NCPs, makes them feel vulnerable and at times powerless to see their children. Their inability to see their children or find a (decent) job and the constant threat of either the CSE agency or the police arresting them further heightens their sense of powerlessness.

Through the PFS program, many NCPs have reported, they start building their reserves up again, gaining back some of the respect, influence, and control they felt they had lost, all of which leads to the beginning of a state of empowerment. Peer support discussions on issues such as dealing with anger and violence, fathering with limited economic resources, and the rights and responsibilities of an NCP (see appendix) help the NCP gain confidence in himself again. These discussions also help some of the NCPs realize that they are capable of success.

The greater source of empowerment for the NCP, however, is employment. Employment allows him to feel more independent. Many NCPs speak of the day when they will get that job that will allow them to move into a place all their own. Some of the men talk about gaining custody of their children when they become gainfully employed. Trane told us that his ex-girlfriend wants him to take his son because it's time for his son to be with his father. He loves his child but refuses to take him because he doesn't have a job, and he feels that would not be good for his son to see. Trane feels this way despite the fact that his girlfriend of seven years thinks that it would be great for the son to live with them. Regardless, Trane is just not comfortable with having his child live with him while he's not working.

FAMILY ISSUES OF POWERLESSNESS   NCPs' feelings of powerlessness in regard to their relationships with their children and the custodial parent seems directly related to their access to economic resources. Many of them state that everything is fine as long as they have some money. It seems to them that when they run into hard times financially, their access to the children and their desire to see the children decline sharply. Trane does not want his son to live with him until he has a decent job, but meanwhile he cannot see his son because the mother, while willing to allow the son to live with Trane, will not allow Trane to come over and visit. As a result, Trane has not seen his son in three years, although he has spoken to him on the telephone a couple of times. This is not an uncommon story among the small sample of NCPs with whom we have interacted. All have discussed how their relationships with their children and their "ex" are to some extent based on their ability to pay support, and how they feel largely powerless to change that dynamic.

Anderson (1994) suggests from his fieldwork that men who become economically viable are able to "play house." Becoming economically viable is one way of gaining access to children. Anderson also suggests that this is a way of controlling the custodial parent. The research that we have conducted to this point supports the thesis that being economically viable helps the noncustodial parent gain access to his children. Moreover, this issue of access has a great deal of saliency among the PFS population. Since most of the men in this study are unemployed or underemployed, few of them can compete with the economic resources that the custodial parent gets from public assistance. Thus, many NCPs perceive that their power to control or even influence family situations and gain access to their children is limited, if not nonexistent.[22]

Despite this perceived dilemma, our observations of peer support sessions and individual conversations with the noncustodial parents in our sample suggest that they have more contact with their children than is often assumed. Preliminary data on the characteristics of the whole PFS sample, including the qualitative sample, suggest that almost two-thirds of the total PFS experimental sample have seen their children at least once a month. Over 50 percent of the overall sample claims to see their children at least twice a month. Those in the qualitative sample appear to have about the same amount of contact with their children as those in the larger sample.

For the noncustodial parent in Parents' Fair Share, however, the ability to see his child is often influenced by his relationship with the custodial parent, the court system, and/or the welfare system. The participants express a feeling of powerlessness that they are unable to change either the custodial parent's or the system's attitude toward them. This often enhances the NCPs' resistance and/or reluctance to meet their legal, social, and emotional obligations as fathers. Some NCPs have tried to circumvent these obstacles in order to be with their children. But more often than not, such efforts wane over time and contact with their children diminishes.

The Parents' Fair Share program, in its effort to convey messages about responsible fathering and economic self-sufficiency, attempts to reduce some of the NCPs' feelings of powerlessness by offering opportunities to mediate situations (which may include the custodial parent) that, in the eyes of the PFS participants, prevent them from being better or more active parents in their child's life. While this formal mediation process is offered from the very beginning of the NCPs' experience in the program, its use has been nominal. Many times either the mediation help requested by the PFS participant has been refused outright by the custodial parent or the latter has chosen not to participate, even after a date has been established. The custodial parent is under no obligation to participate in mediation, and the NCP and PFS program staff have no authority to require participation. That parent's refusal or reluctance is often interpreted by the NCP as another reminder that his role as father is based on financial rather than emotional relationships.

Parents' Fair Share tries to promote the notion that the non-economic components of parenting are an integral part of parenting and will have as much, if not more, impact on children as the money paid in child support (especially when the children are on welfare). Forces outside of PFS (the courts, families, children who want expensive items) challenge the validity of such a proposition and make it extremely difficult for the men to accept. As one case manager for the program recently put it, "It's all about the child support."

Nonetheless, many of the NCPs express love for their children, although some are unaware of how to express or share their love with their children. Through the "Responsible Fatherhood" curriculum used in peer support, PFS staff provide ideas about inexpensive or free activities that NCPs can do with their children. Various PFS programs have sponsored activities to help the NCPs begin this process, including father-child basketball, trips to sporting events, Easter egg hunts, field trips, graduation ceremonies, and picnics. The purpose of the information and activities is to get the NCPs and their children to realize (or remember) that a father is not just a financial provider but also an emotional supporter.

Social and Economic Isolation

Most of the men in this study have some contact with at least one family member, spouse, child, or relative. Even those men who have been homeless have relatives and friends who at times have been willing to assist them. In spite of these limited social networks, the NCPs we have encountered live relatively isolated and insular lives at the time they enter the PFS program. To explain this, the men sometimes point to racial discrimination; some also reflect on their personal limitations. Many men participate in Parents' Fair Share because they are looking for an opportunity to get a job, or at least find where the jobs are. Most of them come from communities where industries have left and a local job is no longer readily available. The lack of mainstream industry in their communities has created levels of unemployment and poverty rates that are much higher than the average for the surrounding city. When these men walk into the PFS office looking for real job leads, they are in fact saying, "We assume that you can help us locate work." Why is this important? Because the resources of the community are so limited and the access to the outside labor market is almost nonexistent within their communities. This section examines how the social and economic isolation the NCPs experience and express is inextricably linked to the inability to make economic and social progress in their lives.[23]

Ironically, despite the fact that these NCPs have family and friends, they are socially isolated. For many of these men, having to rely on their family and friends to make ends meet or just to survive challenges their perceptions of self-worth and reminds them of their inability to be independent. For example, in a conversation with a participant in his midthirties who had been living with his mother for three years, he stated, "I have to call you from a pay phone 'cause my mother don't want me to use her phone." As a result, conversations with him took place on breaks at his job or when he was at a pay phone down the block. Others are similarly stifled because they are living in the home of a relative, parent, or friend.

Sometimes just the living arrangement is enough to make the participant slip into a state of isolation. The NCP knows that he has very limited resources (if he's lucky, he has a part-time job or is receiving some sort of general assistance or relief)[24] and that to keep a roof over his head he must contribute something to the household that is providing him shelter and avoid being a source of trouble. The contributions the men report making vary from $200 per month to in-kind services such as mowing the lawn, fixing things, and doing other household mechanical tasks. As long as the friend, relative, or parent values the contribution the NCP makes and sees little cost to his being there, he is allowed to stay. As a result, an NCP typically tries not to be too noticeable or intrusive so as not to draw too much attention to his presence and wear out his welcome. This in turn limits his ability to participate in social activities that, among other things, may lead to a job.

The reason given by most of the NCPs among our sample for their lack of social interaction is very simple—they have no money. Further, even if they have funds temporarily or find a free way to socialize, they feel real limits on how socially active they should be. Many of the men feel that their living arrangements may be jeopardized if friends and relatives see them "partying" or "hanging out"; they fear that those with whom they are staying will think they have more resources than they say they have. Not willing to risk being asked to leave, many NCPs thus stay close to home.[25]

Personal difficulties, especially problems with the law, are another reason for the social isolation of NCPs. Nearly 80 percent of the qualitative sample have had some encounter with the judicial system and jail. The duration of time they have spent in jail varies, but for the men whom we have observed and spoken with, staying out of jail is a main priority.[26] One way to stay out of jail is to stay away from some of the guys in the neighborhood who are likely to still be getting into trouble.

One quotation summarizes how some NCPs retreat into a social cocoon when their economic resources are limited. As Fila-G from Memphis put it, "I'm just sittin' on the porch. Well, right now, I could truly say I don't foresee much of nothing, you know. Gotta get over, see kids, or something like that, and, uh, you know, it ain't much a broke man can do." NCPs count on very close family members and have few other social resources. One participant who relies on his sister for housing reports the obvious but important reason she is willing to do this: "She is my sister." Since he has no money, no job, and no public assistance, he expects that he would be in trouble and end up in jail if she did not put him up. So he stays close to her home when he's not actively participating in a training component of the program.

Even though these very basic relationships are often stressed, they do persist for many NCPs. The greater challenge is to expand the social network for themselves or for their children. Many of the participants explain that they cannot establish themselves in the home, the neighborhood, or the community without a regular job. Without money, they are unable to stay in one place regularly. Constantly moving, they lose sight of other important things (raising children, participating in continuity activities, and so on) because their primary concern becomes their own survival.

The NCPs' social isolation from family, friends, and the community can be detrimental in several ways. First, it adds to the psychological and emotional feelings of isolation from which they already suffer. Second, it further separates them from economic opportunities. As many job search programs teach, the best sources of job leads are often friends and local contacts in the community. Many job search staff explain to job-seekers that more jobs are found through friends and relatives—31 percent—than through any other source of job leads.

Many of the NCPs in this sample live in very close-knit, poor, urban environments out of necessity, and this further limits their access to information about available jobs. Even those who have found a stable job often grow frustrated over their inability to use it as a stepping-stone to something better for themselves or for others in their family. The following statement by Jasper, a participant in Grand Rapids, indicates some of the economic limitations that the NCPs in the sample feel they are facing:

> That's just it. To me it makes no sense where I work in a job two years, man, two years, and I can't get my son a job. I can't get my little nephew a job, you know, man, where a guy worked there two years, he'll get . . . a job. . . . I've seen people come in the job, they have two and a half years. . . . I've seen people come in there for six months, they put them in an office . . . when I apply for it . . . but you know . . . I still learn something. Applying for the same position that they kept hiring . . . so I finally went to the—I said, listen here, I've been with the company for two and a half years, whatever. I just really don't understand what is the problem with minorities getting into positions. I said, I've never seen anything like it in my life. I said, what do you as an owner have to say about this?

In meetings of peer support groups, facilitators try to show NCPs the habitual nature of their behavior and actions and the contribution that makes to the social and economic isolation they feel. The facilitators try to stress that the participants must think about the long-term consequences of their actions, for themselves and for those with whom they have relationships. The facilitator sometimes asks, "What does it mean to your children that you are not around for them? What does it mean to you if you are constantly leaving jobs?" Many of the men who participate in PFS have not faced up to these issues and, as a result, have isolated themselves from opportunities and people.

Many of the NCPs in PFS enter the program with a passive and skeptical attitude. One of the most common questions that NCPs ask in the first week of the program is, "Are you going to find me a job or do I have to?" This question becomes particularly important in light of their lack of access to and knowledge about the labor market in their community. Though the economic situation has recently improved in many of the PFS sites, the PFS participants—especially the African American males—have not seen this turnaround in their lives. So when the program personnel tell participants, "We are going to help you find a job that you are qualified for," many NCPs in our sample express suspicion and doubt. A large proportion of these men have had full-time jobs before, but they are looking to the program to give them access to a job that is better than the jobs they could find on their own. Some are hoping the program can re-create the "good job" they had at some point in the past.

PFS participants are looking for work that will allow them to start establishing themselves and creating a stable environment so that they can move forward in their lives and possibly take a much more active role in their children's lives.

Breaking the economic isolation the NCPs feel—by helping them find those elusive good jobs—is the key to a favorable reaction to the program. In the eyes of the NCPs, a good job frees them from the constraints of others (the judicial system, family members) and could give them legitimate access to their children and standing in their community. Without such a job, many NCPs report that they resent the "system," the custodial parent, and sometimes even their children.

In conclusion, even though these men have some social interaction with individuals in their community, for the most part they remain socially and economically isolated because their community and associates are also socially isolated or distanced from the mainstream labor market. It should also be noted that for many African Americans, getting and keeping a job does not remove all of the consequences of social and economic isolation, nor does it immediately place them in the mainstream of life in the United States.

EVALUATION OF PARENTS' FAIR SHARE— FINDINGS AND IMPLICATIONS

We have presented a picture of the lives and attitudes of a sample of NCPs in the PFS program. This section discusses the programmatic implications of these findings, highlighting the challenges that this picture presents for the program and briefly describing how project sites and the Manpower Demonstration Research Corporation have responded. The discussion is structured around the three themes presented earlier.

Perception of Opportunity

The clear need that many NCPs express for a job, their anticipation that PFS can be a source of skill development and employment, and their low tolerance for what they see as delays and bureaucratic "screwups," all put the program on the spot in a very concrete and immediate way. Compounding the tension is the challenge of designing a service sequence when many of the NCPs initially lack the skills needed to find a job that provides a wage sufficient to cover their living expenses and child support obligations.

MDRC initially pushed sites to make on-the-job training (OJT) a central part of their program in order to address this problem; the NCPs would be able to earn money while being trained. This original plan has been difficult to achieve for several reasons. First, the Job Training Partnership Act (JTPA) system, the primary provider of OJT placements, was deemphasizing OJT at the time PFS began. Second, many of the NCPs who cannot find work on their own have such sporadic work histories and weak job skills that they are high-risk placements in OJT from the perspective of the employers, who must train them, and of the program, which must subsidize their wage costs and be field-accountable for post-program success in performance standards.

In part because of the difficulty of implementing OJTs, and in part because of a belief that basic skill instruction was needed, several of the PFS sites originally envisioned a sequence of services that addressed the various skill and attitudinal barriers to employment the NCPs faced and then linked them with a job. With growing experience in running the program came a gradual recognition of the economic difficulties the noncustodial parents faced and their unwillingness or inability to pursue a long series of activities prior to employment. A man who lives on—at best—$221 per month (general relief benefits in Los Angeles) does not have the resources or the social mobility to pursue "mainstream objectives." His goals relate to much more basic, daily survival issues: "Do I buy clothes to go to an interview? Do I take the bus to go to the interview? Or do I hold on to the money to buy something to eat and have enough left over to chip in for my housing?" For some the cost of participation becomes too great and they retreat. In their eyes, it has taken them too long to get to a point where they are close to economic self-sufficiency. When the program moves the NCPs quickly through the intervention and into either work or training, the discontent that they express begins to wane.

Sites have responded in several ways. First, programs have worked to improve their ties with the local labor markets and to strengthen their ability to deliver on the promise of improved access to jobs. This has taken the form of increased emphasis on job development services and enhancements to the job club activities originally planned. Without the reality of employment at the end of the program, retaining NCPs in the program becomes very difficult.

Second, programs have sought new ways to mix work, counseling or peer support, and skill-building. One option, tried to varying degrees by sites, is to arrange part-time work while NCPs participate in longer-term training. In addition, sites have worked to maintain contact with the program participants and continue PFS services after an initial job placement, offering help in retaining employment and making a successful transition over time to better jobs by building a work history and learning new skills through employment.

Third, sites have strengthened case management services, so NCPs will be less likely to get lost in the shuffle and program services will be closer to a seamless sequence. If successful, this gives NCPs a personal contact or advocate within the program who can anticipate and address administrative problems as they arise and reduce the frustration level for them.

Fourth, program operators occasionally link NCPs to cash assistance programs (where these are available for single individuals) or in-kind assistance (especially food stamps). These forms of assistance can provide an income floor for NCPs while they attend training to build their skills, and they lessen the chance that crisis situations, like homelessness, will arise.

Finally, the economic vulnerability of the NCPs who participate in PFS heightens the importance of modifying the child support order downward during program participation. For some NCPs, existing orders were set during a past period of employment and are clearly inappropriate under support guidelines. Most NCPs referred to PFS do not know about the option of downward modification of their order or are not knowledgeable enough about court or agency procedures to accomplish this. (Typically, child support enforcement agencies do not provide NCPs with assistance in navigating the legal system.) Further, if a parent does pursue a downward modification, it is relatively common for agencies and courts to impute earnings (full-time work at the minimum wage) when facing an unemployed NCP and to set the support obligation accordingly. Thus, the process involved in the referral to PFS—where the agency recommends to the court a temporary and substantial reduction—is the most realistic way to allow and encourage participation in a program like PFS.

With the near-universal reduction of support orders under PFS comes the need for careful monitoring of participation in the program and a quick procedure to reinstate a higher order if participation ceases or employment is found.[27] Support for PFS programs would quickly evaporate if orders were reduced for all those referred and it proved difficult to reinstate higher orders for those who did not comply with program requirements or found jobs and had the income to pay support.

Powerlessness

NCPs' feelings that they are powerless to influence their economic circumstances, their relations with their families, or their dealings with courts and child support enforcement agencies can produce anger, inaction when presented with opportunities, and occasionally reckless behavior as they strike out at the source of their feelings. Program staff in PFS have tried to walk a fine line between doing things for PFS participants and empowering them to act for themselves. They also have to strike the right balance between letting the NCPs vent their feelings of frustration and anger and pushing them to move on and develop new ways of living.

In some areas, program staff have had to serve as advocates for participants. At the most basic level, the entire concept of PFS represents a challenge to the standard operating procedures of child support agencies and the courts. PFS staff—in designing and implementing the program—often find themselves advocating for the interests of the NCPs. Many NCPs report that they feel PFS represents the first time the child support enforcement system has acknowledged them as individuals and "met them halfway" to help them get their lives in order.

Another important advocacy role for PFS staff is seeking service providers who are willing and able to serve the needs of the NCPs. PFS staff have pushed employment and training agencies to accept clients they might otherwise reject and have sometimes tried out several different service providers before settling on one that can work with this severely disadvantaged group. Staff have also worked to help participants solve problems with bureaucracies and deal with their entrenched ways of handling NCPs. This ombudsmen role can extend to dealings with welfare agencies (which may not initially accept that participation in PFS satisfies the work requirements of their program), criminal courts, and probation departments.

The tension between assistance and empowerment also appears in a program site's choice to emphasize either job development (program staff find job opportunities for participants) or job club services (participants are taught job-seeking skills to market themselves). Initially, sites tended to think that one or the other approach was proper. With growing experience, they often recognized the diversity of NCPs and the need for both approaches in the program.

The peer support component is the forum in which program staff and participants deal most directly with feelings of powerlessness, and in most sites it has emerged as the core of the program and the best chance to help NCPs take charge of their lives. For many participants, the peer support group may feel like one of the few places where they are taken seriously—where the difficulties of their situation are acknowledged, their concerns and feelings are addressed, and their opinions are listened to and respected. The original curriculum for peer support addressed issues related to feelings of powerlessness, such as developing a clearer view of parental rights and responsibilities (legal and otherwise), improving communication skills, and handling anger and conflict. Facilitators often invite important authorities in the lives of NCPs to attend (for example, child support enforcement officials or judges), giving the NCPs a low-pressure, nonadversarial opportunity to discuss issues of concern with the "powers that be." Responding to issues raised by participants, PFS staff added sessions on surviving on the job and responding to racial discrimination.

The need to use the peer support sessions as a vehicle for positive change and not just as a "gripe session" has put a premium on the skills of the group facilitator. It has proven generally easy to get the NCPs talking about deeply felt, troubling issues; sessions often evolve into participant-driven, animated discussions. But the danger is that the sessions will either drift endlessly, with no closure on the lessons to be drawn from the discussion, or that very serious issues will arise that could best be handled by professional counselors.

Though the facilitators are generally quite knowledgeable about the lives and circumstances of the NCPs in the program and good at interacting with them, the funding for such positions usually has prevented programs from hiring professionally trained counselors or very experienced group facilitators. In response, MDRC has revised the peer support curriculum numerous times to strengthen it by adding sessions on topics raised by participants or facilitators, eliminating exercises that did not work, and adding new ones. Further, the facilitators were brought together periodically for multi-day training sessions, and an informal support network for facilitators emerged. In this process, the most experienced and successful facilitators were deeply involved in developing the best materials possible and conducting the training, so that the perspective of site staff was represented.

Social and Economic Isolation

NCPs' social and economic isolation limits their ability to plan a larger parental role and to identify and pursue employment opportunities. These issues have been most directly addressed in the peer support and job club activities of the program.

One of the central messages of peer support is that NCPs are part of the larger community and part of their children's lives, for better or worse. Activities challenge them to recognize the values that their past behavior has conveyed to their children and to rethink their relationship and develop a new plan to help their children develop the values they will need as adults. Other sessions focus on building better relationships with their children and the custodial parent, improving personal communication skills, and learning better parenting techniques. The NCPs in peer support also can provide a social support network for each other (some groups have continued to meet long after the required sessions end or formed spin-off fathers' groups), and sessions seek to help NCPs recognize the value of a larger support network, the existing support network they can build on, and ways in which to strengthen these relationships.

In the peer support curriculum, several of the sessions are devoted to discussions and demonstrations of how to be a father and not just an economic resource. Peer support facilitators try to stress the importance of the emotional ties and give the NCPs suggestions on how to accomplish these goals and spend time with their children in enjoyable ways even though they lack funds for expensive outings or gifts.[28] Peer support facilitators also have organized low-cost or free social events for NCPs and their children to provide a supportive environment in which to try out new parental techniques and roles. They also help the NCPs realize that if they see their children more frequently, each visit will feel less pressured and there will be less of a sense that they have to meet all their children's needs at once.

The job club deals more directly with developing and exploiting social and economic networks to find a good job. Many of the exercises deal with how to seek out job leads through friends and family, how to build an expanding network of contacts, how to present oneself effectively, and how to make a first job the start of a progression to higher-paying positions.

Further, growing emphasis on longer service and continued services after a job placement reflects a realization that many of these NCPs will feel isolated on a job, unsure of expectations or the best way to communicate or raise issues, and lacking in trusted friends on the job who can provide good advice.[29] They also may lack social support outside the job to help them address the issues that arise as the return to work changes their entire routine. Program staff are increasingly trying to maintain enough contact with participants who have found work to be aware of problems they may be having on the job or in other aspects of their lives and to help them develop a constructive plan to address those problems. At this stage in the PFS project, staff are aware that this is both important and difficult to do.

It is too early yet to determine empirically whether Parents' Fair Share is an effective resocializing and skill-building intervention that has worthwhile economic and social impacts. Many of the pieces that could lead to the success of this program are in place. The opportunity for NCPs to discuss issues around being an NCP is a significant part of the intervention and might lead to substantial changes in future behavior. The peer support sessions are particularly helpful in reducing the social and economic isolation experienced by the NCPs. This component gives the NCPs an opportunity within a supportive environment to express and work out some of the obstacles they face. The employment and training component is steadily getting stronger as the intervention progresses and as the site economies improve. The challenge for the sites is to open job opportunities for the NCPs that have otherwise been closed to them. Finally, the enhanced child support enforcement approaches (monitoring of the caseload for eligible participants, referral to the program, lowering of orders during participation, careful monitoring of program participation and employment) are in place in all the project sites.

What is clear is that the stakes in this project are high. As one NCP quoted earlier recounted: "I just went [to the program] to clear the smoke really, because I knew I couldn't run and hide from them all my life."

Staying out of jail is an important reason why some NCPs choose to give PFS and the CSE system a chance. Yet, for most of the men, there was more to their choice to participate than staying out of jail. They want a chance to do something with their lives. Ventura, a young Anglo from Massachusetts, expressed his feelings on why he was participating in PFS.

VENTURA: Yeah, it's better than sitting at home doing nothing. At least here I'm learning something. I'm not getting trouble at home doing nothing.
INTERVIEWER: What do you mean getting into trouble?
VENTURA: I wanna get a better life, and this will probably help me get out … to get my family back. That's what I really—that's my goal, to get my family back. Some people may think it's—I don't really care what them guys think, it's what I want. Some people might not get along with her or anything like that, but it doesn't matter. It's my life, and I want to do with it … a job, you need a good job, and I think

this will help me out. Even if I do go through the class, and if I lose this job, I'll still know how to handle getting another job. Better interviews and write better resumes and stuff like that.

These comments are similar to those that have been expressed by other men in the program. They suggest that the NCPs are indeed expecting the program to help them improve their lives. In a very real way, PFS is about giving NCPs and the enforcement system a new option that has the promise of serving the interests of both and—more important in the long run—of the children both must sustain.

APPENDIX

Employment and training: The centerpiece of Parents' Fair Share programs is a group of activities designed to help participants secure long-term, stable employment at a wage level that will allow them to support themselves and their children. Since noncustodial parents vary in their employability levels, sites are strongly encouraged to offer a variety of services, including job search assistance and opportunities for education and skills training. In addition, since it is important to engage participants in income-producing activities quickly to establish the practice of paying child support, sites are encouraged to offer opportunities for on-the-job training, paid work experience, and other activities that mix skill training or education with part-time employment.

Enhanced child support enforcement: A primary objective of Parents' Fair Share is to increase support payments made on behalf of children living in single-parent welfare households. The demonstration will not succeed unless increases in participants' earnings are translated into regular child support payments. Although a legal and administrative structure already exists to establish and enforce child support obligations, it is critical for demonstration programs to develop new procedures, services, and incentives in this area. These include steps to expedite the establishment of child support awards and/or flexible rules that allow child support orders to be reduced while noncustodial parents participate in Parents' Fair Share and quickly raised when the NCP gets a job or stops participating.

Peer Support: MDRC's background research and the pilot phase experience suggest that employment and training services, by themselves, will not lead to changed attitudes and regular child support payments patterns for all participants. Education, support, and recognition may be needed as well. Thus, demonstration programs are expected to provide regular support groups for participants. The purpose of this component is to inform participants about their rights and obligations as noncustodial parents, to encourage positive parental behavior and sexual responsibility, to strengthen participants' commitment to work, and to enhance participants' life skills. The component is built around a curriculum, known as *Responsible Fatherhood,* that was supplied by MDRC. The groups may also include recreational activities, "mentoring" arrangements using successful Parent's Fair Share graduates, or planned parent-child activities.

Mediation: Often disagreements between custodial and noncustodial parents about visitation, household expenditures, lifestyles, child care, and school arrangements—and the roles and actions of other adults in their children's lives—influence child support payment patterns. Thus, demonstration programs must provide opportunities for parents to mediate their differences using services modeled on those now provided through many family courts in divorce cases.

Table 9A.1   /   Questions for Noncustodial Parents in PFS

A. Experience in Parents' Fair Share

1. What do you think of PFS?
2. What activities have you participated in?
3. How long have you been in PFS?
4. When you were assigned to PFS in court, what did you think was going to happen? What were you told would happen in court?
5. What do you think the purpose of PFS is?
6. What do you like and dislike about PFS? How could PFS be better?
7. What were the reasons that you didn't pay child support in the past?
8. What is the most important reason for not paying child support?
9. Has PFS helped you feel more like paying, and why?

B. Relationship with Custodial Parent(s)

1. How do you and the mother of your child(ren) get along? What is your relationship like now?
2. With how many women have you fathered children?
3. What was your marital status when you had your child(ren)?
4. What was your relationship with the custodial parent(s) before the pregnancy? How did the relationship change after the pregnancy?
5. When did you establish paternity? What were the circumstances (for example voluntary or court established)?
6. What does the custodial parent(s) think about PFS? Has her behavior changed because of PFS? Explain.
7. What are the biggest issues regarding responsibilities and obligations for providing for your child(ren) that you have with the custodial parent(s)?

(Table continues on p. 294.)

Table 9A.1 / *Continued*

C. Relationship with Their Child(ren)

1. How often do you see your child(ren)?

2. Do you have visitation rights? Are you pleased with them? Why? Why not?

3. Do you feel comfortable around your child(ren)?

4. How often does your family (for example, mother, sisters, brothers) interact with your child(ren)?

5. Where do you visit with your child(ren)? At the mother's home or at your home?

6. Does the custodial parent(s) help or get in the way of your relationship with your child(ren)?

7. What activities do you do with your child(ren)? Has this changed since you began PFS?

8. How would you make the relationship between you and your child(ren) better?

9. Are there any problems raising children from two different relationships? What are they?

10. Has PFS helped improve interactions with your child(ren)?

11. Have you taken any steps to improve your interaction with your child(ren)? What were those steps?

12. How could the custodial parent(s) help make your relationship with your child(ren) better?

D. Family Provisions: Socialization in the Home

Has PFS impacted your ability to manage your household and/or parent your child(ren)?

1. Is it more difficult now that you are in the Parents' Fair Share program?

2. Since you started PFS, have you noticed any changes in your child(ren)'s school attendance?

3. What kind of grades do your kids get? Have they always gotten these types of grades?

4. Would you say you are more involved with your child(ren)'s schooling since you entered into the PFS program? Why do you think this is?

Tell me how you feel about the following statements in regard to how you have changed or not changed since entering PFS.

5. I feel better about myself and my family since entering PFS.

Table 9A.1 / *Continued*

6. I am more worried about the kids because I am not around as much.

7. PFS gets in the way of the things I want to do.

8. I have more control of my life since entering PFS.

9. PFS has helped me positively interact with the child(ren)'s mother or father.

10. Since entering PFS I am more helpful in managing my child(ren)'s custodial parent household.

E. Personal Demographics

1. How old are you?

2. How many kids—ages, sex?

3. How old were you when you fathered your first child?

4. How many children live with you?

5. What is your current marital status?

6. What is your highest level of educational attainment?

7. Have you ever been homeless?

8. Are you currently supporting or helping to support another family? (Ferguson, 1990.)

9. What is the number one thing that would help you to be able to pay child support regularly?

F. Personal Economic Condition

1. When was the last time you worked?

2. When was the last time you had a full-time position?

3. What is the longest period of time you ever held a job?

4. Have you ever worked "under the table" or for cash? What kind of job was that? (If yes, then ask question #6.)

5. When you worked "off the books," did you share some of that income with the mother of your child(ren)? If yes, about how much would you give her and how often?

6. About how much did you make last year? What type(s) of jobs did you hold?

7. Do you buy your child(ren) things that are specifically for them? What types of stuff do you buy them?

8. Does your child(ren)'s Mom ever call you or get in touch with you to ask you to purchase things for the child(ren)? What does she usually ask you to purchase? And how often does she make these requests of you?

This chapter is based on a paper prepared for the conference, "The Effects of Child Support Enforcement on Nonresident Fathers," Princeton University, September, 1995.

NOTES

1. Normally, the JOBS program serves the custodial parents of children receiving welfare. Since 1988 the Department of Health and Human Services has granted waivers to more than the initial five states allowing them to use JOBS funds to serve noncustodial parents.

2. The partners in the research endeavor are the Parents' Fair Share Partnership, the Pew Charitable Trusts, the W. K. Kellogg Foundation, the Charles Stewart Mott Foundation, the McKnight Foundation, the Northwest Area Foundation, the Annie E. Casey Foundation, the Ford Foundation, U.S. Department of Health and Human Services, U.S. Department of Labor, U.S. Department of Agriculture, and the Manpower Demonstration Research Corporation. The project began with a two-year pilot phase to test the feasibility of operating the PFS program. The findings from this phase of the project are presented in Bloom and Sherwood (1994). The demonstration phase, with a study of program impacts, began in 1994.

3. The PFS program's success in achieving these goals is being evaluated through four research methods: qualitative research (of which this chapter is an example), implementation and process analysis, impact analysis using random assignment, and benefit/cost analysis.

4. California joined the project in the winter of 1994 and became part of the full-fledged demonstration project in February 1995.

5. The participants in the PFS program are overwhelmingly male. Accordingly, we generally use the male personal pronoun (*his* or *him*) to refer to the noncustodial parent.

6. To initiate and facilitate change (behavioral and attitudinal), a component was developed that was designed to get the NCP thinking about and discussing issues related to parenting. The guide for this process is called the "Responsible Fatherhood" curriculum. It is an eighteen-session guide that helps a group facilitator lead NCPs through issues that might be relevant to their paying child support and connecting or reconnecting with their children.

7. Successful completion of peer support groups varies among sites. Usually it entails the completion of at least ten peer support sessions. Some sites require that the eighteen sessions be completed.

8. The term "ventured" is chosen to highlight a substantial voluntary element in what is legally a mandatory program. This point is discussed in more detail later in the chapter.

9. See Cave et al. (1993) for information on JOBSTART and Orr et al. (1994) for information on the National JTPA study.

10. In some PFS sites, personal service (that is, evidence that the NCP personally received the notice) is required for a hearing on nonpayment, while in others mailed notice with return receipt can be used for these initial hearings. In the latter group of sites, if the NCP fails to appear for the initial hearing, personal service is typically then required as the next enforcement step.

11. The method of active interviewing and network sampling, as well as the use of theoretically grounded sampling (Holstein and Gubrium 1995; Johnson 1990; Glaser and Strauss 1967), was used to allow our research to develop, expand, and explore the themes uncovered within the context of the PFS participants. To ensure that close attention was paid to issues of bias and validity of responses, we used the methods offered by Miles and Huberman (1984), Holstein and Gubrium (1995), and Lofland and Lofland (1984). One method we used to enhance our confidence in the data we collected was careful expansion of the informant pool, using "contrasting cases."

12. College could also mean that they went to a community college to get their GED or possibly an associate's degree.

13. We develop the film, send the participants copies of the prints, and later discuss the photos.

14. Much of this doubt was based on preconceived notions (little of it was based on research) of who the non-child support–paying, primarily minority, noncustodial parents of welfare-receiving children are.

15. The use of focus groups is a standard method for capturing specific data or responses and is often the preferred course of action in developing a theoretically based, qualitative research effort (Kirk and Miller 1986; Miles and Huberman 1984; Glaser and Strauss 1967; Johnson 1990; Daly 1995). These focus groups led to papers published in Furstenburg, Sherwood, and Sullivan (1992).

16. Our focus on the child support system and unreported income during our focus groups did not show us the tenuousness of the living arrangements that many NCPs faced while participating in a program such as PFS. We may initially have underestimated the social and economic vulnerability of the noncustodial parent who participates in PFS. Similarly, we may have misunderstood or overlooked the survival techniques that these individuals have to employ to stay afloat in their communities.

17. The themes and quotations presented in this section were developed through an intensive culling of the data. We had individuals directly related to the project as well as outsiders review the data to support and challenge the validity of the emerging themes. The quotations came from transcripts, observations, and field notes, which were organized so as to highlight themes. Spradley (1979) and Miles and Huberman (1984) served as models in this endeavor.

18. Each site has its own definition of underemployment. Generally speaking, underemployment is defined as working for less than twenty hours a week at less than six dollars an hour.

19. From the program perspective, many of the job developers and job club staff members contacted for this study have suggested that the NCPs with whom they interact are very difficult to place because of their low skill level and because of the nontransferability of the skills they do have. Accordingly, from the service providers' perspective, this makes job placement more difficult and time-consuming.

20. We have heard job developers and others tell us that PFS participants are difficult to place and that when they leave a job, it is difficult to call on that employer again.

21. As discussed earlier, given the laws of child support, typically the only relevant issue is whether the NCP has paid, so the abbreviated nature of the proceedings is understandable from the perspective of the courts.

22. Seltzer and Brandreth (1995) and Furstenberg (1995) indicate that even some nonresident fathers with much higher incomes than the PFS population also have the "difficulty of negotiating their involvement with the children's mother" (168).

23. Our use of the term "social isolation" does not imply that these men live in "caves," out of contact with the general public. Wilson (1987) defines social isolation "as the lack of contact or sustained interaction with individuals and institutions" (60).

24. In our sample, general assistance or relief ranged from a high of $221 per month in Los Angeles to not being available in Memphis, Tennessee.

25. One way to check on whether people are staying as close to home as they say is to try to contact them in the middle of the day. Being able to make contact then is an indication that someone is not moving very far from home. Many of these men have indeed been home when we have contacted them at midday.

26. In fact, their past serious problems in jail heightened their interest in PFS, which they see as a means to avoid further jail time.

27. In PFS, the courts reduce orders only in cases where the custodial parent is receiving AFDC and thus has assigned her rights to child support payment to the state. NCPs can also be eligible for PFS if the custodial parent is not receiving AFDC but the NCP owes the state arrearages for past child support. However, in these cases the child support order is not reduced when the NCP is ordered into PFS.

28. When we asked what they typically do with their children, the NCPs respond with answers such as "playing Nintendo," "going to McDonalds," "watching television," "going to the park," and "just sitting there with them." Very rarely do they talk about spending lots of money or going to exotic places. Thus, they can benefit from new ideas about how to interact with their children.

29. From earlier in the chapter, recall Bob, who felt isolated in his new job and unable to develop a satisfactory way to respond to his supervisor's racist treatment of him.

REFERENCES

Anderson, Elijah. 1990. *Street Wise: Race, Class, and Change in an Urban Community*. Chicago: University of Chicago Press.
———. 1993. "Sex Codes and Family Life Among Poor Inner-City Youths." In *Young Unwed Fathers: Changing Roles and Emerging Policies*, edited by Robert I. Lerman and Theodora J. Ooms. Philadelphia: Temple University Press.
———. 1994. "The Code of the Streets." *Atlantic Monthly* 273(5): 80–110.
Blankenhorn, David. 1995. *Fatherless America: Confronting Our Most Urgent Social Problem*. New York: Basic Books.
Bloom, Dan, and Kay Sherwood. 1994. *Matching Opportunities to Obligations: Lessons for Child Support Reform from Parents' Fair Share Pilot Phase*. New York: Manpower Demonstration Research Corporation.
Bloom, Howard S. 1991. *The National JTPA Study: Baseline Characteristics of the Experimental Sample*. Bethesda, Md. Apt Associates.
Bush, Diane Mitsch, and Robert G. Simmons. 1981. "Socialization Processes over the Life Course." In *Social Psychology: Sociological Perspectives*, edited by Morris Rosenberg and Ralph Turner. New York: Basic Books.

Cave, George, Hans Bos, Fred Doolittle, and Cyril Toussaint. 1993. *JOBSTART: Final Report on a Program for School Dropouts.* New York: Manpower Demonstration Research Corporation.

Clausen, J. A. 1968a. *Socialization and Society.* Boston: Little, Brown.

———. 1968b. "The Life Course of Individuals." In *Aging and Society*, vol. 3, edited by Matilda W. Riley, Marilyn E. Johnson and Anne Foner. New York: Russell Sage Foundation.

Daly, Kerry J. 1995. "Reshaping Fatherhood: Finding the Models." In *Fatherhood: Contemporary Theory, Research, and Social Policy*, edited by William Marsiglio. Thousand Oaks, Calif.: Sage Publications.

Doolittle, Fred, and Suzanne Lynn. 1998. *Working with Low-Income Cases: Lessons for the Child Support Enforcement System from Parent's Fair Share.* New York: Manpower Development Research Corporation.

Ellwood, David T. 1988. *Poor Support: Poverty in the American Family.* New York: Basic Books.

———. 1992 "Child Support Enforcement and Insurance: A Real Welfare Alternative." Paper presented at the Malcolm Weiner Center for Social Policy, John F. Kennedy School of Government, Harvard University, Cambridge, Mass. (March).

Furstenberg, Frank F. Jr. 1993. "Daddies and Fathers: Men Who Do for Their Children and Men Who Don't." Preliminary draft of report. New York: Manpower Demonstration Research.

———. 1995. "Fathering in the Inner City: Paternal Participation and Public Policy." In *Fatherhood: Contemporary Theory, Research, and Social Policy*, edited by William Marsiglio. Thousand Oaks, Calif.: Sage Publications.

Furstenberg, Frank F. Jr., and Kathleen Millan Harris. 1993. "When and Why Fathers Matter: Impacts of Father Involvement on Children of Adolescent Mothers." In *Young Unwed Fathers*, edited by Robert I. Lerman and Theodora J. Ooms. Philadelphia, PA: Temple University Press.

Furstenberg, Frank F., Kay Sherwood, and Mercer Sullivan. 1992. *Caring and Paying: What Fathers and Mothers Say About Child Support.* New York: Manpower Demonstration Research Corporation.

Garfinkel, Irwin. 1992. *Assuring Child Support: An Extension of Social Security.* New York: Russell Sage Foundation.

Gibbs, Jewelle Taylor. 1988. *Young Black and Male in America: An Endangered Species.* Dover, Mass.: Auburn House Publishing.

Glaser, Barney G., and Anselm L. Strauss. 1967. *The Discovery of Grounded Theory: Strategies for Qualitative Research.* New York: Aldine De Gruyter.

Haskins, Ron, Andrew W. Dobelstein, John S. Akin, and Brad J. Schwartz. 1985. "Estimates of National Child Support Collection Potential and Income Security of Female-Headed Families." Final report presented to the Office of Child Support Enforcement, Social Security Administration, Washington (April).

Haskins, Ron, Brad Schwartz, John S. Akin, and Andrew Dobelstein. 1985. "How Much Child Support Can Absent Fathers Pay?" *Policy Studies Journal* 14(2): 201–21.

Holstein, James A., and Jaber F. Gubrium. 1995. *The Active Interviewer.* Thousand Oaks, Calif.: Sage Publications.

Inkeles, Alex. 1968. "Society, Social Structure, and Child Socialization." In *Socialization and Society*, edited by J. A. Clausen. Boston: Little, Brown.

———. 1972. "Social Structure and Socialization." In *The Handbook of Socialization: Theory and Research*, edited by David A. Goslin. Chicago: Sage Publishing.

Jarrett, Robin L. 1992. *A Family Case Study: An Examination of the Under Class Debate.* Thousand Oaks, Calif.: Sage Publications.

———. 1994. "Living Poor: Family Life Among Single-Parent, African-American Women." *Social Problems* 41(1): 73–129.

———. 1995. "Growing Up Poor: The Family Experiences of Socially Mobile Youth in Low-Income African-American Neighborhoods." *Journal of Adolescent Research* 10(1): 111–35.

Johnson, Jeffrey C. 1990. *Selecting Ethnographic Informants*. Newbury Park, Calif.: Sage Publications.

Johnson, Waldo. 1995. "Paternal Identity Among Urban Adolescent Males." *African-American Research Perspectives* 2(1): 82–86.

Joint Center for Political and Economic Studies. 1994. *Young Black Males in Jeopardy: Risk Factors and Intervention Strategies*. Washington: Joint Center for Political and Economic Studies.

Kemple, James J., Fred Doolittle, and John Wallace. 1988. *The National JTPA Study Site Characteristics and Participation Patterns*. New York: Manpower Demonstration Research Corporation.

Kirk, Jerome, and Marc L. Miller. 1986. *Reliability and Validity in Qualitative Research*. Newbury Park, Calif.: Sage Publications.

Lewin, Tamar. 1995. "Creating Fathers Out of Men with Children." *New York Times,* June 18.

Lofland, John, and Lyn H. Lofland. 1984. *Analyzing Social Settings: A Guide to Qualitative Observations and Analysis,* 2d ed. Belmont, Calif.: Wadsworth Publishing.

Marsiglio, William. 1995. "Father's Diverse Life-Course Patterns and Roles: Theory and Social Intervention." In *Fatherhood: Contemporary Theory, Research, and Social Policy*, edited by William Marsiglio. Thousand Oaks, Calif.: Sage Publications.

Massey, Douglas S., and Nancy A. Denton. 1993. *American Apartheid: Segregation and the Making of the Underclass*. Cambridge, Mass.: Harvard University Press.

McLanahan, Sara S. 1994. "The Consequences of Single Motherhood." In *American Prospect* (18): 48–58.

McLanahan, Sara S., and Gary Sandefur. 1995. *Growing Up with a Single Parent*. Cambridge, Mass.: Harvard University Press.

Miles, Matthew B., and Michael A. Huberman. 1984. *Qualitative Data Analysis: A Source Book of New Methods*. Newbury Park, Calif.: Sage Publications.

Orr, Larry, Howard S. Bloom, Stephen H. Bell, Winston Lin, George Cave, and Fred Doolittle. 1994. *The National JTPA Study: Impacts, Benefits, and Costs of Title IIA*. Bethesda, Md.: Apt Associates.

Perkins, William Eric. 1995. "Fathers' Care: A Review of Literature." Unpublished paper. Philadelphia: University of Pennsylvania

Seltzer, Judith A., and Yvonne Brandreth. 1995. "What Fathers Say About Involvement with Children." In *Fatherhood: Contemporary Theory, Research, and Social Policy*, edited by William Marsiglio. Thousand Oaks, Calif.: Sage Publications.

Sorensen, Elaine. 1994. *Noncustodial Fathers: Can They Afford to Pay More Child Support?* Washington: Urban Institute Press.

Spradley, James P. 1979. *Ethnographic Interview*. Fort Worth: Holt, Rinehart, and Winston.

Stack, Carol. 1974. *All Our Kin: Strategies for Survival in a Black Community*. New York: Harper and Row.

Sullivan, Mercer L. 1989. "Absent Fathers in the Inner City." In *Annals of the American Academy of Political and Social Science* 501(January): 48–59.

———. 1990. "Patterns of AFDC Use in a Comparative Ethnographic Study of Young Fathers and Their Children in Three Low-Income Neighborhoods." Paper prepared for the Office of the Assistant Secretary for Planning and Evaluation, U.S. Department of Health and Human Services (June).

————. 1993. "Young Fathers and Parenting in Two Inner-City Neighborhoods." In *Young Unwed Fathers: Changing Roles and Emerging Policies,* edited by Robert I. Lerman and Theodora J. Ooms. Philadelphia: Temple University Press.

U.S. Department of Labor. Various years. *Employment and Earnings.* Washington: U.S. Government Printing Office for U.S. Department of Labor.

Wilson, William J. 1987. *The Truly Disadvantaged: The Inner City, the Underclass, and Public Policy.* Chicago: University of Chicago Press.

Chapter 10

How Should We Think About Child Support Obligations?

Martha Minow

The dramatic increase in rigorous enforcement of laws requiring nonresident parents to support their children financially reflects what seems to be a remarkable degree of consensus about a fundamental norm.[1] People who produce children should provide for their support. Yet vigorous enforcement has also exposed to view many questions that are not resolved by reference to that simple norm.[2] Two persistent questions are unanswered by the basic commitment to enforce child support obligations, and a discussion of these questions can help to illuminate the scope—and limitations—of prevailing normative approaches to issues of law and public policy.

The first question is: What should be the enforceable obligation of indigent nonresident parents? Should they pay a smaller percentage of their income in child support than non-poor nonresident parents?[3] Should indigent parents be excused from making any payments of child support?

The second question grows from the large number of individuals who form successive families, inside and outside of marriage. Should a nonresident parent be able to obtain a downward adjustment of a child support order due to new obligations to a second family?[4]

Some states permit poor nonresident parents to pay either nothing or a lower percentage of their income than what a middle-income parent would owe, while still other states make no adjustment for the poor and therefore require poor nonresident parents to pay high percentages of their income in child support. State courts are massively divided about whether an order should be modified in light of a second family.[5]

To put some human faces on the two questions, consider these stories:

Tom has been only seasonally employed for the past two years; he earns $20,000 a year, but the income is sporadic. He pays child support when he can, but his two children who live with his ex-wife Christine are on public assistance. Tom is furious that whatever child support he can muster goes mostly to the state rather than to the children directly. He lives with Julia, who has a child from a prior relationship; he regrets that he cannot devote more of his paycheck to his current household.

Sam works at a fast-food place and earns minimum wage. He had a child with his high school girlfriend and pays child support for him, but now he is married, with another child on the way. Barbara, the mother of his first child, now has two other children with absent fathers. Sam will not be able to support both households; he is also worried that his child support payments benefit children who are not his own. How should his limited resources be allocated between the two households?

Joanne married Dave, who had a child from a former marriage; her $40,000 income now is figured into his ability to pay child support, but her college debts are not considered in this calculus. She and Dave now would like to have children but do not think they can afford to, at least not until all the college debts are paid.

Maria takes care of her three children through a combination of her part-time job wages and child support payments from their father Michael. Michael's business has done well, giving him an income of more than $100,000 a year, and he recently purchased a large suburban home for his new family. He wants Maria to start working full-time so that she can pay a greater share of the expenses for herself and the children, but she cannot afford the child care needed if she were to work full-time. Maria watches Michael's new children get all the "extras" (summer camp, vacation trips) that she cannot afford for her own children.

Given the continuing high rates of divorce, remarriage, and childbirth outside of marriage, situations like these are increasingly common in this country. As these brief descriptions suggest, solutions are not obvious. Some state laws leave these issues to the discretion of individual judges, while other state laws resolve them—but quite differently from state to state, even under the same circumstances.

This chapter suggests that recourse to the basic norm behind the child support duty offers little guidance to resolve these issues. Normative theories commonly offered to address public policy issues provide some limited guidance, although the review that follows should indicate the sharp limitations in prevailing normative theories when presented with problems about interpersonal obligations.

As a final introductory note, let me emphasize that these two questions are difficult but small compared with some other underlying problems that affect child support enforcement. Those questions include:

1. Do child support guidelines in general set levels of child support too low overall? What do children really need for a fair start in life?

2. Should the state ensure a basic minimum income for all children, even if their parents are unable to produce it? If so, what role should parental child support play for families affected by divorce or nonmarriage?

3. Should the state have any role in telling parents how much more than the minimum to spend on their children?

4. Should the state pursue policies, for example, in favor of population expansion, population control, or gender equality? If so, how should child support laws be crafted to pursue those policies?

5. Should the state try to affect not only the financial contribution parents make toward their children but also the time they spend with them?

Although none of these questions are directly addressed in this chapter, they are all crucial and all implicated by the analysis.

RATIONALES FOR CHILD SUPPORT OBLIGATIONS

Stemming from the law of persons, which evolved into family law, the child support duty has a long history that has produced contrasting and indeed diverging rationales (Fitzgerald 1994, 35–36). The rationales for obliging parents to pay support do not necessarily shed much light on how much support should be paid.

Historically Shifting Rationales

The English common law itself built upon the conception of pater familias under Roman law: the father holds dominion over wife, children, and property (Fitzgerald 1994, 35–36). Accordingly, the father or husband owed support to his children and wife and in exchange secured their services; wives owed husbands domestic and sexual services, while children owed fathers their labor and outside earnings (Lieberman 1986, 1–3); in addition, adult children were expected to support their elderly parents (Garrett 1980, 70–89). The father was dominant but also obligated; even if the spouses disagreed and separated, the father retained a duty to support the children and also enjoyed a presumptive right to their custody (Goodin 1985, 70–89). That custodial presumption shifted in both England and the United States to mothers, but the paternal support obligation persisted, enforceable through the criminal law or through civil actions by any person who provided necessaries, such as food, to the child (Lieberman 1986, 2–5). In addition, for children born out of marriage, states in the early part of the nation's history expanded inheritance rights on the civil side. Yet the states simultaneously maintained bastardy proceedings to fix a child support obligation on a private man rather than on public funds (Grossberg 1985, 211–31).

Legal responses to the Industrial Revolution included protective legislation restricting children's labor-force participation and the imposition of compulsory schooling. These rules and the ideas behind them undermined the idea that the child's labor supplied the basis for the parental support duty. Simultaneously, during the nineteenth and twentieth centuries, children generally became valued less for their economic contributions and more for their ability to elicit and return love and emotional comfort (Zelizer 1985). More recently, during the past two decades, legal and social movements for gender equality have eliminated the father-only quality of child support and converted the duty to a gender-neutral parental duty. Other changes in divorce laws, alimony, and property division followed the trend toward gender-neutrality (Garrison 1991) but have been criticized for perpetuating or exacerbating women's economic disadvantages due to workplace patterns and traditional family roles.[6] One consequence of the ostensibly gender-neutral context is an intense commitment to distinguish child support from any payments between ex-spouses. Similarly, for children born outside of marriage, paternity trials have sought to relieve taxpayer burdens, "not to alter the economic or social standing of the mother of the child" (Grossberg 1985, 217 [discussing the midnineteenth century]).

What, then, is the contemporary rationale for child support? The modern justification seems one of "but-for" causation: but for the parental sexual union, there would be no child, and therefore the parents—both parents—have a duty to provide for that child (Chambers 1982, 1618–21). The loss of the implicit reciprocal exchange—child support for child services—does not alter the reasoning found in William Blackstone (1765–1769), the classic nineteenth-century synthesizer of English common law:

> The duty of parents to provide for the maintenance of their children, is a principle of natural law; an obligation . . . laid on them not only by nature herself but by their own proper act, in bringing them into the world; for they would be in the highest manner injurious to their issue; if they only gave their children life that they might afterwards see them perish. (447–48)

This essential rationale gives no basis for exempting either poor parents or parents who have new obligations to additional children. It also affords little insight into the scope of the child support duty: it does not address how much support is owed and under what conditions that amount should be adjusted. If all that is owed is what would keep the child from perishing, that is a low standard indeed. The interaction between a minimal support payment and the child's eligibility for public assistance further complicates the question. Many nonresident parents earn less than the resident parent receives in public assistance benefits, which themselves fall short of the federally defined poverty level (Center for Social Welfare Policy and Law 1994; American Bar Association 1993). In addition, commonly used formulas for determining child support obligations generate awards that fall short of estimates of the costs of actually maintaining children (Barnow 1994, 18, 24; McLanahan and Sandefur 1994, 139–40 [discussing the decline in the real value of welfare benefits between 1972 and 1992]).

Looking to the ongoing intact family—in which the parents are married—could provide some benchmarks for the support duty. As Dean Herma Hill Kay (1991) has written, "The legal bond between parents and their children is not terminated by divorce; at the least, whatever support obligations are imposed on parents in intact families should survive the family breakup" (765). Yet here the deeply rooted resistance to state intervention in the ongoing family complicates the inquiry. The state scrutinizes parental support of children in the ongoing family only when a deficiency is so great as to amount to child neglect, justifying state intervention (Ellman, Kurtz, and Bartlett 1991, 355; Olsen 1985, 835). Once again, evidence that the support duty at least requires minimal sustenance is not difficult to establish; harder to explain is whether the duty extends beyond that.

Given the resistance to state intervention in ongoing families, the prime enforcement of the child support duty arises following divorce or for children born out of wedlock (Ellman, Kurtz, and Bartlett 1991, 355). Historically, enforcement efforts have been fueled by the risk—or fact—of public dependency. The federal role in child support enforcement stemmed from efforts to offset the public aid paid out through the Aid to Families with Dependent Children (AFDC) entitlement. Congress in 1950 required notice to state child support collection agencies of the recipients of AFDC (42 USC sec. 602[a][11][1950]; Krause 1989, 22). When Congress in 1974 enacted measures to strengthen child support enforcement, with the endorsement of women's groups, those measures pertained entirely to AFDC recipients because the explicit goal was to reduce the federal AFDC cost (Krause 1989, 371).[7] The AFDC recipient has to help identify and locate the noncustodial parent, participate in any paternity or support order action, and assign rights to uncollected child support to the state (42 USC sec. 651–65 [1982]).[8]

Amendments in 1984 and 1988 required participating states to implement wage-withholding from delinquent parents, expedited hearings, and other enforcement mechanisms (Krause 1989, 373–74). The 1984 amendments required states to develop discretionary guidelines for child support awards; the 1988 amendments mandated use of the guidelines as rebuttable presumptions while calling for review of child support orders every three years (Krause 1989, 376; Family Support Act of 1988, 42 USC sec. 667 [1990 supp.]). Designed to yield predictability and gender equity, to offset public welfare payments, and to prevent entry to the welfare rolls, the federal child support enforcement scheme reinforces the conception of child support as grounded in subsistence. Against the general background practice of state noninterference in parental decisions about how much to spend on their children, the federal norms strengthening child support enforcement have done little to specify how to calculate the right level of support owed to particular children.

The measure of support would, of course, vary considerably if the underlying purpose were to achieve savings for the state rather than to meet the child's needs, or to put the child in the same position as one in a two-parent household (Fitzgerald 1994, 39–45). No state currently calls for equalizing the standard of living of the custodial and noncustodial parents as long as the child is a minor (Sawhill 1983; Eden et al. 1986, 353; Eekelaar 1991, 109; Bergmann 1981, 195, 208). What, then, should be the measure of sharing for a child whose parents do not share a household? Fitzgerald (1994) perhaps overstates the difficulty with this question by considering potential constitutional defenses parents could offer to child support orders, but in practice the relatively low levels of child support indicated by most state guidelines reflect the lack of clear, consensual standards for assuring the child's share of parental living standards.

Many courts considering child support issues—and child support guidelines themselves—suggest that the child is entitled to share in the income of both parents (Fitzgerald 1994, 43). One implicit benchmark is the typical practice in a two-parent household. Income and assets are typically shared in such a household. The government generally stays out of fundamental economic distribution issues across households—beyond a welfare safety net and a mildly progressive income tax—because wealth is distributed in our system through families. In this line of reasoning, the accident of a child's birth to parents who are unmarried or who become divorced should not alter the course of events—the distribution of resources—that the private family otherwise would undertake. Therefore, the child should receive child support sufficient to maintain the standard of living the child would have had if the parents had remained in the same family household, without at the same time unduly burdening the noncustodial parent.

Yet there are least four difficulties with this line of reasoning. First, the fact of nonmarriage or divorce requires spreading resources between two households that otherwise would be devoted to one. This basic fact means that the two households, in most circumstances, will be unable to achieve the standard of living available to the one (Garrison 1991; Kay 1991). Similarly, the economies of scale achieved for each additional child in one household cannot be achieved over two. Estimates suggest that 16 percent of white custodial parents and 28 percent of black custodial parents who became poor during the 1980s after moving to a single-parent household did so because of the loss of scale economies (Garrison 1994). The total income of the two parents must rise between 10 and 24 percent, according to one estimate, to keep the standard of living of each member unchanged (Giampetro 1986).

Second, if the parents had stayed together in one household, regardless of their resources they would have had no legal obligation to support their children beyond subsistence because of the state's respect for parental prerogatives under the rubric of family privacy (Krause 1989, 384–85). Noncustodial parents thus often object if ordered to pay for a child's college expenses on the grounds that no married parents have such an obligation (Krause 1989, 384–85).

Third, child support is intended to benefit the child, not the custodial parent, and yet providing the child the standard of living that the two parents together would have had is difficult if not impossible to disentangle from the custodial parent's standard of living. Consider, as a basic example, housing. It is impossible to provide the post-divorce or nonmarital child housing comparable to what the two-parent household would have had without also providing it to the custodial parent (Chambers 1991, 773). Yet child support is supposed to avoid windfalls to the custodial parent.[9]

Finally, to base child support on what the child would have shared had the parents stayed together is to treat as irrelevant any differences in emotional commitment and day-to-day involvement between these two situations. Prominent observers of family life and child support enforcement have come to question precisely this view. They counter that child support duties should diminish or even end for a noncustodial parent who lacks a social relationship—an ongoing, reciprocal, emotional connection—with the child.[10] They claim that otherwise massive and probably unproductive state regulation of family relations would be required. Given the large declines in actual contact between noncustodial parents and their children, this view would have dramatic consequences for child support obligations (Chambers 1982, 1623).

In sum, the basic rationale for obliging parents to support their children stems from the parents' literal responsibility for bringing the children into existence. A modern rationale for child support is to prevent reliance on the state's safety net. Both of these rationales point toward, at a minimum, provision of support sufficient to meet children's subsistence needs so that the state does not have to do so. A contrasting guide for setting the level of support uses the baseline comparison of the two-parent household and obliges parents to share their incomes in order to provide as much as possible the same standard of living that the child would have if the parents lived together with the child. Yet this approach is quickly undermined by the practical difficulties of achieving the single household's standard of living with resources stretched over two homes, the desire to prevent windfalls to the custodial parent, and the risk that by living in two different households, the child and noncustodial parent lack the emotional commitments that serve as a predicate for income-sharing. Ascertaining what amounts to too much of a burden on the non-resident parent remains a task unanswered by reference solely to the basic duty to support one's children or the effort to approximate the two-parent household living standard. When the nonresident parent is poor, what counts as an unacceptable burden is especially unclear.

A national panel established to advise the states on guidelines urges some level of child support order even when the parents cannot meet the child's subsistence needs; the principles also direct that each child should have an equal right to share in the parental income, with adjustments for the child's age, parental income, spousal income, and other dependents.[11] Yet unanswered are what precisely it should mean to "share" in parental income—by a percentage, by a progressively increasing percentage with higher-income parents, or through some other measure. Another question is whether an "equal right" to share should approximate at all "equal shares." Does sharing imply a fixed percentage, unaltered by the class or income of each or both parents? Does sharing imply a lower percentage for lower-income parents? Also unaddressed is how duties to children acquired after the child support order should adjust an existing child support order—through the equal-right-to-share principle or through some other notion.

Competing Values

The basic purposes of making parents financially responsible for the children they produce—reducing the burden on the state to support dependents, helping children share in the income and assets even when their parents do not cohabit, and preventing undue burdens on nonresident parents—potentially point in different directions when applied. Indeed, these purposes support conflicting arguments about the two questions at issue in this chapter.

Thus, setting a child support obligation for an indigent nonresident parent can impose an undue burden, exposing that parent to sanctions for nonpayment. Threats of fines and incarceration will push some nonresident parents into compliance, but for those who are truly indigent, such threats become sheer expressions of brute power. Punishment with no hope of inducement is an insufficient reason to use the power of the state against a parent. It may also alienate the parent from the child and make it more difficult for the parent to get a paying job, enabling payment of child support in the future. An unpaid obligation mounts into arrears, and the parent would then be liable upon obtaining a job. Finally, getting a paycheck does not necessarily amount to an ability to pay up the arrears and instead may again expose the parent to sanctions without hope of securing compliance.

The argument on the other side simply notes how bad it would be to exempt the indigent parent from the child support obligation or even to reduce that obligation below the minimum set in a state guideline. It would give a sorry moral statement if one's parental duties evaporated if one only descended to a low enough income bracket. It could create a perverse incentive for some people to avoid taking or holding jobs that would give them enough income to enable them to pay child support. Some people might also hide income—by taking under-the-table payments for work, for example—and thereby seem to escape the support obligation. Even a small symbolic payment of child support would be better than an exemption for poor parents. The small payment underscores the obligatory quality of child support and promotes the pattern of regular, financial commitment that is crucial to parental responsibility.[12]

There are also competing arguments about the purposes of child support from the parent who seeks to reduce a support obligation after voluntarily assuming other responsibilities to a new family. Are the children in the two families to be treated the same, with a similar claim on the parent's resources, or are the children from the first family entitled to be given higher priority?[13]

Implicit in the first question is treatment of child support as a nondisclaimable duty that should not be altered by activities chosen by the obligor. In other words, a child support duty attaches upon the birth or adoption of a child; it does not diminish or disappear when the parent wants to pursue other duties, whether to another child, or to mortgage payments on a house, or to loan payments on a motorcycle. This notion of "first families first" has received approval traditionally in state courts (Williams 1994, 1, 13).

The opposing argument calls for "equal treatment" of all the children of a particular parent; first-in-time children should not have a priority. Had the parents stayed together and produced additional children, there would have been adjustments and a likely reduction in the resources available for the first child. The sheer fact that the parents no longer cohabit or share parenting should make no difference; the duty of support and notions of sharing apply equally to each child. Moreover, it would be an undue burden on the nonresident parent to prevent reallocation of resources to support later children. Freezing the duty of support in place for the children in the first family unfairly curbs the nonresident parent's freedom to form a new family, the argument would continue.

Defenders of "first families first" would respond that the possibility of adjusting child support means that a nonresident parent loses the sense of commitment to the existing children and fails to take seriously the cost to them of subsequent children. Because there is no longer one household but two (or three, or more), the parent no longer has the good of all in mind. A nonresident parent in particular is likely to care more about the children he sees everyday. The other children are already deprived of his regular presence. Further depriving them of the child support already found due to them is unfair. Removing the disincentive to take on new obligations only works to the disadvantage of the existing children.

Factual variations only further illustrate how conflicting arguments about the purposes of child support duties can be built. Should it matter whether the new child is biologically the parent's or a stepchild? Should it matter whether the parent's new family arises within or outside of marriage? Should it matter whether the downward adjustment of the award to the first children would prevent them from approximating the same standard of living as the child in the second family— or induce their custodial parent to enter full-time employment?

One's intuitions about such arguments are undoubtedly affected by one's own situation and tendency to identify with some people and not others (Coltrane and Hickman 1992). If one is concerned about the noncustodial parent's freedom to move on and form a new family, surely he should be able to reduce his preexisting child support duty. If one is concerned about the child in the first relationship and worried that even the original child support order fails to bring that child up to the nonresident parent's standard of living, a downward adjustment seems unfair and unwise. If one is troubled by family instability and the prospect of men fathering children with a series of different women, reinforcing the responsibilities of fatherhood seems important. Yet if one imagines that both parents have moved on to new relationships with new lovers and new children, the economic burdens the child support duty imposes on the nonresident parent seem unfair.

NORMATIVE APPROACHES

Trying to make law mirror conventional practices helps make law seem a legitimate expression of popularly held values and also increases the likelihood of compliance. When conventional practices are themselves confused or unclear, however, we must take a look at the fundamental purposes of the law.

As an alternative to trying to make law mirror social conventions, normative theories about law try to ensure that law pursues justice or visions of the good life. Thus at odds with conventionalism are five standard normative theories: Utilitarianism, Kantian commitments to rights and duties, virtue ethics, the ethics of care and relationships, and the expressive view of law. These theories diverge among themselves, but each offers norms to guide law and policy.[14] A review reveals that none of these theories directly answers the questions at hand about child support, but they do frame some of the basic choices crucial to addressing those issues.[15]

Norms to Set Obligations of Poor Nonresident Parents

Some theorists defend social convention as the guide for policy.[16] In this discussion, that could mean using estimates of actual parental expenditures to peg support orders for parents who do not cohabit. The idea is to direct law to reflect actual social practices. Compared with estimates of expenditures on children, child support orders for low-income families fall considerably short (Pirog-Good 1993, 42, 453–62; Tjaden, Thoennes, and Pearson 1989). Yet such estimates by necessity look to intact families to resolve disputes over children who do not live with both parents.

Thus, trying to answer questions about child support by reference to conventions observed by intact families runs into problems. One immediate problem is that practices within a single household do not anticipate the loss of economies of scale and increased expenses with two households. Other elements, including emotional commitments and the absence of commitments to family members in other households, make practices in two-parent households without divorce diverge from those of single-parent households, households following divorce, and other permutations.[17] Once the reference point to establish the convention is itself in dispute, conventionalism loses its chief virtues: avoiding normative conflict and securing both legitimacy and compliance.

As an alternative to conventionalism, utilitarianism focuses on consequences for the sum of all individuals' utility and seeks to maximize happiness and minimize unhappiness for the greatest number of people.[18] Probably this theory would argue for taking whatever a poor nonresident parent could pay to defray public expenditures to support the child, but calculating the possible damage to the parent-child relationship would be part of the analysis.[19] Utilitarians might also worry about perverse incentives created against accepting paying work should the law exempt unemployed nonresident parents from child support duties. These perverse incentives are especially troubling in light of evidence that many unmarried fathers who are poor at the time of their child's birth have modest to dramatic income increases over the next three years without producing increases in child support awards (Meyer 1995). A utilitarian concern with achieving compliance with rules—and reducing the costs of enforcement—could justify reducing support obligations of poor nonresident parents to low amounts but not exempting them altogether (Bartfeld and Meyer 1993).

Most often contrasted with utilitarianism are the theories inspired by Immanuel Kant. Kantian theory, also often known as deontological or, simply, rights theory, resists a central or exclusive focus on consequences in normative theorizing.[20] Two versions of the Kantian legacy are pertinent to this question: the conception of a duty that should be followed simply because it is a duty and the duty to treat persons not only as means but also as ends.[21] While contemporary Kantians would debate whether child support is the kind of duty that should be followed simply because it is a duty, Immanuel Kant himself had no doubt that is just that kind of duty.[22] Therefore, the poor parent should pay child support because it is the right thing to do, even if the amount paid is too little to support the child—or even if the law directs that the payment go toward repaying the state and thus it never reaches the child at all.

The categorical imperative might argue against letting the state devise a child support rule that treats the obligor parent only as a means, for example, to reduce the general taxpayer burden or to finance the child's trip to summer camp. Yet the imperative is not directed so much to the state constructing or applying the rule as it is to the individual who has a duty to another individual. In this view, the imperative directs the obligor parent to remember to treat the child as an end, not merely as a means for doing battle or competing with the other parent. This idea generates intriguing ideas about the right conduct between parent and child and between parents, but it offers little direction about how to set specific levels of financial support.

Virtue theorists call for thinking and acting in the right way at the right time and for cultivating good character.[23] Unlike Kantians, virtue theorists tend to resist duties detached from feeling, but they do urge the cultivation of the disposition to do good and to act responsibly. This view would probably endorse imposing some child support duty even on indigent parents while also urging parents to cultivate children's own capacities for personal responsibility. But virtue theories would not help to set the size of the award, nor would they offer much help in dealing with the problem of arrears for the poor parent who cannot pay the child support obligation.

Ethic-of-care theories urge the strengthening of human relationships of care and connection, especially to protect vulnerable people (Gilligan 1982; Tronto 1993),[24] and would be likely to test a child support policy in terms of its impact on the interpersonal connections of mutual care and concern within the family relationships, including ex-spouses (Regan 1994, 443–44). Probably ethic-of-care advocates would reject the question about poor nonresidents' support obligations by asking what larger networks of relationships could be identified and used to meet the children's needs (Gilligan 1982; Tronto 1993, 118; Goodin 1985, 70–89, 186).

Expressive theories of law emphasize the symbolic significance of the law rather than its ability to produce results in human conduct (Bobbitt 1992, 196–219; West 1993; Feinberg 1970, 95; White 1990; Sunstein 1994). Considerable attention to the expressive value of law appears in recent scholarship on family law (Glendon 1987; Bartlett 1981; Weisbrod 1989). Some expressive theorists hope that law may have an educative effect and help teach people about attitudes, relationships, and morals (Glendon 1987, 7–9). But most advocates of this view emphasize the importance in and of themselves of the stories and images contained in law. For this reason, expressive theorists may urge imposing obligations even on parents who cannot pay because it gives the right message about obligations, though debates over the messages law should give could well emerge.

In short, the theories divide over whether the law's ability to produce compliance matters to the judgment of poor parents' child support duties. Yet all but perhaps the ethic of care would urge imposition of some—if modest—support duty on even very poor nonresident parents. The ethic-of-care approach would urge some support obligation if the poor parent had any capacity to respond to the children's vulnerability, but the capacity of other people—and society—to respond would figure importantly in the rule as well.[25] All of the theories support enforcement of child support on even poor fathers who have an ability to pay the amount ordered.[26]

The Impact of the Arrival of Children in a Second Family on the Child Support Order

The treatment of the existing child support obligation after the creation of a second family is undoubtedly a contested issue precisely because conventional methods of reasoning do not point in a clear direction. Common sense is unavailing here because it supports conflicting intuitions. The first is to analogize the additional child in a second family to an additional child in the original family; presumably, the children would share in the family resources and there would probably be economies of scale. The conflicting intuition treats the child support obligations as a commitment that remains whatever else the parent does. Just as a car loan cannot be modified because the debtor has decided to buy another car, a child support order cannot be modified simply because the parent has decided to have another child.

Legal doctrine supports both intuitions. Thus, *Zablocki v. Redhail* (434 U.S. 374 [1978] [overturning as a violation of equal protection and due process a Wisconsin statute requiring compliance with child support orders prior to marriage]) protects individual liberty to marry against even legitimate state efforts to ensure child support enforcement; the cases protecting reproductive freedom similarly warn against state efforts to burden reproductive choice by making a prior child support obligation unmodifiable.[27] Yet bankruptcy law treats child support payments as beyond modification (Whelan, Cohen, and Wexler 1994); child support similarly is nondisclaimable and nonwaivable.[28] Modifications of court-ordered support may be permitted, but they must be based on discretionary, individualized judicial judgments, producing the variety of commonsense interpretations of local judges.[29]

Not much insight is forthcoming from a further tact of conventional reasoning: asking what rational actors would have agreed upon prior to a controversy. Although this approach offers some illumination in the context of property division and alimony between the adults in an intimate relationship, the very premise of rational actors with equal bargaining power is missing when the interests of future children are at stake. If the parents are viewed as fiduciaries for these children, their usually conflicting interests undermine the premises of the rational-actor ex ante bargaining model. Thus, it may not be rational to bind oneself against modification of child support obligations even in the face of subsequent children, nor does it seem rational to accept a reduction of support for a child simply because the nonresident obligor has chosen to take on new obligations.

Moreover, this very line of thought presumes that a rational bargain is a proper way to imagine the norms in this context. That presumption conflicts with the conception of child support as a duty that arises from the fact of parentage. Further, this line of thought neglects the societal as well as private interests at stake; remaining normative theories offer more help in this direction.

The alternative of utilitarian analysis would ask what consequences follow if the nonresident parent could reduce the child support obligations upon the arrival of a second family; would such a modification improve the well-being of more people than an alternative practice? Predicting consequences here depends considerably on estimates of the impact of financial incentives or burdens on how people become parents.[30] Some people plan parenthood; many do not. People become parents by engaging in unprotected sexual intercourse as part of spontaneous passion; people become parents after participating in a marriage ceremony or entering a committed nonmarital relationship with the intent to produce or acquire and raise children as a couple. People become parents through arduous adoption procedures or elaborate new reproductive technologies. People become parents by developing romantic relationships with another adult who already has children.

How much would any of these methods of becoming a parent be affected if the individual knows he or she has a preexisting and unchangeable financial obligation to a child living in another household? (see chapter 5 in this volume). Some people might switch from a lifestyle that involves spontaneous, unprotected sexual activity; some would plan and budget in advance, perhaps forgoing new children or delaying or spacing subsequent children further apart. Others would not change their lifestyle and as a result would risk producing more children; they would then have to either live frugally to meet the child support payments or fall into noncompliance. Still others might decide to adopt or become involved with a partner who already has children for reasons of love and commitment to those individuals, unaffected by other incentives or sanctions.

Utilitarians, who sum the consequences in search of the greatest good for the greatest number, would then probably divide the question into ex ante and ex post analysis. That is, before the second family has been formed, what rule would maximize utility? Assuming that at the margin a rule concerning modification of a child support order would affect the actions leading to a second set of children, the optimal rule would deny modification in order to lead that parent to internalize the costs of having more children. Those parents who can afford more than one set of children could proceed to do so; those for whom this would pose a financial strain or impossibility would be helped by the rule to anticipate this fact. The nonresident parent should neither be insulated from costs nor given an incentive to shift them to the resident parent, to the children, or to the larger society.

Those who seek to promote more responsible reproductive actions and decisions would view these potential consequences as desirable. The needs of the first set of children remain unchanged, while the ability and willingness of the nonresident parent would change with the arrival of a second family; if that change puts the children in a worse position, it should be deterred. Moreover, reducing the volatility of the income for the children in the first family would be a benefit in and of itself.

One could take a broader view and consider noneconomic consequences, however. Then, even reasoning ex ante, one would consider the loss to the nonresident father in terms of reproductive freedom and realization of life dreams to form a new family. Thus the inquiry turns to whether the forgone opportunities for these individuals who postpone or avoid having further children produce a loss that is outweighed by the benefits to the preexisting children and the larger society. Those benefits include undisrupted child support for the first set of children (assuming compliance) and elimination of the legal and administrative costs of efforts to modify support. A greater number of existing children will have greater economic security, but a greater number of adults will forgo the joys and tribulations of further parenthood. The burdens on the public assistance system could decrease with more children able to receive adequate child support. In reality, I suspect, each of these potentially positive consequences would be modest in amount, given the resistance of the relevant behaviors to change.

Once the second family has been formed, utilitarians are likely to argue for modification to permit efficient allocations of existing resources between the two sets of dependent children. This would reflect both a basic view of sharing as fairness and a prediction that refusals to modify could produce resentment that would render compliance with the order more difficult to secure. Some comparison between the children's needs and the ability to pay by the nonresident parent (and new partner) would be necessary to make any adjustment. If the resulting analysis yields the conclusion that the initial child support order should be reduced, this modification can be understood as a subsidy from the first set of children to the second set of children.

Of course, one cannot adopt one rule ex ante and another ex post in a legal system devoted to treating like cases alike and giving people notice about the laws that affect them. Permitting retrospective modifications in light of second families would give the nonresident parent no future incentive to avoid additional children. Denying retrospective modifications in light of second families could cramp nonresident parents' abilities to support additional children comfortably. Given the choice between the two rules, some may take the economic issues more seriously than the noneconomic ones. It would also be plausible to see the interests of existing children more seriously than the interests of as yet nonexisting children. Again, utilitarian analysis would try to estimate the greatest good for the most people. That estimate requires judgments about the actual effect of a no-modification rule in deterring additional children for people lacking sufficient financial resources to support more than one set of children.

Developing that estimate becomes even more complicated in light of the multiple actors and points in time that are relevant here. Thus, promoting responsible parenting decisions could be a reason to free the nonresident parent to form new responsible family relationships. The first child may have resulted from an irresponsible decision to become a parent by an individual who is now more mature and wants to become a responsible parent in a new household. The preexisting child support obligation could be a hindrance toward that end. Similarly, individual freedom should be a value not only for the noncustodial parent but also for the custodial parent, and for the children as well.

Ultimately, utilitarian analysis is likely to place a priority on compliance issues. What rule is likely to produce compliance rather than avoidance? Study of behavior would help, as would study of attitudes, but attitudes themselves could be influenced by clearly announced and enforced rules, one way or the other. Attention to compliance also highlights perverse consequences that should be avoided.

Thus, a rule should not link reductions of support duties to declines in contact between child and nonresident parent. Such a rule would encourage loss of contact. Other perverse consequences should also be anticipated. A nonresident parent may obtain a second job and refuse to report it for fear that the income will not go to the second family but be demanded as support payments for the first family; some nonresident parents may refuse to work a second job for this same reason. Another troubling consequence would be pressure on the custodial parent to take a second job to meet expenses—and then be less available to give time to the children, who already may see little of the nonresident parent.

In contrast, a Kantian approach suggests initially that the child support duty should be obeyed because it is right, and concerns about negative consequences for children acquired in a different household should not affect the conception of the duty to children in the first household. Yet the parent surely has a comparable and equally compelling duty to support children in the second household. If those children already exist, it is difficult to see how their claims are less than those of the children who happened to be born earlier. Nonetheless, a Kantian analysis could support a rule against modifying the support order for the first set of children simply because it is right and not worry about consequences for children in a later household.

Similarly, it would be wrong to treat the children in the second household as a means for reducing obligations to the first set of children. Adopting the children of one's new companion in order to reduce one's obligation to one's own children, for example, would violate Kant's categorical imperative. Yet if the adoption also reflects a desire to become the parent of these additional children and to provide them with love and companionship, they would no longer be only a means but also ends in themselves. In short, the Kantian concerns highlight the significance of reasons for acting—or reasons not to take an action—even more than the actions themselves when it comes to the nonresident parent who acquires children in a new household.

Another way to consider the imperative emphasizes that all of the children—in both households—should be ends, not merely means. This invites construction of a rule that is likely to ensure fairness between the households and equal status or standards of living. Reasoning backward from the ultimate living standards, then, all the resources available to the adults in the two households—including those derived from a new spouse—should be allocated to yield as much comparability as possible. In some circumstances, this would require downward modifications of prior child support awards. In others, the income and wealth brought in by the new spouse or parent in the second household would justify an increase in the support obligation to the first family.

Virtue theories would ask: Which rule promotes the disposition to do good, one permitting modification of child support orders in light of obligations to a new family, or one refusing such modification?[31] Which would promote responsible action? If taking on new family responsibilities would make a nonresident parent unable to provide for already existing children, this would be irresponsible conduct.[32] Yet virtue could also be exhibited by agreeing to share fully and equally the available resources across two households.

The dominant direction of inquiry from an ethic of care would focus on maintaining and strengthening relationships; sorting out the interaction between financial ties and emotional ties would be crucial to this inquiry. The ethic of care would oppose a rule that encourages nonresident parents to withdraw from the lives of their children. Downward modifications of child support to a first family in light of a second family could have that effect. The effect attributable to the modification of support might be small relative to the common shift in parental time and affection produced by the sheer fact of the second household, yet financial contributions communicate much to children who live in another household (U.S. House of Representatives 1983b, 355). An ethic of care would also consider whether the nonresident parent's resentment about nonmodification could strain relations.

The second contribution of the ethic of care is to shift from a focus on conflicting claims to address the wider web of relationships within which some harmonious resolution could be achieved.[33] Could other people, such as grandparents, contribute to the financial needs of the children and reduce the strain between the two households? Public policies providing family allowances or other social supports for parents raising children might also be sought under an ethic of care.

Looking for other resources would be crucial under Robert Goodin's (1985) theory of duties to protect the vulnerable. Thus, without ever discussing child support as an issue, Goodin offers this analysis that is strikingly relevant to the competing claims of two households on a parent:

> The dilemmas arise because discharging our responsibilities with respect to some of those who are vulnerable to us entails defaulting on our responsibilities with respect to some others who are also vulnerable. Whom we should favor depends, according to this analysis, upon the relative vulnerability of each party to us. We must determine: (1) how strongly that party's interests would be affected by our alternative actions and choices; and (2) whether or not he would be able to find other sources of assistance or protection if we failed him. (119)

According to this analysis, a nonresident parent should not seek to reduce his obligations to support children in a first household if they are highly dependent on that support and could not find other sources of support—unless fulfilling that obligation leaves the children in the second household even more destitute and without alternative sources of support. Time limits on public assistance and other parts of the social safety net would dramatically affect this analysis. If the parents have any ability to participate in political action to mobilize more public support for children in need, they should do so, whether to help their own children or others who would benefit from changes in public policy. Thus, the ethic of care and concerns for protecting the vulnerable challenge the framework that locates only the parents and the two households and instead reaches for other sources of support for children.

Concerns for the values expressed by law, regardless of their consequences on behavior, would probably oppose a rule permitting modification of child support in the face of a second family. Such a rule condones financial withdrawal from one's own children and thus conflicts with symbolic endorsements of parental duty.

Limiting Judicial Discretion

A normative question in law independent of the content of any particular rule concerns the degree to which it grants discretionary authority to decision-makers, such as judges and administrators (Sullivan 1992; Kennedy 1976; Scalia 1989). The benefits of a discretionary rule include the ability to be flexible, to respond to varying circumstances, and to consign controversial questions to the less visible area of case-by-case judgments. The drawbacks of discretionary rules, not surprisingly, are unpredictability, exposure to the biases of the decision-makers, results that treat like cases differently, and the obfuscation of important value choices in the details of particular cases.

The history of child support rules in this country demonstrates disillusionment with the promise of judicial discretion and growing preference for restricting that discretion. This trend is amply supported by the chaos produced by unpredictable rules, the unfairness of leaving important judgments to the biases of particular, varied judges, the perception that similar situations obtained quite different results in the courts, and the general tendency to order insufficient levels of support on a case-by-case basis insulated from democratic accountability. These same considerations justify erring on the side of restricted discretion with regard to the treatment of poor nonresident parents and requests to modify support in light of subsequent families. The temptation to grant discretion for case-by-case resolution of these issues is great, but the need for uniform, predictable rules that implement chosen values is even greater.

RECOMMENDATIONS

The contemporary purposes of child support give priority to a child's subsistence but leave ambiguous how much the child should be assured participation in the same standard of living as the nonresident parent. The purposes also leave confused the relative importance of payment by very poor parents made directly to the child and payments to defray the expense of public assistance. Besides conventionalism, I have canvassed five normative frameworks: utilitarianism, Kantian approaches, virtue theories, the ethic of care, and law as expression of values. I have also identified the independent value of predictable rules that restrict local discretion.

Based on this review, I recommend the following responses to the two issues about child support.

Should Poor Parents Pay a Smaller Percentage of Their Income in Child Support Than Non-Poor Parents?

Requiring all parents, even poor parents, to provide financial support for their children comports with otherwise diverging normative frameworks, ranging from utilitarianism and Kantianism to virtue theories and the ethic of care. What exact level of support should be imposed is less obvious from these frameworks of analysis. Here, common sense may provide some help. Imposing a support obligation that is beyond the nonresident parent's means is futile and at times counterproductive, as when arrears mount and trigger contempt citations that make it even more difficult for the parent to meet any support obligation. At the same time, no rule should create a perverse incentive for nonresident parents to avoid paying work (or above-the-table income) in order to avoid child support duties. Therefore, even poor parents should have to pay child support, set where necessary at a lower rate than would be applicable to higher-income parents, in order to meet children's needs. Devising general rules for this population of parents, whether based on percentages or flat amounts, would be better than case-by-case determinations. Periodic reviews and adjustments should focus on raising the award level even more than lowering it on the assumption, borne out by evidence, that over time most nonresident parents earn more rather than less.

Those nonresident parents who cannot even provide for their children's subsistence should still pay something in order to comport with widely held and converging conceptions of parental child support duties. These purposes are not fully advanced if this payment goes entirely to defray public expenses rather than to the family itself, and that approach may actually harm general social utility if that parent then is unable to contribute to the support of additional children in another household. Therefore, ensuring a "pass-through" of at least some set amount to be paid directly to the child rather than to reimburse the state would be an important aspect of child support payments toward supporting children who receive public assistance.

Yet, as informed by an ethic of care as well as a broader analysis of poverty policies, debates over child support too often neglect pursuit of other public policies to guarantee all children's basic subsistence and to promote higher standards of living. In terms of practical politics, this neglect is understandable. But the resulting pressure on child support debates displaces concerns about children's well-being that can never be resolved through the child support system alone. Not even full enforcement of ambitious child support policies would remedy child poverty, and other policies must be pursued to accomplish that end.

Should a Nonresident Parent Be Able to Reduce a Child Support Award After Having Children in a Second Family?

Permitting reductions of child support if the nonresident parent starts a new family gains support from the conventional analogy to how one household responds to additional children, as well as from the utilitarian desire to achieve compliance, from Kantian and virtue-based commitments to treat all the children equally as ends and not means, and from commitments to promote the individual freedom of nonresident parents. Yet reductions of support due to a second family diverge from Kantian and virtue-based conceptions of the child support duty as nondisclaimable, from the ethic of care's commitment to maintaining relationships, and from expressive theories seeking consistent depictions of parental duties.

As is often the case, the normative theories do more to clarify what is at stake than to resolve competing values.[34] In light of this review of normative theories, the decision about modifications for subsequent families should be framed as follows:

1. Does the rule about modifying child support obligations seek to deter nonresident parents from creating subsequent families, to promote their creation of subsequent families, or to be neutral on this issue?

2. If the goal is deterrence, should it be relevant to all nonresident parents or only to those who risk lacking sufficient resources to support fully more than one set of children?

3. Does empirical evidence support the influence of child support rules on reproductive and family-creating activities for the nonresident parents whose conduct is under regulation, and if not, are symbolic messages in law important independent of their influence on behavior?

4. Does the rule seek to send a clear message, for deterrence or symbolic purposes, or instead does it seek to permit discretionary accommodations based on how much both sets of children would gain or suffer and whether alternative sources of support could be available?

I offer here my own answers, in full acknowledgment that contrasting answers have much to commend them and in hope that the questions clarify what is up for debate. In my view, there is no a priori reason that the child support rule should either deter or promote subsequent families for nonresident parents except when such new obligations put existing child support obligations at risk. The risk of concern here is not merely failure to meet children's subsistence needs but also failure to extend to a first set of children the living standard enjoyed by the nonresident parent. In the face of these risks, the government should indeed play the role of helping adults anticipate the danger of failing to provide fully for children who already exist. In addition, the government should make it clear that child support duties persist regardless of contact between parent and child or emotional commitment between parent and child.

Sending signals on these issues requires clear rules. Rules in this area are unlikely to influence behavior unless they are simple and transparent, such as "no modification due to subsequent family duties." While discretionary accommodations would be more likely to produce fair results in individual cases, they would further blur the clarity of the rule. That clarity is of importance even apart from efforts to influence behavior, because it also expresses values formally for the society. It is worth remembering how limited law is when it comes to guiding the behavior of people within families. As Carol Weisbrod (1989) has written, the reality of family law is that "we care so much, and that law, finally can do so little" (1007). If this is the case, then how we think about child support may have as much to do with the values our society presents as the behaviors we hope to shape.

I prefer a rule against abandoning obligations to children simply because the nonresident parent wants to take on new obligations.[35] I acknowledge that a plausible alternative rule would permit modifications of an existing support obligation if the reduction did not deprive the children of the chance to share equally with subsequent children the nonresident parent's resources, yet negative experiences with the kind of judicial discretion required by such a rule is precisely what led to the federal legislation requiring state guidelines. As is often true in law, the ideal content for a rule may require a form that is too costly to administer, with costs measured in terms of confusions impeding compliance as well as administrative burdens.

Returning to the stories offered at the beginning of this chapter, this analysis suggests that Tom, who earns $20,000 a year, should continue to pay child support but that a set amount should be passed through directly to those children before reimbursing the state for public assistance. If his income sharply declines, he could seek an adjustment on that basis, followed by periodic reviews that assume future increases in income. The Melson formula, rather than the income-shares or flat percentage models, would be much better in accommodating his need to support himself and his new household by ensuring a self-support reserve. A similar kind of self-support reserve should be adopted—as a general rule, not on a case-by-case basis—if the state uses income shares or a flat percentage formula to determine the level of child support. This would permit Tom to ensure support for the child currently in his household who is the offspring of his girlfriend.

Sam, who earns minimum wage, will not have enough money to support two sets of children, but he should still be obliged to pay support for the child he fathered with his high school girlfriend—though not for her children who have other fathers. This will make it financially difficult for him to have additional children, but this is an accurate reflection of the duties he already has. If he proceeds to have additional children and finds he cannot support them, public assistance may well become needed, but the burden to the state would not be significantly lightened if he were able to divert his income from his existing children, already dependent upon public assistance, to future children. No doubt both households would be helped by a more sensible set of policies assisting families with young children to provide for child care and other basic needs and to help low-earning individuals achieve more marketable skills; child support policies cannot cure the larger issues of inadequate family supports or poor economic opportunities for large sectors.

Joanne's income is indeed appropriate to consider as part of her husband's available resources to meet his preexisting child support duties, but her income figure should deduct her college debt payments. Only the resources actually available to the household should figure into the calculation of the nonresident parent's ability to support existing children. This approach might make it seem more possible to be able to finance additional children in the current household.

Maria's children should receive considerable child support from their father, Michael; since he is doing well financially, they should share in his success. Maria should not be obliged to move from part-time to full-time work without calculating the in-kind contribution she makes to the care of the children as part of her share, under any of the child support formulas. Certainly if she takes a paying job and then needs to pay for child care, Michael should help defray that expense.[36]

I reach these conclusions basically in an effort to put children's interests ahead of adults' interests. This includes children in subsequent families, but in general their interests are less in jeopardy than the interests of children who do not live with the parent who owes child support. Interestingly, none of the prevailing normative frameworks articulates children's rights as the central concern. Under American law, child support is widely understood as a parental duty, not a child's right. Perhaps articulating children's rights would help refocus discussion on their basic needs and entitlement to share in parental—and societal—fortunes.[37] Yet opposition to the very concept of children's rights in the United States has persisted for decades (Minow 1995). Not the least reason for this opposition is the practical one: How should a child's rights be enforced when they depend on the behaviors of adults?

Absent resolution of the practical and philosophic problems with children's rights, child support will remain a legal duty of parents. This chapter offers a frame for analysis that makes that duty aim to ensure not only children's subsistence but also their opportunity to share in the fortunes and standards of living of both of their parents. I also urge the use of rules that avoid creating perverse incentives to reduce parental income and contact with children living in another household or to produce more children in order to avoid existing child support obligations. Finally, I urge clear and simple rules that give little discretion to local decisionmakers. General rules establishing lower levels of support for poor nonresident parents than for middle- and upper-income ones would be consistent with these criteria. So would general rules permitting modification of support duties in light of the nonresident parent's increases in income and the access of both parents to the income of new spouses or cohabitants. Even if such rules do not produce direct compliance or changes in behavior, they express important values about the permanence of parental responsibilities. Child support rules cannot, however, remedy the larger problems of child poverty. The political will to adopt a more comprehensive set of child allowances and income maintenance policies—and to structure better work opportunities for low-earning individuals—might be strengthened, however, after society renews its commitment to enforce parental support duties.

Thanks to Liza Vertinsky for research assistance and to Irving Garfinkel, Kate Bartlett, David Chambers, Elizabeth Spelman, Philip Heymann, Joe Singer, Diane Ring, and the Harvard Law Faculty summer colloquium discussion for comments.

NOTES

1. In light of bipartisan critiques of massive nonpayment of support when ordered and widely disparate orders produced under a system of judicial discretion, federal law stimulated all states to promulgate guidelines establishing child support guidelines,

keying awards to parental income, number of children, and similar factors. State and federal enforcement techniques now include automatic wage-withholding, intercepts of federal tax refunds, and interstate enforcement agreements. See *Family Support Act of 1988*, U.S. Public Law 102–485, 102 Stat. 2343; *Sorenson v. Secretary of Treasury*, 475 U.S. 851 (1986) (approving intercept of tax refund to pay child support).

2. How to improve overall enforcement is no longer a question, except for parents who do not receive a regular wage but work in fields such as construction or receive under-the-table income. As one of the leading contributors to the law reforms commented in 1989, "I think that the 'better enforcement debate' is all but over. With mandated, formula-based setting of support obligations, with payroll deduction of support owed, and with computer-provided nationwide access to support-owing parents, the law now provides an effective arsenal for imposing the obligation as well as collecting child support" (Krause 1989, 367). Given high levels of enforcement, the new questions for child support law, as Krause notes, involve (1) parents who lack the means to comply; (2) whether absent parents should foot the entire bill for children with whom they have little involvement; and (3) what role the state or society should play in financially supporting such children (380). Other contestable issues include: whether the support duty should extend to children after the age of majority owing to their disability, higher education costs, or unemployment; whether stepparents incur a support obligation; what impact increasingly shared custody or expanded visitation should have on support obligations; and whether any further changes in child support law can improve progress toward gender equality.

3. A logically related question is: Should rich nonresident parents pay a larger percentage of their income in child support then those with fewer resources? Currently, no state has a progressive rate structure, although a few permit increased percentage rates for higher-income parents. I think a progressive rate structure warrants attention because it connects insights about the marginal value of the dollar with the underlying normative question: Should a child share in the standard of living enjoyed by a parent or should he or she simply be assured a basic level of support? Child support guidelines could be revamped to provide either a proportional percentage-of-income measure, with no minimum or maximum, or a progressive measure, with poor parents paying a lower percentage of income than richer parents, but I will leave the analysis of this issue for another day.

4. Although the traditional rule favored the first set of children (see Garfinkel, Melli, and Robertson 1994), judicial responses show considerable disagreement about how to handle requests for modification in the face of a second family (Gregory, Swisher, and Scheible 1993). The courts are similarly split about modifications sought when the nonresident parent switches to a lower-paying job (Gregory, Swisher, and Scheible, 272–73).

5. Compare *In re the Marriage of Billie Joe Ladeley and Kenneth Leroy Ladeley*, 469 N.W.2d 663 (Iowa 1991) (no modification), *Hoover v. Hoover*, 793 P.2d 1329 (Nev. 1990) (no modification), and *Hockenberry v. Hockenberry*, 600 N.E.2d 839 (Ohio Ct. App. 1992) (no modification) with *Haverstock v. Haverstock*, 599 N.E.2d 617, 619 (Ind. Ct. App. 1992) (same duty to support children in both households), *Bergman v. Bergman*, 486 N.W.2d 243, 245 (N.D. 1992) (reductions permitted because of subsequent family), and *Howard v. Hisemon*, 826 S.W.2d 314 (Ark. Ct. App. 1992). See also *Brown v. Brown*, 503 N.W.2d 280 (Wis. Ct. App. 1993) (earlier-born children have a priority). Thus, the states are split between the "first families first" view and the view supporting equal treatment for all offspring of the same parent (see Williams 1994, 1, 13).

6. Weitzman (1985) argues that the shift to no-fault divorce deprived dependent women of bargaining leverage with husbands who left them; she described, based on California data, a dramatic contrast in the post-divorce standard of living of men and women. Others have disputed the magnitude of her finding; see Duncan and Hoffman (1985), Jacob (1986), and Sugarman (1990).

7. The mechanism used by the legislation is to threaten states with loss of federal funding while also supplying additional federal funds to cover substantial portions of those support enforcement programs that meet federal standards (Jacob 1986).

8. The federal government itself maintains a computerized locator service using Social Security, Internal Revenue Service, and other federal information.

9. But see Eekelaar and Maclean (1986) and Glendon (1987, 63–111).

10. See Chambers (1982) and Krause (1989, 385–88, 398). Chambers does not advocate eliminating child support obligations today but would if current trends of noncontact continue (1633). Both Chambers and Krause would support increased governmental aid to children (based on general taxpayer revenues). There are two possible rejoinders to their basic view: the lack of an emotional relationship in no way diminishes the parent's responsibility for the child's existence, and the laws could seek to promote social relationships between children and noncustodial parents rather than take their absence as inevitable. See Czpanskiy (1991, 1415) and Minow (1992–93, 318–21, 327–29).

11. The eight principles are: "(1) Both parents share legal responsibility for supporting their children. The economic responsibility should be divided in proportion to their available income. (2) The subsistence needs of each parent should be taken into account in setting child support, but in virtually no event should the child support obligation be set at zero. (3) Child support must cover a child's basic needs as a first priority, but, to the extent either parent enjoys a higher than subsistence level standard of living, the child is entitled to share the benefit of that improved status. (4) Each child of a given parent has an equal right to share in that parent's income, subject to factors such as age of the child, income of each parent, income of current spouses, and the presence of other dependents. (5) Each child is entitled to determination of support without respect to the marital status of the parents at the time of the child's birth. Consequently, any guidelines should be equally applicable to determining child support related to paternity determinations, separations, and divorces. (6) Application of a guideline should be sexually nondiscriminatory. Specifically, it should be applied without regard to the gender of the custodial parent. (7) A guideline should not create extraneous negative effects on the major life decisions of either parent. In particular, the guideline should avoid creating economic disincentives for remarriage or labor-force participation. (8) A guideline should encourage the involvement of both parents in the child's upbringing. It should take into account the financial support provided directly by parents in shared physical custody or extended visitation arrangements, recognizing that even a fifty percent sharing of physical custody does not necessarily obviate the child support obligation" (Williams 1987, 309–10).

12. Even this gesture could be defective. Reducing the support obligation below the statutory minimum owing to parental poverty conveys the message that a child's basic needs can be reduced or ignored when a parent is poor. Of course, in the absence of a social safety net, this message is widespread regardless of the child support rule.

13. See *Feltman v. Feltman,* 434 N.W.2d 590 (S.D. 1989) (J. Henderson dissenting) ("Are children of a second marriage 'children of a lesser god'?"). The majority in that case preferred the "equal treatment" approach.

14. No doubt the normative schools I will describe could be recast along different lines and still others could be added. I cannot provide a thorough treatment of any of these approaches, especially since each has variations and complex applications across a broad range of contexts. Since, to my knowledge, none of the theories has been specifically applied to the questions raised in this chapter about child support, I am drawing on their guiding ideas to suggest how they might direct normative inquiry about these questions.

15. These normative theories simply were not designed to address issues within families. Instead, they speak to relations between two individuals, between the individual and the state, or between justice and social organization. Historically, most of these theories presumed competent adult males as the focus for concern. By definition, the interest here involves dependent children and their relationships with their biological parents and, potentially, the partners and spouses of those parents.

    More generally, family law routinely poses problems among more than two people but fewer than the entire population of a society. Family law problems fall within a conventionally conceived private sphere and only indirectly implicate individuals' relations with the state. Child support issues in particular raise problems of fairness between households that have a parent in common, in a society that is increasingly familiar with serial polygamy; the prevailing normative theories do not focus on this kind of issue.

16. See Sidgewick (1974/1874, 338). Unfortunately, commonsense appeals to convention do not offer resolutions for contentious issues, nor do they help with recognition of new conventions. Sidgewick himself noted the shift from the commonly recognized duty of children to their elderly parents to collective provision for the aged, obviating the duties of individual adult children (see Williams 1985, 247).

17. Matters really can get complicated; it is not uncommon to have a custodial parent who is remarried and raising stepchildren with her own, and a noncustodial parent who is remarried and raising both his own younger children and stepchildren brought to the household by his new wife. One of these households may break up and still further households and children come and go; what sharing principles should apply across potentially three or four households with children from potentially six or more adult relationships?

18. Jeremy Bentham and John Stuart Mill are the classic utilitarian theorists. Utilitarianism frameworks include those that attend solely to monetizable benefits and those that consider other benefits.

19. See Oldham (1994, 585, 605 n. 142): "[P]roponents of child support argue that, among other benefits, requiring some child support contribution will encourage the noncustodial parent to remain in contact with the child" (citing Seltzer, Scheaffer, and Charng 1989, 1013–14 [noncustodial parents who pay child support visit their children more often than those who do not]). But see Furstenberg, Morgan, and Allison 1987, 695, 699–700 (finding that there is no strong evidence to suggest that children benefit from paternal participation apart from economic support).

20. Contemporary theorists influenced by Kant, including John Rawls (1970), deploy the heuristic device of a social contract to consider the right way to order a society without knowing specifically where one's own place in it will be. It is not lack of interest in consequences that is notable for Kantians but, instead, a strong opposition to doing something bad in order to achieve something good; one simply should not do something bad; see Goodin (1985, 116) for more on the Kantian view.

21. "Now I say that man, and in general every rational being, exists as an end in himself and not merely as a means to be arbitrarily used by this or that will. He must in all his actions, whether directed to himself or to other rational beings, always be regarded at the same time as an end" (Kant 1966, 90). See also Williams (1985, 64).

22. "[F]rom the fact of *procreation* in the union [constituted by marriage], there follows the duty of preserving and rearing *children* as the products of this union" (Kant 1952). See also Sullivan (1989), who describes inner-city communities where fathers have no honor if they do not try to support their children.

23. Many observers trace virtue theory to Greek philosophers such as Plato and Aristotle. Contemporary virtue theorists include Foot (1978) and MacIntyre (1984); related themes appear in Jean-Paul Sartre's concern with authenticity and Iris Murdock's writings about character. See, for example, Murdoch (1970, 1985). See also Blum (1990, 173).

    Bearing some relationship to both utilitarianism and virtue ethics is a theory that takes the good of the community as primary. Sometimes called communitarianism, its theorists include Michael Walzer, *Spheres of Justice*; Mary Ann Glendon, *Rights Talk*; and Amatai Ezioni, *The Morality of Community*. See generally Rosenstand, Nina. 1994. *The Moral of the Story*, 190 (discussing virtue theory).

24. This view treats responsibilities as embedded in a set of relationships and cultural practices rather than formal rules or promises. A related notion urges responsiveness to vulnerable people by those who are able to respond (Goodin 1985).

25. See also Garfinkel, Melli, and Robertson (1994, 96) (emphasizing the limited effects of even a perfectly efficient child support enforcement system in eliminating the poverty gap for children eligible for child support).

26. Given the evidence that child support awards do not keep pace with increases in the income of nonresident poor parents, improvements in periodic monitoring and upward modifications in awards for poor fathers are warranted (see Meyer 1995).

27. See *Roe v. Wade*, 410 U.S. 113 (1973); *Griswold v. Connecticut*, 381 U.S. 479 (1965). Actually, the shrinking protections for abortion choices might point in the other direction. See *Webster v. Reproductive Health Services*, 109 S.Ct. 3040 (1989).

28. It cannot be bargained away, for example, in an antenuptial agreement.

29. This guideline does not even begin to reach the variety of private agreements or de facto arrangements that parties live with; if the state is not involved through public assistance, private parties can and do negotiate or put up with a wide range of child support terms after divorce or paternity actions.

30. One might further try to model other decision points related to parenthood—decisions to become romantically involved, to marry or not marry, to break up a relationship, to remarry—and consider how amenable any of these stages are to cultural, legal, or economic incentives.

31. This sets aside a different question about whether legal rules are good devices for promoting dispositions or instead risk engendering resentment, noncompliance, or reliance on external authority rather than internal virtue.

32. Also, does the disposition to do good and to act responsibly include not only protection of the first set of children's subsistence needs but also their share of a higher standard of living? Again, if the answer is affirmative, and if a rule can promote the right disposi-

tion, a rule refusing modification would be advisable even for a parent who could still cover the first set of children's basic needs.

33. Some people interpret this as a call for mediation or other nonadversarial dispute resolution processes. Such processes still take place under the shadow of prevailing law, so the choice of a nonadversarial process cannot replace an answer to the modification question.

34. Many of these ideas presume certain relationships among norms, behaviors, and dispositions that may not be correct. Empirical study could challenge those assumptions and also invite more concreteness in normative reasoning. The failure of most of the normative theories to close in on specific issues of practical policy is striking but due only in part to uncertainty about social practices, human attitudes, and the effects of rules on human behavior and dispositions.

35. For a similar view, see U.S. House of Representatives (1983a, 137) ("Remarriage of the absent parent should in no way absolve that parent from providing regular support to their children. That responsibility transcends other financial obligations which an absent parent may incur").

36. Datina Herd (1995) recently wrote a column criticizing the child support rules for forcing herself and her husband to pay to support children from a former relationship while the mother of those children received welfare rather than working for pay. The sense of inequity she expresses about having to work outside the home when the other mother does not is real and troubling, but the defect here was in the welfare rules governing work for pay, not in the child support obligation itself.

37. One commentator suggests that upon divorce (and perhaps other family reorganizations) the family wealth or "estate" should be divided, with a share for the children (Fitzgerald 1994). Since most family's wealth is expected future earnings, however, this would come down to a right to share in the parents' future earnings streams, much like contemporary child support. Yet perhaps this way of thinking about it could help elevate the share accorded to the child.

REFERENCES

American Bar Association. 1993. *America's Children at Risk: A National Agenda for Legal Action.* ABA Presidential Working Group on the Unmet Needs of Children and Their Families. Chicago: American Bar Association.

Barnow, Burt S. 1994. "Economic Studies of Expenditures on Children and Their Relationship to Child Support Guidelines." In *Child Support Guidelines: The Next Generation,* edited by Margaret Campbell Haynes. Washington: U.S. Department of Health and Human Services, Administration for Children and Families, Office of Child Support Enforcement.

Bartfeld, Judi, and Daniel R. Meyer. 1993. "Are There Really Deadbeat Dads? The Relationship Between Ability to Pay, Enforcement, and Compliance in Nonmarital Child Support Cases." Institute for Research on Poverty Discussion Paper 994–93. Madison: University of Wisconsin.

Bartlett, Katherine. 1981. "Re-Expressing Parenthood." *Yale Law Journal* 98(2): 293–340.

Bergmann, Barbara. 1981. "The Economic Support of 'Fatherless' Children." In *Income Support: Conceptual and Policy Issues,* edited by Peter G. Brown, Conrad Johnson, and Paul Vernier. Totowa, N.J.: Rowman and Littlefield.

Blackstone, William. 1765–69. *Commentaries on the Law of England.* Oxford: Clarendon Press.

Blum, Laurence. 1990. "Vocation, Friendship, and Community: Limitations of the Personal-Impersonal Framework." In *Identity, Character, and Morality,* edited by Owen Flanagan and Amelie Rorty. Cambridge, Mass.: MIT Press.

Bobbitt, Philip. 1992. *Constitutional Fate.* New York: Oxford University Press.

Center for Social Welfare Policy and Law. 1994. *Living at the Bottom: An Analysis of 1994 AFDC Benefit Levels.* Publication 210-2. New York: Center for Social Welfare Policy and Law.

Chambers, David. 1982. "Comment—The Coming Curtailment of Compulsory Child Support." *Mich. Law Review* 80(8): 1614–34.

———. 1991. "Meeting the Financial Needs of Children." *Brooklyn Law Review* 57(3): 769–75.

Coltrane, Scott, and Neal Hickman. 1992. "The Rhetoric of Rights and Needs: Moral Discourse in the Reform of Child Custody and Child Support Laws." *Social Problems* 39(4): 400–420.

Czpanskiy, Karen. 1991. "Volunteers and Draftees: The Struggle for Parental Equality." *UCLA Law Review* 38(6): 1415–81.

Duncan, Greg, and Saul Hoffman. 1985. "A Reconsideration of the Economic Consequences of Divorce." *Demography* 22(4): 485–97.

Eden, Philip, et al. 1986. "In the Best Interests of Children: A Simplified Model for Equalizing the Living Standards of Parental Households." In *Essentials of Child Support Guidelines Development: Economic Issues and Policy Consequences.* Proceedings of the Women's Legal Defense Fund's National Conference on the Development of Child Support Guidelines. Queensboro, Md., 1986.

Eekelaar, John. 1991. *Regulating Divorce.* New York: Oxford University Press.

Eekelaar, John, and Mavis Maclean. 1986. *Maintenance After Divorce.* Oxford: Clarendon Press.

Ellmann, Ira, Paul M. Kurtz, and Katharine T. Bartlett. 1991. *Family Law: Cases, Text, Problems.* Charlottesville, Va.: Michie Company.

Feinberg, Joel. 1970. *Doing and Deserving.* Princeton, N.J.: Princeton University Press.

Fitzgerald, Wendy Anton. 1994. "Maturity, Difference, and Mystery: Children's Perspectives and the Law." *Arizona Law Review* 36(1): 11–111.

Foot, Phillippa. 1978. *Virtues and Vices.* Berkeley: University of California Press.

Furstenberg, Frank, Jr., S. P. Morgan, and P. D. Allison. 1987. "Paternal Participation and Children's Well-being After Marital Dissolution." *American Sociological Review* 52(5): 695–702.

Garfinkel, Irwin, Marygold S. Melli, and John G. Robertson. 1994. "Child Support Orders: A Perspective on Reform." *Future of Children* 4 (Spring): 84–100.

Garrett, W. Walton. 1980. "Filial Responsibility Laws." *Journal of Family Law* 18(4): 793–818.

Garrison, Marsha. 1991. "Good Intentions Gone Awry: The Impact of New York's Equitable Distribution Law on Divorce Outcomes." *Brooklyn Law Review* 57(3): 621–754.

———. 1994. "Book Review: Child Support and Children's Poverty—A Review of Small Change and America's Children." *Family Law Quarterly* 28(3): 475.

Giampetro, Andrea. 1986. "Mathematical Approaches to Calculating Child Support Payments: Stated Objectives, Practical Results, and Hidden Policies." *Family Law Quarterly* 20(3): 373–91.

Gilligan, Carol. 1982. *In a Different Voice.* Cambridge, Mass.: Harvard University Press.

Glendon, Mary Ann. 1987. *Abortion and Divorce in Western Law.* Cambridge, Mass.: Harvard University Press.

Goodin, Robert E. 1985. *Protecting the Vulnerable.* Chicago: University of Chicago Press.

Gregory, John De Witt, Peter N. Swisher, and Sheryl L. Scheible. 1993. *Understanding Family Law*. New York: Matthew Bender.

Grossberg, Michael. 1985. *Governing the Hearth: Law and the Family in Nineteenth-Century America*. Chapel Hill: University of North Carolina Press.

Herd, Datina M. 1995. "Unsupported Support." *Newsweek*, April 22, p. 16.

Jacob, Herbert. 1986. "Faulting No-Fault." *American Bar Foundation Research Journal*.

Kant, Immanuel. 1952. *The Science of Right*. Translated by W. Hastie. Great Books edition. Edinburgh: T. & T. Clark.

———. 1966. *Grounding for the Metaphysics of Morals*. Translated by H. J. Paton, London: Hutchinson University Library.

Kay, Herma Hill. 1991. "Commentary: Toward a Theory of Fair Distribution." *Brooklyn Law Review* 57(3): 755–67.

Kennedy, Duncan. 1976. "Form and Substance in Private Law Adjudication." *Harvard Law Review* 89(8): 1685.

Krause, Harry D. 1989. "Child Support Reassessed: The Limits of Private Responsibility and the Public Interest." *University of Illinois Law Review* (2): 367–98.

Lieberman, Joseph I. 1986. *Child Support in America*. New Haven, Conn.: Yale University Press.

MacIntyre, Alasdair. 1984. *After Virtue*. Notre Dame, Ind.: University of Notre Dame Press.

McLanahan, Sara, and Gary Sandefur. 1994. *Growing up with a Single Parent: What Hurts, What Helps*. Cambridge, Mass.: Harvard University Press.

Meyer, Daniel R. 1995. "Supporting Children Born Outside of Marriage: Do Child Support Awards Keep Pace with Changes in Father's Incomes?" *Social Sciences Quarterly* 76(3): 577.

Minow, Martha. 1992–93. "All in the Family and in All Families: Membership, Loving, and Owing." *Virginia Law Review* 95(2): 275–332.

———. 1995. "What Ever Happened to Children's Rights." *Minnesota Law Review* 80(2): 267–98.

Murdoch, Iris. 1970/1985. *The Sovereignty of the Good*. Boston: Ark Paperbacks.

Oldham, J. Thomas. 1994. "The Appropriate Child Support Award When the Noncustodial Parent Earns Less Than the Custodial Parent." *Houston Law Review* 31(2): 585–616.

Olsen, Frances. 1985. "The Myth of State Intervention in the Family." *University of Michigan Journal of Law Reform* 18(4): 835–64.

Pirog-Good, Maureen A. 1993. "Child Support Guidelines and the Economic Well-being of Children in the United States." *Family Relations* 42(4): 453–62.

Rawls, John. 1971. *A Theory of Justice*. Cambridge, Mass.: Belknap Press.

Regan, Milton J., Jr. 1994. "The Boundaries of Care: Constructing Community After Divorce." *Houston Law Review* 31(2): 425–50.

Sawhill, Isabel V. 1983. "Developing Normative Standards for Child Support Payments." In *The Parental Child Support Obligation*, edited by Judith Cassetty. Lexington, Mass.: Lexington Books.

Scalia, Antonin. 1989. "The Rule of Law as a Law of Rules." *University of Chicago Law Review* 56(4): 1175–88.

Seltzer, Judith A., Nora C. Scheaffer, and Hong-wen Charng. 1989. "Family Ties After Divorce: The Relationship Between Visiting and Paying Child Support." *Journal of Marriage and the Family* 51(4): 1013–22.

Sidgewick, Henry. 1874/1974. *The Methods of Ethics*. London: Macmillan.

Sugarman, Stephen. 1990. "Dividing Financial Interests at Divorce." In *Divorce Reform at the Crossroads*, edited by Stephen Sugarman and Herma Hill Kay. New Haven: Yale University Press.

Sullivan, Kathleen. 1992. "Foreword: The Justices of Rules and Standards (the Supreme Court, 1991 Term)." *Harvard Law Review* 106(1): 22–123.

Sullivan, Mercer L. 1989. "Absent Fathers in the Inner City." *Annals of the American Academy* 501 (January): 48–58.

Sunstein, Cass. 1994. "Conflicting Values in Law." *Fordham Law Review* 62(6): 1661–73.

Tjaden, Patricia G., Nancy Thoennes, and Jessica Pearson. 1989. "Will These Children Be Supported Adequately? The Impact of Current Guidelines." *Judges' Journal* 28(4): 4–13.

Tronto, Joan. 1993. *Moral Boundaries: A Political Argument for an Ethic of Care.* New York: Routledge.

U.S. House of Representatives. 1983a. "National Women's Law Center Responses to Questions on Child Support Enforcement." *Child Support Legislation: Hearing Before the Subcommittee on Public Assistance and Unemployment Compensation of the Committee on Ways and Means.* 98th Cong., 1st sess., July 14.

————. 1983b. "Statement of the Women's Legal Defense Fund." *Child Support Enforcement Legislation: Hearing Before the Subcommittee on Public Assistance and Unemployment Compensation of the Committee on Ways and Means.* 98th Cong., 1st sess, July 14.

Weisbrod, Carol. 1989. "On the Expressive Functions of Family Law." *University of California at Davis Law Review* 22(3): 991–1007.

Weitzman, Lenore. 1985. *The Divorce Revolution.* New York: Free Press.

West, Robin. 1993. *Narrative, Authority, and Law.* Ann Arbor: University of Michigan Press.

Whelan, Roger M., Mandy B. Cohen, and Karen F. Wexler. 1994. "Consumer Bankruptcy Reform: Balancing the Equities in Chapter 13." *American Bankruptcy Institute Law Review* 2(1): 165–91.

White, James Boyd. 1990. *Justice as Translation: An Essay in Cultural and Legal Criticism.* Chicago: University of Chicago Press.

Williams, Bernard. 1985. *Ethics and the Limits of Philosophy.* Cambridge, Mass.: Harvard University Press.

Williams, Robert G. 1994. "An Overview of Child Support Guidelines in the United States." In *Child Support Guidelines: The Next Generation,* edited by Margaret Campbell Haynes. Washington: U.S. Department of Health and Human Services, Administration for Children and Families, Office of Child Support Enforcement.

Zelizer, Viviana. 1985. *Pricing the Priceless Child.* New York: Basic Books.

Conclusion

Irwin Garfinkel, Sara S. McLanahan, Daniel R. Meyer, and Judith A. Seltzer

D uring the last twenty-five years, federal and state governments have enacted increasingly strong legislation to compel nonresident fathers to pay child support. This legislative thrust has been supported by two research streams, one depicting the plight of single mothers and their children and the other documenting the ability of nonresident fathers to pay substantially more child support. In the popular media, fathers who fail to pay child support have been labeled "deadbeat dads." Child support enforcement has gained widespread political support because of its potential both to reduce public welfare expenditures and to improve the economic security of single mothers and their children.

In this drama, which we have labeled *Fathers Under Fire*, policy-makers and the public have focused primarily on fathers' ability to pay child support, with little attention being given to their other responsibilities and concerns. Moreover, as described in chapter 2, even the research on fathers' ability to pay has often been oversimplified and/or misinterpreted. Just because nonresident fathers as a whole can afford to pay substantially more child support than they currently pay does not mean that the fathers of children on welfare can afford to pay substantially more. This book attempts to redress this imbalance by focusing explicitly on nonresident fathers and their responses to stronger child support enforcement.

The book addresses three major questions: Do child support policies make sense in light of the characteristics, capabilities, and circumstances of nonresident fathers? Will stronger enforcement have adverse effects on these fathers and, ultimately, children? And finally, should we take more positive action toward helping fathers meet their child support obligations and other parental responsibilities? In this concluding chapter, we summarize the answers to these questions, point to areas that merit further research, and provide specific recommendations for improving the current child support system.

THE QUESTIONS

Are Policy Developments Compatible with Fathers' Capabilities?

Child support policy in the last twenty-five years has been characterized by increasing stringency and uneven application. Routine withholding of child support obligations, statewide registries of obligations, reporting of new hires, new interstate enforcement mechanisms, seizure of assets, and forfeiture of driver's licenses and professional licenses have made it increasingly difficult and costly for fathers to avoid paying child support. Because a large part of the impetus for stronger enforcement has been to reduce welfare expenditures, however, enforcement has focused disproportionately on the fathers of children on welfare, who are likely to be poor themselves. Because these men lack legal representation and political clout, their child support obligations are much higher, relative to their income, than the obligations of middle-income fathers. Finally, new paternity establishment practices, such as in-hospital paternity establishment, are bringing increasing numbers of low-income fathers into the formal child support system.

In view of what we know about fathers' capabilities and circumstances, do these policy developments make sense? The answer is both yes and no. Stronger child support enforcement as a general policy makes sense. Harsher treatment of low-income fathers, however, is perverse and could be dangerous. Nonresident fathers pay about $15 billion in child support. According to the values embodied in current state child support guidelines, they should be paying $45 billion to $50 billion. A large minority of fathers who pay no child support—between 30 and 40 percent, according to chapter 2—have very low incomes. Without help, they will not be able to contribute very much money. At the same time, an equally large minority of non-paying fathers can afford to pay substantial amounts of child support. Furthermore, according to state guidelines, most fathers who are currently paying child support should be required to pay more. As a whole, fathers who live apart from their children have lower incomes than fathers who live with their biological children. But because nonresident fathers are less likely to live with dependent children, their standard of living is somewhat higher than that of resident fathers. More important, their standard of living is *much* higher than that of their nonresident children. Finally, Daniel Meyer's research (chapter 3) shows that requiring fathers to meet their child support obligations would not reshuffle poverty from old families to new families. All of this suggests that more child support from nonresident fathers would reduce the economic insecurity of children and might reduce public costs.

Although the uneven application of child support enforcement is understandable, even predictable, it still is a matter of concern. The concern is not that low-income fathers are being brought into the formal child support system. As we argue later, we think this could be a healthy development. Rather, the concern is with the disproportionately high (relative to income) child support obligations imposed on these men and with the disproportionate use of harsh enforcement tools against them. To begin with, there is the simple question of equity. Few people would say that it is fair or just for low-income fathers to be treated more severely than well-to-do fathers, including being jailed for failure to pay child support. Similarly, few people would agree that low-income fathers should be required to pay half or more of their incomes when much less is expected of middle- and upper-income fathers.

Besides being unfair, the harsh treatment of low-income fathers is likely to be ineffective. The cost of collecting child support from these men is likely to be as great as (or greater than) the total amount of dollars collected. Twenty percent of all nonresident fathers are estimated to earn less than $6,000 (chapter 2). To insist that these men pay as much child support as a man with a full-time, full-year minimum-wage job is unduly onerous. Even worse, expecting these men to reimburse past Medicaid and AFDC payments to their children over and above their child support obligations established by state guidelines is a recipe for failure. These men simply cannot pay these debts, and no child support agency can make them do so. The inevitable result, as depicted in chapter 9, is the accumulation of child support arrearages, periodic jailing, and the buildup of hostility and resentment toward mothers and children as well as government authority. As we discuss later, there may be good reasons for insisting that even very poor fathers pay some child support. But enforcement of unrealistic and onerous obligations among these men is not likely to save money and could do a lot more harm than good.

Does Enforcement Have Adverse Unintended Effects?

Strengthening public enforcement of private child support is not likely to have much adverse effect on the poverty rates of fathers with new families or on the work behavior of nonresident fathers. The new laws, however, are likely to deter out-of-wedlock births. And they *may* deter remarriage and increase children's exposure to serious parental conflict. These are the major findings reported in the chapters in part II of this volume. Although none of these results should be taken as the last word on the subject, they do raise concerns, and they do suggest that there are likely to be trade-offs associated with stronger child support enforcement.

Deterring out-of-wedlock births strengthens the case for stronger enforcement (chapter 7). We are relatively confident in Anne Case's results since they have been replicated by other studies (Garfinkel et al. 1998; Plotnick et al. 1998). Similarly, because Richard Freeman and Jane Waldfogel's findings (chapter 4) are similar to those of Marieka Klawitter (1994), it does not appear that child support orders or enforcement reduces nonresident fathers' labor supply.

The results for remarriage and conflict go in the opposite direction. Indeed, if David Bloom and his colleagues are correct that most of the income gains to children of nonresident fathers are offset by income losses resulting from declines in remarriage (chapter 5), and if Judith Seltzer and her colleagues are correct that increases in child support payments may lead to more serious conflict between parents (chapter 6), then stronger enforcement may make children worse off overall. Because the data Bloom and his colleagues use provide such small samples, and because the results reported by Seltzer and her colleagues depend on the sample and analytic strategy adopted, we hope their work will be replicated by other researchers. Until the findings are replicated, we believe their results should be viewed more cautiously. Even if the losses in children's income due to declines in remarriage offset the gains in income due to higher child support payments, other indirect effects, such as the deterrent effect of child support on divorce (Nixon 1997) and nonmarital childbearing, go in the opposite direction. Delays in remarriage also may reduce children's exposure to serious conflict. We know that conflict is relatively common in stepparent families (Hanson, McLanahan, and Thomson 1996), and it is possible that delays in remarriage might result in better matches and less conflict.

All four editors of this volume have advocated stronger child support enforcement, and the findings about remarriage and conflict have not persuaded us to abandon our position. What these chapters do suggest, however, is that the indirect effects of child support enforcement on fathers' behaviors could turn out to be more important than the direct effects. Finally, if the negative effects of child support enforcement on remarriage are concentrated among low-income fathers, this reinforces the cautions we raised in part III about overzealous enforcement among poor fathers and fathers of children on welfare. Overburdening these men and using their payments solely to reduce welfare costs are two strategies that are likely to increase negative behavioral responses without increasing children's economic security.

Should We Do More to Help Nonresident Fathers?

Part III of the book considers four strategies for helping nonresident fathers: (1) helping fathers gain access to their children, (2) providing low-income fathers with services to improve their earnings capacity and fathering capabilities, (3) reducing or eliminating obligations for very low–income fathers, and (4) reducing obligations for fathers who live with other children. The first two proposals are examined from an empirical–social science perspective that asks whether interventions are effective. The last two are assessed from an ethical-theoretical perspective that asks whether they are just.

HELPING FATHERS GAIN ACCESS TO THEIR CHILDREN   Stronger child support enforcement weakens nonresident fathers' bargaining power vis-à-vis resident mothers and may reduce their ability to spend time with their child. Under the old system, a father could trade child support for visitation, whereas under the new system he is forced to pay but the mother is not required to reciprocate. Collective attempts by fathers to redress this imbalance are to be expected. Jessica Pearson and Nancy Thoennes (chapter 8) find that mediation and other services can increase fathers' access without increasing serious conflict, at least among parents who do not have serious, long-standing disagreements. They recommend that services be provided quickly before disagreements have had time to become entrenched. In our judgment, the shift in OCSE policy from a pure enforcement approach to including services to promote access is an appropriate policy response. If child support enforcement is to succeed, it must be perceived as fair and balanced. Rights normally go along with responsibilities. This is consistent with the behavior of parents in national surveys as well—when fathers pay child support, this increases their influence in decisions about their children's lives (chapter 6). However, because of the potential harm that violent fathers might inflict on mothers and/or children, strengthening access must be done with care.

HELPING FATHERS MEET THEIR OBLIGATIONS   The preliminary findings from the Parents' Fair Share program, as reported by Earl Johnson and Fred Doolittle (chapter 9), are discouraging insofar as they underscore the desperate conditions of many low-income fathers who are not paying child support. Most troubling is the fact that many men appear to have come to accept the notion that they are little more than a breadwinner and have withdrawn from their children out of a sense of failure. Also noteworthy is the fact that many of these fathers believe that their child support dollars are going to the government rather than to their children. It is not surprising that these men feel a greater responsibility toward the children in their current households, who may not be eligible for welfare, than they feel toward their nonresident children. These results suggest that, at a minimum, low-income fathers should not be required to pay a higher percentage of their income than middle-income fathers. They also suggest that it would be worthwhile to examine the effects of establishing even lower obligations for low-income fathers. Similarly, the federal government or state governments should experiment with incentives for low-income fathers to pay support and with giving credit for in-kind payments. Although it is too early to evaluate the success of the Parents' Fair Share demonstration program, continued experimentation with efforts to assist low-income fathers to increase their earnings and their interest and competence in fathering is warranted.

EXEMPTING VERY POOR FATHERS FROM CHILD SUPPORT OBLIGATIONS   A large minority of nonresident fathers are so poor that they can afford to pay, at most, small to meager amounts of child support. The costs of collecting support from these men are likely to be as large or larger than the amounts collected. However, the fact that extreme poverty is usually not a permanent phenomenon, and the fact that enforcement deters nonmarital childbearing, improves the benefit-cost ratio of stronger enforcement among the very poor. Conversely, the fact that the negative effects of enforcement on remarriage may be concentrated among low-income parents reduces the benefit-cost ratio.

Perhaps the clearest conclusion that emerges from Martha Minow's normative analyses (chapter 10) is that all fathers, including the very poorest men, should be required to contribute something toward their child's support. Her argument is consistent with the Pearson-Thoennes suggestion that setting expectations and resolving disputes early in the process leads to more cooperation between parents in the long run. We find these arguments convincing. Even a small child support obligation at the beginning may reduce the possibility of future disagreements about whether the father should pay any support at all. We also agree that the obligation must be fair and reasonable. Low-income nonresident fathers should be brought into the formal child support system, but the system must be reformed. Increasing the number of low-income fathers who are legally liable for child support without reducing the harshness of their treatment is likely to result in substantial harm to children. The fathers will not be able to meet their obligations; the children will experience no financial gain; and serious conflict between the parents may increase. Surely this is not good public policy.

REDUCING OBLIGATIONS IN RESPONSE TO NEW DEPENDENTS   About one-third of nonresident fathers live with other children. It is possible that the percentage would be higher if child support enforcement were weaker or if child support obligations were reduced in the event that nonresident fathers began sharing their income with other children. Certainly the circumstances of these fathers would be improved if child support obligations were reduced, or eliminated, as a consequence of the new children. However, the position of the nonresident father can be improved only by worsening the position of his child and the child's mother or by increasing the costs to taxpayers. Moreover, Meyer (chapter 3) has shown that even without an allowance for new dependents, there would be very little "reshuffling of poverty" from fathers' first families to new families if current child support legislation were fully enforced. Thus, we agree with Minow's conclusion that although normative theories provide no unambiguous answer to this dilemma, in the end government should help parents anticipate the danger of failing to provide for their existing children by sending a clear signal of "no modification due to subsequent duties."

DIRECTIONS FOR FUTURE RESEARCH

The chapters in this volume have done an excellent job of using existing data and methodologies to answer our questions about nonresident fathers' characteristics and reactions to stronger child support enforcement. They also have highlighted many limitations in our data and methods. First, and perhaps most important, many of our best surveys undercount or misclassify a substantial proportion of nonresident fathers, especially low-income fathers and fathers of children born outside of marriage. To draw a truly accurate—as opposed to a "patchwork"—portrait of nonresident fathers, we must do a better job of including these men in our surveys, and we must do a better job of persuading the men who are in our surveys to acknowledge their paternity status. Finally, we must learn more about the *missing* fathers by designing special studies that target these men. Getting accurate information on unwed fathers is particularly important since this group of men is the fastest-growing part of the nonresident fathers' population, and since they are most likely to be underrepresented in our existing surveys. A particular concern is whether the omission of so many nonresident fathers from survey samples biases conclusions about the factors that predict child support and related outcomes, such as employment, remarriage, and paternal involvement. The Fragile Families and Child Wellbeing Study, which is currently under way in multiple cities throughout the country is one example of such a study.[1] By interviewing unmarried parents at the maternity ward (or shortly after the birth of their baby) and by following both parents for up to four years, the new study will provide previously unavailable information on unwed fathers' capabilities, their attitudes about fathers' rights and responsibilities, and their relationships with mothers and children. The fragile families' data will also provide important information on how unwed parents respond to the new child support policies and practices that are being implemented in different states.

Along with bringing more nonresident fathers into our samples, we need to gather more information about these men from the mothers, including information on the fathers' education, occupation, work history, and marital histories. Such information would help us sort out which fathers are missing from the data and allow us to test our assumptions about assortative mating used in studies that rely on mothers' reports about fathers' characteristics. We should ask mothers more questions about their exposure to domestic violence, distinguishing between experiences with their own fathers (or father figures), the fathers of their children, and other sexual partners. Asking questions only about the current relationship between the mother and nonresident father may seriously underestimate the potential for violence, since parents who do not get along are less likely to have any contact with one another (chapter 6). Asking questions about *all* past relationships may seriously overestimate the potential abuse of nonresident fathers since they are only one potential source of violence. To obtain reliable estimates of exposure to domestic violence, and to address the problems of small samples discussed in part II of this volume, may require special sampling strategies and reliance on state-based samples from vital records. The analyses of national survey data for outcomes, such as employment, in which reporting bias is probably smaller than for domestic violence, show that national surveys without very large oversamples of important subpopulations do not provide sample sizes large enough to support the statistical analyses necessary.

We also need to follow fathers over time. Many of the factors that determine fathers' ability to pay child support are likely to change as fathers grow older. For example, fathers' ability to pay increases with age (Phillips and Garfinkel 1993; Lerman and Ooms 1993). Such data are very expensive, and attrition is always a problem. This is especially true in studies that attempt to follow fathers after the breakup of a marriage or union when residential mobility is very high. The NLSY-1979 cohort has done a very good job of keeping track of nonresident fathers, and the new NLSY-1997 cohort will provide an excellent opportunity for following a new cohort of men who are coming of age in the late 1990s and early 2000s.

Finally, couple data are essential if we want to understand the relationship between parents who live apart. While mothers can provide reasonably accurate information on child support payments and visitation, they cannot report on the father-child relationship or on many other aspects of nonresident fathers' lives. Similarly, fathers cannot provide good information on mothers' attitudes and expectations or on mother-child relationships. Even information about the parents' relationship is likely to be biased if obtained from only one party. If we really want to learn how to promote more cooperative relationships between parents who live apart, we must have information from both parents, rather than from individuals only. The Fragile Families and Child Wellbeing Study, which was described earlier, will help fill this gap by collecting data from fathers as well as mothers on parents' expectations and relationships.

In addition to highlighting the limitations of existing data, the chapters in this volume point to some of the analytical problems that researchers face when they try to determine how fathers will respond to stronger child support enforcement.

All of the authors in part II agree that extrapolating from correlational evidence is likely to yield biased estimates of fathers' reactions. To deal with this problem, they treat cross-state differences in child support laws and practices as "natural" experiments and argue that estimates based on these experiments are superior to those based on simple correlations. Anne Case, however, raises serious questions about this strategy when she shows that cross-state differences in child support policies may not be random after all. Her findings imply that researchers need to be cautious in their choice of "natural" experiments, and they need to test for the robustness of their results under different assumptions.

The findings in chapters 3 through 7 should be replicated by other researchers using other data sets. We see this set of analyses as a first step toward assessing the effects of stronger child support enforcement on fathers' behavior. Although the results for nonmarital childbearing have been replicated, and the findings on employment are consistent with some past work, those for other outcomes— employment, remarriage, and father involvement—need the scrutiny of further research and replication.

In addition to replicating the analyses in this book and demonstrating the robustness of the estimates, we encourage researchers to build models that include multiple indirect effects for fathers (or mothers) and to examine outcomes across multiple actors. Bloom and his colleagues have taken a step in this direction by simulating the effects of fathers' remarriage on the economic well-being of their children. In doing so, they have mapped out a research agenda for the future that is both ambitious and essential.

Finally, the chapters in this volume only begin to address the question of whether we could (or should) do more to assist nonresident fathers in meeting their child support obligations. With respect to the empirical question of whether programs work, we must wait for the formal evaluation of Parents' Fair Share before drawing conclusions about this particular program. In addition to these demonstrations, fatherhood initiatives are springing up throughout the country with different emphases and different clientele. New and better data on fathers can inform these new initiatives by highlighting the areas where fathers need the most help. The next generation of initiatives will provide numerous opportunities for evaluating the effectiveness of programs designed to help fathers meet their paternal obligations. Similarly, the access demonstrations examined here represent only a small part of a larger set of initiatives designed to reduce conflict and increase cooperation between parents. Parent education programs and mediation for divorcing couples have gained widespread support in some parts of the country, and these efforts need to be described and carefully evaluated in terms of both their effectiveness and costs (Emery 1994). Conflict resolution among low-income parents is a particularly important topic for future research, given that the new welfare legislation pushes unmarried parents toward more contact and greater interdependence.

Social scientists qua scientists cannot answer the question of whether we *should* do more for nonresident fathers. The best we can do is to provide information to policymakers and citizens on whether a policy is effective and on the distribution of benefits and costs across different groups—fathers, mothers, children, and taxpayers. This book was motivated by a concern that fathers' interests were being neglected by social scientists in the assessment of child support policies. But we do not mean to imply that fathers' interests should take precedence over those of mothers and children. In order to be complete, the evidence in this book must be combined with research on the effects of stronger enforcement on mothers and children, and these, in turn, must be balanced against the costs to taxpayers of different interventions.

POLICY RECOMMENDATIONS

As is always the case in a research endeavor, many questions remain unanswered. But policy cannot wait until knowledge is perfect. A number of policy recommendations are more or less implicit in the previous discussion in this chapter. The purpose of this section is to make those recommendations explicit.

We distinguish between two types of policy—those that affect families who are already separated, either due to marital disruption or because they have children born outside of marriage, and those that affect families who will experience marital disruption or bear out-of-wedlock children in the future. That is, we consider both policies that affect the stock of families in which fathers and children are already living apart and the flow of families into the child support system. The distinction between these families is important, because families already in the child support system, or who are already separated, have established expectations about how the parents will deal with each other. Changing the "rules" midstream may increase conflict and dissatisfaction among parents. Introducing new rules before parents decide to live apart means that their decision to separate is made in the context of clear rules and expectations about each parent's rights and responsibilities to the children. Although most of our recommendations apply to both the stock of families in the child support system and the flow of new families into it, changes are often applied first to new cases owing to limited organizational resources or personnel limitations. Our recommendations about access, however, make theoretical as well as practical distinctions between the stock and flow of child support–eligible families.

A Universal Enforcement System

In principle, the American child support enforcement system is universal, offering similar services to all who request them, irrespective of income or welfare status. In practice, however, many state enforcement offices provide only limited or no services to mothers and children not on welfare. Furthermore, many fathers who are unwed or extremely poor escape the system entirely. In our judgment, the system should be universal. As we argued earlier, even very poor fathers should be required to pay a token amount of child support. At the same time, pursuing only fathers of children on welfare is neither fair nor wise. Many children of middle-class fathers also receive inadequate or irregular support. Some of the mothers of these children receive no help from state child support agencies and are forced to hire a lawyer and take the father to court in order to obtain what they are owed. Lacking the time and money to pursue the father, many mothers simply give up and forgo the support they are due. Dealing with these claims on a case-by-case basis is inefficient and should be redressed. Other mothers not on welfare may have initially believed that they did not need collection services from the child support agency only to find that, over time, payments became irregular or stopped. While services should be available to all families who request them when having difficulties, a policy that sought to provide services to all from the outset might prevent this type of scenario. Society has an interest in ensuring that *all* nonresident fathers support their children.

Special Treatment of Low-Income Fathers

At the very least, child support enforcement policy should not treat low-income fathers worse than middle- and upper-income nonresident fathers. Two practices are especially onerous—making low-income fathers liable for repaying welfare costs and assuming that they earn at least the full-time equivalent of the minimum wage. Such practices, which lead to large arrearages and small payments, should be abolished.

Child support guidelines should also be amended to ensure that low-income fathers are required to pay no higher a fraction of their income in child support than middle- and upper-income fathers. Consideration should be given to requiring fathers with incomes below the poverty line to pay an even lower proportion of their income in child support.

Consideration also should be given to expressing child support orders in percentage terms. Expressing orders in percentage terms would provide automatic relief to the minority of fathers who have temporarily low income. Fathers who experience an income loss due to unemployment or illness are not in a position to go to court to seek a reduction in their child support orders. Thus, expressing orders in percentage terms would also help prevent the accrual of large arrearages. At the same time, because most fathers' incomes go up over time, expressing orders in percentage terms would lead to larger child support orders and payments in the vast majority of cases (Bartfeld and Garfinkel 1996).[2]

Child support policy should go beyond eliminating unrealistic and unduly onerous child support obligations for low-income fathers to providing them with incentives and assistance to meet their child support obligations. Further experimentation with programs like Parents' Fair Share should be undertaken. Under PRWORA, states are allowed to eliminate the fifty-dollar child support pass-through to mothers and children on welfare, and most have done so. The federal government—or failing that, individual states—should reverse this policy and reinstate the pass-through. For instance, the state of Wisconsin is now giving 100 percent of child support paid to all welfare recipients in the state (except for a small experimental group). It is important for fathers to know that their children derive some benefit from their child support payments. Even more important, we should reward mothers and fathers who establish private child support obligations by guaranteeing that children receive a minimum amount of support every month (Garfinkel 1994). This would encourage both paternity establishment and child support orders. Finally, we should experiment with programs that match very low private child support payments with public funds—something akin to the earned income tax credit, which subsidizes earnings. This policy would encourage very poor fathers to pay support and would also increase the economic security of poor children.

Policies to Promote Nonresident Fathers' Access

We believe that fathers have a right to see their children, but we do not believe that there should be a direct policy link between child support and access. That is, we believe that nonpayment is *not* a valid reason for a resident parent to deny access, nor do we believe that denial of access is a valid reason for nonpayment. Both payments and access are highly contested and unreliable, so to link the two would increase the chances of both breaking down. Children would be held hostage to their parents' disagreements, as they were in the past, prior to the new child support legislation. Evidence from the demonstration projects that Jessica Pearson and Nancy Thoennes (chapter 8) review supports our pessimism about attempts to enforce access in families with long-term conflicts about child support or access.

Nonetheless, we believe there is an imbalance in policy: child support obligations are publicly enforced, but access is not. Policy-makers attempting to enforce access face the difficulty that fathers without access come from two types of families: some nonresident fathers seek greater access than resident mothers may permit, and in other families fathers themselves avoid access even though resident mothers may prefer nonresident fathers to spend more time with their children (for example, see Bruch 1978 and Czapanskiy 1989 for proposals to increase financial obligations of nonresident parents when they fail to spend regular time with their children). Ascertaining whether the mother or father is acting irresponsibly in a particular case is no easy matter. Furthermore, the possibility of spouse or child abuse compounds the difficulties. Thus, we believe we must proceed cautiously, experimenting first with early education, mediation, and other services before trying bold new initiatives to enforce access.

We believe that the best hope to increase access of fathers from both types of families is to work toward establishing new expectations about access and child support so that both mothers and fathers start off with a better understanding of what the other's rights are. This is a longer-term strategy than most of our other policy recommendations. It focuses attention on families in which parents are in the process of deciding to live apart. We suspect that revised parental expectations explain in part why Pearson and Thoennes find that access problems decrease when a visitation schedule is established early in the separation period, before serious conflict becomes entrenched. This long-term strategy is also consistent with

Seltzer's (1998) argument that joint legal custody increases nonresident fathers' contact with children because it clarifies that both parents have the right to participate in children's lives after divorce.

Private and Public Child Support

This book is about nonresident fathers and child support policy. Although we have attempted to approach the policy issues primarily from the nonresident father's point of view, it is obvious that child support policy must also take account of the interests of children, resident mothers, and society as a whole. And our recommendations reflect these other interests. Similarly, just as child support policy should not be shaped by only one set of interests, it must be considered in light of broader social policies affecting families and children.

At the most general level, child support policy reflects the extent to which the support of children is a private rather than a public responsibility. Some people take the position that child support enforcement is unnecessary because the costs of child-rearing are a public responsibility. They argue that if public benefits were more generous, children would not need private child support. We do not share this position, and we would point out that no country has totally socialized the costs of children. Hence, not enforcing private child support obligations implicitly means shifting more of the costs of children onto resident mothers. The public responsibility argument, in practice, becomes a smoke screen for excusing nonresident fathers from their responsibilities.

Other people take the position that the support of children is purely a private responsibility. We do not agree with this position either. To begin with, society has an interest in making sure that children's basic needs are met. This means, at a minimum, that government has a responsibility to enforce private child support obligations. Even more important, just as the need for private child support enforcement would not evaporate if we had a better public income maintenance system, even a perfectly efficient private child support enforcement system would not obviate the need for better income maintenance, public education, health care, and child care. In short, we see these two systems—public and private support for children—as complementing one another and as reinforcing the social norm that raising healthy and secure children is a shared responsibility.

NOTES

1. The Fragile Families and Child Wellbeing Study is directed by Irwin Garfinkel and Sara McLanahan. Coinvestigators include Jeanne Brooks-Gunn, Marta Tienda, Sheila Ards, Waldo Johnson, Yolanda Padillo, Lauren Rich, Mark Turner, Maureen Waller, and Melvin Wilson. The study is funded by NICHD and a consortium of foundations including the Ford Foundation, the Robert Wood Johnson Foundation, the Public Policy Institute of California, the Hogg Foundation, the Fund for New Jersey, St. David's Hospital Foundation, the Commonwealth Fund, and Newark-Beth Israel Healthcare Foundation.

2. Percentage-expressed orders do have some disadvantages. One difficulty is that child support enforcement workers do not know whether the amount of child support that was paid in a particular case was the correct amount unless they know income. Similarly, if a nonresident parent's income falls to zero, no child support is due, but without knowing income, a child support enforcement worker does not know whether a payment is appropriate or whether an enforcement action should be taken. Some simple steps could make the administration of these percentage-expressed orders easier. Nonresident parents could be required to provide the child support agency with their tax returns so that the amount of child support paid could be reconciled with annual income, or nonresident parents could be asked to report loss of income to the child support agency. A second difficulty is that percentage-expressed orders are difficult to administer in states whose guidelines consider the resident parent's income as well as the nonresident parent's. Nonetheless, we believe the advantages of percentage-expressed orders outweigh their disadvantages, and we would like to see them used more extensively and evaluated more rigorously.

REFERENCES

Bartfeld, Judi, and Irwin Garfinkel. 1996. "The Impact of Percentage-Expressed Child Support Orders on Payments over Time." *Journal of Human Resources* (Fall): 794–815.

Bruch, Carol S. 1978. "Making Visitation Work: Dual Parenting Orders." *Family Advocate* 1: 22–26, 41–42.

Czapanskiy, Karen. 1989. "Child Support and Visitation: Rethinking the Connections." *Rutgers Law Journal* 20(3): 619–65.

Emory, Robert E. 1994. *Renegotiating Family Relationships: Divorce, Child Custody and Mediation.* New York: Guilford Press.

Garfinkel, Irwin. 1994. *Assuring Child Support: An Extension of Social Security.* New York: Russell Sage Foundation.

Garfinkel, Irwin, Daniel Gaylin, Sara McLanahan, and Chien Huang. 1998. "Will Child Support Enforcement Reduce Nonmarital Childbearing?" Revision of paper presented at 1996 Population Association meeting, New Orleans (May 9–11, 1998).

Hanson, Thomas, Sara S. McLanahan, and Elizabeth Thomson. 1996. "Double Jeopardy: Parental Conflict and Stepfamily Outcomes for Children." *Journal of Marriage and the Family* 58(1): 141–54.

Klawitter, Marieka. 1994. "Child Support Awards and the Earnings of Divorced Nonresident Fathers." *Social Service Review* 68(3): 351–68.

Lerman, Robert I., and Theodora J. Ooms. 1993. *Young Unwed Fathers: Changing Roles and Emerging Policies.* Philadelphia: Temple University Press.

Nixon, Lucia A. 1997. "The Effect of Child Support Enforcement on Marital Dissolution." *Journal of Human Resources* 32(1): 159–81.

Phillips, Elizabeth, and Irwin Garfinkel. 1993. "Income Growth Among Nonresident Fathers: Evidence from Wisconsin." *Demography* 30(2): 227–41.

Plotnick, Robert, Irwin Garfinkel, Daniel Gaylin, Sara McLanahan, and Inhoe Ku. 1998. "Can Child Support Enforcement Reduce Teenage Premarital Childbearing?" Paper presented at the Population Association meetings, Chicago (April 2–4, 1998).

Seltzer, Judith A. 1998. "Father by Law: Effects of Joint Legal Custody on Fathers' Involvement with Children." *Demography* 35(2): 135–46.

Index

Numbers in **boldface** refer to tables and figures.

Index